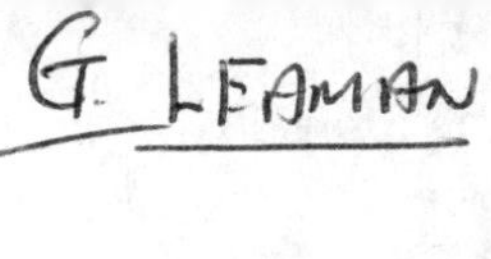
G. LEAMAN

M68000

8-/16-/32-Bit Microprocessors User's Manual

seventh edition

PRENTICE HALL, Englewood Cliffs, N.J. 07632

Previously published under the title *M68000 8-/16-/32-Bit Microprocessors Programmer's Reference Manual*

Printed in the United States of America

10 9 8 7 6 5 4 3 2 1

ISBN 0-13-567074-8 {MOTOROLA}

Prentice-Hall International (UK) Limited, *London*
Prentice-Hall of Australia Pty. Limited, *Sydney*
Prentice-Hall Canada Inc., *Toronto*
Prentice-Hall Hispanoamericana, S.A., *Mexico*
Prentice-Hall of India Private Limited, *New Delhi*
Prentice-Hall of Japan, Inc., *Tokyo*
Simon & Schuster Asia Pte. Ltd., *Singapore*
Editora Prentice-Hall do Brasil, Ltda., *Rio de Janeiro*

TABLE OF CONTENTS

TABLE OF CONTENTS (Continued)

TABLE OF CONTENTS (Continued)

Section 6
Exception Processing

TABLE OF CONTENTS (Continued)

Section 7
M6800 Peripheral Interface

Section 8
MC68000 and MC68HC000 Instruction Execution Times

Section 9
MC68008 Instruction Execution Times

TABLE OF CONTENTS (Continued)

TABLE OF CONTENTS (Concluded)

LIST OF ILLUSTRATIONS

LIST OF ILLUSTRATIONS (Continued)

LIST OF ILLUSTRATIONS (Concluded)

LIST OF TABLES

LIST OF TABLES (Continued)

LIST OF TABLES (Concluded)

SECTION 1
INTRODUCTION

In 1979, Motorola introduced the first implementation of the M68000 16-/32-bit microprocessor architecture — the MC68000. With a 16-bit data bus and 24-bit address bus, the MC68000 was the first in a microprocessor family to implement a comprehensive, extensible computer architecture. The MC68000 was soon followed by the MC68008, with an 8-bit data bus and a 20-bit address bus, and the MC68010, which introduced the virtual machine aspects of the M68000 architecture. The MC68HC000, an HCMOS implementation of the MC68000, dissipates an order-of-magnitude less power than the MC68000. The MC68020 and the MC68030, which retain the M68000 Family characteristics with 32-bit buses, have on-chip caches and coprocessor interfaces to provide additional capabilities and increased performance.

This manual, which includes hardware details and programming information for the MC68000, the MC68HC000, the MC68008, and the MC68010, combines the *M68000 8-/16-/32-Bit Microprocessors Programmer's Reference Manual* with the advance information data sheets for these microprocessors. All the information needed by system designers, systems programmers, and writers of assemblers and compilers who use the MC68000, MC68HC000, MC68008 and/or the MC68010 is now in one book.

The four microprocessors are very similar. The MC68008 differs from the others in that the data bus size is eight bits, and the address range is smaller. The MC68010 has a few additional instructions, and instructions that operate differently than the corresponding instructions of the other devices.

To simplify the organization of this manual, the MC68000 has been chosen as the representative microprocessor. The operations and characteristics of the MC68HC000 are identical, and all MC68000 information applies directly to this low-power version. A thin bar in the outside margin identifies additional information that applies only to the MC68008; a heavy bar identifies additional information that applies only to the MC68010.

Execution timing information for the MC68000 and the MC68HC000 has been combined in one section. To avoid confusion, separate sections for the MC68008 and the MC68010 have been included.

Several sections of this manual refer to assembler syntax for instructions and addressing modes. The syntax shown is that of the current Motorola assembler for the M68000 Family processors. Older versions of the Motorola assembler use a syntax that differs in minor ways, and the syntax for other assemblers may also differ.

SECTION 2
ARCHITECTURAL DESCRIPTION

The MC68000 and the MC68HC000 have identical architectures. The MC68000 and the MC68008 are identical from the programmer's viewpoint, except that the MC68000 can directly access 16 megabytes (24-bit address) and the MC68008 can directly access 1 megabyte (20-bit address). The MC68010, which also uses a 24-bit address, has much in common with the other devices; however, it supports additional instructions and registers and provides full virtual machine/memory capability.

2.1 PROGRAMMER'S MODEL

The MC68000 executes instructions in one of two modes - user mode or supervisor mode. The user mode provides the execution environment for the majority of application programs. The supervisor mode, which allows some additional instructions and privileges, is used by the operating system and other system software. **SECTION 6 EXCEPTION PROCESSING** provides further details.

To provide upward compatibility of code written for a specific implementation of the MC68000, the user programmer's model, shown in Figure 2-1, is common to all implementations. In the user programmer's model, the MC68000 offers 16, 32-bit, general-purpose registers (D0-D7, A0-A7), a 32-bit program counter, and an 8-bit condition code register. The first eight registers (D0-D7) are used as data registers for byte (8-bit), word (16-bit), and long-word (32-bit) operations. The second set of seven registers (A0-A6) and the user stack pointer (USP) can be used as software stack pointers and base address registers. In addition, the address registers can be used for word and long-word operations. All of the 16 registers can be used as index registers.

The supervisor programmer's model consists of supplementary registers used in the supervisor mode. The MC68000 and the MC68008 contain identical supervisor mode register resources, which are shown in Figure 2-2, including the status register (high-order byte) and the supervisor stack pointer (SSP/A7').

The supervisor programmer's model supplement of the MC68010 is shown in Figure 2-3. In addition to the supervisor stack pointer and status register, it includes the vector base register and the alternate function-code registers.

The vector base register is used to determine the location of the exception vector table in memory to support multiple vector tables. The alternate function code registers allow the supervisor to access user data space or emulate CPU space cycles. For more information about data space and CPU space, refer to **5.1.9 Processor Function Codes (FC0, FC1, FC2).**

The status register, shown in Figure 2-4, contains the interrupt mask (eight levels available) and the condition codes: overflow (V), zero (Z), negative (N), carry (C), and extend (X). Additional status bits indicate that the processor is in the trace (T) mode and/or in the supervisor (S) state.

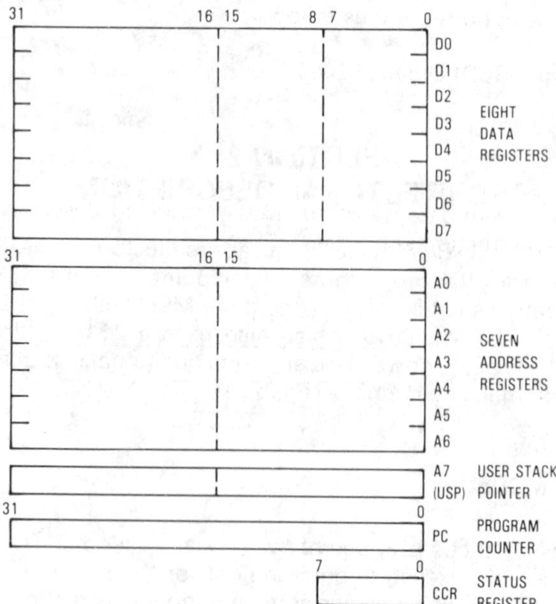

Figure 2-1. User Programmer's Model (MC68000/MC68HC000/MC68008/MC68010)

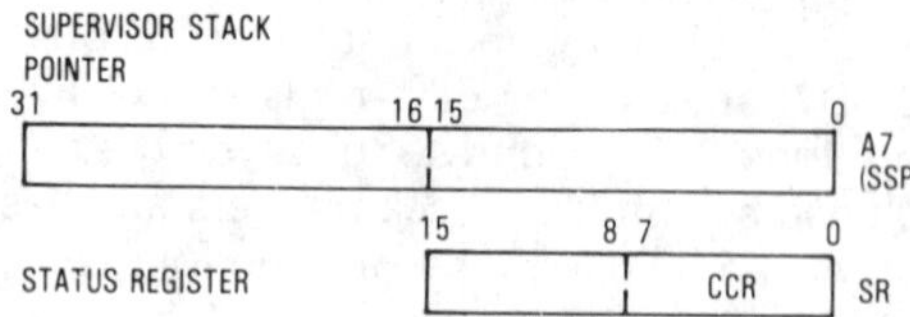

Figure 2-2. Supervisor Programmer's Model Supplement (MC68000/MC68HC000/MC68008)

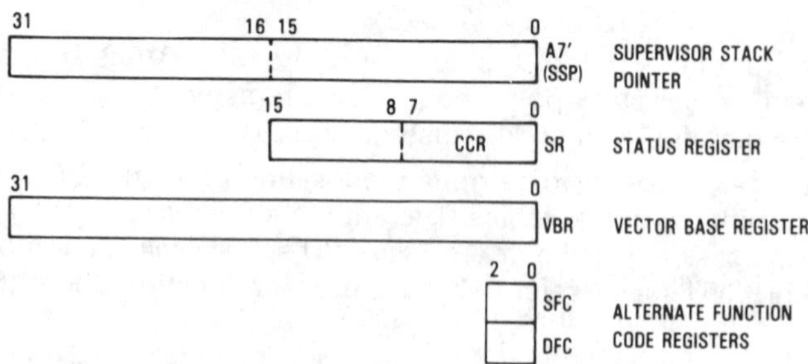

Figure 2-3. Supervisor Programmer's Model Supplement (MC68010)

The five basic data types supported are as follows:

- Bits
- Binary-coded-decimal (BCD) Digits (4 Bits)
- Bytes (8 Bits)
- Words (16 Bits)
- Long Words (32 Bits)

In addition, operations on other data types, such as memory addresses, status word data, etc., are provided in the instruction set.

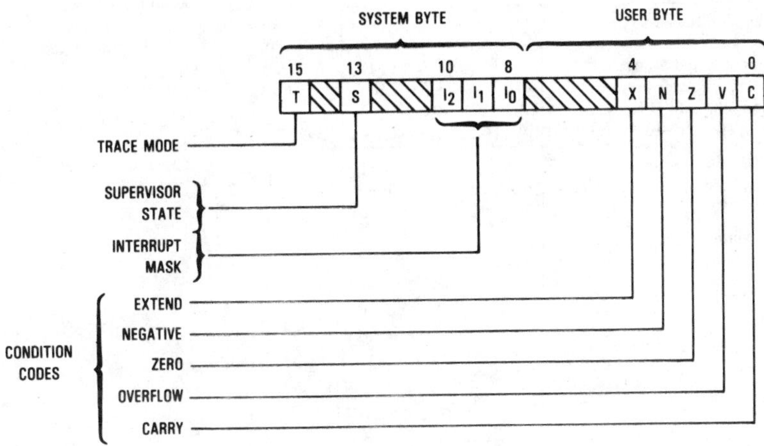

Figure 2-4. Status Register

The 14 flexible addressing modes, shown in Table 2-1, include six basic types:

- Register Direct
- Register Indirect
- Absolute
- Immediate
- Program Counter Relative
- Implied

The register indirect addressing modes provide postincrementing, predecrementing, offsetting, and indexing capabilities. The program counter relative mode also supports indexing and offsetting.

The basic M68000 Family instruction set is shown in Table 2-2. The complete set includes variations of several of the basic instructions. These additional instructions are listed in Table 2-3. Design of the instruction set gives special emphasis to support of structured, high-level languages and to ease of assembly language programming. Each instruction, with a few exceptions, operates on bytes, words, and long words, and most instructions can use any of the 14 addressing modes. Combining instruction types, data types, and addressing modes, over 1000 useful instructions are provided. These instructions include signed and unsigned multiply and divide, "quick" arithmetic operations, BCD arithmetic, and expanded operations (through traps). Additionally, the highly symmetric, proprietary microcoded structure of the instruction set provides a sound, flexible base for the future.

2

Table 2-1. Data Addressing Modes

Mode	Generation
Register Direct Addressing	
Data Register Direct	EA = Dn
Address Register Direct	EA = An
Absolute Data Addressing	
Absolute Short	EA = (Next Word)
Absolute Long	EA = (Next Two Words)
Program Counter Relative Addressing	
Relative with Offset	EA = (PC) + d_{16}
Relative with Index and Offset	EA = (PC) + d_8
Register Indirect Addressing	
Register Indirect	EA = (An)
Postincrement Register Indirect	EA = (An), An ⧫ An + N
Predecrement Register Indirect	An ⧫ An – N, EA = (An)
Register Indirect with Offset	EA = (An) + d_{16}
Indexed Register Indirect with Offset	EA = (An) + (Xn) + d_8
Immediate Data Addressing	
Immediate	DATA = Next Word(s)
Quick Immediate	Inherent Data
Implied Addressing	
Implied Register	EA = SR, USP, SSP, PC, VBR, SFC, DFC

NOTES:
EA = Effective Address
Dn = Data Register
An = Address Register
( ) = Contents of
PC = Program Counter
d_8 = 8-Bit Offset (Displacement)
d_{16} = 16-Bit Offset (Displacement)
N = 1 for byte, 2 for word, and 4 for long word. If An is the stack pointer and the operand size is byte, N = 2 to keep the stack pointer on a word boundary.
⧫ = Replaces
Xn = Address or Data Register used as Index Register
SR = Status Register

Table 2-2. Instruction Set Summary

Mnemonic	Description
ABCD*	Add Decimal with Extend
ADD*	Add
AND*	Logical AND
ASL*	Arithmetic Shift Left
ASR*	Arithmetic Shift Right
Bcc	Branch Conditionally
BCHG	Bit Test and Change
BCLR	Bit Test and Clear
BRA	Branch Always
BSET	Bit Test and Set
BSR	Branch to Subroutine
BTST	Bit Test
CHK	Check Register Against Bounds
CLR*	Clear Operand
CMP*	Compare
DBcc	Decrement and Branch Conditionally
DIVS	Signed Divide
DIVU	Unsigned Divide
EOR*	Exclusive OR
EXG	Exchange Registers
EXT	Sign Extend
JMP	Jump
JSR	Jump to Subroutine
LEA	Load Effective Address
LINK	Link Stack
LSL*	Logical Shift Left
LSR*	Logical Shift Right

*These instructions available in loop mode on MC68010. See **APPENDIX D MC68010 LOOP MODE OPERATION**.

Mnemonic	Description
MOVE*	Move Source to Destination
MULS	Signed Multiply
MULU	Unsigned Multiply
NBCD*	Negate Decimal with Extend
NEG*	Negate
NOP	No Operation
NOT*	One's Complement
OR*	Logical OR
PEA	Push Effective Address
RESET	Reset External Devices
ROL*	Rotate Left without Extend
ROR*	Rotate Right without Extend
ROXL*	Rotate Left with Extend
ROXR*	Rotate Right with Extend
RTD	Return and Deallocate
RTE	Return from Exception
RTR	Return and Restore
RTS	Return from Subroutine
SBCD*	Subtract Decimal with Extend
Scc	Set Conditional
STOP	Stop
SUB*	Subtract
SWAP	Swap Data Register Halves
TAS	Test and Set Operand
TRAP	Trap
TRAPV	Trap on Overflow
TST*	Test
UNLK	Unlink

Table 2-3. Variations of Instruction Types

Instruction Type	Variation	Description
Add	**ADD*** ADDA* ADDQ ADDI ADDX*	Add Add Address Add Quick Add Immediate Add with Extend
AND	**AND*** ANDI ANDI to CCR ANDI to SR	Logical AND AND Immediate AND Immediate to Condition Codes AND Immediate to Status Register
CMP	**CMP*** CMPA* CMPM* CMPI	Compare Compare Address Compare Memory Compare Immediate
EOR	**EOR*** EORI EORI to CCR EORI to SR	Exclusive OR Exclusive OR Immediate Exclusive OR Immediate to Condition Codes Exclusive OR Immediate to Status Register
MOVE	**MOVE*** MOVEA* MOVEC MOVEM MOVEP MOVEQ MOVES MOVE from SR MOVE to SR MOVE from CCR MOVE to CCR MOVE USP	Move Source to Destination Move Address Move Control Register Move Multiple Registers Move Peripheral Data Move Quick Move Alternate Address Space Move from Status Register Move to Status Register Move from Condition Codes Move to Condition Codes Move User Stack Pointer
NEG	**NEG*** NEGX*	Negate Negate with Extend
OR	**OR*** ORI ORI to CCR ORI to SR	Logical OR OR Immediate OR Immediate to Condition Codes OR Immediate to Status Register
SUB	**SUB*** SUBA* SUBI SUBQ SUBX*	Subtract Subtract Address Subtract Immediate Subtract Quick Subtract with Extend

*These instructions available in loop mode on MC68010. See **APPENDIX D MC68010 LOOP MODE OPERATION**.

2.2 SOFTWARE DEVELOPMENT

Many innovative features have been incorporated to make programming easier, faster, and more reliable. These features are discussed in the following paragraphs.

2.2.1 Consistent Structure

The highly regular structure of the MC68000 simplifies writing programs in assembly language. Operations on integer data in registers and memory are independent of the data. Separate, special instructions that operate on byte (8 bit), word (16 bit), and long-word (32 bit) integers are not necessary. The instruction format (an instruction mnemonic plus data size, source addressing mode, and destination addressing mode) has helped to minimize the number of instructions.

The dual operand nature of many of the instructions significantly increases the flexibility and power of the MC68000. Consistency is again maintained since any data register or memory location may be either a source or a destination for most operations on integer data.

The addressing modes are simple without sacrificing efficiency. All 14 addressing modes operate consistently and independently of the instruction operation. Furthermore, all address registers can be used for the direct, register indirect, and indexed addressing modes.

(By definition, immediate, program counter relative, and absolute addressing do not use address registers.) For increased flexibility, any address or data register may be used as an index register. Using the register indirect postincrement/predecrement addressing modes, any of the eight address registers can be pointer registers for user program stacks. Address register A7 functions as the system stack pointer in addition to its normal addressing capabilities. The system stack stores the program counter for subroutine calls; in the supervisor mode, the system stack stores the program counter and status register for traps and interrupts.

2.2.2 Structured Modular Programming

The art of programming microprocessors has evolved rapidly in past years as numerous advanced techniques have been developed for easier, more consistent and reliable generation of software. These techniques require the programmer to be more disciplined and to use a defined programming structure such as modular programming, which involves programming each function or small process in a concise module or subroutine that is easily programmed and tested. The availability of advanced, structured assemblers and block-structured high-level languages such as Pascal simplifies modular programming. Such concepts are virtually useless, however, unless parameters are easily transferred between and within software modules that operate on a re-entrant and recursive basis. (To be re-entrant, a routine must be usable by interrupt- and noninterrupt-driven programs without loss of data. A recursive routine may call or use itself.) The MC68000 provides architectural features that allow efficient re-entrant modular programming. Two complementary instructions, link and allocate (LINK) and unlink (UNLK), reduce subroutine call overhead by manipulating linked lists of data areas on the stack. The move multiple register (MOVEM) instruction also reduces subroutine call programming overhead. This instruction moves multiple registers specified by the programmer to or from consecutive locations at an effective address in memory. Calls to the operating system or to user subroutines can use the trap (TRAP) instruction, which accesses one of sixteen software trap vectors. Other instructions that support modern structured programming techniques are push effective address (PEA), load effective address (LEA), return and restore (RTR), return from exception (RTE), jump to subroutine (JSR), branch to subroutine (BSR), and return from subroutine (RTS).

The powerful vectored priority interrupt structure of the microprocessor allows straightforward generation of re-entrant modular input/output (I/O) routines. Seven maskable levels of priority with 192 vector locations and seven autovector locations provide maximum flexibility for I/O control. (A total of 255 vector locations is available for interrupts, hardware traps, and software traps.)

2.2.3 Improved Software Testing

The MC68000 incorporates several features that reduce the chance for errors. Some of these features, such as consistent architecture and the structured modular-programming capability, have already been discussed.

Features that have been incorporated specifically to detect the occurrence of programming errors (bugs) are very important to programmers. Several hardware traps are provided to indicate abnormal internal conditions:

- Word Access with an Odd Address
- Illegal Instructions

- Unimplemented Instructions
- Ilegal Memory Access (Bus Error)
- Divide by Zero
- Overflow Condition Code (Separate Instruction TRAPV)
- Register Out of Bounds (CHK Instruction)
- Spurious Interrupt

Additionally, the 16 software TRAP instructions are available to the programmer to provide applications-oriented error detection or correction routines.

An additional error-detection tool is the check register against bounds (CHK) instruction used for array bound checking by verifying that a data register contains a valid subscript. A trap occurs if the register contents are negative or greater than a limit.

Finally, the MC68000 includes a facility allowing instruction-by-instruction tracing of a program being debugged. This trace mode results in a trap being made to a tracing routine after each instruction is executed.

2.3 VIRTUAL MEMORY/MACHINE CONCEPTS

In most systems using the MC68010 as the central processor, only a fraction of the 16-megabyte address space actually contains physical memory. However, by using virtual memory techniques, the system can be made to appear to the user to have 16 megabytes of physical memory available. These techniques have been used for several years in large, mainframe computers and more recently in minicomputers. Now, with the MC68010, virtual memory can be fully supported in microprocessor-based systems.

Similarly, a system can be designed to allow user programs to access types of devices that are not physically present in the system, such as tape drives, disk drives, printers, or CRTs. With proper software emulation, a physical system can be made to appear to a user program like any other computer system, and the program can be given full access to all the resources of that emulated system. Such an emulated system is called a virtual machine; it can be implemented with an MC68010 microprocessor.

2.3.1 Virtual Memory

The basic mechanism for supporting virtual memory in computers is to provide only a limited amount of high-speed physical memory that can be accessed directly by the processor while maintaining an image of a much larger virtual memory on secondary storage devices such as large-capacity disk drives. When the processor attempts to access a location in the virtual memory map that is not currently residing in physical memory (referred to as a page fault), the access to that location is temporarily suspended while the necessary data are fetched from the secondary storage and placed in physical memory; the suspended access is then completed. Hardware support for virtual memory consists of the capability of suspending execution of an instruction when a bus error is signaled and of completing the instruction after the physical memory has been updated as necessary.

The MC68010 uses instruction continuation rather than instruction restart to support virtual memory. With instruction restart, the processor must remember the exact state of the system before each instruction is started in order to restore that state if a page fault occurs during execution of the instruction. After the page fault has been repaired, the entire instruction that caused the fault is re-executed. With instruction continuation, when a page fault occurs, the processor stores the internal state and, after the page fault is repaired, restores that internal state and continues execution of the instruction. To utilize instruction continuation, the MC68010 stores the internal state on the supervisor stack when a bus cycle is terminated with a bus-error signal. The MC68010 then loads the program counter from vector table entry number two (offset $008) and resumes program execution at that new address. When the bus-error exception-handler routine has completed execution, an RTE instruction is executed. This instruction reloads the MC68010 with the internal state stored on the stack, reruns the faulted bus cycle, and continues the suspended instruction. Instruction continuation has the additional advantage of allowing hardware support for virtual I/O devices. Since virtual registers can be simulated in the memory map, an access to such a register causes a fault, and the function of the register can be emulated by software.

2.3.2 Virtual Machine

One typical use for a virtual machine system is in the development of an operating system for a machine that is under development and not available for programming use. In such a system, the operating system of the existing computer (the governing operating system) emulates the hardware of the new system to allow the new operating system to be executed and debugged as though it were running on the new hardware. Since the new operating system is controlled by the governing operating system, any attempts by the new operating system to use virtual resources not physically present are trapped by the governing operating system and handled in software. In the MC68010, a virtual machine can be fully supported by running the new operating system in the user mode and the governing operating system in the supervisor mode. Thus, any attempts by the new operating system to access supervisor resources or to execute privileged instructions cause a trap to the governing operating system.

To fully support a virtual machine, the MC68010 must protect the supervisor resources from access by user programs. The one supervisor resource that is not fully protected in the MC68000 is the system byte of the status register. In the MC68000 and MC68008, the move from the status register (MOVE from SR) instruction allows user programs to test the S bit (in addition to the T bit and interrupt mask) and to determine that they are running in the user mode. For full virtual machine support, a new operating system must not be aware that it is running in the user mode and should not be allowed to access the S bit. By making the MOVE from SR instruction privileged, when the new operating system attempts to access the S bit, a trap to the governing operating system occurs, and the SR image passed to the new operating system by the governing operating system has the S bit set. The move from the condition code register (MOVE from CCR) instruction has been added to allow unhindered user-program access to the condition codes.

SECTION 3
DATA ORGANIZATION AND ADDRESSING CAPABILITIES

This section describes the data organization and addressing capabilities of the M68000 architecture.

3.1 OPERAND SIZE

Operand sizes are defined as follows: a byte consists of 8 bits, a word consists of 16 bits, and a long word consists of 32 bits. The operand size for each instruction is either explicitly encoded in the instruction or implicitly defined by the instruction operation. All explicit instructions support byte, word, or long-word operands. Implicit instructions support some subset of all three sizes.

3.2 DATA ORGANIZATION IN REGISTERS

The eight data registers support data operands of 1, 8, 16, or 32 bits. The seven address registers and the active stack pointer support address operands of 32 bits.

3.2.1 Data Registers

Each data register is 32 bits wide. Byte operands occupy the low-order 8 bits, word operands the low-order 16 bits, and long-word operands, the entire 32 bits. The least significant bit is addressed as bit zero; the most significant bit is addressed as bit 31.

When a data register is used as either a source or a destination operand, only the appropriate low-order portion is changed; the remaining high-order portion is neither used nor changed.

3.2.2 Address Registers

Each address register (and the stack pointer) is 32 bits wide and holds a full, 32-bit address. Address registers do not support byte-sized operands. Therefore, when an address register is used as a source operand, either the low-order word or the entire long-word operand is used, depending upon the operation size. When an address register is used as the destination operand, the entire register is affected, regardless of the operation size. If the operation size is word, operands are sign extended to 32 bits before the operation is performed.

3.3 DATA ORGANIZATION IN MEMORY

Bytes are individually addressable. As shown in Figure 3-1, the high-order byte of a word has the same address as the word. The low-order byte has an odd address, one count

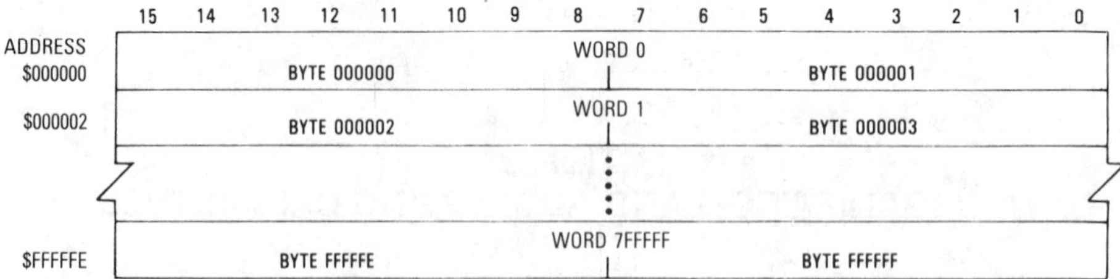

Figure 3-1. Word Organization in Memory

higher. Instructions and multibyte data are accessed only on word (even byte) boundaries. If a long-word operand is located at address n (n even), then the second word of that operand is located at address n+2.

The data types supported by the M68000 microprocessors are bit data, integer data of 8, 16, and 32 bits, 32-bit addresses, and binary-coded-decimal data. Each data type is stored in memory as shown in Figure 3-2. The numbers indicate the order of accessing the data from the processor. For the MC68008 with its 8-bit bus, the appearance of data in memory is identical to the MC68000 and MC68010. The organization of data in the memory of the MC68008 is shown in Figure 3-3.

3.4 ADDRESSING

Instructions for the M68000 microprocessors contain two kinds of information: (1) the type of operation to be performed and (2) the location of the operand(s) on which to perform that function. The methods used to address the operand(s) are described in the following paragraphs.

Instructions specify an operand location in one of three ways:

1. Register Specification — the number of the register is given in the register field of the instruction.
2. Effective Address — the effective address mode is specified.
3. Implicit Reference — the definition of certain instructions implies the use of specific registers.

3.5 INSTRUCTION FORMAT

Instructions are from one to five words long as shown in Figure 3-4. The length of the instruction and the operation to be performed is specified by the first word of the instruction, which is called the operation word. The additional words further specify the operands. These words are either immediate operands or extensions to the effective address mode specified in the operation word.

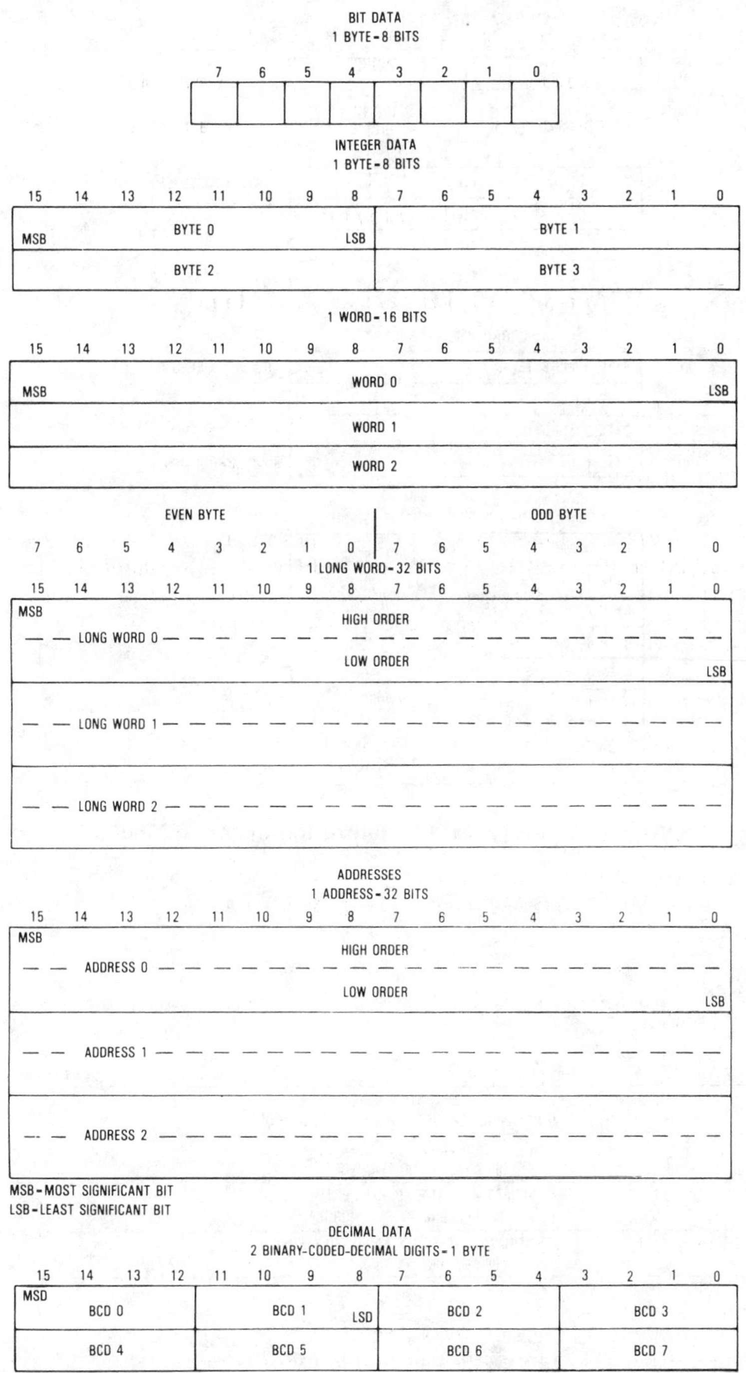

Figure 3-2. Data Organization in Memory

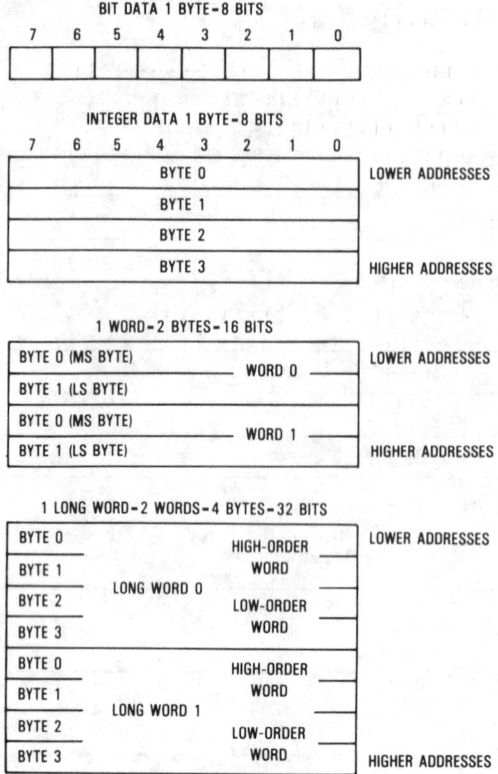

Figure 3-3. Memory Data Organization of the MC68008

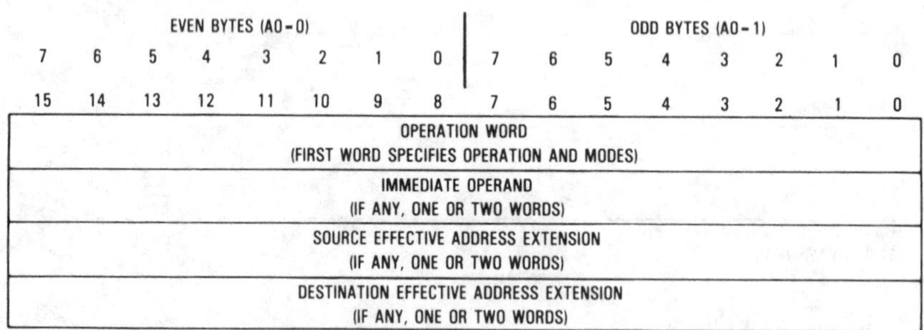

Figure 3-4. Instruction Format

3.6 PROGRAM/DATA REFERENCES

The MC68000 separates memory references into two classes: program references and data references. Program references refer to the section of memory that contains the program being executed; data references refer to the section of memory that contains data. Generally, operand reads are from the data space, but all operand writes are to the data space.

3

3.7 REGISTER NOTATION

APPENDIX B INSTRUCTION SET DETAILS contains a description of each instruction and identifies the registers using the following mnemonics:

An — Address Register (n specifies the register number)
Dn — Data Register (n specifies the register number)
Rn — Any Register, Address or Data (n specifies the register number)
Xn — Any Index Register, Address or Data (n specifies the register number)
PC — Program Counter
SR — Status Register
CCR — Condition Code Half of the Status Register
SP — Active Stack Pointer (either user or supervisor)
USP — User Stack Pointer
SSP — Supervisor Stack Pointer
d — Displacement Value
N — Operand Size in Bytes (1, 2, 4)
SFC, DFC — Source/Destination Function Code Register
VBR — Vector Base Register

3.8 ADDRESS REGISTER INDIRECT NOTATION

When an address register is used to point to a memory location, the addressing mode is called address register indirect. The term indirect is used because the register does not contain the operand, but contains the address of the operand in memory. The descriptive symbol for the indirect mode is an address register designation in parentheses, e.g., (An).

3.9 REGISTER SPECIFICATION

The register field within an instruction specifies the register to be used. Other fields within the instruction specify whether the register selected is an address or data register and how the register is to be used.

3.10 EFFECTIVE ADDRESS

Most instructions specify the location of an operand by using the effective address field in the operation word. For example, Figure 3-5 shows the general format of the operation word of the single, effective address instruction. The effective address is composed of two, 3-bit fields: the mode field and the register field. The value in the mode field selects the different address modes. The register field contains the number of a register.

The effective address field may require additional information to fully specify the operand. This additional information, called the effective address extension, is contained in a following word or words and is considered part of the instruction as shown in Figure 3-4.

The effective address modes are grouped into three categories: register direct, memory addressing, and special.

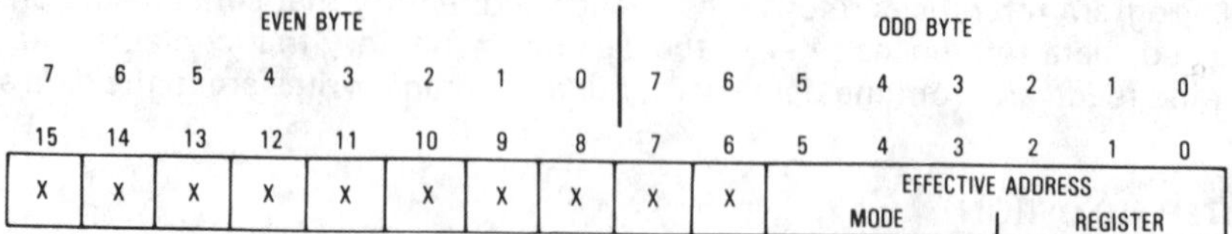

Figure 3-5. Single Effective-Address-Instruction Operation - General Format

3.10.1 Register Direct Modes

These effective address modes specify that the operand is in one of the 16 multifunction registers.

3.10.1.1 DATA REGISTER DIRECT. The operand is in the data register specified by the effective address register field.

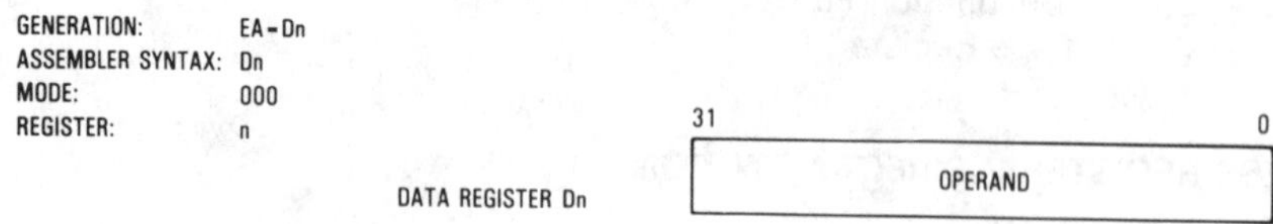

3.10.1.2 ADDRESS REGISTER DIRECT. The operand is in the address register specified by the effective address register field.

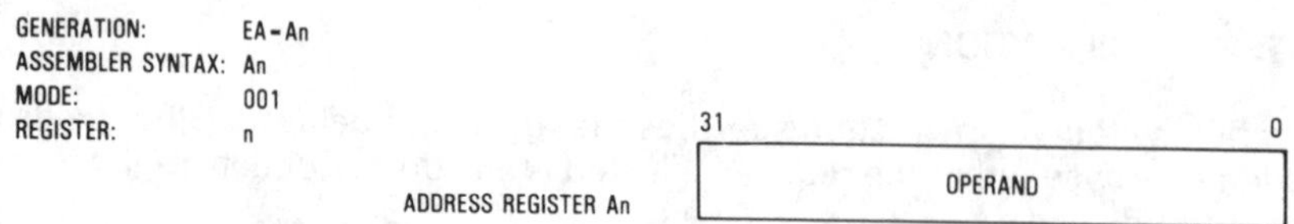

3.10.2 Memory Address Modes

These effective address modes specify that the operand is in memory and provide the specific address of the operand.

3.10.2.1 ADDRESS REGISTER INDIRECT. The address of the operand is in the address register specified by the register field. The reference is classified as a data reference with the exception of the jump and jump-to-subroutine instructions.

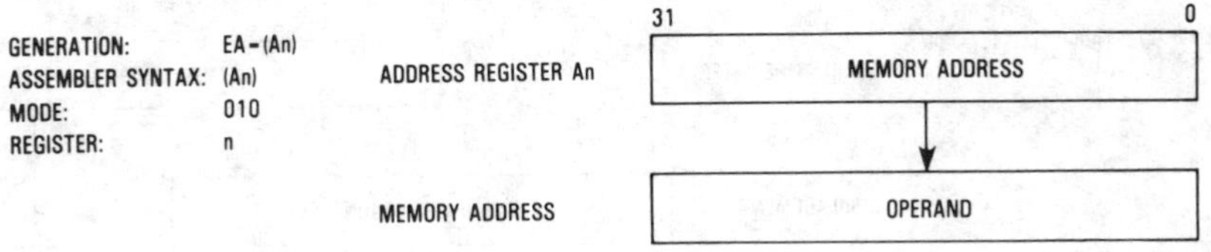

3.10.2.2 ADDRESS REGISTER INDIRECT WITH POSTINCREMENT. The address of the operand is in the address register specified by the register field. After the operand address is used, it is incremented by one, two, or four, depending on whether the size of the operand is byte, word, or long word. If the address register is the stack pointer and the operand size is byte, the address is incremented by two rather than one to keep the stack pointer on a word boundary. The reference is classified as a data reference.

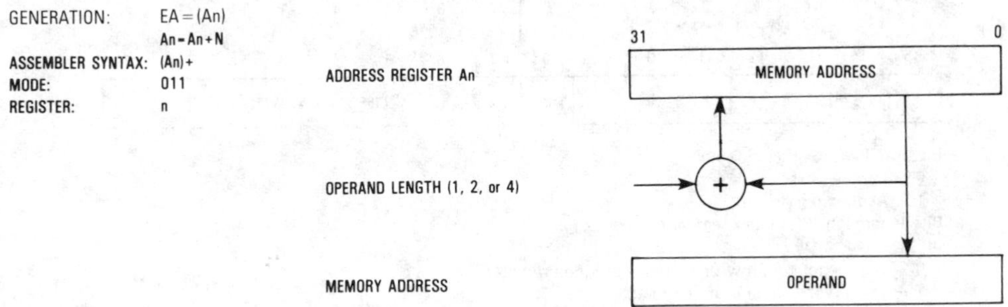

3.10.2.3 ADDRESS REGISTER INDIRECT WITH PREDECREMENT. The address of the operand is in the address register specified by the register field. Before the operand address is used, it is decremented by one, two, or four, depending on whether the operand size is byte, word, or long word. If the address register is the stack pointer and the operand size is byte, the address is decremented by two rather than one to keep the stack pointer on a word boundary. The reference is classified as a data reference.

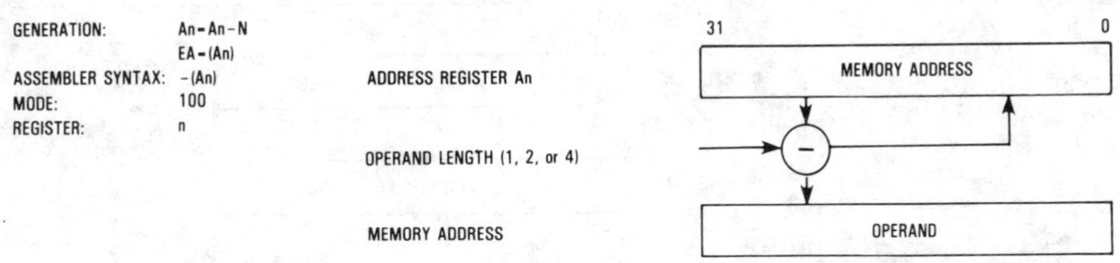

3.10.2.4 ADDRESS REGISTER INDIRECT WITH DISPLACEMENT. This address mode requires one word of extension. The address of the operand is the sum of the address in the address register and the sign-extended, 16-bit displacement integer in the extension word. The reference is classified as a data reference with the exception of the jump and jump-to-subroutine instructions.

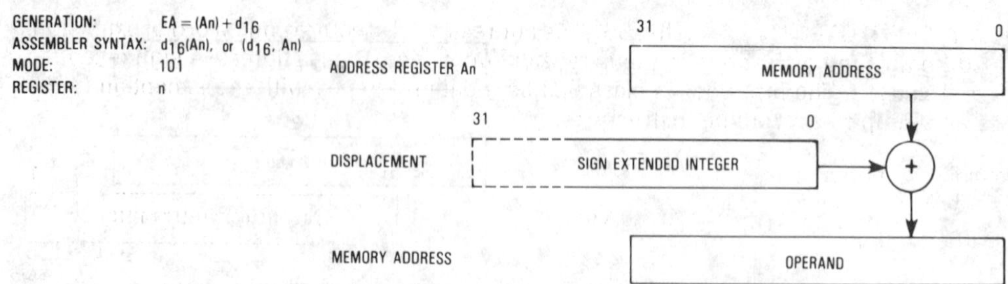

3.10.2.5 ADDRESS REGISTER INDIRECT WITH INDEX. This address mode requires one word of extension formatted as follows:

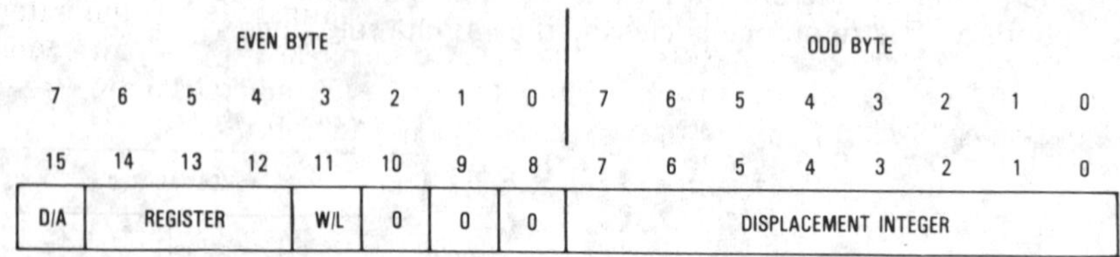

Bit 15 — Index register indicator
- 0 — Data register
- 1 — Address register

Bits 14 through 12 — Index register number

Bit 11 — Index size
- 0 — Sign-extended, low order word in index register
- 1 — Long-word value in index register

The address of the operand is the sum of the address in the address register, the sign-extended displacement integer in the low-order eight bits of the extension word, and the contents of the index register. The reference is classified as a data reference with the exception of the jump and jump-to-subroutine instructions. The size of the index register does not affect the execution time of the instructions.

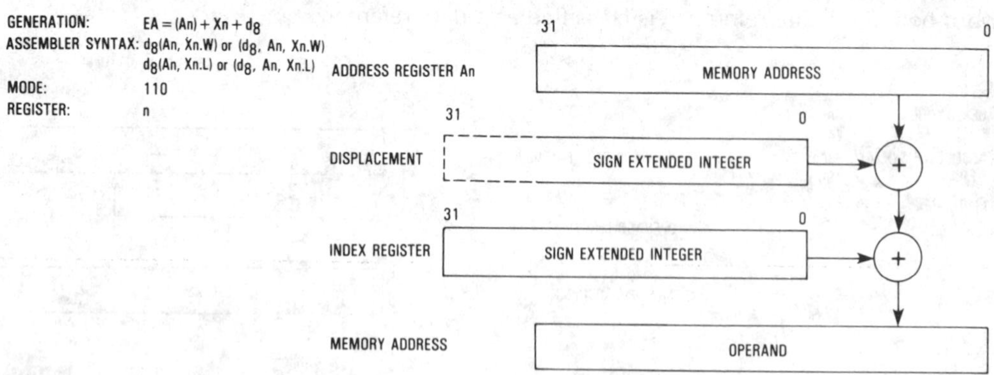

3.10.3 Special Address Modes

The special address modes use the effective address register field to specify the special addressing mode instead of a register number.

3.10.3.1 ABSOLUTE SHORT ADDRESS. This address mode requires one word of extension. The address of the operand is in the extension word. The 16-bit address is sign extended before it is used. The reference is classified as a data reference with the exception of the jump and jump-to-subroutine instructions.

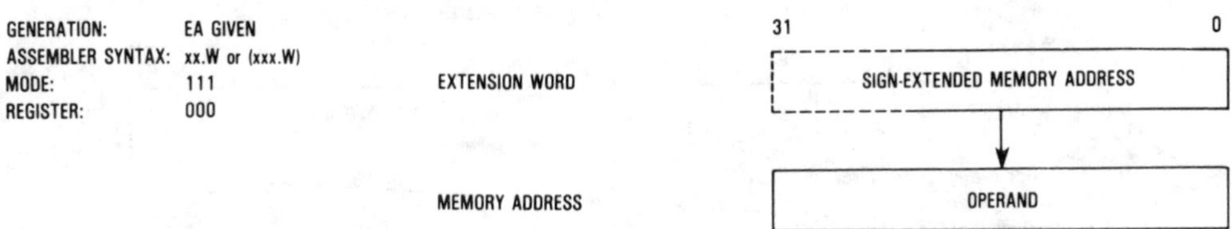

3.10.3.2 ABSOLUTE LONG ADDRESS. The absolute long-address mode requires two words of extension. The address of the operand is developed by concatenating the extension words. The high-order part of the address is the first extension word; the low-order part of the address is the second extension word. The reference is classified as a data reference with the exception of the jump and jump-to-subroutine instructions.

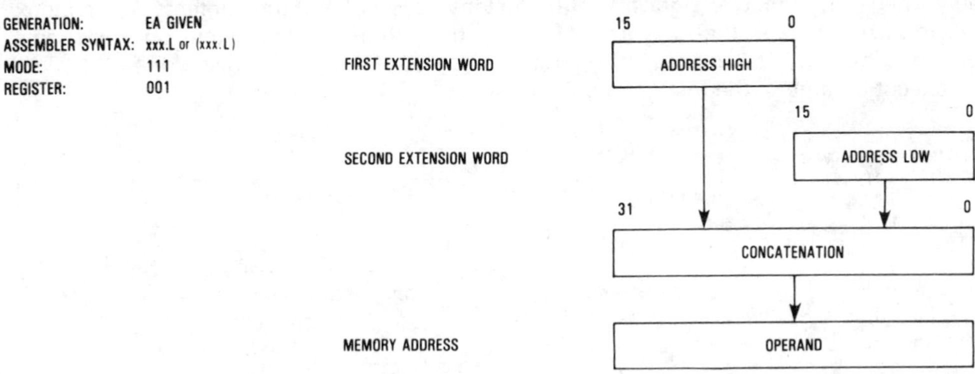

3.10.3.3 PROGRAM COUNTER WITH DISPLACEMENT. This address mode requires one word of extension. The address of the operand is the sum of the address in the program counter and the sign-extended, 16-bit displacement integer in the extension word. The value in the program counter is the address of the extension word. The reference is classified as a program reference.

GENERATION: $EA = (PC) + d_{16}$
ASSEMBLER SYNTAX: $d_{16}(PC)$
MODE: 111
REGISTER: 010

PROGRAM COUNTER — 31 … 0 — ADDRESS OF EXTENSION WORD
EXTENSION WORD — 31 … 0 — SIGN EXTENDED INTEGER — +
MEMORY ADDRESS — OPERAND

3.10.3.4 PROGRAM COUNTER WITH INDEX. This address mode requires one word of extension formatted as follows:

EVEN BYTE								ODD BYTE							
7	6	5	4	3	2	1	0	7	6	5	4	3	2	1	0
15	14	13	12	11	10	9	8	7	6	5	4	3	2	1	0
D/A	REGISTER			W/L	0	0	0	DISPLACEMENT INTEGER							

Bit 15 — Index register indicator
  0 — Data register
  1 — Address register
Bits 14 through 12 — Index register number
Bit 11 — Index size
  0 — Sign-extended, low-order word in index register
  1 — Long-word value in index register

The address is the sum of the address in the program counter, the sign-extended displacement integer in the lower eight bits of the extension word, and the contents of the index register. The value in the program counter is the address of the extension word. This reference is classified as a program reference. The size of the index register does not affect the execution time of the instruction.

GENERATION: EA = (PC) + (Xn) + d
ASSEMBLER SYNTAX: d_8(PC,Xn.W)
d_8(PC,Xn.L)
MODE: 111
REGISTER: 011

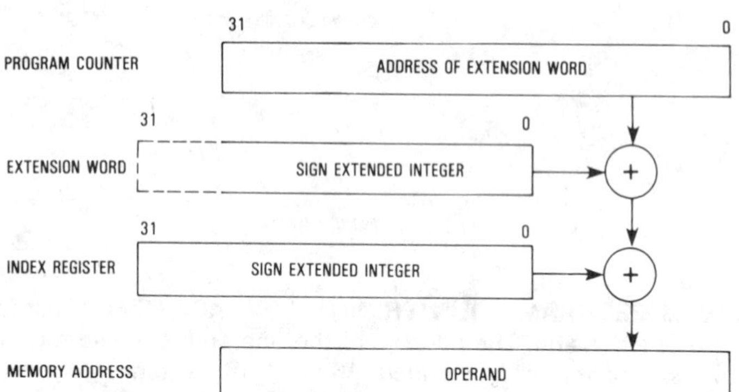

3.10.3.5 IMMEDIATE DATA. This address mode requires either one or two words of extension depending on the size of the operation.

Byte Operation — operand is low-order byte of extension word
Word Operation — operand is extension word
Long-Word Operation — operand is in the two extension words; high-order 16 bits are in the first extension word; low-order 16 bits are in the second extension word.

The extension word formats are as follows:

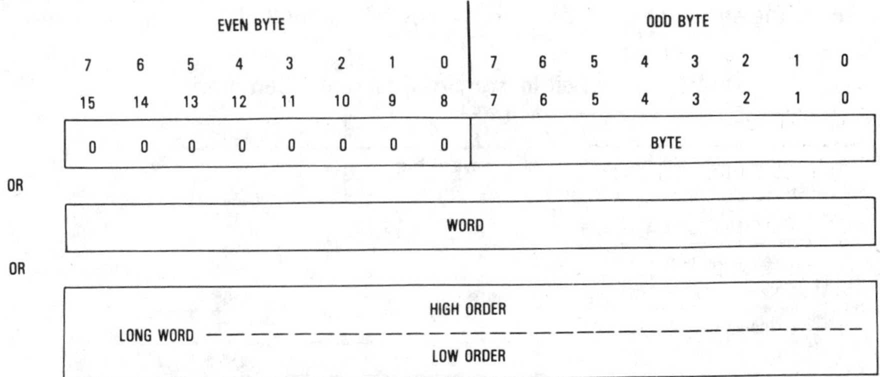

3.10.4 Effective Address Encoding Summary

Table 3-1 is a summary of the effective address modes discussed in the previous paragraphs.

Table 3-1. Effective Address Encoding Summary

Addressing Mode	Mode	Register
Data Register Direct	000	Register Number
Address Register Direct	001	Register Number
Address Register Indirect	010	Register Number
Address Register Indirect with Postincrement	011	Register Number
Address Register Indirect with Predecrement	100	Register Number
Address Register Indirect with Displacement	101	Register Number
Address Register Indirect with Index	110	Register Number
Absolute Short	111	000
Absolute Long	111	001
Program Counter with Displacement	111	010
Program Counter with Index	111	011
Immediate	111	100

3.11 IMPLICIT REFERENCE

Some instructions make implicit reference to the program counter (PC), the system stack pointer (SP), the supervisor stack pointer (SSP), the user stack pointer (USP), or the status register (SR). Table 3-2 provides a list of these instructions and the implied registers.

3.12 STACKS AND QUEUES

In addition to supporting the array data structure with the index addressing mode, the MC68000 also supports stack and queue data structures with the address-register indirect postincrement and predecrement addressing modes. A stack is a last-in first-out (LIFO) list; a queue is a first-in first-out (FIFO) list. Data are added to a stack or queue by being "pushed" onto the structure; data are removed by being "pulled" from the structure.

3

Table 3-2. Implicit Instruction Reference Summary

Instruction	Implied Register(s)
Branch Conditional (Bcc), Branch Always (BRA)	PC
Branch to Subroutine (BSR)	PC, SP
Check Register Against Bounds (CHK)	SSP, SR
Test Condition, Decrement and Branch (DBcc)	PC
Signed Divide (DIVS)	SSP, SR
Unsigned Divide (DIVU)	SSP, SR
Jump (JMP)	PC
Jump to Subroutine (JSR)	PC, SP
Link and Allocate (LINK)	SP
Move Alternate Address Space (MOVES)	SFC, DFC
Push Effective Address (PEA)	SP
Return and Deallocate (RTD)	PC, SP
Return from Exception (RTE)	PC, SP, SR
Return and Restore Condition Codes (RTR)	PC, SP, SR
Return from Subroutine (RTS)	PC, SP
Trap (TRAP)	SSP, SR
Trap on Overflow (TRAPV)	SSP, SR
Unlink (UNLK)	SP

The system stack is used implicitly by many instructions; user stacks and queues can be created and maintained using the addressing modes.

3.12.1 System Stack

Address register seven (A7), or SP, is either SSP or USP. The state of the S bit in the status register determines which stack pointer is accessed as A7. If the S bit indicates supervisor mode, SSP is SP and USP cannot be referenced as an address register. If the S bit indicates user mode, USP is SP and SSP cannot be referenced. Each system stack fills from high memory to low memory. The address mode –(SP) creates a new item on the active system stack; the address mode (SP)+ deletes an item from the active system stack.

A subroutine call saves the program counter on the active system stack, and a return restores the program counter from the active system stack. Both the program counter and the status register are saved on the supervisor stack during the processing of traps and interrupts. Thus, the correct execution of the supervisor-mode code is not dependent on the behavior of user code. USP is available to user programs without restrictions.

To maintain proper data alignment on the system stack, data entry on the stack is restricted. Data is always put in the stack on a word boundary. Thus, byte data is pushed on or pulled from the system stack in the high half of the word; the lower half is unchanged.

3

3.12.2 User Stacks

User stacks can be implemented and manipulated by employing the address-register indirect with postincrement and predecrement addressing modes. Using an address register (one of A0 through A6), the user may implement stacks filled either from high memory to low memory, or vice versa. Important items to remember are as follows:

1. Using predecrement, the register is decremented before its contents are used as the pointer into the stack.
2. Using postincrement, the register is incremented after its contents are used as the pointer into the stack.
3. Byte data must be put on the stack in pairs when mixed with word or long-word data so that the stack does not get misaligned when the data is retrieved. Word and long-word accesses must be on word-boundary (even) addresses.

Stack growth from high to low memory is implemented with
 –(An) — to push data on the stack
 (An)+ — to pull data from the stack

After either a push or a pull operation, register An points to the last (top) item on the stack. This operation is illustrated as follows:

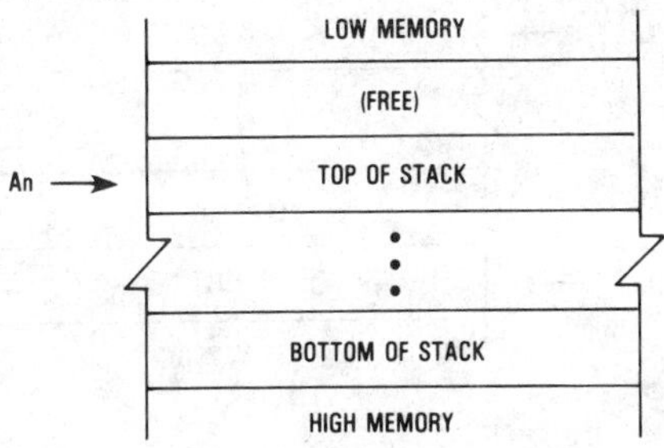

Stack growth from low to high memory is implemented with
 (An)+ — to push data on the stack,
 –(An) — to pull data from the stack.

After either a push or pull operation, register An points to the next available space on the stack. This operation is illustrated as follows:

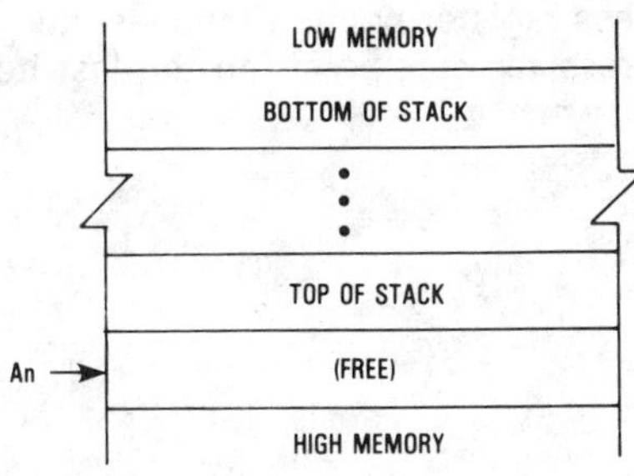

3.12.3 Queues

User queues can be implemented and manipulated with the postincrement or predecrement address-register indirect modes. Using a pair of address registers (two of A0 through A6), the user may implement queues that are filled either from high to low memory, or vice versa. Because queues are pushed from one end and pulled from the other, two registers are used: the put and get pointers.

Queue growth from low to high memory is implemented with
(An)+ — to put data into the queue,
(Am)+ — to get data from the queue.

After a put operation, the put address register points to the next available space in the queue, and the unchanged get address register points to the next item to remove from the queue. After a get operation, the get address register points to the next item to remove from the queue and the unchanged put address register points to the next available space in the queue. This operation is illustrated as follows:

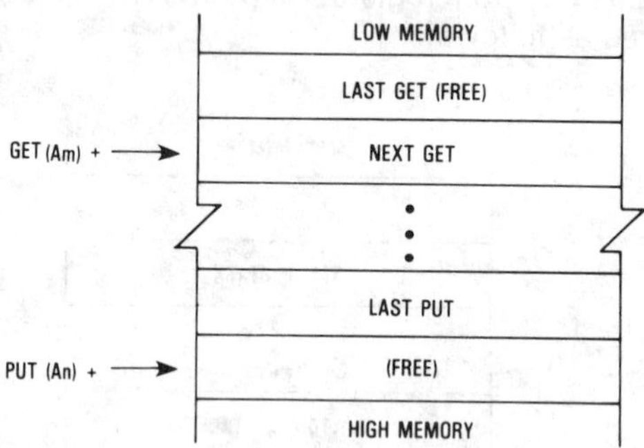

If the queue is to be implemented as a circular buffer, the address register should be checked and adjusted, if necessary, before the put or get operation is performed. The address register is adjusted by subtracting the buffer length (in bytes).

Queue growth from high to low memory is implemented with
–(An) — to put data into the queue,
–(Am) — to get data from the queue.

After a put operation, the put address register points to the last item put in the queue, and the unchanged get address register points to the last item removed from the queue. After a get operation, the get address register points to the last item removed from the queue, and the unchanged put address register points to the last item put in the queue. This operation is illustrated as follows:

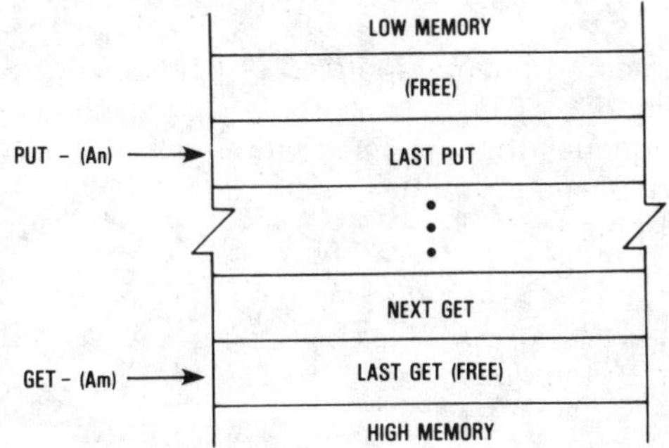

3

If the queue is to be implemented as a circular buffer, the get or put operation should be performed first, and then the address register should be checked and adjusted, if necessary. The address register is adjusted by adding the buffer length (in bytes).

SECTION 4
INSTRUCTION SET SUMMARY

4

This section contains an overview of the M68000 architecture instruction set. The instructions form a set of tools to perform the following operations:

Data Movement	Bit Field Manipulation
Integer Arithmetic	Binary-Coded-Decimal Arithmetic
Logical	Program Control
Shift and Rotate	System Control
Bit Manipulation	Multiprocessor Communications

The complete range of instruction capabilities combined with the flexible addressing modes described previously provide a very flexible base for program development. Information about each instruction is given in **Appendix B Instruction Set Details**. Instructions that are available only on the MC68010 or that are different on the MC68010 are identified with solid bars.

The following notations are used throughout this section:

An = any address register, A0-A7
Dn = any data register, D0-D7
Rn = any address or data register
CCR = condition code register (lower byte of status register)
cc = condition codes from CCR
SP = active stack pointer
USP = user stack pointer
SSP = supervisor stack pointer
DFC = destination function code register
SFC = source function code register
Rc = control register (VBR, SFC, DFC)
d = displacement; d_{16} is a 16-bit displacement
⟨ea⟩ = effective address
list = list of registers, e.g., D0-D3
#⟨data⟩ = immediate data; a literal integer
label = assembly program label
[7] = bit 7 of respective operand
[31:24] = bits 31 through 24 of operand; i.e., high-order byte of a register
X = extend (X) bit in CCR
N = negative (N) bit in CCR
Z = zero (Z) bit in CCR
~ = invert; operand is logically complemented
Λ = logical AND
v = logical OR
o = logical exclusive OR

4.1 DATA MOVEMENT OPERATIONS

Address and data manipulation (transfer and storage) are accomplished by the move (MOVE) instruction and by the associated addressing modes. Data movement instructions allow byte, word, and long-word operands to be transferred from memory to memory, memory to register, register to memory, and register to register. Address movement instructions (MOVE or MOVEA) allow word and long-word operand transfers to ensure that only legal address manipulations are executed. In addition to the general MOVE instruction, there are several special data movement instructions: move multiple registers (MOVEM), move peripheral data (MOVEP), move quick (MOVEQ), exchange registers (EXG), load effective address (LEA), push effective address (PEA), link stack (LINK), unlink stack (UNLK). Table 4-1 is a summary of the data movement operations.

Table 4-1. Data Movement Operations

Instruction	Operand Syntax	Operand Size	Operation
EXG	Rx, Ry	32	Rx — Ry
LEA	⟨ea⟩, An	32	⟨ea⟩ → An
LINK	An, #⟨d⟩	16, 32	SP – 4 → SP; An → (SP); SP → An; SP + d → SP
MOVE MOVEA	⟨ea⟩, ⟨ea⟩ ⟨ea⟩, An	8, 16, 32 16, 32 → 32	Source → Destination
MOVEM	list, ⟨ea⟩ ⟨ea⟩, list	16, 32 16, 32 → 32	Listed Registers → Destination Source → Listed Registers
MOVEP	Dx, (d_{16}, Ay) (d_{16}, Ay), Dx	16, 32	Dx [31:24] → (Ay + d); Dx [23:16] → (Ay + d + 2); Dx [15:8] – (Ay + d + 4); Dx [7:0] → (Ay + d + 6) (Ay + d) → Dx [31:34]; (Dy + d + 2) → Dx [23:16]; (Ay + d + 4) → Dx [15:8]; (Ay + d + 6) → Dx [7:0]
MOVEQ	#⟨data⟩, Dn	8 → 32	Immediate Data → Destination
PEA	⟨ea⟩	32	SP – 4 → (SP); ⟨ea⟩ → (SP)
UNLK	An	32	An → SP; (SP) → An; SP + 4 → SP

4.2 INTEGER ARITHMETIC OPERATIONS

The arithmetic operations include the four basic operations of add (ADD), subtract (SUB), multiply (MUL), and divide (DIV) as well as arithmetic compare (CMP, CMPM), clear (CLR), and negate (NEG). The ADD, CMP, and SUB instructions are available for both address and data operations, with data operations accepting all operand sizes. Address operations are limited to 16- or 32-bit operands (legal address sizes). The clear and negate instructions may be used on all sizes of data operands.

The MUL and DIV operations are available for signed and unsigned operands, using word multiply to produce a long-word product, and using a long-word dividend with word divisor to produce a word quotient with a word remainder.

Multiprecision and mixed-sized arithmetic can be accomplished using a set of extended instructions. These instructions are add extended (ADDX), subtract extended (SUBX), sign extend (EXT), and negate binary with extend (NEGX).

Table 4-2 is a summary of the integer arithmetic operations.

Table 4-2. Integer Arithmetic Operations

Instruction	Operand Syntax	Operand Size	Operation
ADD ADDA	Dn, ⟨ea⟩ ⟨ea⟩, Dn ⟨ea⟩, An	8, 16, 32 8, 16, 32 16, 32	Source + Destination ➧ Destination
ADDI ADDQ	#⟨data⟩, ⟨ea⟩ #⟨data⟩, ⟨ea⟩	8, 16, 32 8, 16, 32	Immediate Data + Destination ➧ Destination
ADDX	Dy, Dx – (Ay), – (Ax)	8, 16, 32 8, 16, 32	Source + Destination + X ➧ Destination
CLR	⟨ea⟩	8, 16, 32	0 ➧ Destination
CMP CMPA	⟨ea⟩, Dn ⟨ea⟩, An	8, 16, 32 16, 32	Destination — Source
CMPI	#⟨data⟩, ⟨ea⟩	8, 16, 32	Destination — Immediate Data
CMPM	(Ay) + , (Ax) +	8, 16, 32	Destination — Source
DIVS/DIVU	⟨ea⟩, Dn	32/16 ➧ 16:16	Destination/Source ➧ Destination (Signed or Unsigned)
EXT	Dn Dn	8 ➧ 16 16 ➧ 32	Sign Extended Destination ➧ Destination
MULS/MULU	⟨ea⟩, Dn	16 × 16 ➧ 32	Source*Destination ➧ Destination (Signed or Unsigned)
NEG	⟨ea⟩	8, 16, 32	0 — Destination ➧ Destination
NEGX	⟨ea⟩	8, 16, 32	0 — Destination — X ➧ Destination
SUB SUBA	⟨ea⟩, Dn Dn, ⟨ea⟩ ⟨ea⟩, An	8, 16, 32 8, 16, 32 16, 32	Destination — Source ➧ Destination
SUBI SUBQ	#⟨data⟩, ⟨ea⟩ #⟨data⟩, ⟨ea⟩	8, 16, 32 8, 16 ,32	Destination — Immediate Data ➧ Destination
SUBX	Dx, Dy – (Ax), – (Ay)	8, 16, 32 8, 16, 32	Destination — Source — X ➧ Destination

4.3 LOGICAL OPERATIONS

Logical-operation instructions and logical (AND), inclusive or logical (OR), exclusive or logical (EOR), and logical complement (NOT) are available for all sizes of integer data operands. A similar set of immediate instructions and immediate (ANDI), inclusive or (ORI), and exclusive or immediate (EORI) provide these logical operations with all sizes of immediate data. Test an operand (TST) is an arithmetic comparison of the operand with zero, which is then reflected in the condition codes. Table 4-3 is a summary of the logical operations.

Table 4-3. Logical Operations

Instruction	Operand Syntax	Operand Size	Operation
AND	⟨ea⟩, Dn Dn, ⟨ea⟩	8, 16, 32 8, 16, 32	Source Λ Destination ➧ Destination
ANDI	#⟨data⟩, ⟨ea⟩	8, 16, 32	Immediate Data Λ Destination ➧ Destination
EOR	Dn, ⟨ea⟩	8, 16, 32	Source ⊗ Destination ➧ Destination
EORI	#⟨data⟩, ⟨ea⟩	8, 16, 32	Immediate Data ⊗ Destination ➧ Destination
NOT	⟨ea⟩	8, 16, 32	~Destination ➧ Destination
OR	⟨ea⟩, Dn Dn, ⟨ea⟩	8, 16, 32 8, 16, 32	Source V Destination ➧ Destination
ORI	#⟨data⟩, ⟨ea⟩	8, 16, 32	Immediate Data V Destination ➧ Destination
TST	⟨ea⟩	8, 16, 32	Source – 0 to Set Condition Codes

4.4 SHIFT AND ROTATE OPERATIONS

Shift operations in both directions are provided by the arithmetic shift right (ASR) and arithmetic shift left (ASL) instructions, and logical shift right (LSR) and logical shift left (LSL) instructions. The available rotate instructions (with and without extend) are rotate right (ROR), rotate left (ROL), rotate right with extend (ROXR), and rotate left with extend (ROXL). All shift and rotate operations can be performed on either registers or memory.

Register shifts and rotates support all operand sizes and allow a shift count (from one to eight) to be specified in the instruction operation word or a shift count (modulo 64) to be specified in a register.

Memory shifts and rotates are only for word operands and allow only single-bit shifts or rotates. The swap register halves (SWAP) instruction exchanges the 16-bit halves of a register. Performance of shift/rotate instructions is enhanced so that use of the ROR or ROL instructions with a shift count of eight allows fast byte swapping. Table 4-4 is a summary of the shift and rotate operations.

Table 4-4. Shift and Rotate Operations

Instruction	Operand Syntax	Operand Size	Operation
ASL	Dx, Dy #⟨data⟩, Dy ⟨ea⟩	8, 16, 32 8, 16, 32 16	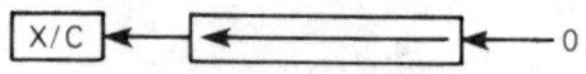 X/C 0
ASR	Dx, Dy #⟨data⟩, Dy ⟨ea⟩	8, 16, 32 8, 16, 32 16	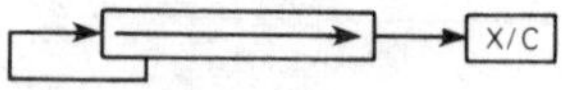 X/C
LSL	Dx, Dy #⟨data⟩, Dy ⟨data⟩	8, 16, 32 8, 16, 32 16	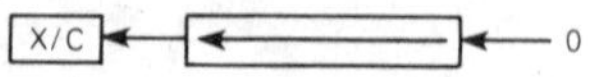 X/C 0
LSR	Dx, Dy #⟨data⟩, Dy ⟨ea⟩	8, 16, 32 8, 16, 32 16	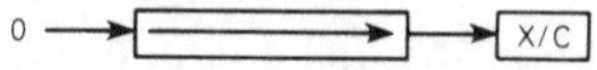 0 X/C
ROL	Dx, Dy #⟨data⟩, Dy ⟨ea⟩	8, 16, 32 8, 16, 32 16	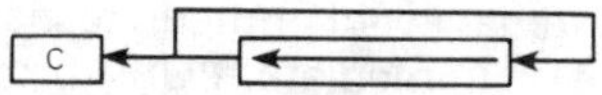 C
ROR	Dx, Dy #⟨data⟩, Dy ⟨ea⟩	8, 16, 32 8, 16, 32 16	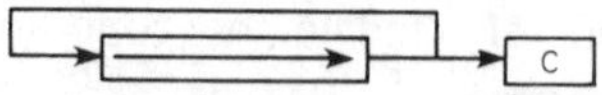 C
ROXL	Dx, Dy #⟨data⟩, Dy ⟨ea⟩	8, 16, 32 8, 16, 32 16	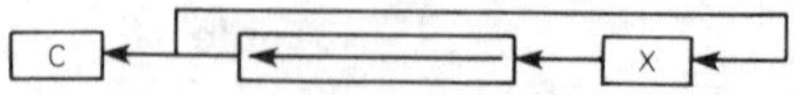 C X
ROXR	Dx, Dy #⟨data⟩, Dy ⟨ea⟩	8, 16, 32 8, 16, 32 16	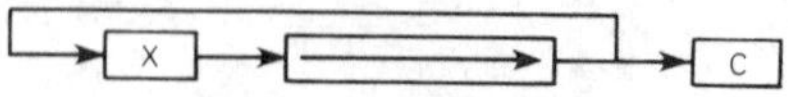 X C
SWAP	Dx	32	 MSW LSW

4.5 BIT-MANIPULATION OPERATIONS

Bit-manipulation operations are accomplished using the following instructions: bit test (BTST), bit test and set (BSET), bit test and clear (BCLR), and bit test and change (BCHG).

All bit-manipulation operations can be performed on either registers or memory, with the bit number specified as immediate data or by the contents of a data register. Register operands are always 32 bits; memory operands are always 8 bits. Table 4-5 is a summary of the bit-manipulation operations. (Z is bit 2, the "zero" bit, of the status register.)

Table 4-5. Bit-Manipulation Operations

Instruction	Operand Syntax	Operand Size	Operation
BCHG	Dn, ⟨ea⟩ #⟨data⟩	8, 32 8, 32	~(<Bit Number>of Destination) → Z → Bit of Destination
BCLR	Dn, ⟨ea⟩ #⟨data⟩, ⟨ea⟩	8, 32 8, 32	~(<Bit Number>of Destination) → Z; 0 → Bit of Destination
BSET	Dn, ⟨ea⟩ #⟨data⟩, ⟨ea⟩	8, 32 8, 32	~(<Bit Number>of Destination) → Z; 1 → Bit of Destination
BTST	Dn, ⟨ea⟩ #⟨data⟩, ⟨ea⟩	8, 32 8, 32	~(<Bit Number>of Destination) → Z

4.6 BINARY-CODED-DECIMAL OPERATIONS

Multiprecision arithmetic operations on binary-coded-decimal numbers are accomplished using the following instructions: add decimal with extend (ABCD), subtract decimal with extend (SBCD), and negate decimal with extend (NBCD). Table 4-6 is a summary of the binary-coded-decimal operations.

Table 4-6. Binary-Coded-Decimal Operations

Instruction	Operand Syntax	Operand Size	Operation
ABCD	Dy, Dx –(Ay), –(Ax)	8 8	$Source_{10} + Destination_{10} + X$ → Destination
NBCD	⟨ea⟩	8	$0 - Destination_{10} - X -$ → Destination
SBCD	Dx, Dy –(Ax), –(Ay)	8 8	$Destination_{10} - Source_{10} - X$ → Destination

4.7 PROGRAM CONTROL OPERATIONS

Program control operations are accomplished using a set of conditional and unconditional branch instructions and return instructions. Table 4-7 summarizes these instructions.

The conditional instructions provide testing and branching for the following conditions:

- CC —Carry clear
- CS —Carry set
- EQ —Equal
- F —Never true*
- GE —Greater or equal
- GT —Greater than
- HI —High
- LE —Less or equal
- LS —Low or same
- LT —Less than
- MI —Minus
- NE —Not equal
- PL —Plus
- T —Always true*
- VC —Overflow clear
- VS —Overflow set

*Not available for the branch conditionally (Bcc) instructions; use branch always (BRA) for T and no operation (NOP) for F.

Table 4-7. Program Control Operations

Instruction	Operand Syntax	Operand Size	Operation
Conditional			
Bcc	⟨label⟩	8, 16	If Condition True, Then PC + d ▶ PC
DBcc	Dn, ⟨label⟩	16	If Condition False, Then Dn − 1 ▶ Dn If Dn ≠ − 1, Then PC + d ▶ PC
Scc	⟨ea⟩	8	If Condition True, Then 1's ▶ Destination; Else 0's ▶ Destination
Unconditional			
BRA	⟨label⟩	8, 16	PC + d ▶ PC
BSR	⟨label⟩	8, 16	SP − 4 ▶ SP; PC ▶ (SP); PC + d ▶ PC
JMP	⟨ea⟩	none	Destination ▶ PC
JSR	⟨ea⟩	none	SP − 4 ▶ SP; PC ▶ (SP); Destination ▶ PC
NOP	none	none	PC + 2 ▶ PC
Returns			
RTD	#⟨d⟩	16	(SP) ▶ PC; SP + 4 + d ▶ SP
RTR	none	none	(SP) ▶ CCR; SP + 2 ▶ SP; (SP) ▶ PC; SP + 4 ▶ SP
RTS	none	none	(SP) ▶ PC; SP + 4 ▶ SP

4.8 SYSTEM CONTROL OPERATIONS

System control operations are accomplished by using privileged instructions, trap-generating instructions, and instructions that use or modify the condition code register. These instructions are summarized in Table 4-8. In the MC68010, the move from the status register (MOVE from SR) instruction has been made privileged, and the move from the condition code register (MOVE from CCR) has been added. For more detail see **2.3 VIRTUAL MEMORY/MACHINE CONCEPTS.**

4.9 MULTIPROCESSOR OPERATIONS

Communication between the M68000 Family of microprocessors is supported by the test and set an operand (TAS) instruction,which executes indivisible read-modify-write bus cycles (see Table 4-9).

Table 4-8. System Control Operations

Instruction	Operand Syntax	Operand Size	Operation
		Privileged	
ANDI	#⟨data⟩, SR	16	Immediate Data Λ SR → SR
EORI	#⟨data⟩, SR	16	Immediate Data ⊗ SR → SR
MOVE	⟨ea⟩, SR SR, ⟨ea⟩	16 16	Source → SR SR → Destination
MOVE	USP, An An, USP	32 32	USP → An An → USP
MOVEC	Rc, Rn Rn, Rc	32 32	Rc → Rn Rn → Rc
MOVES	Rn, ⟨ea⟩ ⟨ea⟩, Rn	8, 16, 32	Rn → Destination Using DFC Source Using SFC → Rn
ORI	#⟨data⟩, SR	16	Immediate Data V SR → SR
RESET	none	none	Assert $\overline{\text{RESET}}$ line
RTE	none	none	(SP) → SR; SP+2 → SP; (SP) → PC; SP+4 → SP; Restore Stack According to Format
STOP	#⟨data⟩	16	Immediate Data → SR; STOP
		Trap Generating	
BKPT	#⟨data⟩	none	Execute Breakpoint Acknowledge Bus Cycle; . . . Trap as Illegal Instruction
CHK	⟨ea⟩, Dn	16	If Dn<0 or Dn>(ea), Then CHK Exception
Illegal	none	none	SSP − 2 → SSP; Vector Offset → (SSP); . . . SSP − 4 → SSP; PC → (SSP); SSP − 2 → SSP; SR → (SSP); Illegal Instruction Vector Address → PC
TRAP	#⟨data⟩	none	SSP − 2 → SSP; Format and Vector Offset → (SSP); . . . SSP − 4 → SSP; PC → (SSP); SSP − 2 → SSP; SR → (SSP); Vector Address → PC
TRAPV	none	none	If V Then Take Overflow TRAP Exception
		Condition Code Register	
ANDI	#⟨data⟩, CCR	8	Immediate Data Λ CCR → CCR
EORI	#⟨data⟩, CCR	8	Immediate Data ⊗ CCR → CCR
MOVE	⟨ea⟩, CCR CCR, ⟨ea⟩	16 16	Source → CCR CCR → Destination
ORI	#⟨data⟩, CCR	8	Immediate Data V CCR → CCR

Table 4-9. Multiprocessor Operations

Instruction	Operand Syntax	Operand Size	Operation
TAS	⟨ea⟩	8	Destination − 0; Set Condition Codes; 1 → Destination [7]

4

SECTION 5
SIGNAL AND BUS OPERATION DESCRIPTION

This section, which contains brief descriptions of the input and output signals, also discusses bus operation during the various machine cycles.

5

NOTE

The terms **assertion** and **negation** are used extensively in this manual to avoid confusion when describing a mixture of "active-low" and "active-high" signals. The term assert or assertion is used to indicate that a signal is active or true, independently of whether that level is represented by a high or low voltage. The term negate or negation is used to indicate that a signal is inactive or false.

5.1 SIGNAL DESCRIPTIONS

The input and output signals can be functionally organized into the groups shown in Figure 5-1 (for the MC68000, the MC68HC000, and the MC68010), Figure 5-2 (for the MC68008, 48-pin version), and Figure 5-3 (for the MC68008, 52-pin version). The following paragraphs provide brief descriptions of the signals and references (where applicable) to other paragraphs that contain more information about the signals.

5.1.1 Address Bus (A1 through A23)

This 23-bit, unidirectional, three-state bus in the MC68000, MC68HC000, and the MC68010 is capable of addressing 16 megabytes of data. This bus provides the address for bus operation during all cycles except interrupt acknowledge cycles. During interrupt acknowledge cycles, address lines A1, A2, and A3 provide the level number of the interrupt being acknowledged, and address lines A4 through A23 are driven to logic high.

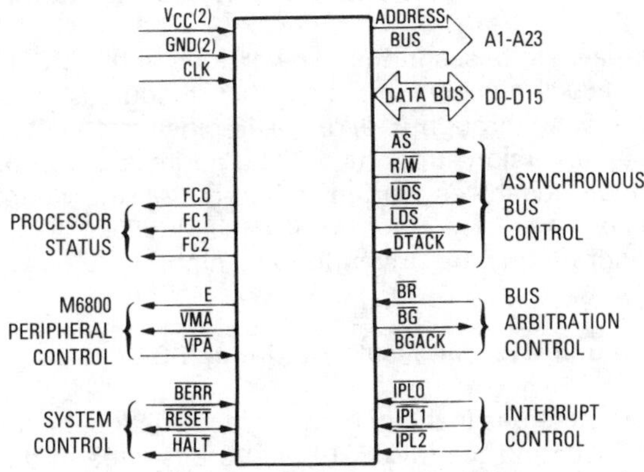

Figure 5-1. Input and Output Signals (MC68000, MC68HC000, and MC68010)

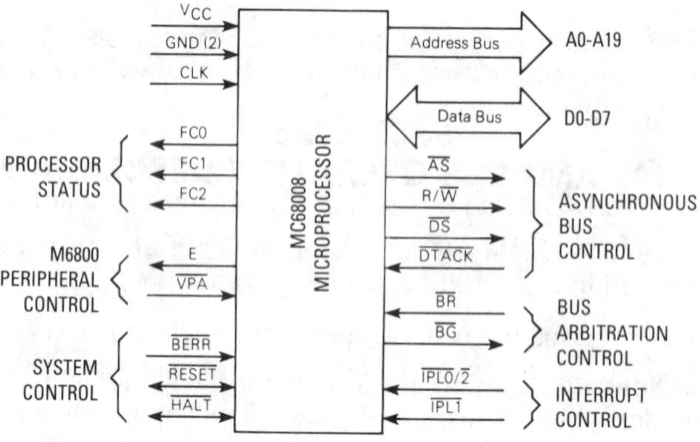

Figure 5-2. Input and Output Signals (MC68008, 48-Pin Version)

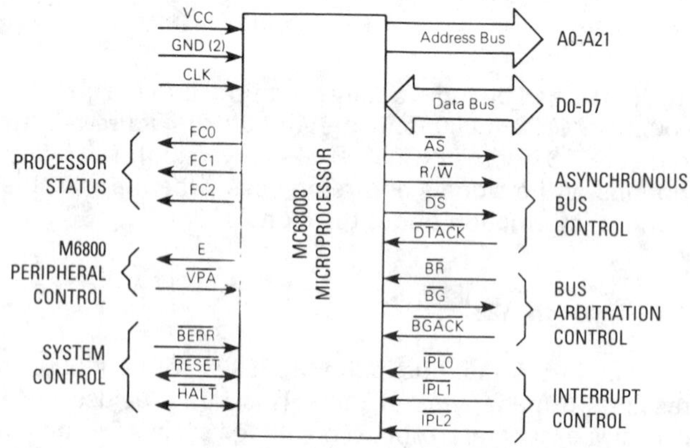

Figure 5-3. Input and Output Signals (MC68008, 52-Pin Version)

5.1.2 MC68008 Address Bus (48-Pin: A0 through A19; 52-Pin: A0 through A21)

The unidirectional, three-state buses in the two versions of the MC68008 differ from each other and from the MC68000 bus only in the number of address lines and the addressing range. The 20-bit address (A0 through A19) of the 48-pin version provides a one-megabyte address space; the 52-pin version supports a 22-bit address (A0 through A21), extending the address space to four megabytes. During an interrupt-acknowledge cycle, the interrupt level number is placed on lines A1, A2, and A3 (like the MC68000). Lines A0 and A4 through the most significant address line are driven to logic high.

5.1.3 Data Bus (D0 through D15; MC68008: D0 through D7)

This bidirectional, three-state bus is the general-purpose data path. It is 16 bits wide in the MC68000, the MC68HC000, and the MC68010, and 8 bits wide in the MC68008. The bus can transfer and accept data of either word or byte length. During an interrupt-acknowledge cycle, the external device supplies the vector number on data lines D0 through D7.

5.1.4 Asynchronous Bus Control

Asynchronous data transfers are controlled by the following signals: address strobe, read/write, upper and lower data strobes, and data transfer acknowledge. These signals are described in the following paragraphs.

5.1.4.1 ADDRESS STROBE (AS). This three-state signal indicates that the information on the address bus is a valid address.

5.1.4.2 READ/WRITE (R/W). This three-state signal defines the data-bus transfer as a read or write cycle. The R/W signal relates to the data strobe signals described in the following paragraphs.

5.1.4.3 UPPER AND LOWER DATA STROBES (UDS, LDS). These three-state signals and R/W, control the flow of data on the data bus of the MC68000, the MC68HC000, and the MC68010. Table 5-1 lists the combinations of these signals and the corresponding data on the bus. When the R/W line is high, the processor reads from the data bus. When the R/W line is low, the processor drives the data bus.

Table 5-1. Data Strobe Control of Data Bus (MC68000, MC68HC000, and MC68010)

UDS	LDS	R/W	D8-D15	D0-D7
High	High	—	No Valid Data	No Valid Data
Low	Low	High	Valid Data Bits 8-15	Valid Data Bits 0-7
High	Low	High	No Valid Data	Valid Data Bits 0-7
Low	High	High	Valid Data Bus 8-15	No Valid Data
Low	Low	Low	Valid Data Bits 8-15	Valid Data Bits 0-7
High	Low	Low	Valid Data Bits 0-7*	Valid Data Bits 0-7
Low	High	Low	Valid Data Bits 8-15	Valid Data Bits 8-15*

*These conditions are a result of current implementation and may not appear on future devices.

5.1.4.4 DATA STROBE (MC68008: DS). This three-state signal and R/W control the flow of data on the data bus of the MC68008. Table 5-2 lists the combinations of these signals and the corresponding data on the bus. When the R/W line is high, the processor reads from the data bus. When the R/W line is low, the processor drives the data bus.

Table 5-2. Data Strobe Control of Data Bus (MC68008)

DS	R/W	D0-D7
1	—	No Valid Data
0	1	Valid Data Bits 0-7 (Read Cycle)
0	0	Valid Data Bits 0-7 (Write Cycle)

5.1.4.5 DATA TRANSFER ACKNOWLEDGE ($\overline{\text{DTACK}}$). This input signal indicates the completion of the data transfer. When the processor recognizes $\overline{\text{DTACK}}$ during a read cycle, data is latched, and the bus cycle is terminated. When $\overline{\text{DTACK}}$ is recognized during a write cycle, the bus cycle is terminated. (Refer to **5.2.7 Asynchronous Operation** and **5.2.8 Synchronous Operation**.)

5.1.5 Bus Arbitration Control

The bus request, bus grant, and bus grant acknowledge signals form a bus arbitration circuit to determine which device becomes the bus master device. In the 48-pin version of the MC68008, no pin is available for the bus grant acknowledge signal; this microprocessor uses a two-wire bus arbitration scheme.

5.1.5.1 BUS REQUEST ($\overline{\text{BR}}$). This input can be wire-ORed with bus request signals from all other devices that could be bus masters. This signal indicates to the processor that some other device needs to become the bus master. Bus requests can be issued at any time during a cycle or between cycles.

5.1.5.2 BUS GRANT ($\overline{\text{BG}}$). This output signal indicates to all other potential bus-master devices that the processor will relinquish bus control at the end of the current bus cycle.

5.1.5.3 BUS GRANT ACKNOWLEDGE ($\overline{\text{BGACK}}$). This input indicates that some other device has become the bus master. This signal should not be asserted until the following conditions are met:

1. A bus grant has been received.
2. Address strobe is inactive, which indicates that the microprocessor is not using the bus.
3. Data transfer acknowledge is inactive, which indicates that neither memory nor peripherals are using the bus.
4. Bus grant acknowledge is inactive, which indicates that no other device is still claiming bus mastership.

The 48-pin version of the MC68008 has no pin available for the bus grant acknowledge signal and uses a two-wire bus arbitration scheme instead. If another device in a system supplies a bus grant acknowledge signal, the bus request input signal to the processor should be asserted when either the bus request or the bus grant acknowledge from that device is asserted.

5.1.6 Interrupt Control ($\overline{\text{IPL0}}$, $\overline{\text{IPL1}}$, $\overline{\text{IPL2}}$)

These input signals indicate the encoded priority level of the device requesting an interrupt. Level seven, which cannot be masked, has the highest priority; level zero indicates that no interrupts are requested. $\overline{\text{IPL0}}$ is the least significant bit of the encoded level, and $\overline{\text{IPL2}}$ is the most significant bit. For each interrupt request, these signals must remain asserted until the processor signals interrupt acknowledge (FC0 through FC2 and A16 through A19 high) for that request to ensure that the interrupt is recognized.

The 48-pin version of the MC68008 has only two interrupt control signals: IPL0/IPL2 and IPL1. IPL0/IPL2 is internally connected to both IPL0 and IPL2, which provides four interrupt priority levels: levels 0, 2, 5, and 7. In all other respects, the interrupt priority levels in this version of the MC68008 are identical to those levels in the other microprocessors described in this manual.

5.1.7 System Control

The system control inputs are used to reset the processor, to halt the processor, and to signal a bus error to the processor. The outputs reset the external devices in the system and signal a processor error halt to those devices. The three system control signals are described in the following paragraphs.

5

5.1.7.1 BUS ERROR (BERR). This input signal indicates a problem in the current bus cycle. The problem may be

1. No response from a device;
2. No interrupt vector number returned;
3. An illegal access request rejected by a memory management unit; or
4. Some other application-dependent error.

Either the processor retries the bus cycle or performs exception processing, as determined by interaction between the bus error signal and the halt signal. Refer to **5.2.4 Bus Error and Halt Operation** for additional information.

5.1.7.2 RESET (RESET). The external assertion of this bidirectional signal along with the assertion of HALT starts a system initialization sequence by resetting the processor. The processor assertion of RESET (from executing a RESET instruction) resets all external devices of a system without affecting the internal state of the processor. To reset both the processor and the external devices, the RESET and HALT input signals must be asserted at the same time. Refer to **5.2.5 Reset Operation** for further information.

5.1.7.3 HALT (HALT). An input to this bidirectional signal causes the processor to stop bus activity at the completion of the current bus cycle. This operation places all control signals in the inactive state and places all three-state lines in the high-impedance state (refer to Table 5-4). For additional information about the interaction between HALT and RESET, refer to **5.2.5 Reset Operation** and for more information on HALT and BERR, refer to **5.2.4 Bus Error and Halt Operation**.

When the processor has stopped executing instructions (in the case of a double bus fault condition, for example), the HALT line is driven by the processor to indicate the condition to external devices. Refer to **5.2.4.4 DOUBLE BUS FAULTS.**

5.1.8 M6800 Peripheral Control

These control signals are used to interface the asynchronous M68000 processors with the synchronous M6800 peripheral devices. These signals are described in the following paragraphs.

5.1.8.1 ENABLE (E). This signal is the standard enable signal common to all M6800 Family peripheral devices. A single period of clock E consists of ten MC68000 clock periods (six clocks low, four clocks high). This signal is generated by an internal ring counter that may come up in any state. (At power on, it is impossible to guarantee phase relationship of E to CLK.) The E signal is a free-running clock that runs regardless of the state of the MPU bus.

5.1.8.2 VALID PERIPHERAL ADDRESS ($\overline{\text{VPA}}$). This input signal indicates that the device or memory area addressed is an M6800 Family device or a memory area assigned to M6800 Family devices and that data transfer should be synchronized with the E signal. This input also indicates that the processor should use automatic vectoring for an interrupt. Refer to **SECTION 7 M6800 PERIPHERAL INTERFACE.**

5.1.8.3 VALID MEMORY ADDRESS ($\overline{\text{VMA}}$). This output signal indicates to M6800 peripheral devices that the address on the address bus is valid and that the processor is synchronized to the E signal. This signal only responds to a $\overline{\text{VPA}}$ input that identifies an M6800 Family device.

The MC68008 does not supply a $\overline{\text{VMA}}$ signal. This signal can be produced by a transistor-to-transistor logic (TTL) circuit; an example is described in **7.1 DATA TRANSFER OPERATION.**

5.1.9 Processor Function Codes (FC0, FC1, FC2)

These function code outputs indicate the mode (user or supervisor) and the address space type currently being accessed, as shown in Table 5-3. The function code outputs are valid whenever $\overline{\text{AS}}$ is active.

Table 5-3. Function Code Outputs

Function Code Output			Address-Space Type
FC2	FC1	FC0	
Low	Low	Low	(Undefined, Reserved)
Low	Low	High	User Data
Low	High	Low	User Program
Low	High	High	(Undefined, Reserved)
High	Low	Low	(Undefined, Reserved)
High	Low	High	Supervisor Data
High	High	Low	Supervisor Program
High	High	High	CPU Space

5.1.10 Clock (CLK)

The clock input is a TTL-compatible signal that is internally buffered for development of the internal clocks needed by the processor. This clock signal is a constant frequency square wave that requires no stretching or shaping. The clock input should not be gated off at any time, and the clock signal must conform to minimum and maximum pulse-width times listed in **11.5 AC ELECTRICAL SPECIFICATIONS — CLOCK TIMING.**

5.1.11 Power Supply (V_{CC} and GND)

Power is supplied to the processor using these connections. The positive output of the power supply is connected to the V_{CC} pins and ground is connected to the GND pins.

5.1.12 Signal Summary

Table 5-4 summarizes the signals discussed in the preceding paragraphs.

Table 5-4. Signal Summary

Signal Name	Mnemonic	Input/Output	Active State	Hi-Z	
				On $\overline{HALT}$	On $\overline{BGACK}$
Address Bus	A1-A23	Output	High	Yes	Yes
Data Bus	D0-D15	Input/Output	High	Yes	Yes
Address Strobe	$\overline{AS}$	Output	Low	No	Yes
Read/Write	R/$\overline{W}$	Output	Read-High Write-Low	No	Yes
Data Strobe	$\overline{DS}$	Output	Low	No	Yes
Upper and Lower Data Strobes	$\overline{UDS}$, $\overline{LDS}$	Output	Low	No	Yes
Data Transfer Acknowledge	$\overline{DTACK}$	Input	Low	No	No
Bus Request	$\overline{BR}$	Input	Low	No	No
Bus Grant	$\overline{BG}$	Output	Low	No	No
Bus Grant Acknowledge	$\overline{BGACK}$	Input	Low	No	No
Interrupt Priority Level	$\overline{IPL0}$, $\overline{IPL1}$, $\overline{IPL2}$	Input	Low	No	No
Bus Error	$\overline{BERR}$	Input	Low	No	No
Reset	$\overline{RESET}$	Input/Output	Low	No[1]	No[1]
Halt	$\overline{HALT}$	Input/Output	Low	No[1]	No[1]
Enable	E	Output	High	No	No
Valid Memory Address	$\overline{VMA}$	Output	Low	No	Yes
Valid Peripheral Address	$\overline{VPA}$	Input	Low	No	No
Function Code Output	FC0, FC1, FC2	Output	High	No	Yes
Clock	CLK	Input	High	No	No
Power Input	V_{CC}	Input	—	—	—
Ground	GND	Input	—	—	—

NOTE 1. Open drain.

5.2 BUS OPERATION

The following paragraphs describe control signal and bus operation during data transfer operations, bus arbitration, bus error and halt conditions, and reset operation.

5.2.1 Data Transfer Operations

Transfer of data between devices involves the following signals:

1. Address bus A1 through highest numbered address line
2. Data bus D0 through highest numbered data line
3. Control signals

The address and data buses are separate parallel buses used to transfer data using an asynchronous bus structure. In all cases, the bus master must deskew all signals it issues at both the start and end of a bus cycle. In addition, the bus master must deskew the acknowledge and data signals from the slave device.

The following paragraphs describe the read, write, read-modify-write, and CPU space cycles. The indivisible read-modify-write cycle implements interlocked multiprocessor communications. A CPU space cycle is a special processor cycle.

5.2.1.1 READ CYCLE. During a read cycle, the processor receives either one or two bytes of data from the memory or from a peripheral device. If the instruction specifies a word or long-word operation, the MC68000, MC68HC000, or MC68010 processor reads both upper and lower bytes simultaneously by asserting both upper and lower data strobes. When the instruction specifies byte operation, the processor uses the internal A0 bit to determine which byte to read and issues the appropriate data strobe. When A0 equals zero, the upper data strobe is issued; when A0 equals one, the lower data strobe is issued. When the data is received, the processor internally positions the byte appropriately.

The MC68008 must perform two or four read cycles to access a word or long word, asserting the data strobe to read a single byte during each cycle. The address bus on the MC68008 includes A0, which selects the appropriate byte for each read cycle.

The word read-cycle flowchart in Figure 5-4 applies to the MC68000, MC68HC000, and MC68010. The byte read-cycle flowchart shown in Figure 5-5 and the read and write-cycle timing shown in Figure 5-6 apply to the MC68000, MC68HC000, MC68008, and MC68010, except that the MC68008 uses $\overline{DS}$ instead of either $\overline{UDS}$ or $\overline{LDS}$. The details of word and byte read cycle timing shown in Figure 5-7 do not apply to the MC68008.

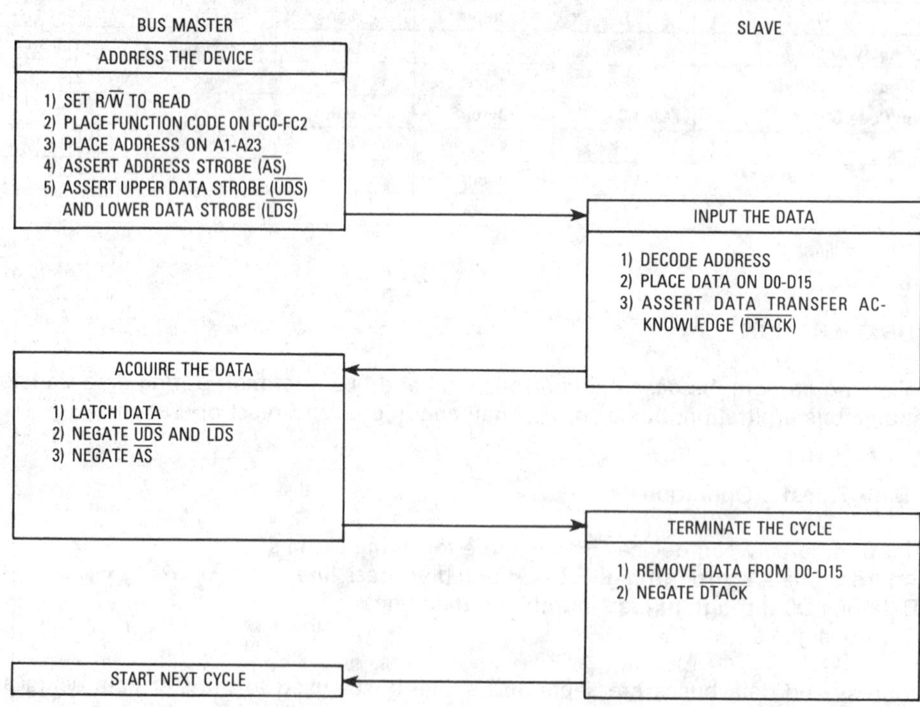

Figure 5-4. Word Read-Cycle Flowchart (MC68000, MC68HC000, and MC68010)

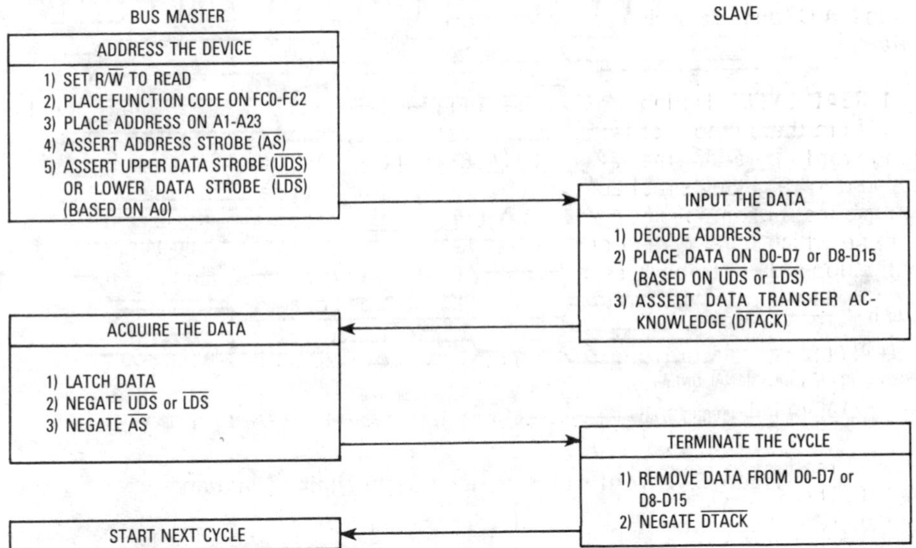

Figure 5-5. Byte Read-Cycle Flowchart

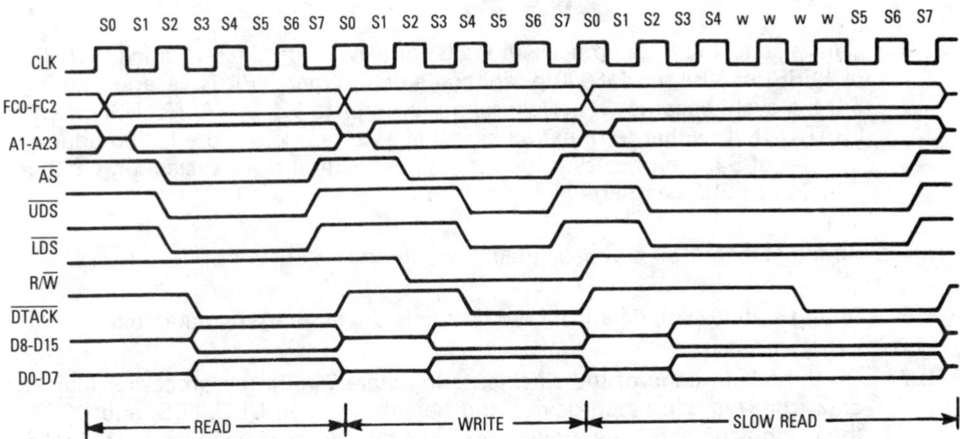

Figure 5-6. Read- and Write-Cycle Timing Diagram

A bus cycle consists of eight states. The various signals are asserted during specific states of a read cycle, as follows:

STATE 0 The read cycle starts in state 0 (S0). The processor places valid function codes on FC0-FC2 and drives R/W high to identify a read cycle.

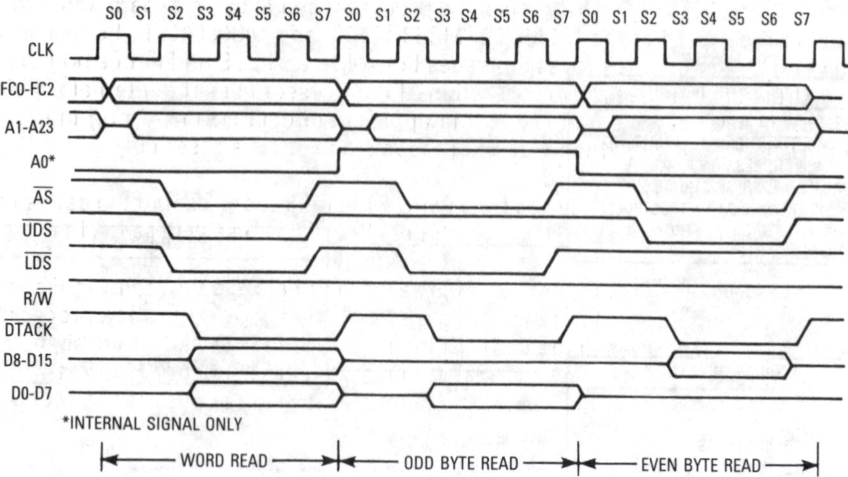

Figure 5-7. Word and Byte Read-Cycle Timing Diagram

STATE 1 Entering state 1 (S1), the processor drives a valid address on the address bus.

STATE 2 On the rising edge of state 2 (S2), the processor asserts $\overline{AS}$ and $\overline{UDS}$, $\overline{LDS}$, or $\overline{DS}$.

STATE 3 During state 3 (S3), no bus signals are altered.

STATE 4 During state 4 (S4), the processor waits for a cycle termination signal ($\overline{DTACK}$ or $\overline{BERR}$) or $\overline{VPA}$, an M6800 peripheral signal. When $\overline{VPA}$ is asserted during S4, the cycle becomes a peripheral cycle (refer to **7.1 DATA TRANSFER OPERATION**). If neither termination signal is asserted before the falling edge at the end of S4, the processor inserts wait states (full clock cycles) until either $\overline{DTACK}$ or $\overline{BERR}$ is asserted.

STATE 5 During state 5 (S5), no bus signals are altered.

STATE 6 During state 6 (S6), data from the device is driven onto the data bus.

STATE 7 On the falling edge of the clock entering state 7 (S7), the processor latches data from the addressed device and negates $\overline{AS}$ and $\overline{UDS}$, $\overline{LDS}$, and $\overline{DS}$. At the rising edge of S7, the processor places the address bus in the high-impedance state. The device negates $\overline{DTACK}$ or $\overline{BERR}$ at this time.

NOTE

During an active bus cycle, $\overline{VPA}$ and $\overline{BERR}$ are sampled on every falling edge of the clock beginning with S4, and data is latched on the falling edge of S6 during a read cycle. The bus cycle terminates in S7, except when $\overline{BERR}$ is asserted in the absence of $\overline{DTACK}$. In that case, the bus cycle terminates one clock cycle later in S9.

5.2.1.2 WRITE CYCLE. During a write cycle, the processor sends bytes of data to the memory or peripheral device. For the MC68000, MC68HC000, and MC68010, if the instruction specifies a word operation, the processor issues both UDS and LDS and writes both bytes. When the instruction specifies a byte operation, the processor uses the internal A0 bit to determine which byte to write and issues the appropriate data strobe. When the A0 bit equals zero, UDS is asserted; when the A0 bit equals one, LDS is asserted.

The MC68008 performs two write cycles for a word write operation, issuing the data strobe signal during each cycle. The address bus includes the A0 bit to select the desired byte.

For the MC68000, MC68HC000, and MC68010, the word write-cycle flowchart in Figure 5-8 applies. The byte write-cycle flowchart in Figure 5-9 applies to all four microprocessors, except that in the MC68008 the single data strobe is DS, and the data bus consists of lines D0 through D7. The word and byte write-cycle timing in Figure 5-10 applies directly to the MC68000, the MC68HC000, and MC68010. The byte write portion applies to the MC68008, except that the data strobe is DS and the data bus consists of D0 through D7.

The descriptions of the eight states of a write cycle are as follows:

STATE 0 The write cycle starts in S0. The processor places valid function codes on FC0-FC2 and drives R/W high (if a preceding write cycle has left R/W low).

STATE 1 Entering S1, the processor drives a valid address on the address bus.

STATE 2 On the rising edge of S2, the processor asserts AS and drives R/W low.

STATE 3 During S3, the data bus is driven out of the high-impedance state as the data to be written is placed on the bus.

STATE 4 At the rising edge of S4, the processor asserts UDS, LDS, or DS. The processor waits for a cycle termination signal (DTACK or BERR) or VPA, an M6800 peripheral signal. When VPA is asserted during S4, the cycle becomes a peripheral cycle (refer to **7.1 DATA TRANSFER OPERATION**). If neither termination signal

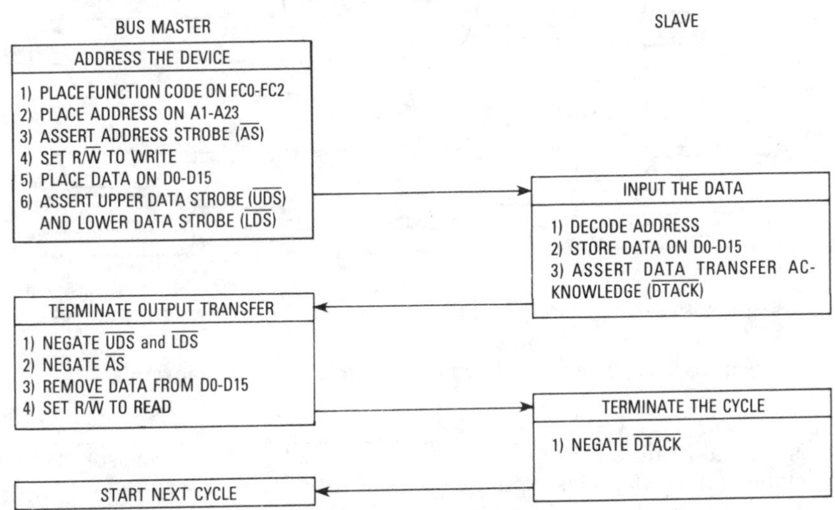

Figure 5-8. Word Write-Cycle Flowchart (MC68000, MC68HC000, and MC68010)

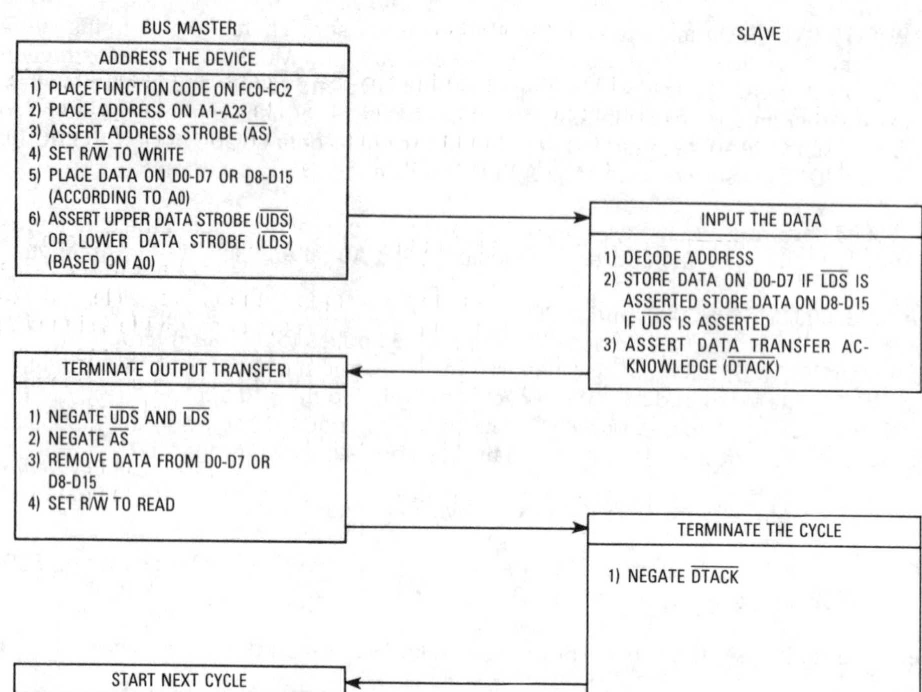

Figure 5-9. Byte Write-Cycle Flowchart

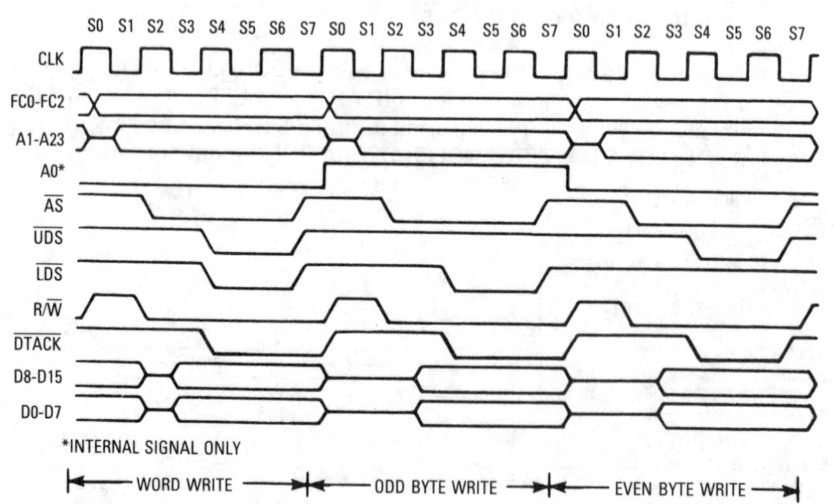

Figure 5-10. Word and Byte Write-Cycle Timing Diagram

is asserted before the falling edge at the end of S4, the processor inserts wait states (full clock cycles) until either $\overline{DTACK}$ or $\overline{BERR}$ is asserted.

STATE 5 During S5, no bus signals are altered.

STATE 6 During S6, no bus signals are altered.

STATE 7 On the falling edge of the clock entering S7, the processor negates $\overline{AS}$, $\overline{UDS}$, $\overline{LDS}$, and $\overline{DS}$. As the clock rises at the end of S7, the processor places the address and data buses in the high-impedance state, and drives R/$\overline{W}$ high. The device negates $\overline{DTACK}$ or $\overline{BERR}$ at this time.

5.2.1.3 READ-MODIFY-WRITE CYCLE. The read-modify-write cycle performs a read operation, modifies the data in the arithmetic logic unit, and writes the data back to the same address. The address strobe ($\overline{AS}$) remains asserted throughout the entire cycle, making the cycle indivisible. The test and set (TAS) instruction uses this cycle to provide a signaling capability without deadlock between processors in a multiprocessing environment. The TAS instruction (the only instruction that uses the read-modify-write cycle) only operates on bytes. Thus, all read-modify-write cycles are byte operations. The read-modify-write flowchart shown in Figure 5-11 and the timing diagram, Figure 5-12, apply to the MC68008 as well as to the MC68000, MC68HC000, and MC68010. The data strobe signal in the MC68008 is $\overline{DS}$, the address bus includes A0 to select the correct byte, and the data bus lines are D0 through D7.

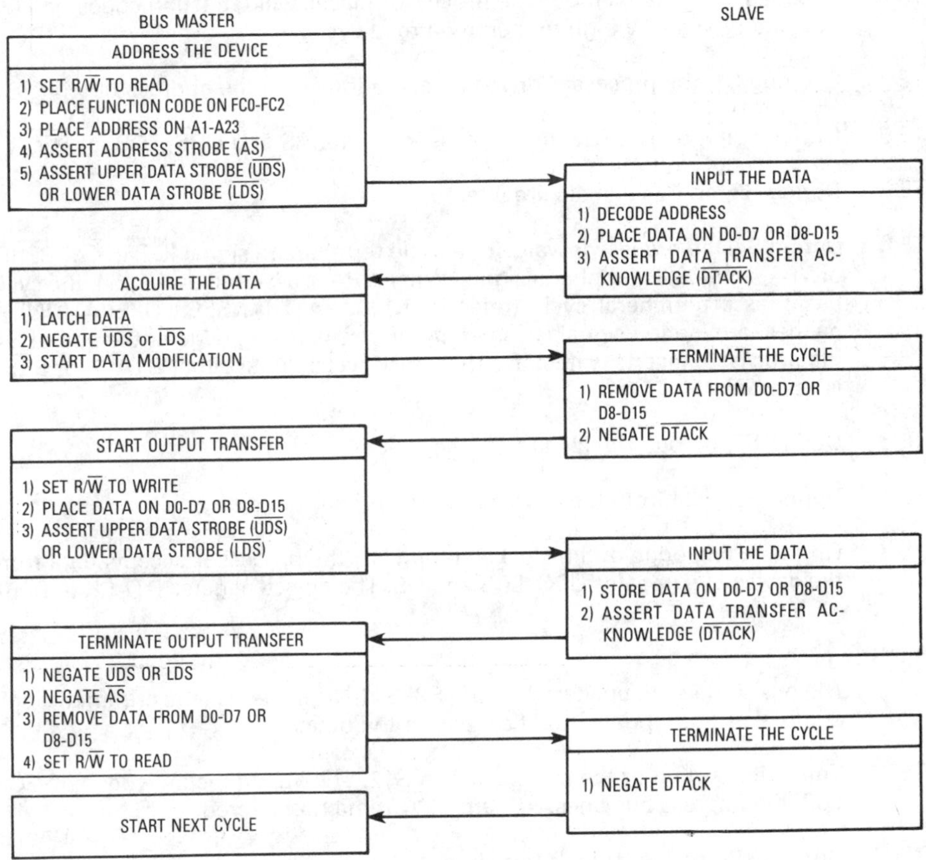

Figure 5-11. Read-Modify-Write-Cycle Flowchart

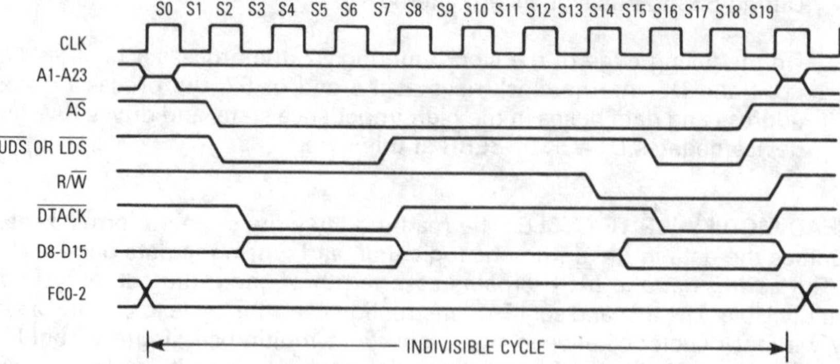

Figure 5-12. Read-Modify-Write-Cycle Timing Diagram

The descriptions of the read-modify-write cycle states are as follows:

STATE 0 — The read cycle starts in S0. The processor places valid function codes on FC0-FC2 and drives R/W high to identify a read cycle.

STATE 1 — Entering S1, the processor drives a valid address on the address bus.

STATE 2 — On the rising edge of S2, the processor asserts AS and UDS, LDS, or DS.

STATE 3 — During S3, no bus signals are altered.

STATE 4 — During S4, the processor waits for a cycle termination signal (DTACK or BERR) or VPA, an M6800 peripheral signal. When VPA is asserted during S4, the cycle becomes a peripheral cycle (refer to **7.1 DATA TRANSFER OPERATION**). If neither termination signal is asserted before the falling edge at the end of S4, the processor inserts wait states (full clock cycles) until either DTACK or BERR is asserted.

STATE 5 — During S5, no bus signals are altered.

STATE 6 — During S6, data from the device are driven onto the data bus.

STATE 7 — On the falling edge of the clock entering S7, the processor accepts data from the device and negates UDS, LDS and DS. The device negates DTACK or BERR at this time.

STATES 8–11 — The bus signals are unaltered during S8–S11, during which the arithmetic logic unit makes appropriate modifications to the data.

STATE 12 — The write portion of the cycle starts in S12. The valid function codes on FC0-FC2, the address bus lines, AS, and R/W remain unaltered.

STATE 13 — During S13, no bus signals are altered.

STATE 14 — On the rising edge of S14, the processor drives R/W low.

STATE 15 During S15, the data bus is driven out of the high-impedance state as the data to be written are placed on the bus.

STATE 16 At the rising edge of S16, the processor asserts $\overline{\text{UDS}}$ and $\overline{\text{LDS}}$ or $\overline{\text{DS}}$. The processor waits for $\overline{\text{DTACK}}$ or $\overline{\text{BERR}}$ or $\overline{\text{VPA}}$, an M6800 peripheral signal. When $\overline{\text{VPA}}$ is asserted during S16, the cycle becomes a peripheral cycle (refer to **7.1 DATA TRANSFER OPERATION**). If neither termination signal is asserted before the falling edge at the close of S16, the processor inserts wait states (full clock cycles) until either $\overline{\text{DTACK}}$ or $\overline{\text{BERR}}$ is asserted.

STATE 17 During S17, no bus signals are altered.

STATE 18 During S18, no bus signals are altered.

STATE 19 On the falling edge of the clock entering S19, the processor negates $\overline{\text{AS}}$, $\overline{\text{UDS}}$, $\overline{\text{LDS}}$, and $\overline{\text{DS}}$. As the clock rises at the end of S19, the processor places the address and data buses in the high-impedance state, and drives R/$\overline{\text{W}}$ high. The device negates $\overline{\text{DTACK}}$ or $\overline{\text{BERR}}$ at this time.

5.2.1.4 CPU SPACE CYCLE. A CPU space cycle, indicated when the function codes are all high, is a special processor cycle. Bits A16 through A19 of the address bus identify eight types of CPU space cycles. Only the interrupt acknowledge cycle, in which A16 through A19 are high, applies to all the microprocessors described in this manual. The MC68010 defines an additional type of CPU space cycle, the breakpoint acknowledge cycle, in which A16 through A19 are all low. Other configurations of A16 through A19 are reserved by Motorola to define other types of CPU cycles used in other M68000 Family microprocessors. Figure 5-13 shows the encoding of CPU space addresses.

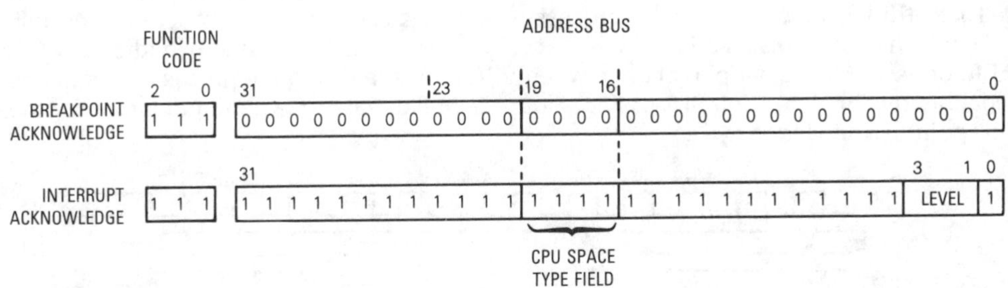

Figure 5-13. CPU Space Address Encoding

The interrupt acknowledge cycle places the level of the interrupt being acknowledged on address bits A1 through A3 and drives all other address lines high. The interrupt acknowledge cycle reads a vector number when the device places a vector number on the data bus.

The timing diagram for an interrupt acknowledge cycle is shown in Figure 5-14. In the MC68008, the data strobe is $\overline{\text{DS}}$ and the address bus includes A0. The data bus consists of D0 through D7. In all other respects, Figure 5-14 applies to the MC68008. Refer to **6.3.2 Interrupt** for more information about interrupt processing.

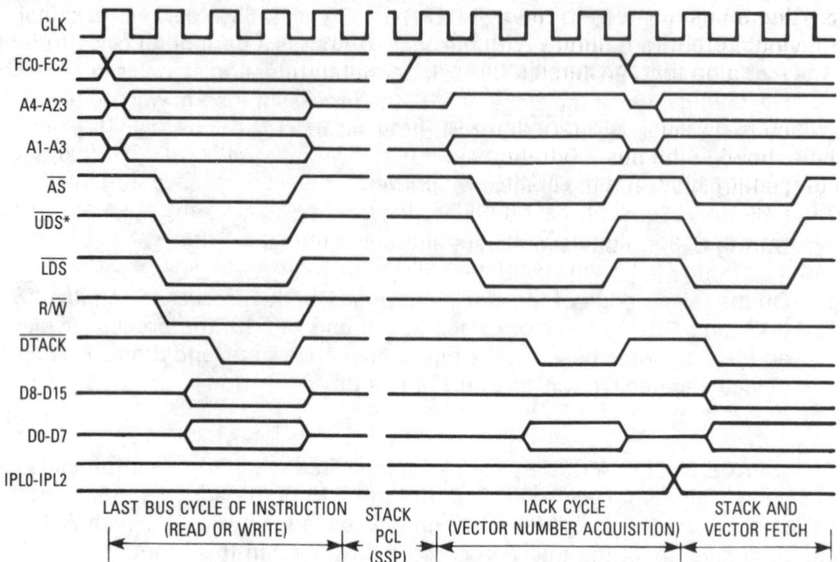

*Although a vector number is one byte, both data strobes are asserted due to the microcode used for exception processing. The processor does not recognize anything on data lines D8 through D15 at this time.

Figure 5-14. Interrupt Acknowledge Cycle Timing Diagram

The breakpoint acknowledge cycle is performed by the MC68010 to provide an indication to hardware that a software breakpoint is being executed when the processor executes a breakpoint (BKPT) instruction. The processor neither accepts nor sends data during this cycle, which is otherwise similar to a read cycle. The cycle is terminated by either DTACK, BERR, or as an M6800 peripheral cycle when VPA is asserted, and the processor continues illegal instruction exception processing. Figure 5-15 illustrates the timing diagram for the breakpoint acknowledge cycle.

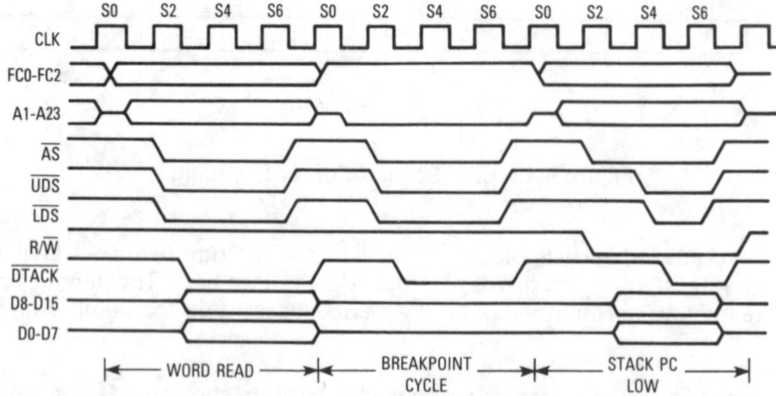

Figure 5-15. Breakpoint Acknowledge Cycle Timing Diagram

5.2.2 Bus Arbitration

Bus arbitration is a technique used by bus-master devices to request, to be granted, and to acknowledge bus mastership. Bus arbitration consists of the following:

1. Asserting a bus mastership request
2. Receiving a grant indicating that the bus is available at the end of the current cycle
3. Acknowledging that mastership has been assumed

Step 3, which is optional, is omitted in the 48-pin version of the MC68008. Figure 5-16 is a flowchart showing the bus arbitration cycle of the MC68000, the MC68HC000, the 52-pin version of the MC68008, and the MC68010. Figure 5-17 is a flowchart of the bus arbitration cycle of the 48-pin version of the MC68008. Figure 5-18 is a timing diagram of the bus arbitration cycle charted in Figure 5-16. Figure 5-19 is a timing diagram of the bus arbitration cycle charted in Figure 5-17. This technique allows processing of bus requests during data transfer cycles.

5

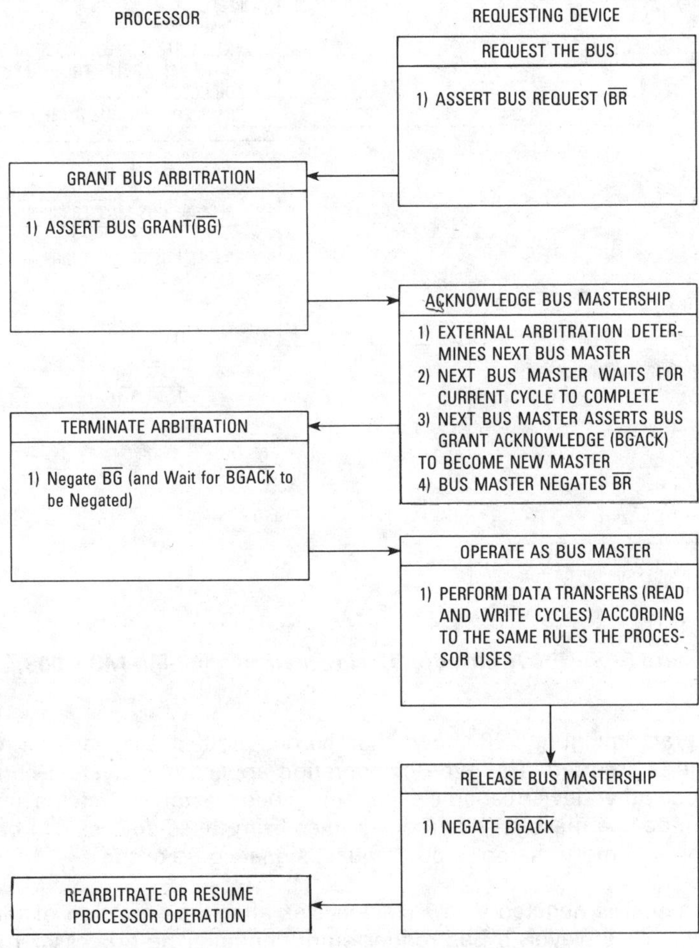

PROCESSOR
REQUESTING DEVICE
REQUEST THE BUS
1) ASSERT BUS REQUEST (BR
GRANT BUS ARBITRATION
1) ASSERT BUS GRANT(BG)
ACKNOWLEDGE BUS MASTERSHIP
1) EXTERNAL ARBITRATION DETERMINES NEXT BUS MASTER
2) NEXT BUS MASTER WAITS FOR CURRENT CYCLE TO COMPLETE
3) NEXT BUS MASTER ASSERTS BUS GRANT ACKNOWLEDGE (BGACK) TO BECOME NEW MASTER
4) BUS MASTER NEGATES BR
TERMINATE ARBITRATION
1) Negate BG (and Wait for BGACK to be Negated)
OPERATE AS BUS MASTER
1) PERFORM DATA TRANSFERS (READ AND WRITE CYCLES) ACCORDING TO THE SAME RULES THE PROCESSOR USES
RELEASE BUS MASTERSHIP
1) NEGATE BGACK
REARBITRATE OR RESUME PROCESSOR OPERATION

Figure 5-16. Bus Arbitration Cycle Flowchart (MC68000, MC68HC000, 52-Pin MC68008, and MC68010)

5

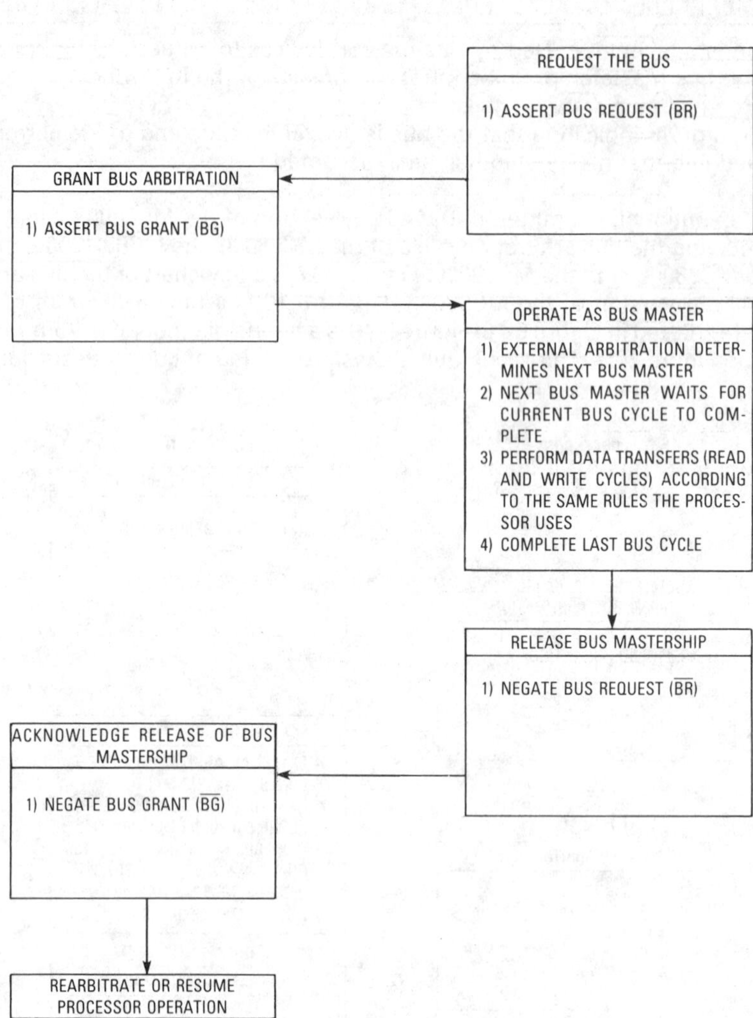

PROCESSOR
REQUESTING DEVICE
REQUEST THE BUS
1) ASSERT BUS REQUEST (BR)
GRANT BUS ARBITRATION
1) ASSERT BUS GRANT (BG)
OPERATE AS BUS MASTER
1) EXTERNAL ARBITRATION DETERMINES NEXT BUS MASTER
2) NEXT BUS MASTER WAITS FOR CURRENT BUS CYCLE TO COMPLETE
3) PERFORM DATA TRANSFERS (READ AND WRITE CYCLES) ACCORDING TO THE SAME RULES THE PROCESSOR USES
4) COMPLETE LAST BUS CYCLE
RELEASE BUS MASTERSHIP
1) NEGATE BUS REQUEST (BR)
ACKNOWLEDGE RELEASE OF BUS MASTERSHIP
1) NEGATE BUS GRANT (BG)
REARBITRATE OR RESUME PROCESSOR OPERATION

Figure 5-17. Bus Arbitration Cycle Flowchart (48-Pin MC68008)

The timing diagram in Figure 5-18 shows that the bus request is negated at the time that an acknowledge is asserted. This type of operation applies to a system consisting of a processor and one other device capable of becoming bus master. In systems having several devices that can be bus masters, bus request lines from these devices can be wire-ORed at the processor, and more than one bus request signal could occur.

The bus grant signal is negated a few clock cycles after the assertion of the bus grant acknowledge signal. However, if bus requests are pending, the processor reasserts bus grant for another request a few clock cycles after bus grant (for the previous request) is negated. In response to this additional assertion of bus grant, external arbitration circuitry selects the next bus master before the current bus master has completed the bus activity.

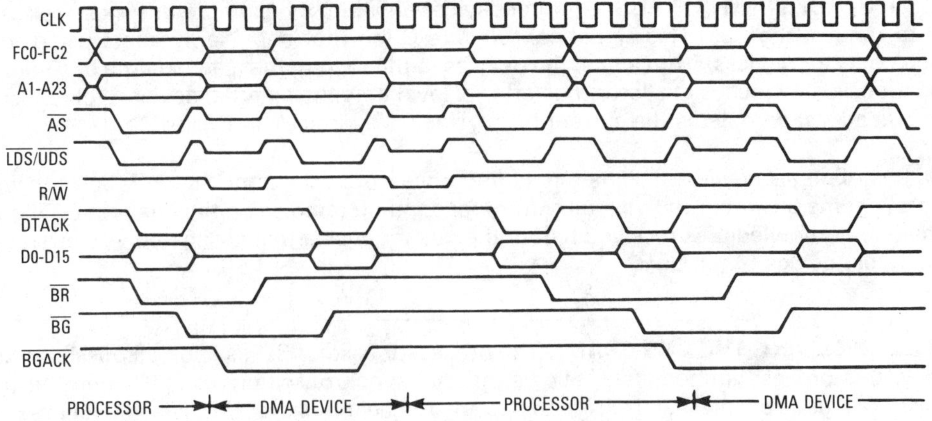

Figure 5-18. Bus Arbitration Timing Diagram (MC68000, MC68HC000, 52-Pin MC68008, and MC68010)

The timing diagram in Figure 5-19 also applies to a system consisting of a processor and one other device capable of becoming bus master. Since the 48-pin version of the MC68008 does not recognize a bus grant acknowledge signal, this processor does not negate bus grant until the current bus master has completed the bus activity.

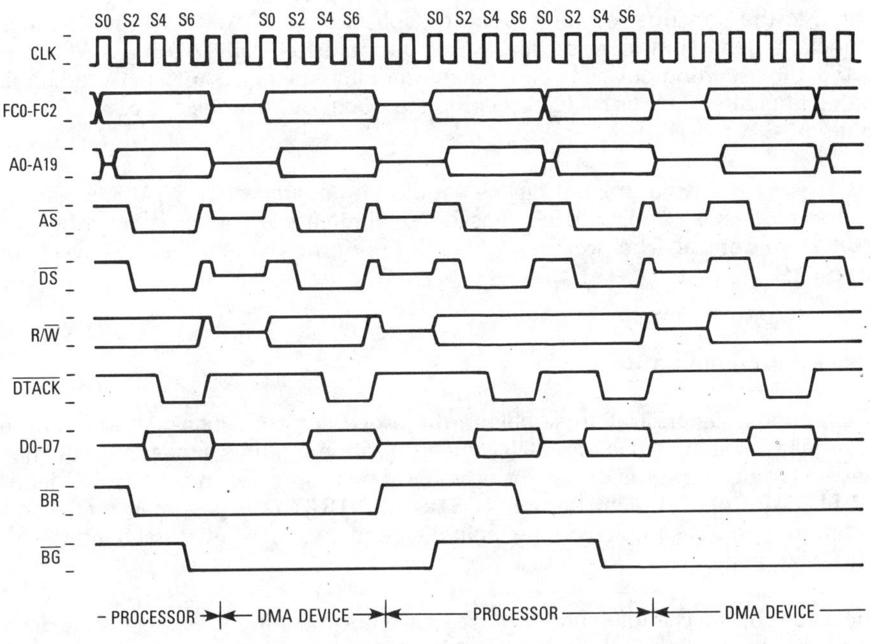

Figure 5-19. Bus Arbitration Timing Diagram (48-Pin MC68008)

5.2.2.1 REQUESTING THE BUS. External devices capable of becoming bus masters assert BR to request the bus. This signal can be wire-ORed (not necessarily constructed from open-collector devices) from any of the devices in the system that can become bus master. The processor, which is at a lower bus priority level than the external devices, relinquishes the bus after it completes the current bus cycle.

The bus grant acknowledge signal on all the processors except the 48-pin MC68008 helps to prevent the bus arbitration circuitry from responding to noise on the bus request signal. When no acknowledge is received before the bus request signal is negated, the processor continues the use of the bus.

5.2.2.2 RECEIVING THE BUS GRANT. The processor asserts BG as soon as possible. Normally, this process immediately follows internal synchronization, except when the processor has made an internal decision to execute the next bus cycle but has not yet asserted AS for that cycle. In this case, BG is delayed until AS is asserted to indicate to external devices that a bus cycle is in progress.

BG can be routed through a daisy-chained network or through a specific priority-encoded network. Any method of external arbitration that observes the protocol can be used.

5.2.2.3 ACKNOWLEDGEMENT OF MASTERSHIP (MC68000, MC68HC000, 52-PIN MC68008, AND MC68010). Upon receiving BG, the requesting device waits until AS, DTACK, and BGACK are negated before asserting BGACK. The negation of AS indicates that the previous bus master has completed its cycle. (No device is allowed to assume bus mastership while AS is asserted.) The negation of BGACK indicates that the previous master has released the bus. The negation of DTACK indicates that the previous slave has terminated the connection to the previous master. (In some applications, DTACK might not be included in this function; general-purpose devices would be connected using AS only.) When BGACK is asserted, the asserting device is bus master until it negates BGACK. BGACK should not be negated until after the bus cycle(s) is complete. A device relinquishes control of the bus by negating BGACK.

The bus request from the granted device should be negated after BGACK is asserted. If another bus request is pending, BG is reasserted within a few clocks, as described in **5.2.3 Bus Arbitration Control**. The processor does not perform any external bus cycles before reasserting BG.

5.2.3 Bus Arbitration Control

All asynchronous bus arbitration signals to the processor are synchronized before being used internally. As shown in Figure 5-20, synchronization requires a maximum of one cycle of the system clock, assuming that the asynchronous input setup time (#47, defined in **11.8 AC ELECTRICAL SPECIFICATIONS — BUS ARBITRATION)** has been met. The input asynchronous signal is sampled on the falling edge of the clock and is valid internally after the next falling edge.

Bus arbitration control is implemented with a finite state machine. One of the state diagrams in Figure 5-21 applies to the MC68000, the MC68HC000, the 52-pin version of the MC68008, and the MC68010. The other diagram applies to the 48-pin version of the MC68008, in

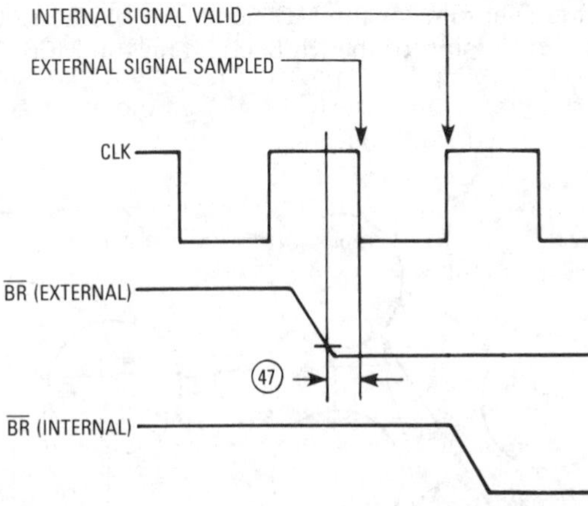

Figure 5-20. External Asynchronous Signal Synchronization

which BGACK is permanently negated internally. The same finite state machine is used, but it is effectively a two-state machine because BGACK is always negated.

In Figure 5-21, input signals R and A are the internally synchronized versions of BR and BGACK. The BG output is shown as G, and the internal three-state control signal is shown as T. If T is true, the address, data, and control buses are placed in the high-impedance state when AS is negated. All signals are shown in positive logic (active high), regardless of their true active voltage level. State changes (valid outputs) occur on the next rising edge of the clock after the internal signal is valid.

A timing diagram of the bus arbitration sequence during a processor bus cycle is shown in Figure 5-22. The bus arbitration timing while the bus is inactive (e.g., the processor is performing internal operations for a multiply instruction) is shown in Figure 5-23.

When a bus request is made after the MPU has begun a bus cycle and before AS has been asserted (S0), the special sequence shown in Figure 5-24 applies. Instead of being asserted on the next rising edge of clock, BG is delayed until the second rising edge following its internal assertion.

Figures 5-22, 5-23, and 5-24 apply directly to the MC68000, the MC68HC000, the 52-pin version of the MC68008, and the MC68010. The figures also apply to the 48-pin version of the MC68008, except that BR remains asserted while the external device has control of the bus, and BG remains asserted for two additional clock cycles.

5.2.4. Bus Error and Halt Operation

In a bus architecture that requires a handshake from an external device, such as the asynchronous bus used in the M68000 Family, the handshake may not always occur. A bus error input is provided to terminate a bus cycle in error when the expected signal is not asserted. Different systems and different devices within the same system require different maximum-response times. External circuitry can be provided to assert the bus error signal after the appropriate delay following the assertion of address strobe.

(a) State Diagram for the MC68000, the MC68HC000, the 52-pin Version of the MC68008, and the MC68010

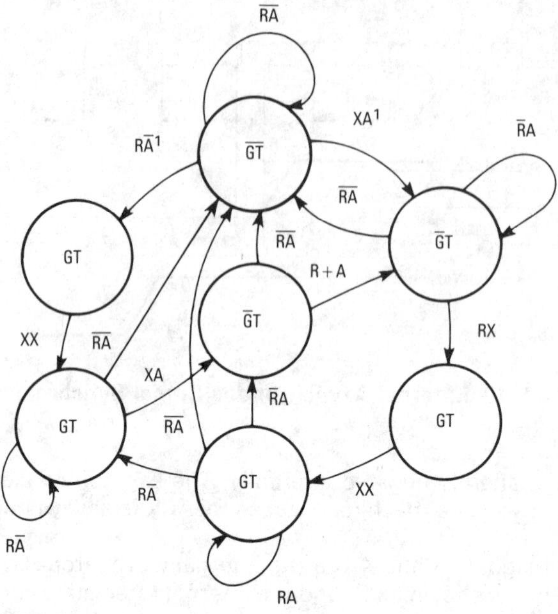

(b) State Diagram for the 48-Pin Version of the MC68008

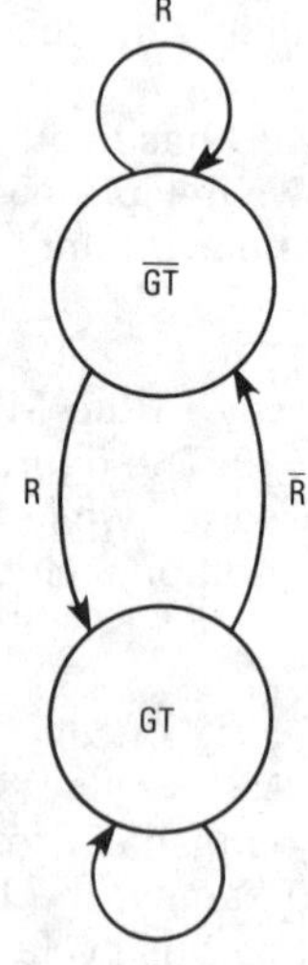

R = Bus Request Internal
A = Bus Grant Acknowledge Internal
G = Bus Grant
T = Three-State Control to Bus Control Logic[2]
X = Don't Care

NOTES:
1. State machine will not change if the bus is S0 or S1. Refer to **5.2.3. BUS ARBITRATION CONTROL.**
2. The address bus will be placed in the high-impedance state if T is asserted and $\overline{AS}$ is negated.

Figure 5-21. Bus Arbitration Unit State Diagrams

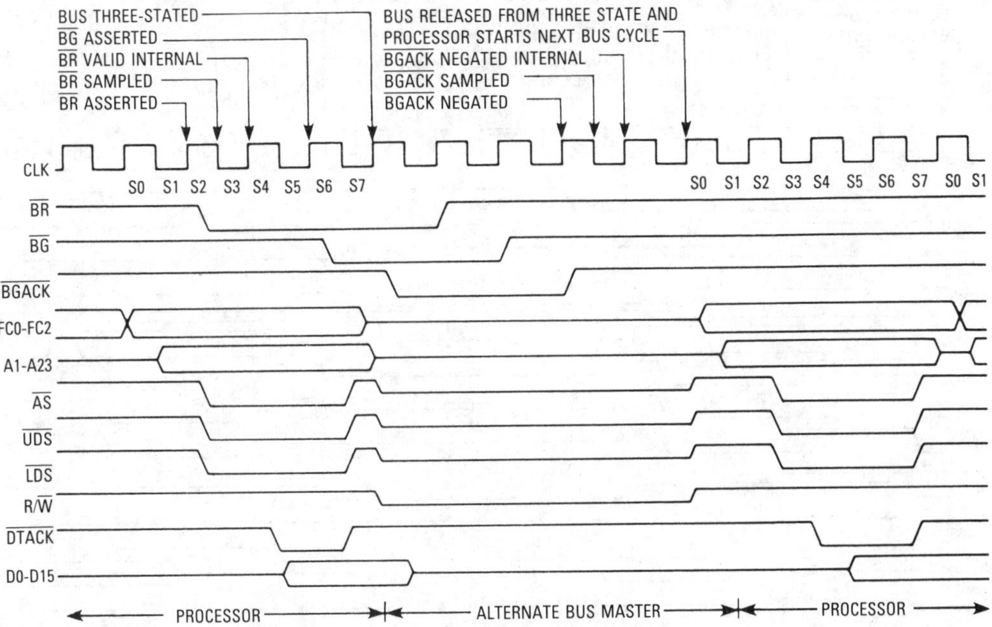

Figure 5-22. Bus Arbitration Timing Diagram — Processor Active

5

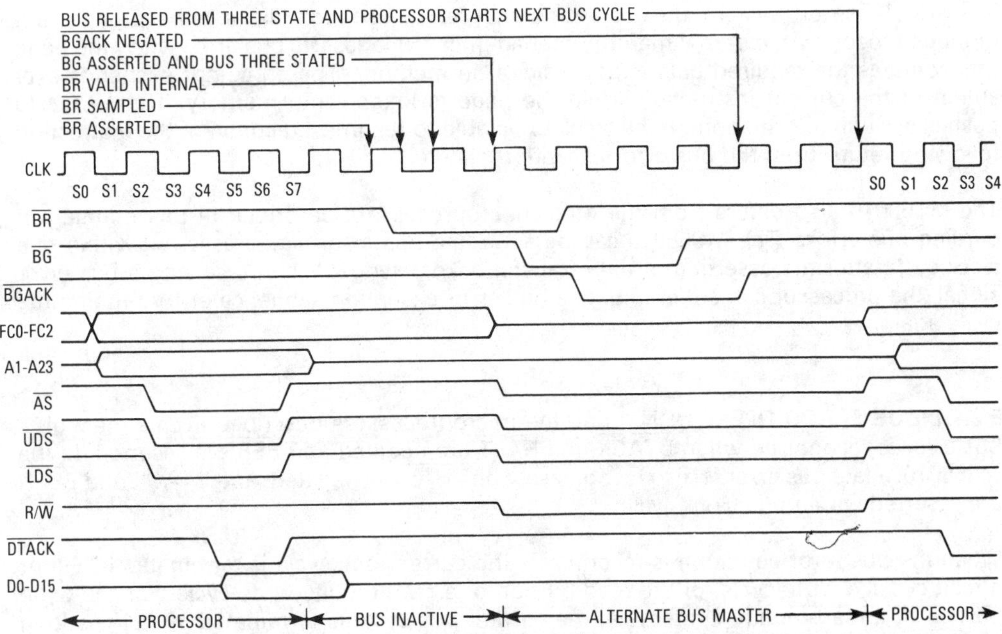

Figure 5-23. Bus Arbitration Timing Diagram — Bus Inactive

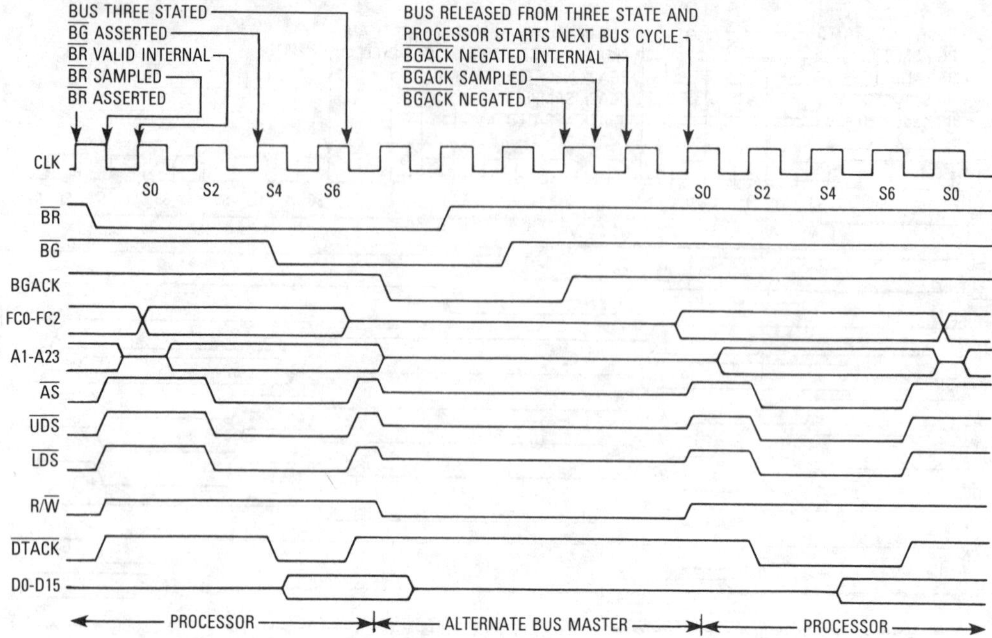

Figure 5-24. Bus Arbitration Timing Diagram — Special Case

In a virtual memory system, the bus error signal can be used to indicate either a page fault or a bus timeout. An external memory management unit asserts bus error when the page that contains the required data is not resident in memory. The processor suspends execution of the current instruction while the page is loaded into memory. The MC68010 pushes enough information on the stack to be able to resume execution of the instruction following return from the bus error exception handler.

The MC68010 also differs from the other microprocessors described in this manual regarding bus errors. The MC68010 can detect a late bus error signal asserted within one clock cycle after the assertion of data transfer acknowledge. When receiving a bus error signal, the processor can either initiate a bus error exception sequence or try running the cycle again.

5.2.4.1 BUS ERROR OPERATION. In all the microprocessors described in this manual, a bus error is recognized when DTACK and HALT are negated and BERR is asserted. In the MC68010, a late bus error is also recognized when HALT is negated, and DTACK and BERR are asserted within one clock cycle.

When the bus error condition is recognized, the current bus cycle is terminated in S9 for a read cycle, a write cycle, or the read portion of a read-modify-write cycle. For the write portion of a read-modify-write cycle, the current bus cycle is terminated in S21. As long as BERR remains asserted, the data and address buses are in the high-impedance state. Figure 5-25 shows the timing for the normal bus error, and Figure 5-26 shows the timing for the MC68010 late bus error.

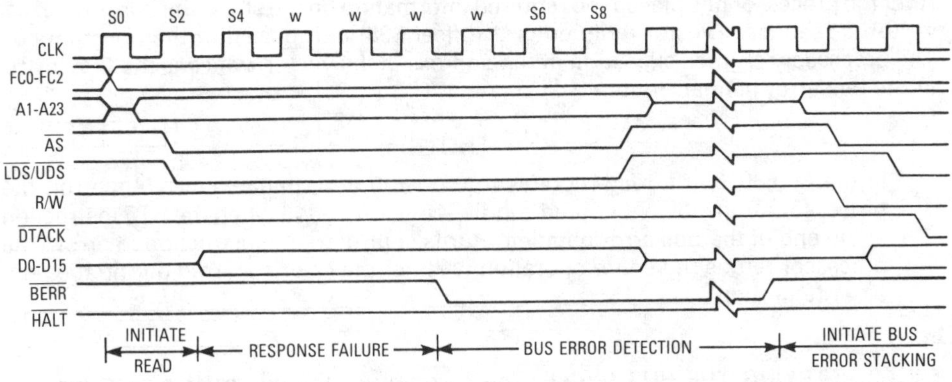

Figure 5-25. Bus Error Timing Diagram

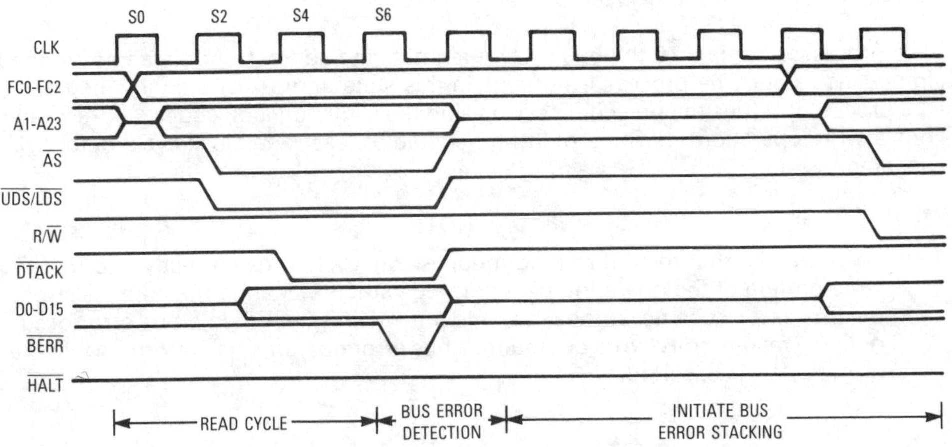

Figure 5-26. Delayed Bus Error Timing Diagram (MC68010)

After the aborted bus cycle is terminated and BERR is negated, the processor enters exception processing for the bus error exception. During the exception processing sequence, the following information is placed on the supervisor stack:

1. Status register
2. Program counter (two words, which may be up to five words past the instruction being executed)
3. Error information

The first two items are identical to the information stacked by any other exception. The error information differs for the MC68010. The MC68000, MC68HC000, and MC68008 stack bus error information to help determine and to correct the error. The MC68010 stacks the frame format and the vector offset followed by 22 words of internal register information. The return from exception (RTE) instruction restores the internal register information so that the MC68010 can continue execution of the instruction after the error handler routine completes. Refer to **6.3.9 Bus Error** for further information.

After the processor has placed the required information on the stack, the bus error exception vector is read from vector table entry 2 (offset $08) and placed in the program counter. The processor resumes execution at the address in the vector, which is the first instruction in the bus error handler routine.

NOTE

In the MC68010, if a read-modify-write operation terminates in a bus error, the processor reruns the entire read-modify-write operation when the RTE instruction at the end of the bus error handler returns control to the instruction in error. The processor reruns the entire operation whether the error occurred during the read or write portion.

5

5.2.4.2 RETRYING THE BUS CYCLE. The assertion of the bus error signal during a bus cycle in which HALT is also asserted by an external device initiates a retry operation. Figure 5-27 is a timing diagram of the retry operation. The delayed BERR signal in the MC68010 also initiates a retry operation when HALT is asserted by an external device. Figure 5-28 shows the timing of the delayed operation.

The processor terminates the bus cycle, then puts the address and data lines in the high-impedance state. The processor remains in this state until HALT signal is negated. Then the processor retries the preceding cycle using the same function codes, address, and data (for a write operation). BERR should be negated at least one clock cycle before HALT is negated.

NOTE

To guarantee that the entire read-modify-write cycle runs correctly and that the write portion of the operation is performed without negating the address strobe, the processor does not retry a read-modify-write cycle. When a bus error occurs during a read-modify-write operation, a bus error operation is performed whether or not HALT is asserted.

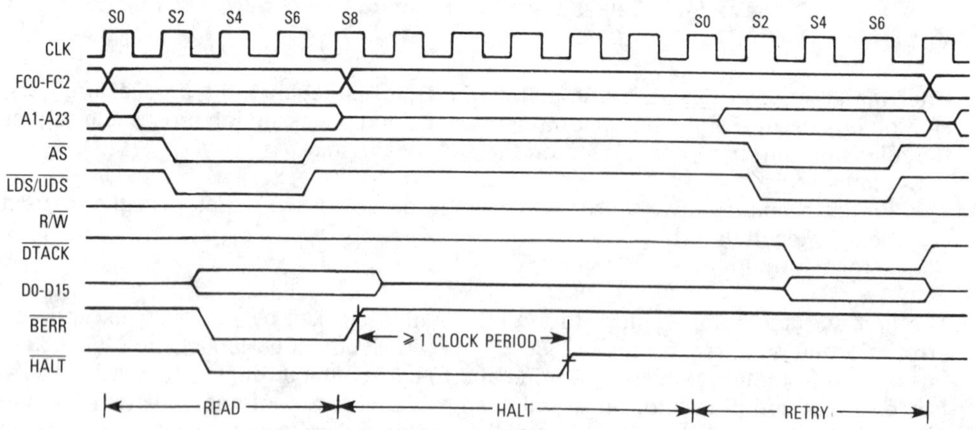

Figure 5-27. Retry Bus Cycle Timing Diagram

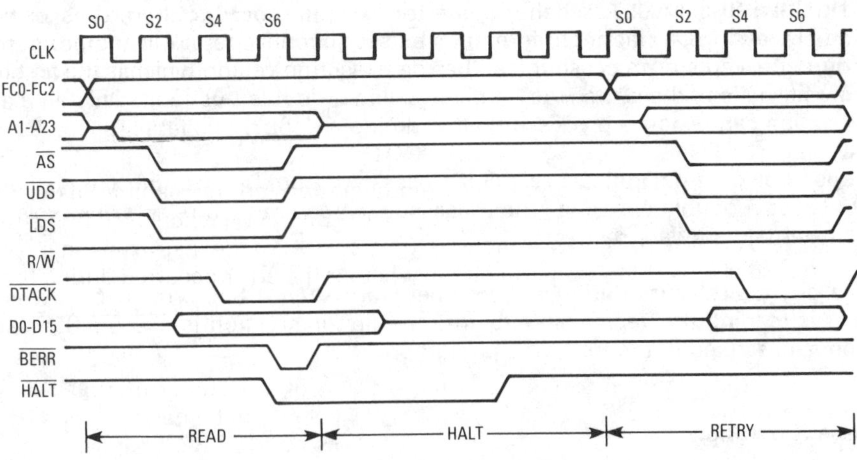

Figure 5-28. Delayed Retry Bus Cycle Timing Diagram

5.2.4.3 HALT OPERATION. HALT performs a halt/run/single-step operation similar to the halt operation of an MC6800. When HALT is asserted by an external device, the processor halts and remains halted as long as the signal remains asserted, as shown in Figure 5-29.

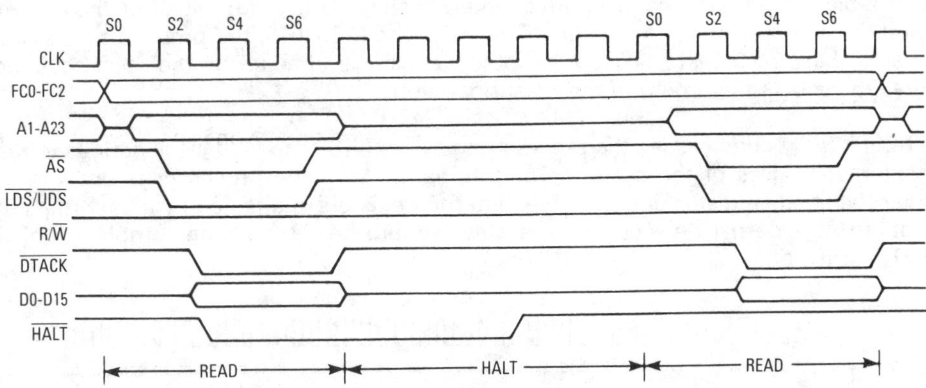

Figure 5-29. Halt Operation Timing Diagram

While the processor is halted, the address bus and the data bus signals are placed in the high-impedance state. Bus arbitration is performed as usual. Should a bus error occur while HALT is asserted, the processor performs the retry operation previously described.

The single-step mode is derived from correctly timed transitions of HALT. HALT is negated to allow the processor to begin a bus cycle, then asserted to enter the halt mode when the cycle completes. The single-step mode proceeds through a program one bus cycle at a time for debugging purposes. The halt operation and the hardware trace capability allow tracing of either bus cycles or instructions one at a time. These capabilities and a software debugging package provide total debugging flexibility.

5.2.4.4 DOUBLE BUS FAULT. When a bus error exception occurs, the processor begins exception processing by stacking information on the supervisor stack. If another bus error occurs during exception processing (i.e., before execution of another instruction begins) the processor halts and asserts HALT. This is called a double bus fault. Only an external reset operation can restart a processor halted due to a double bus fault.

A retry operation does not initiate exception processing; a bus error during a retry operation does not cause a double bus fault. The processor can continue to retry a bus cycle indefinitely if external hardware requests.

A double bus fault occurs during a reset operation when a bus error occurs while the processor is reading the vector table (before the first instruction is executed). The reset operation is described in the following paragraph.

5.2.5 Reset Operation

RESET is asserted externally for the initial processor reset. Subsequently, the signal can be asserted either externally or internally (executing a RESET instruction). For proper external reset operation, HALT must also be asserted.

When RESET and HALT are driven by an external device, the entire system, including the processor, is reset. Resetting the processor initializes the internal state. The processor reads the reset vector table entry (address $00000), and loads the contents into the supervisor stack pointer (SSP). Next, the processor loads the contents of address $00004 (vector table entry 1) into the program counter. Then the processor initializes the interrupt level in the status register to a value of seven. In the MC68010, the processor also clears the vector base register to $00000. No other register is affected by the reset sequence. Figure 5-30 shows the timing of the reset operation.

The RESET instruction causes the processor to assert RESET for 124 clock periods to reset the external devices of the system. The internal state of the processor is not affected. Neither the status register nor any of the internal registers is affected by an internal reset operation. All external devices in the system should be reset at the completion of the RESET instruction.

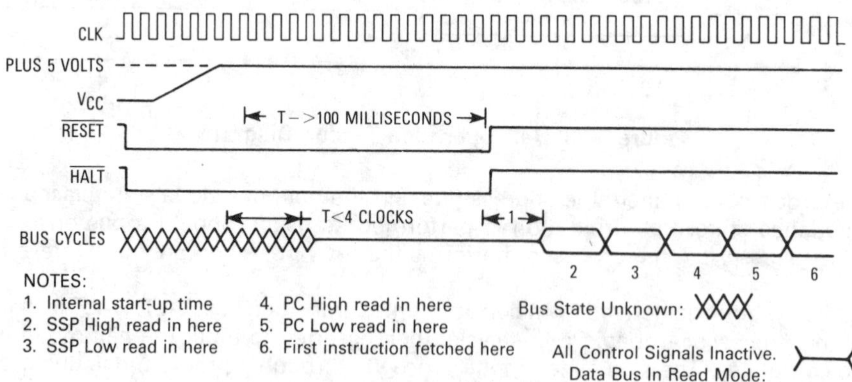

Figure 5-30. Reset Operation Timing Diagram

For the initial reset, RESET and HALT must be asserted for at least 100 milliseconds. For a subsequent external reset, asserting these signals for ten clock cycles or longer resets the processor. However, an external reset signal that is asserted while the processor is executing a RESET instruction is ignored. Since the processor asserts the RESET signal for 124 clock cycles during execution of a RESET instruction, an external reset should assert RESET for at least 132 clock periods.

5.2.6 The Relationship of DTACK, BERR, and HALT

To properly control termination of a bus cycle for a retry or a bus error condition, DTACK, BERR, and HALT should be asserted and negated on the rising edge of the processor clock. This relationship assures that when two signals are asserted simultaneously, the required setup time (specification #47, **11.6 AC ELECTRICAL SPECIFICATIONS — READ AND WRITE CYCLES)** for both of them is met during the same bus state. External circuitry should be designed to incorporate this precaution. A related specification, #48, can be ignored when DTACK, BERR, and HALT are asserted and negated on the rising edge of the processor clock.

The possible bus cycle terminations can be summarized as follows (case numbers refer to Table 5-5).

Normal Termination: DTACK is asserted. BERR and HALT remain negated (case 1).

Halt Termination: HALT is asserted coincident with, or preceding DTACK, and BERR remains negated (case 2).

Bus Error Termination: BERR is asserted in lieu of, coincident with, or preceding DTACK (case 3). In the MC68010, the late bus error also, BERR is asserted following DTACK (case 4). HALT remains negated and BERR is negated coincident with or after DTACK.

Retry Termination: HALT and BERR asserted in lieu of, coincident with, or before DTACK (case 5). In the MC68010, the late retry also, BERR and HALT are asserted following DTACK (case 6). BERR is negated coincident with or after DTACK. HALT must be held at least one cycle after BERR.

Table 5-5 shows the details of the resulting bus cycle terminations in the MC68000, MC68HC000, MC68008 and MC68010 for various combinations of signal sequences.

The negation of BERR and HALT under several conditions is shown in Table 5-6. (DTACK is assumed to be negated normally in all cases; for reliable operation, both DTACK and BERR should be negated when address strobe is negated).

EXAMPLE A:
A system uses a watchdog timer to terminate accesses to unused address space. The timer asserts BERR after timeout (case 3).

EXAMPLE B:
A system uses error detection on random-access memory (RAM) contents. The system designer may:

1. Delay DTACK until the data is verified. If data is invalid, return BERR and HALT simultaneously to retry the error cycle (case 5).

2. Delay DTACK until the data is verified. If data is invalid, return BERR at the same time as DTACK (case 3).
3. For an MC68010, return DTACK before data verification. If data is invalid, assert BERR and HALT to retry the error cycle (case 6).
4. For an MC68010, return DTACK before data verification. If data is invalid, assert BERR on the next clock cycle (case 4).

Table 5-5. DTACK, BERR, and HALT Assertion Results

Case No.	Control Signal	Asserted on Rising Edge of State N	Asserted on Rising Edge of State N+2	MC68000/MC68HC000/ MC68008 Results	MC68010 Results
1	DTACK BERR HALT	A NA NA	S NA X	Normal cycle terminate and continue.	Normal cycle terminate and continue.
2	DTACK BERR HALT	A NA A/S	S NA S	Normal cycle terminate and halt. Continue when HALT negated.	Normal cycle terminate and halt. Continue when HALT negated.
3	DTACK BERR HALT	X A NA	X S NA	Terminate and take bus error trap.	Terminate and take bus error trap.
4	DTACK BERR HALT	A NA NA	S A NA	Normal cycle terminate and continue.	Terminate and take bus error trap.
5	DTACK BERR HALT	X A A/S	X S S	Terminate and retry when HALT removed.	Terminate and retry when HALT removed.
6	DTACK BERR HALT	A NA NA	S A A	Normal cycle terminate and continue.	Terminate and retry when HALT removed.

LEGEND:
- N - The number of the current even bus state (e.g., S4, S6, etc.)
- A - Signal is asserted in this bus state
- NA - Signal is not asserted in this bus state
- X - Don't care
- S - Signal was asserted in preceding bus state and remains asserted in this state

NOTE: All operations are subject to relevant setup and hold times.

Table 5-6. BERR and HALT Negation Results

Conditions of Termination in Table 4-4	Control Signal	Negated on Rising Edge of State N		N+2	Results – Next Cycle
Bus Error	BERR HALT	• •	or or	• •	Takes bus error trap.
Rerun	BERR HALT	• •	or	•	Illegal sequence; usually traps to vector number 0.
Rerun	BERR HALT	•		 •	Reruns the bus cycle.
Normal	BERR HALT	• •	 or	 •	May lengthen next cycle.
Normal	BERR HALT	 •	 or	• none	If next cycle is started it will be terminated as a bus error.

• = Signal is negated in this bus state.

5.2.7 Asynchronous Operation

To achieve clock frequency independence at a system level, the bus can be operated in an asynchronous manner. Asynchronous bus operation uses the bus handshake signals to control the transfer of data. The handshake signals are AS, UDS, LDS, DS (MC68008 only), DTACK, BERR, HALT, and VPA (only for M6800 peripheral cycles). AS indicates the start of the bus cycle, and UDS, LDS, and DS signal valid data for a write cycle. After placing the requested data on the data bus (read cycle) or latching the data (write cycle), the slave device (memory or peripheral) asserts DTACK to terminate the bus cycle. If no device responds or if the access is invalid, external control logic asserts BERR, or BERR and HALT, to abort or retry the cycle. Figure 5-31 shows the use of the bus handshake signals in a fully asynchronous read cycle. Figure 5-32 shows a fully asynchronous write cycle.

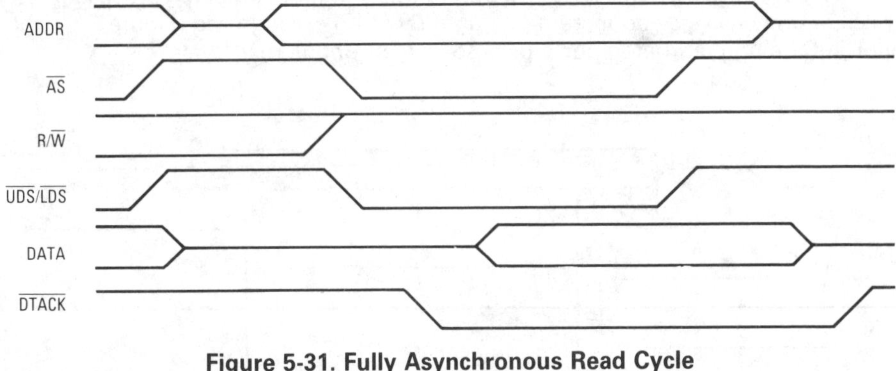

Figure 5-31. Fully Asynchronous Read Cycle

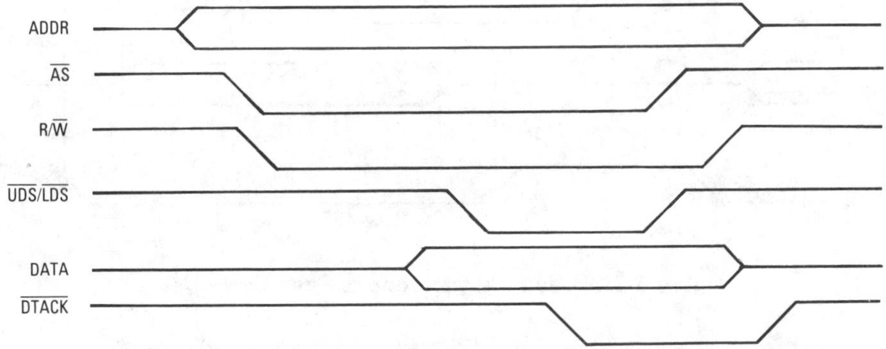

Figure 5-32. Fully Asynchronous Write Cycle

In the asynchronous mode, the accessed device operates independently of the frequency and phase of the system clock. For example, the MC68681 dual universal asynchronous receiver/transmitter (DUART) does not require any clock-related information from the bus master during a bus transfer. Asynchronous devices are designed to operate correctly with processors at any clock frequency when relevant timing requirements are observed.

A device can use a clock at the same frequency as the system clock (e.g., 8, 10, or 12.5 MHz), but without a defined phase relationship to the system clock. This mode of operation is pseudo-asynchronous; it increases performance by observing timing parameters related to the system clock frequency, without being completely synchronous with that clock. A memory array designed to operate with a particular frequency processor but not driven by the processor clock is a common example of a pseudo-asynchronous device.

The designer of a fully asynchronous system can make no assumptions about address setup time, which could be used to improve performance. With the system clock frequency known, the slave device can be designed to decode the address bus before recognizing an address strobe. Parameter #11 (refer to **11.6 AC ELECTRICAL SPECIFICATIONS — READ AND WRITE CYCLES**) specifies the minimum time before address strobe during which the address is valid.

In a pseudo-asynchronous system, timing specifications allow DTACK to be asserted for a read cycle before the data from a slave device is valid. The length of time that DTACK may precede data is specified as parameter #31. This parameter must be met to ensure the validity of the data latched into the processor. No maximum time is specified from the assertion of AS to the assertion of DTACK. During this unlimited time, the processor inserts wait cycles in one-clock-period increments until DTACK is recognized. Figure 5-33 shows the important timing parameters for a pseudo-asynchronous read cycle.

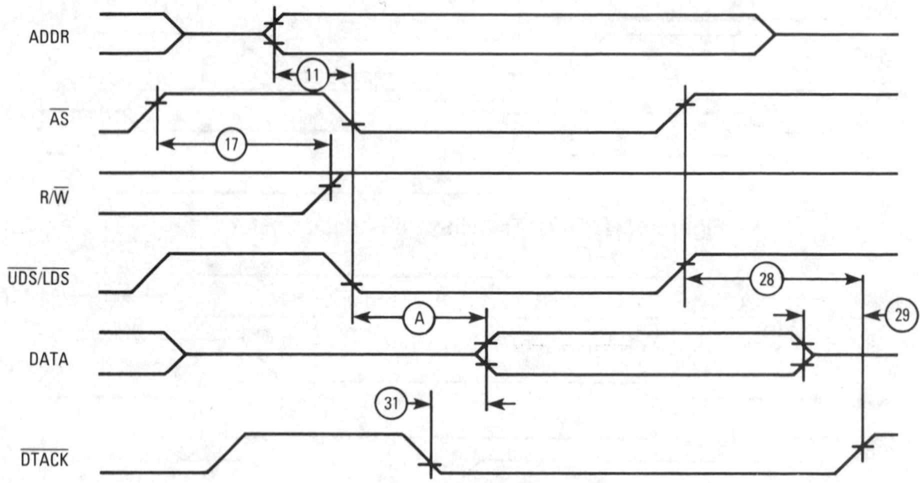

Figure 5-33. Pseudo-Asynchronous Read Cycle

During a write cycle, after the processor asserts AS but before driving the data bus, the processor drives R/W low. Parameter #55 specifies the minimum time between the transition of R/W and the driving of the data bus, which is effectively the maximum turnoff time for any device driving the data bus.

After the processor places valid data on the bus, it asserts the data strobe signal(s). A data setup time, similar to the address setup time previously discussed, can be used to improve performance. Parameter #26 is the minimum time a slave device can accept valid data before recognizing a data strobe. The slave device asserts DTACK after it accepts the data. Parameter #25 is the minimum time after negation of the strobes during which the valid data remains on the address bus. Parameter #28 is the maximum time between the negation of the strobes by the processor and the negation of DTACK by the slave device. If DTACK remains asserted past the time specified by parameter #28, the processor may recognize it as being asserted early in the next bus cycle and may terminate that cycle prematurely. Figure 5-34 shows the important timing specifications for a pseudo-asynchronous write cycle.

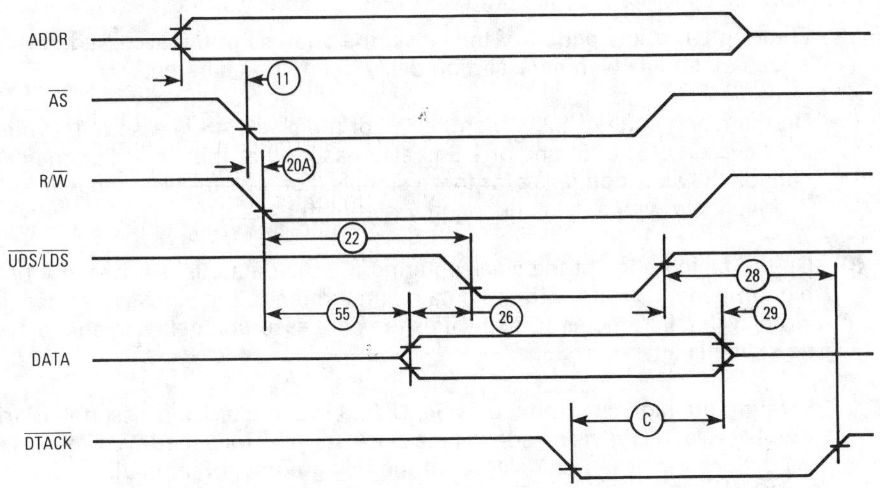

Figure 5-34. Pseudo-Asynchronous Write Cycle

In the MC68010, the BERR signal can be delayed after the assertion of DTACK. Specification #48 is the maximum time between assertion of DTACK and assertion of BERR. If this maximum delay is exceeded, operation of the processor may be erratic.

5.2.8 Synchronous Operation

In some systems, external devices use the system clock to generate DTACK and other asynchronous input signals. This synchronous operation provides a closely coupled design with maximum performance, appropriate for frequently accessed parts of the system. For example, memory can operate in the synchronous mode, but peripheral devices operate asynchronously. For a synchronous device, the designer uses explicit timing information shown in **11.6 AC ELECTRICAL SPECIFICATIONS — READ AND WRITE CYCLES**. These specifications define the state of all bus signals relative to a specific state of the processor clock.

The standard M68000 bus cycle consists of four clock periods (eight bus cycle states) and, optionally, an integral number of clock cycles inserted as wait states. Wait states are inserted as required to allow sufficient response time for the external device. The following state-by-state description of the bus cycle differs from those descriptions in **5.2.1.1 READ CYCLE** and **5.2.1.2 WRITE CYCLE** by including information about the important timing parameters that apply in the bus cycle states.

STATE 0 The bus cycle starts in S0, during which the clock is high. At the rising edge of S0 the function code for the access is driven externally. Parameter #6A defines the delay from this rising edge until the function codes are valid. Also, the R/$\overline{\text{W}}$ signal is driven high; parameter #18 defines the delay from the same rising edge to the transition of R/$\overline{\text{W}}$. The minimum value for parameter #18 applies to a read cycle preceded by a write cycle and this value is the maximum hold time for a low on R/$\overline{\text{W}}$ beyond the initiation of the read cycle.

STATE 1 Entering S1, a low period of the clock, the address of the accessed device is driven externally with an assertion delay defined by parameter #6.

STATE 2 On the rising edge of S2, a high period of the clock, $\overline{\text{AS}}$ is asserted. During a read cycle, $\overline{\text{UDS}}$, $\overline{\text{LDS}}$, and/or $\overline{\text{DS}}$ is also asserted at this time. Parameter #9 defines the assertion delay for these signals. For a write cycle, the R/$\overline{\text{W}}$ signal is driven low with a delay defined by parameter #20.

STATE 3 On the falling edge of the clock entering S3, the data bus is driven out of the high-impedance state with the data being written to the accessed device (in a write cycle). Parameter #23 specifies the data assertion delay. In a read cycle, no signal is altered in S3.

STATE 4 Entering the high clock period of S4, $\overline{\text{UDS}}$, $\overline{\text{LDS}}$, and/or $\overline{\text{DS}}$ is asserted (during a write cycle) on the rising edge of the clock. As in S2 for a read cycle, parameter #9 defines the assertion delay from the rising edge of S4 for $\overline{\text{UDS}}$, $\overline{\text{LDS}}$, and/or $\overline{\text{DS}}$. In a read cycle, no signal is altered by the processor during S4.

Until the falling edge of the clock at the end of S4 (beginning of S5), no response from any external device except $\overline{\text{RESET}}$ is acknowledged by the processor. If either $\overline{\text{DTACK}}$ or $\overline{\text{BERR}}$ is asserted before the falling edge of S4 and satisfies the input setup time defined by parameter #47, the processor enters S5 and the bus cycle continues. If either $\overline{\text{DTACK}}$ or $\overline{\text{BERR}}$ is asserted but without meeting the setup time parameter #47, the processor may recognize the signal and continue the bus cycle; the result is unpredictable. If neither $\overline{\text{DTACK}}$ nor $\overline{\text{BERR}}$ is asserted before the next rise of clock, the bus cycle remains in S4, and wait states (complete clock cycles) are inserted until one of the bus cycle terminations is met.

STATE 5 S5 is a low period of the clock, during which the processor does not alter any signal.

STATE 6 S6 is a high period of the clock, during which data for a read operation is setup relative to the falling edge (entering S7). Parameter #27 defines the minimum period by which the data must precede the falling edge. For a write operation, the processor changes no signal during S6.

STATE 7 On the falling edge of the clock entering S7, the processor latches data and negates $\overline{\text{AS}}$ and $\overline{\text{UDS}}$, $\overline{\text{LDS}}$, and/or $\overline{\text{DS}}$ during a read cycle. The hold time for these strobes from this falling edge is specified by parameter #12. The hold time for data relative to the negation of $\overline{\text{AS}}$ and $\overline{\text{UDS}}$, $\overline{\text{LDS}}$, and/or $\overline{\text{DS}}$ is specified by parameter #29. For a write cycle, only $\overline{\text{AS}}$ and $\overline{\text{UDS}}$, $\overline{\text{LDS}}$, and/or $\overline{\text{DS}}$ are negated; timing parameter #12 also applies.

On the rising edge of the clock, at the end of S7 (which may be the start of S0 for the next bus cycle), the processor places the address bus in the high-impedance state. During a write cycle, the processor also places the data bus in the high-impedance state and drives R/$\overline{W}$ high. External logic circuitry should respond to the negation of the $\overline{AS}$ and $\overline{UDS}$, $\overline{LDS}$, and/or $\overline{DS}$ by negating $\overline{DTACK}$ and/or $\overline{BERR}$. Parameter #28 is the hold time for $\overline{DTACK}$, and parameter #30 is the hold time for $\overline{BERR}$.

Figure 5-35 shows a synchronous read cycle and the important timing parameters that apply. The timing for a synchronous read cycle, including relevant timing parameters, is shown in Figure 5-36.

A key consideration when designing in a synchronous environment is the timing for the assertion of $\overline{DTACK}$ and $\overline{BERR}$ by an external device. To properly use external inputs, the processor must synchronize these signals to the internal clock. The processor must sample the external signal, which has no defined phase relationship to the CPU clock, which may be changing at sampling time, and must determine whether to consider the signal high or low during the succeeding clock period. Successful synchronization requires that the internal machine receives a valid logic level (not a metastable signal), whether the input is high, low, or in transition. Metastable signals propagating through synchronous machines can produce unpredictable operation.

Figure 5-37 is a conceptual representation of the input synchronizers used by the M68000 Family processors. The input latches allow the input to propagate through to the output when E is high. When low, E latches the input. The three latches require one cycle of CLK to synchronize an external signal. The high-gain characteristics of the devices comprising the latches quickly resolve a marginal signal into a valid state.

Parameter #47 of **11.6 AC ELECTRICAL SPECIFICATIONS — READ AND WRITE CYCLES** is the asynchronous input setup time. Signals that meet parameter #47 are guaranteed to be recognized at the next falling edge of the system clock. However, signals that do not

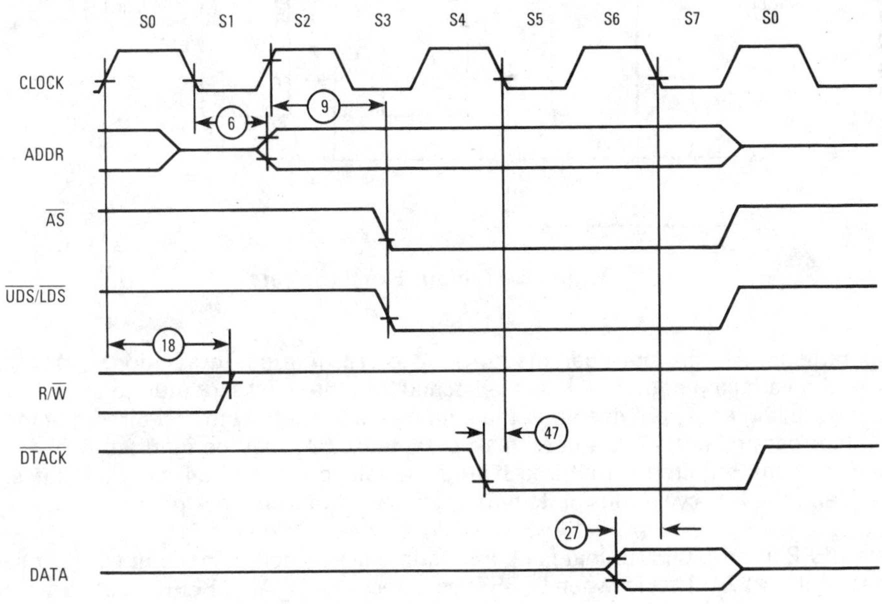

Figure 5-35. Synchronous Read Cycle

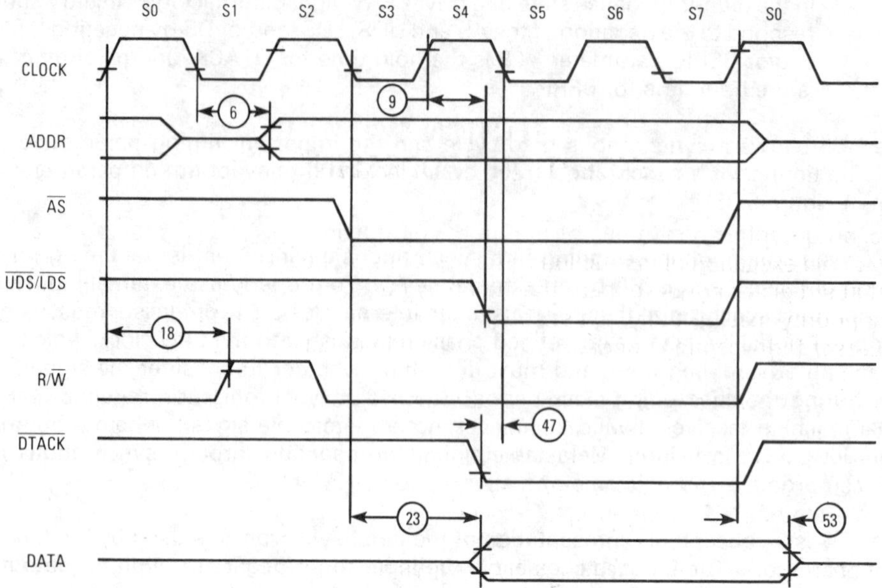

Figure 5-36. Synchronous Write Cycle

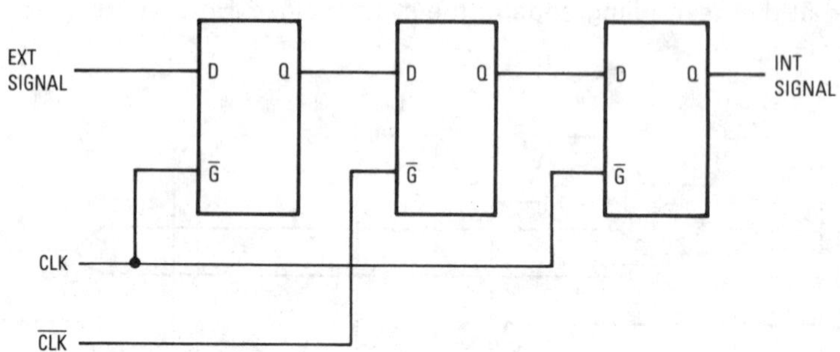

Figure 5-37. Input Synchronizers

meet parameter #47 are not guaranteed not to be recognized. In addition, if DTACK is recognized on a falling edge, valid data is latched into the processor (during a read cycle) on the next falling edge, provided that the data meets the setup time required (parameter #27). When parameter #27 has been met, parameter #31 may be ignored. If DTACK is asserted with the required setup time before the falling edge of S4, no wait states are incurred, and the bus cycle runs at its maximum speed of four clock periods.

The late BERR in an MC68010 that is operating in a synchronous mode must meet setup time parameter #27A. That is, when BERR is asserted after DTACK, BERR must be asserted before the falling edge of the clock, one clock cycle after DTACK is recognized. Violating this requirement may cause the MC68010 to operate erratically.

SECTION 6
EXCEPTION PROCESSING

This section describes operations of the processor outside the normal processing associated with the execution of instructions. The functions of the bits in the supervisor portion of the status register are described: the supervisor/user bit, the trace enable bit, and the interrupt priority mask. Finally, the sequence of memory references and actions taken by the processor for exception conditions is described in detail.

6

The processor is always in one of three processing states: normal, exception, or halted. The normal processing state is associated with instruction execution; the memory references are to fetch instructions and operands and to store results. A special case of the normal state is the stopped state, resulting from execution of a STOP instruction. In this state, no further memory references are made.

An additional, special case of the normal state is the loop mode of the MC68010, optionally entered when a test condition, decrement, and branch (DBcc) instruction is executed. In the loop mode, only operand fetches occur. See **APPENDIX D MC68010 LOOP MODE OPERATION**.

The exception processing state is associated with interrupts, trap instructions, tracing, and other exceptional conditions. The exception may be internally generated by an instruction or by an unusual condition arising during the execution of an instruction. Externally, exception processing can be forced by an interrupt, by a bus error, or by a reset. Exception processing provides an efficient context switch so that the processor can handle unusual conditions.

The halted processing state is an indication of catastrophic hardware failure. For example, if during the exception processing of a bus error another bus error occurs, the processor assumes the system is unusable and halts. Only an external reset can restart a halted processor. Note that a processor in the stopped state is not in the halted state, nor vice versa.

6.1 PRIVILEGE MODES

The processor operates in one of two levels of privilege: the supervisor mode or the user mode. The privilege mode determines which operations are legal. The mode is optionally used by an external memory management device to control and translate accesses. The mode is also used to choose between the supervisor stack pointer (SSP) and the user stack pointer (USP) in instruction references.

The privilege mode is a mechanism for providing security in a computer system. Programs should access only their own code and data areas and should be restricted from accessing information that they do not need and must not modify. The operating system executes in the supervisor mode, allowing it to access all resources required to perform the overhead tasks for the user-mode programs. Most programs execute in user mode, in which the accesses are controlled and the effects on other parts of the system are limited.

6.1.1 Supervisor Mode

The supervisor mode has the higher level of privilege. The mode of the processor is determined by the S bit of the status register; if the S bit is set, the processor is in the supervisor mode. All instructions can be executed in the supervisor mode. The bus cycles generated by instructions executed in the supervisor mode are classified as supervisor references. While the processor is in the supervisor mode, those instructions that use either the system stack pointer implicitly or address register seven explicitly access the SSP.

6.1.2 User Mode

6

The user mode has the lower level of privilege. If the S bit of the status register is clear, the processor is executing instructions in the user mode.

Most instructions execute identically in either mode. However, some instructions having important system effects are designated privileged. For example, user programs are not permitted to execute the STOP instruction or the RESET instruction. To ensure that a user program cannot enter the supervisor mode except in a controlled manner, the instructions that modify the entire status register are privileged. To aid in debugging systems software, the move to user stack pointer (MOVE to USP) and move from user stack pointer (MOVE from USP) instructions are privileged. To implement virtual machine concepts in the MC68010, the move from status register (MOVE from SR), move to/from control register (MOVEC), and move alternate address space (MOVES) instructions are also privileged.

The bus cycles generated by an instruction executed in user mode are classified as user references. Classifying a bus cycle as a user reference allows an external memory management device to translate the addresses of and control access to protected portions of the address space. While the processor is in the user mode, those instructions that use either the system stack pointer implicitly or address register seven explicitly access the USP.

6.1.3 Privilege Mode Changes

Once the processor is in the user mode and executing instructions, only exception processing can change the privilege mode. During exception processing, the current state of the S bit of the status register is saved, and the S bit is set, putting the processor in the supervisor mode. Therefore, when instruction execution resumes at the address specified to process the exception, the processor is in the supervisor privilege mode.

The transition from supervisor to user mode can be accomplished by any of four instructions: return from exception (RTE) (MC68010 only), move to status register (MOVE to SR), AND immediate to status register (ANDI to SR), and exclusive OR immediate to status register (EORI to SR). The RTE instruction in the MC68010 fetches the new status register and program counter from the supervisor stack and loads each into its respective register. Next, it begins the instruction fetch at the new program counter address in the privilege mode determined by the S bit of the new contents of the status register. The MOVE to SR, ANDI to SR, and EORI to SR instructions fetch all operands in the supervisor mode, perform the appropriate update to the status register, and then fetch the next instruction at the next sequential program counter address in the privilege mode determined by the new S bit.

6.1.4 Reference Classification

When the processor makes a reference, it classifies the reference according to the encoding of the three function code output lines. This classification allows external translation of addresses, control of access, and differentiation of special processor states, such as CPU space (used by interrupt acknowledge cycles). Table 6-1 lists the classification of references.

Table 6-1. Reference Classification

Function Code Output			Address Space
FC2	FC1	FC0	
0	0	0	(Undefined, Reserved)*
0	0	1	User Data
0	1	0	User Program
0	1	1	(Undefined, Reserved)*
1	0	0	(Undefined, Reserved)*
1	0	1	Supervisor Data
1	1	0	Supervisor Program
1	1	1	CPU Space

*Address space 3 is reserved for user definition, while 0 and 4 are reserved for future use by Motorola.

6

6.2 EXCEPTION PROCESSING

The processing of an exception occurs in four steps, with variations for different exception causes:

1. Make a temporary copy of the status register and set the status register for exception processing.
2. Obtain the exception vector.
3. Save the current processor context.
4. Obtain a new context and resume instruction processing.

6.2.1 Exception Vectors

An exception vector is a memory location from which the processor fetches the address of a routine to handle an exception. Each exception type requires a handler routine and a unique vector. All exception vectors are two words in length (Figure 6-1), except for the reset vector, which is four words long. All exception vectors reside in the supervisor data space, except for the reset vector, which is in the supervisor program space. A vector number is an 8-bit number that is multiplied by four to obtain the offset of an exception vector. Vector numbers are generated internally or externally, depending on the cause of the exception. For interrupts, during the interrupt acknowledge bus cycle, a peripheral provides an 8-bit vector number (Figure 6-2) to the processor on data bus lines D0 through D7.

The processor forms the vector offset by left-shifting the vector number two bit positions and zero-filling the upper-order bits to obtain a 32-bit long-word vector offset. In the MC68000, the MC68HC000, and the MC68008, this offset is used as the absolute address to obtain the exception vector itself, which is shown in Figure 6-3.

In the MC68010, the vector offset is added to the 32-bit vector base register (VBR) to obtain the 32-bit absolute address of the exception vector. See Figure 6-4. Since the VBR is set to zero upon reset, the MC68010 functions identically to the MC68000, MC68HC000, and MC68008 until the VBR is changed via the move control register MOVEC instruction.

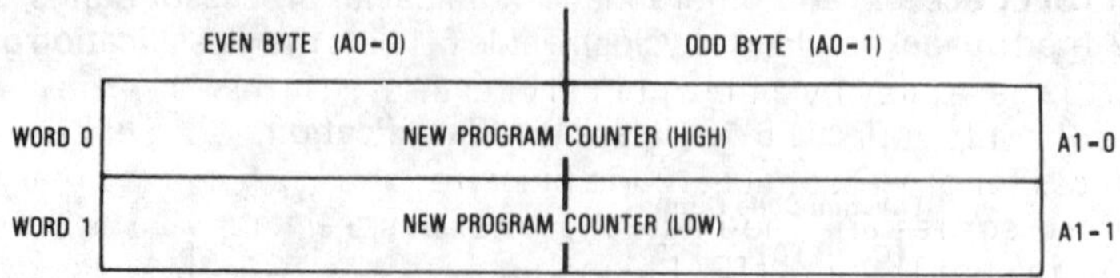

Figure 6-1. Exception Vector Format

6

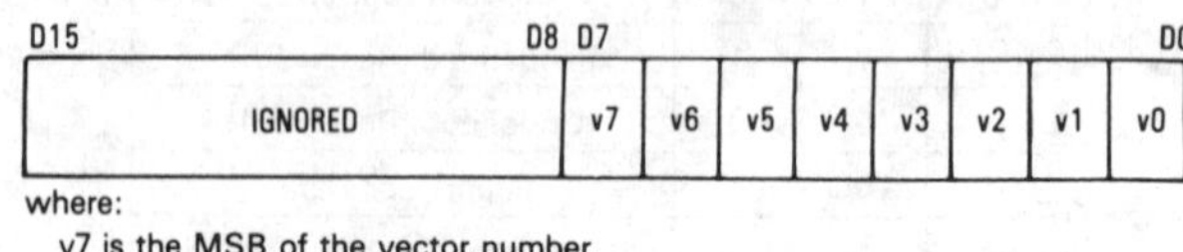

Figure 6-2. Peripheral Vector Number Format

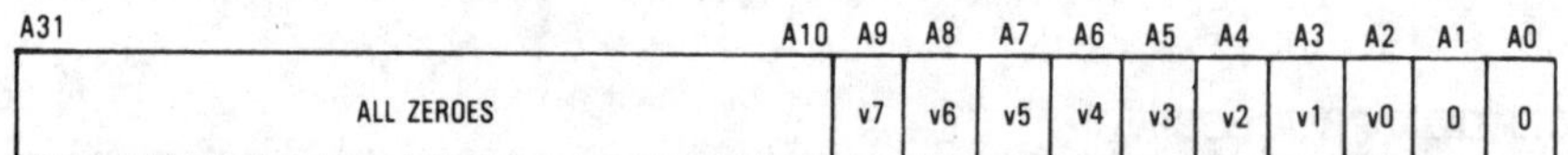

Figure 6-3. Address Translated from 8-Bit Vector Number (MC68000, MC68HC000, and MC68008)

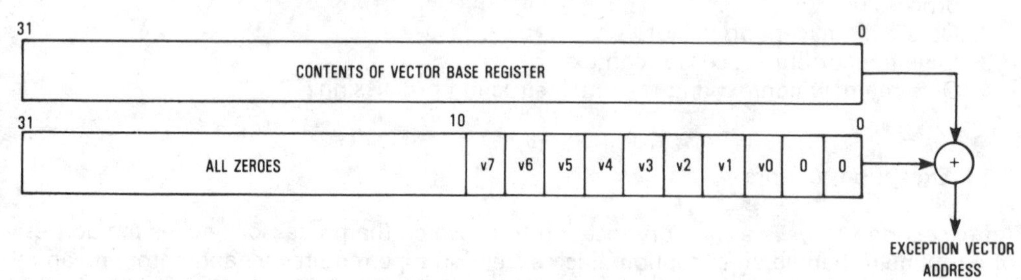

Figure 6-4. Exception Vector Address Calculation (MC68010)

The actual address on the address bus is truncated to the number of address bits available on the bus of the particular implementation of the M68000 architecture. In the MC68000, the MC68HC000, and the MC68010, this is 24 address bits. (A0 is implicitly encoded in the data strobes.) In the MC68008, the address is 20 or 22 bits in length. The memory map for exception vectors is shown in Table 6-2.

The vector table, Table 6-2, is 512 words long (1024 bytes), starting at address 0 (decimal) and proceeding through address 1023 (decimal). The vector table provides 255 unique vectors, some of which are reserved for trap and other system function vectors. Of the

255, 192 are reserved for user interrupt vectors. However, the first 64 entries are not protected, so user interrupt vectors may overlap at the discretion of the systems designer.

6.2.2 Kinds of Exceptions

Exceptions can be generated by either internal or external causes. The externally generated exceptions are the interrupts, the bus error, and reset. The interrupts are requests from peripheral devices for processor action; the bus error and reset inputs are used for access control and processor restart. The internal exceptions are generated by instructions, address errors, or tracing. The trap (TRAP), trap on overflow (TRAPV), check register against bounds (CHK), and divide (DIV) instructions can generate exceptions as part of their instruction execution. In addition, illegal instructions, word fetches from odd addresses, and privilege violations cause exceptions. Tracing is similar to a very high priority, internally-generated interrupt following each instruction.

6.2.3 Multiple Exceptions

These paragraphs describe the processing that occurs when multiple exceptions arise simultaneously. Exceptions can be grouped by their occurrence and priority. The group 0 exceptions are reset, bus error, and address error. These exceptions cause the instruction currently being executed to abort and the exception processing to commence within two clock cycles. The group 1 exceptions are trace and interrupt, privilege violations, and illegal instructions. Trace and interrupt exceptions allow the current instruction to execute to completion, but pre-empt the execution of the next instruction by forcing exception processing to occur. A privilege-violating instruction or an illegal instruction is detected when it is the next instruction to be executed. The group 2 exceptions occur as part of the normal processing of instructions. The TRAP, TRAPV, CHK, and zero divide exceptions are in this group. For these exceptions, the normal execution of an instruction may lead to exception processing.

Group 0 exceptions have highest priority, whereas group 2 exceptions have lowest priority. Within group 0, reset has highest priority, followed by address error and then bus error. Within group 1, trace has priority over external interrupts, which in turn takes priority over illegal instruction and privilege violation. Since only one instruction can be executed at a time, no priority relationship applies within group 2.

The priority relationship between two exceptions determines which is taken, or taken first, if the conditions for both arise simultaneously. Therefore, if a bus error occurs during a TRAP instruction, the bus error takes precedence, and the TRAP instruction processing is aborted. In another example, if an interrupt request occurs during the execution of an instruction while the T bit is asserted, the trace exception has priority and is processed first. Before instruction execution resumes, however, the interrupt exception is also processed, and instruction processing finally commences in the interrupt handler routine. A summary of exception grouping and priority is given in Table 6-3.

As a general rule, the lower the priority of an exception, the sooner the handler routine for that exception executes. For example, if simultaneous trap, trace, and interrupt exceptions are pending, the exception processing for the trap occurs first, followed immediately by exception processing for the trace and then for the interrupt. When the processor resumes normal instruction execution, it is in the interrupt handler, which returns to the

Table 6-2. Exception Vector Assignment

Vector Number(s)	Address		Space[6]	Assignment
	Dec	Hex		
0	0	000	SP	Reset: Initial SSP[2]
1	4	004	SP	Reset: Initial PC[2]
2	8	008	SD	Bus Error
3	12	00C	SD	Address Error
4	16	010	SD	Illegal Instruction
5	20	014	SD	Zero Divide
6	24	018	SD	CHK Instruction
7	28	01C	SD	TRAPV Instruction
8	32	020	SD	Privilege Violation
9	36	024	SD	Trace
10	40	028	SD	Line 1010 Emulator
11	44	02C	SD	Line 1111 Emulator
12[1]	48	030	SD	(Unassigned, Reserved)
13[1]	52	034	SD	(Unassigned, Reserved)
14	56	038	SD	Format Error[5]
15	60	03C	SD	Uninitialized Interrupt Vector
16-23[1]	64	040	SD	(Unassigned, Reserved)
	92	05C		—
24	96	060	SD	Spurious Interrupt[3]
25	100	064	SD	Level 1 Interrupt Autovector
26	104	068	SD	Level 2 Interrupt Autovector
27	108	06C	SD	Level 3 Interrupt Autovector
28	112	070	SD	Level 4 Interrupt Autovector
29	116	074	SD	Level 5 Interrupt Autovector
30	120	078	SD	Level 6 Interrupt Autovector
31	124	07C	SD	Level 7 Interrupt Autovector
32-47	128	080	SD	TRAP Instruction Vectors[4]
	188	0BC		—
48-63[1]	192	0C0	SD	(Unassigned, Reserved)
	255	0FF		—
64-255	256	100	SD	User Interrupt Vectors
	1020	3FC		—

NOTES:

1. Vector numbers 12, 13, 16 through 23, and 48 through 63 are reserved for future enhancements by Motorola. No user peripheral devices should be assigned these numbers.
2. Reset vector (0) requires four words, unlike the other vectors which only require two words, and is located in the supervisor program space.
3. The spurious interrupt vector is taken when there is a bus error indication during interrupt processing. Refer to Paragraph 4.4.4.
4. TRAP #n uses vector number 32 + n.
5. MC68010 only. See Return from Exception Section.
   This vector is unassigned, reserved on the MC68000 and MC68008.
6. SP denotes supervisor program space, and SD denotes supervisor data space.

Table 6-3. Exception Grouping and Priority

Group	Exception	Processing
0	Reset Address Error Bus Error	Exception Processing Begins Within Two Clock Cycles
1	Trace Interrupt Illegal Privilege	Exception Processing Begins Before The Next Instruction
2	TRAP, TRAPV, CHK Zero Divide	Exception Processing Is Started By Normal Instruction Execution

trace handler, which returns to the trap execution handler. This rule does not apply to the reset exception; its handler is executed first even though it has the highest priority, because the reset operation clears all other exceptions.

6

6.2.4 Exception Stack Frames

Exception processing saves the most volatile portion of the current processor context on the top of the supervisor stack. This context is organized in a format called the exception stack frame. Although this information varies with the particular processor and type of exception, it always includes the status register and program counter of the processor when the exception occurred.

The amount and type of information saved on the stack is determined by the processor type and exception type. Exceptions are grouped by type according to priority of the exception.

Of the group 0 exceptions, the reset exception does not stack any information. The information stacked by a bus error or address error exception in the MC68000, MC68HC000, or MC68008 is described in **6.3.9.1 BUS ERROR (MC68000/MC68HC000/MC68008)** and shown in Figure 6-7.

The MC68000, MC68HC000, and MC68008 group 1 and 2 exception stack frame is shown in Figure 6-5. Only the program counter and status register are saved. The program counter points to the next instruction to be executed after exception processing.

The MC68010 exception stack frame is shown in Figure 6-6. The number of words actually stacked depends on the exception type. Group 0 exceptions (except reset) stack 29 words

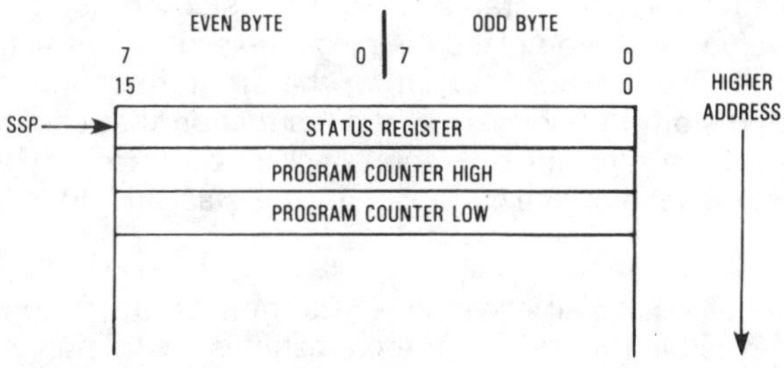

Figure 6-5. MC68000, MC68HC000, and MC68008 Group 1 and 2 Exception Stack Frame

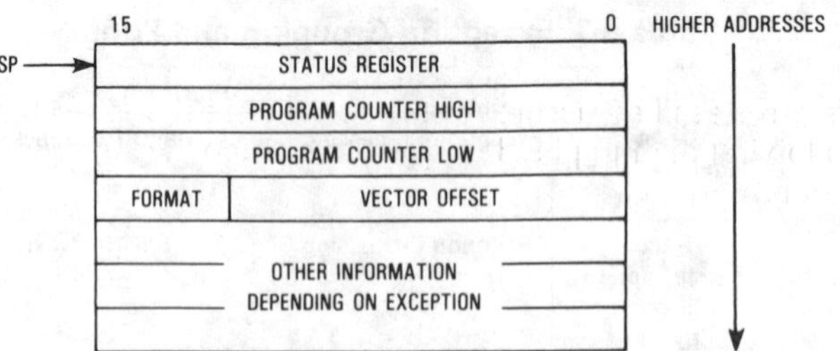

Figure 6-6. MC68010 Stack Frame

and group 1 and 2 exceptions stack four words. To support generic exception handlers, the processor also places the vector offset in the exception stack frame. The format code field allows the return from exception (RTE) instruction to identify what information is on the stack so that it can be properly restored. Table 6-4 lists the MC68010 format codes. Although some formats are specific to a particular M68000 Family processor, the format 0000 is always legal and indicates that just the first four words of the frame are present.

Table 6-4. MC68010 Format Codes

Format Code	Stacked Information
0000	Short Format (4 Words)
1000	Long Format (29 Words)
All Others	Unassigned, Reserved

6.2.5 Exception Processing Sequence

In the first step of exception processing, an internal copy is made of the status register. After the copy is made, the S bit of the status register is set, putting the processor into the supervisor mode. Also, the T bit is cleared, which allows the exception handler to execute unhindered by tracing. For the reset and interrupt exceptions, the interrupt priority mask is also updated appropriately.

In the second step, the vector number of the exception is determined. For interrupts, the vector number is obtained by a processor bus cycle classified as an interrupt acknowledge cycle. For all other exceptions, internal logic provides the vector number. This vector number is then used to calculate the address of the exception vector.

The third step, except for the reset exception, is to save the current processor status. (The reset exception does not save the context and skips this step.) The current program counter value and the saved copy of the status register are stacked using the SSP. The stacked program counter value usually points to the next unexecuted instruction. However, for bus error and address error, the value stacked for the program counter is unpredictable and may be incremented from the address of the instruction that caused the error. Group 1 and 2 exceptions use a short format exception stack frame (format = 0000 on the MC68010). Additional information defining the current context is stacked for the bus error and address error exceptions.

The last step is the same for all exceptions. The new program counter value is fetched from the exception vector. The processor then resumes instruction execution. The instruction at the address in the exception vector is fetched, and normal instruction decoding and execution is started.

6.3 PROCESSING OF SPECIFIC EXCEPTIONS

The exceptions are classified according to their sources, and each type is processed differently. The following paragraphs describe the types of exceptions and the processing of each type in detail.

6.3.1 Reset

The reset exception corresponds to the highest exception level. The processing of the reset exception is performed for system initiation and recovery from catastrophic failure. Any processing in progress at the time of the reset is aborted and cannot be recovered. The processor is forced into the supervisor state, and the trace state is forced off. The interrupt priority mask is set at level seven. In the MC68010, VBR is forced to zero. The vector number is internally generated to reference the reset exception vector at location 0 in the supervisor program space. Because no assumptions can be made about the validity of register contents, in particular the SSP, neither the program counter nor the status register is saved. The address in the first two words of the reset exception vector is fetched as the initial SSP, and the address in the last two words of the reset exception vector is fetched as the initial program counter. Finally, instruction execution is started at the address in the program counter. The initial program counter should point to the power up/restart code.

The RESET instruction does not cause a reset exception; it asserts the $\overline{\text{RESET}}$ signal to reset external devices, which allows the software to reset the system to a known state and continue processing with the next instruction.

6.3.2 Interrupts

Seven levels of interrupt priorities are provided, numbered from one to seven. In the MC68000, MC68HC000, MC68008 52-pin version, and MC68010 all seven levels are available. The MC68008 48-pin version supports only three interrupt levels: two, five, and seven. Level seven has the highest priority. Devices can be chained externally within interrupt priority levels, allowing an unlimited number of peripheral devices to interrupt the processor. The status register contains a three-bit mask indicating the current interrupt priority, and interrupts are inhibited for all priority levels less than or equal to the current priority.

An interrupt request is made to the processor by encoding the interrupt request level on the interrupt request lines; a zero indicates no interrupt request. Interrupt requests arriving at the processor do not force immediate exception processing, but the requests are made pending. Pending interrupts are detected between instruction executions. If the priority of the pending interrupt is lower than or equal to the current processor priority, execution continues with the next instruction, and the interrupt exception processing is postponed until the priority of the pending interrupt becomes greater than the current processor priority.

If the priority of the pending interrupt is greater than the current processor priority, the exception processing sequence is started. A copy of the status register is saved; the privilege mode is set to supervisor mode; tracing is suppressed; and the processor priority level is set to the level of the interrupt being acknowledged. The processor fetches the vector number from the interrupting device by executing an interrupt acknowledge cycle, which displays the level number of the interrupt being acknowledged on the address bus.

If external logic requests an automatic vector, the processor internally generates a vector number corresponding to the interrupt level number. If external logic indicates a bus error, the interrupt is considered spurious, and the generated vector number references the spurious interrupt vector. The processor then proceeds with the usual exception processing, saving the format/offset word (MC68010 only), program counter, and status register on the supervisor stack. The offset value in the format/offset word on the MC68010 is the vector number multiplied by four. The format is all zeroes. The saved value of the program counter is the address of the instruction that would have been executed had the interrupt not been taken. The appropriate interrupt vector is fetched and loaded into the program counter, and normal instruction execution commences in the interrupt handling routine. Priority level seven is a special case. Level seven interrupts cannot be inhibited by the interrupt priority mask, thus providing a "nonmaskable interrupt" capability. An interrupt is generated each time the interrupt request level changes from some lower level to level seven. A level seven interrupt may still be caused by the level comparison if the request level is a seven and the processor priority is set to a lower level by an instruction.

6.3.3 Uninitialized Interrupt

An interrupting device provides an M68000 interrupt vector number and asserts data transfer acknowledge ($\overline{DTACK}$), or asserts valid peripheral address ($\overline{VPA}$) or bus error ($\overline{BERR}$) during an interrupt acknowledge cycle by the MC68000. If the vector register has not been initialized, the responding M68000 Family peripheral provides vector number 15, the uninitialized interrupt vector. This response conforms to a uniform way to recover from a programming error.

6.3.4 Spurious Interrupt

During the interrupt acknowledge cycle, if no device responds by asserting $\overline{DTACK}$ or $\overline{VPA}$, $\overline{BERR}$ should be asserted to terminate the vector acquisition. The processor separates the processing of this error from bus error by forming a short format exception stack and fetching the spurious interrupt vector instead of the bus error vector. The processor then proceeds with the usual exception processing.

6.3.5 Instruction Traps

Traps are exceptions caused by instructions; they occur when a processor recognizes an abnormal condition during instruction execution or when an instruction is executed that normally traps during execution.

Exception processing for traps is straightforward. The status register is copied; the supervisor mode is entered; and tracing is turned off. The vector number is internally generated; for the TRAP instruction, part of the vector number comes from the instruction itself. The format/offset word (MC68010 only), the program counter and the copy of the status register are saved on the supervisor stack. The offset value in the format/offset word on the MC68010 is the vector number multiplied by four. The saved value of the program counter is the address of the instruction following the instruction that generated the trap. Finally, instruction execution commences at the address in the exception vector.

Some instructions are used specifically to generate traps. The TRAP instruction always forces an exception and is useful for implementing system calls for user programs. The

TRAPV and CHK instructions force an exception if the user program detects a runtime error, which may be an arithmetic overflow or a subscript out of bounds.

A signed divide (DIVS) or unsigned divide (DIVU) instruction forces an exception if a division operation is attempted with a divisor of zero.

6.3.6 Illegal and Unimplemented Instructions

Illegal instruction is the term used to refer to any of the word bit patterns that do not match the bit pattern of the first word of a legal M68000 instruction. If such an instruction is fetched, an illegal instruction exception occurs. Motorola reserves the right to define instructions using the opcodes of any of the illegal instructions. Three bit patterns always force an illegal instruction trap on all M68000-Family-compatible microprocessors. The patterns are: $4AFA, $4AFB, and $4AFC. Two of the patterns, $4AFA and $4AFB, are reserved for Motorola system products. The third pattern, $4AFC, is reserved for customer use (as the take illegal instruction trap (ILLEGAL) instruction).

In addition to the previously defined illegal instruction opcodes, the MC68010 defines eight breakpoint (BKPT) instructions with the bit patterns $4848-$484F. These instructions cause the processor to enter illegal instruction exception processing as usual. However, a breakpoint acknowledge bus cycle in which the function code lines (FC0-FC2) are high and the address lines are all low, is also executed before the stacking operations are performed. The processor does not accept or send any data during this cycle. Whether the breakpoint acknowledge cycle is terminated with a $\overline{\text{DTACK}}$, $\overline{\text{BERR}}$ or $\overline{\text{VPA}}$ signal, the processor continues with the illegal instruction processing. The purpose of this cycle is to provide a software breakpoint that signals to external hardware when it is executed. Timing for the breakpoint acknowledge cycle is shown in **5.2.1.4 CPU SPACE CYCLE**.

Word patterns with bits 15 through 12 equaling 1010 or 1111 are distinguished as unimplemented instructions, and separate exception vectors are assigned to these patterns to permit efficient emulation. Opcodes beginning with bit patterns equaling 1111 (line F) are implemented in the MC68020 as coprocessor instructions. These separate vectors allow the operating system to emulate unimplemented instructions in software.

Exception processing for illegal instructions is similar to that for traps. After the instruction is fetched and decoding is attempted, the processor determines that execution of an illegal instruction is being attempted and starts exception processing. The exception stack frame for group 2 is then pushed on the supervisor stack, and the illegal instruction vector is fetched.

6.3.7 Privilege Violations

To provide system security, various instructions are privileged. An attempt to execute one of the privileged instructions while in the user mode causes an exception. The privileged instructions are:

AND Immediate to SR
EOR Immediate to SR
MOVE to SR
MOVE from SR
MOVEC
MOVES
MOVE USP
OR Immediate to SR
RESET
RTE
STOP

Exception processing for privilege violations is nearly identical to that for illegal instructions. After the instruction is fetched and decoded and the processor determines that a privilege violation is being attempted, the processor starts exception processing. The status register is copied; the supervisor mode is entered; and tracing is turned off. The vector number is generated to reference the privilege violation vector, and the current program counter and the copy of the status register are saved on the supervisor stack. If the processor is an MC68010, the format/offset word is also saved. The saved value of the program counter is the address of the first word of the instruction causing the privilege violation. Finally, instruction execution commences at the address in the privilege violation exception vector.

6.3.8 Tracing

6

To aid in program development, the M68000 Family includes a facility to allow tracing following each instruction. When tracing is enabled, an exception is forced after each instruction is executed. Thus, a debugging program can monitor the execution of the program under test.

The trace facility is controlled by the T bit in the supervisor portion of the status register. If the T bit is clear (off), tracing is disabled and instruction execution proceeds from instruction to instruction as normal. If the T bit is set (on) at the beginning of the execution of an instruction, a trace exception is generated after the instruction is completed. If the instruction is not executed because an interrupt is taken or because the instruction is illegal or privileged, the trace exception does not occur. The trace exception also does not occur if the instruction is aborted by a reset, bus error, or address error exception. If the instruction is executed and an interrupt is pending on completion, the trace exception is processed before the interrupt exception. During the execution of the instruction, if an exception is forced by that instruction, the exception processing for the instruction exception occurs before that of the trace exception.

As an extreme illustration of these rules, consider the arrival of an interrupt during the execution of a TRAP instruction while tracing is enabled. First, the trap exception is processed, then the trace exception, and finally the interrupt exception. Instruction execution resumes in the interrupt handler routine.

After the execution of the instruction is completed and before the start of the next instruction, exception processing for a trace begins. A copy is made of the status register. The transition to supervisor mode is made, and the T bit of the status register is turned off, disabling further tracing. The vector number is generated to reference the trace exception vector, and the current program counter and the copy of the status register are saved on the supervisor stack. On the MC68010, the format/offset word is also saved on the supervisor stack. The saved value of the program counter is the address of the next instruction. Instruction execution commences at the address contained in the trace exception vector.

6.3.9 Bus Error

A bus error exception occurs when the external logic requests that a bus error be processed by an exception. The current bus cycle is aborted. The current processor activity, whether instruction or exception processing, is terminated and the processor immediately begins exception processing. The bus error facility is identical on the MC68000, MC68HC000, and

MC68008; however, the stack frame produced on the MC68010 contains more information. The larger stack frame supports instruction continuation, which supports virtual memory on the MC68010 processor. Bus errors for the MC68000/MC68HC000/MC68008 and for the MC68010 are described separately in subsequent paragraphs.

6.3.9.1 BUS ERROR (MC68000/MC68HC000/MC68008). Exception processing for a bus error follows the usual sequence of steps. The status register is copied, the supervisor mode is entered, and tracing is turned off. The vector number is generated to refer to the bus error vector. Since the processor is fetching the instruction or an operand when the error occurs, the context of the processor is more detailed. To save more of this context, additional information is saved on the supervisor stack. The program counter and the copy of the status register are saved. The value saved for the program counter is advanced two to ten bytes beyond the address of the first word of the instruction that made the reference causing the bus error. If the bus error occurred during the fetch of the next instruction, the saved program counter has a value in the vicinity of the current instruction, even if the current instruction is a branch, a jump, or a return instruction. In addition to the usual information, the processor saves its internal copy of the first word of the instruction being processed and the address being accessed by the aborted bus cycle. Specific information about the access is also saved: type of access (read or write), processor activity (processing an instruction), and function code outputs when the bus error occurred. The processor processing an instruction if it is in the normal state or processing a group 2 exception; the processor is not processing an instruction if it is processing a group 0 or a group 1 exception. Figure 6-7 illustrates how this information is organized on the supervisor stack. If a bus error occurs during the last step of exception processing, while either reading the exception vector or fetching the instruction, the value of the program counter is the address of the exception vector. Although this information is not generally sufficient to effect full recovery from the bus error, it does allow software diagnosis. Finally, the processor commences instruction processing at the address in the vector. It is the responsibility of the error handler routine to clean up the stack and determine where to continue execution.

If a bus error occurs during the exception processing for a bus error, an address error, or a reset, the processor halts and all processing ceases. This halt simplifies the detection of a catastrophic system failure, since the processor removes itself from the system to protect memory contents from erroneous accesses. Only an external reset operation can restart a halted processor.

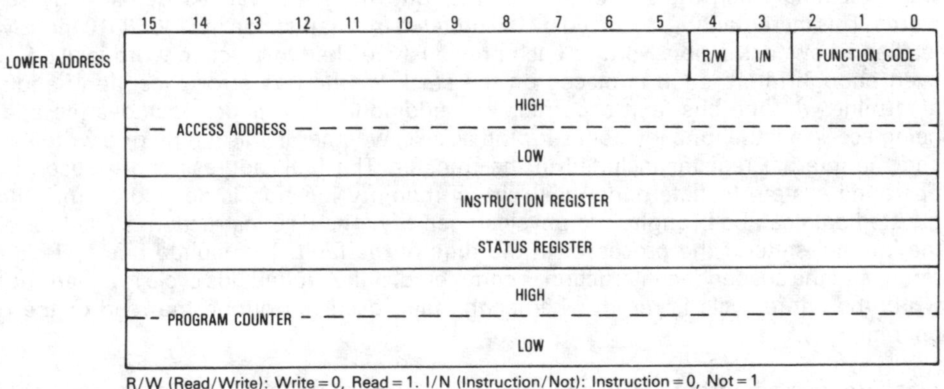

Figure 6-7. Supervisor Stack Order for Bus or Address Error Exception

6.3.9.2 BUS ERROR (MC68010). Exception processing for a bus error follows a slightly different sequence than the sequence for group 1 and 2 exceptions. In addition to the four steps executed during exception processing for all other exceptions, 22 words of additional information are placed on the stack. This additional information describes the internal state of the processor at the time of the bus error and is reloaded by the RTE instruction to continue the instruction that caused the error. Figure 6-8 shows the order of the stacked information.

	15 14 13 12	11 10 9 8 7 6 5 4 3 2 1 0
SP	STATUS REGISTER	
	PROGRAM COUNTER (HIGH)	
	PROGRAM COUNTER (LOW)	
	1000	VECTOR OFFSET
	SPECIAL STATUS WORD	
	FAULT ADDRESS (HIGH)	
	FAULT ADDRESS (LOW)	
	UNUSED, RESERVED	
	DATA OUTPUT BUFFER	
	UNUSED, RESERVED	
	DATA INPUT BUFFER	
	UNUSED, RESERVED	
	INSTRUCTION INPUT BUFFER	
	|VERSION| |NUMBER|	
	INTERNAL INFORMATION, 16 WORDS	

NOTE: The stack pointer is decremented by 29 words, although only 26 words of information are actually written to memory. The three additional words are reserved for future use by Motorola.

Figure 6-8. Exception Stack Order (Bus and Address Error)

The value of the saved program counter does not necessarily point to the instruction that was executing when the bus error occurred, but may be advanced by as many as five words. This incrementing is caused by the prefetch mechanism on the MC68010 that always fetches a new instruction word as each previously fetched instruction word is used. However, enough information is placed on the stack for the bus error exception handler to determine why the bus fault occurred. This additional information includes the address being accessed, the function codes for the access, whether it was a read or a write access, and the internal register included in the transfer. The fault address can be used by an operating system to determine what virtual memory location is needed so that the requested data can be brought into physical memory. The RTE instruction is used to reload the internal state of the processor at the time of the fault. The faulted bus cycle is then rerun, and the suspended instruction is completed. If the faulted bus cycle is a read-modify-write, the entire cycle is rerun, whether the fault occurred during the read or the write operation.

An alternate method of handling a bus error is to complete the faulted access in software. Using this method requires the special status word, the instruction input buffer, the data input buffer, and the data output buffer image. The format of the special status word is shown in Figure 6-9. If the bus cycle is a read, the data at the fault address should be written to the images of the data input buffer, instruction input buffer, or both according to the data fetch (DF) and instruction fetch (IF) bits.* In addition, for read-modify-write cycles, the status register image must be properly set to reflect the read data if the fault occurred during the read portion of the cycle and the write operation (i.e., setting the most significant bit of the memory location) must also be performed. These operations are required because the entire read-modify-write cycle is assumed to have been completed by software. Once the cycle has been completed by software, the rerun (RR) bit in the special status word is set to indicate to the processor that it should not rerun the cycle when the RTE instruction is executed. If the RR bit is set when an RTE instruction executes, the MC68010 reads all the information from the stack, as usual.

15	14	13	12	11	10	9	8	7–3	2 1 0
RR	*	IF	DF	RM	HB	BY	RW	*	FC2-FC0

RR — Re-run flag; 0 = processor re-run (default), 1 = software rerun.
IF — Instruction fetch to the Instruction Input Buffer.
DF — Data fetch to the Data Input Buffer.
RM — Read-Modify-Write cycle.
HB — High byte transfer from the Data Output Buffer or to the Data Input Buffer.
BY — Byte transfer flag; HB selects the high or low byte of the transfer register. If BY is clear, the transfer is word.
RW — Read/Write flag; 0 = write, 1 = read.
FC — The function code used during the faulted access.
* — These bits are reserved for future use by Motorola and will be zero when written by the MC68010.

Figure 6-9. Special Status Word Format

6.3.10 Address Error

An address error exception occurs when the processor attempts to access a word or long-word operand or an instruction at an odd address. An address error is similar to an internally generated bus error. The bus cycle is aborted, and the processor ceases current processing and begins exception processing. The exception processing sequence is the same as that for a bus error including the information to be stacked, except that the vector number refers to the address error vector. Likewise, if an address error occurs during the exception processing for a bus error, address error, or reset, the processor is halted.

On the MC68010, the address error exception stacks the same information stacked by a bus error exception. Therefore, the RTE instruction can be used to continue execution of the suspended instruction. However, if the RR flag is not set, the fault address is used when the cycle is retried, and another address error exception occurs. Therefore, the user must be certain that the proper corrections have been made to the stack image and user registers before attempting to continue the instruction. With proper software handling, the address error exception handler could emulate word or long-word accesses to odd addresses if desired.

*If the faulted access was a byte operation, the data should be moved from or to the least significant byte of the data output or input buffer images, unless the high-byte transfer (HB) bit is set. This condition occurs if a MOVEP instruction caused the fault during transfer of bits 8-15 of a word or long word or bits 24-31 of a long word.

6.4 RETURN FROM EXCEPTION (MC68010)

In addition to returning from any exception handler routine on the MC68010, the RTE instruction resumes the execution of a suspended instruction by returning to the normal processing state after restoring all of the temporary register and control information stored during a bus error. For the RTE instruction to execute properly, the stack must contain valid and accessible data. The RTE instruction checks for data validity in two ways. First, the format/offset word is checked for a valid stack format code. Second, if the format code indicates the long stack format, the validity of the long stack data is checked as it is loaded into the processor. In addition, the data is checked for accessibility when the processor starts reading the long data. Because of these checks, the RTE instruction executes as follows:

6

1. Determine the stack format. This step is the same for any stack format and consists of reading the status register, program counter, and format/offset word. If the format code indicates a short stack format, execution continues at the new program counter address. If the format code is not an MC68010-defined stack format code, exception processing starts for a format error.

2. Determine data validity. For a long-stack format, the MC68010 begins to read the remaining stack data, checking for validity of the data. The only word checked for validity is the first of the 16 internal information words (SP + 26) shown in Figure 6-8. This word contains a processor version number (in bits 10 through 13) and proprietary internal information that must match the version number of the MC68010 attempting to read the data. This validity check is used to ensure that the data is properly interpreted by the RTE instruction. If the version number is incorrect for this processor, the RTE instruction is aborted and exception processing begins for a format error exception. Since the stack pointer is not updated until the RTE instruction has successfully read all the stack data, a format error occurring at this point does not stack new data over the previous bus error stack information.

3. Determine data accessibility. If the long stack data is valid, the MC68010 performs a read from the last word (SP + 56) of the long stack to determine data accessibility. If this read is terminated normally, the processor assumes that the remaining words on the stack frame are also accessible. If a bus error is signaled before or during this read, a bus error exception is taken. After this read, the processor must be able to load the remaining data without receiving a bus error; therefore, if a bus error occurs on any of the remaining stack reads, the error becomes a double bus fault, and the MC68010 enters the halted state.

SECTION 7
M6800 PERIPHERAL INTERFACE

Motorola's extensive line of M6800 peripherals is directly compatible with the M68000 Family. Since both the M6800 processors and the M68000 processors use memory-mapped I/O, interfacing the synchronous M6800 peripherals with the asynchronous M68000 Family processors works very well. The processor modifies its bus cycle to meet the M6800 cycle requirements whenever an M6800 device address is detected. Figure 7-1 is a flowchart of the data transfer between the processor and M6800 devices.

7.1 DATA TRANSFER OPERATION

Three signals on the processor provide the M6800 interface. They are: enable (E), valid memory address ($\overline{\text{VMA}}$), and valid peripheral address ($\overline{\text{VPA}}$). Enable corresponds to the E or phase 2 signal in M6800 systems. The bus frequency is one tenth of the MC68000 system clock frequency. The timing of E allows 1 megahertz peripherals to be used with 8 megahertz processors. Enable has a 60/40 duty cycle; that is, it is low for six system clocks, and high for four system clocks. This duty cycle allows $\overline{\text{VPA}}$ accesses on successive E pulses.

In the MC68000 and the MC68010, $\overline{\text{VMA}}$ is provided to indicate synchronization with E. The MC68008 does not provide a $\overline{\text{VMA}}$ signal; external circuitry similar to that shown in Figure 7-2 using transistor-to-transistor (TTL) logic must be included in the system to provide $\overline{\text{VMA}}$. The $\overline{\text{VMA}}$ signal indicates to the M6800 devices that the address on the

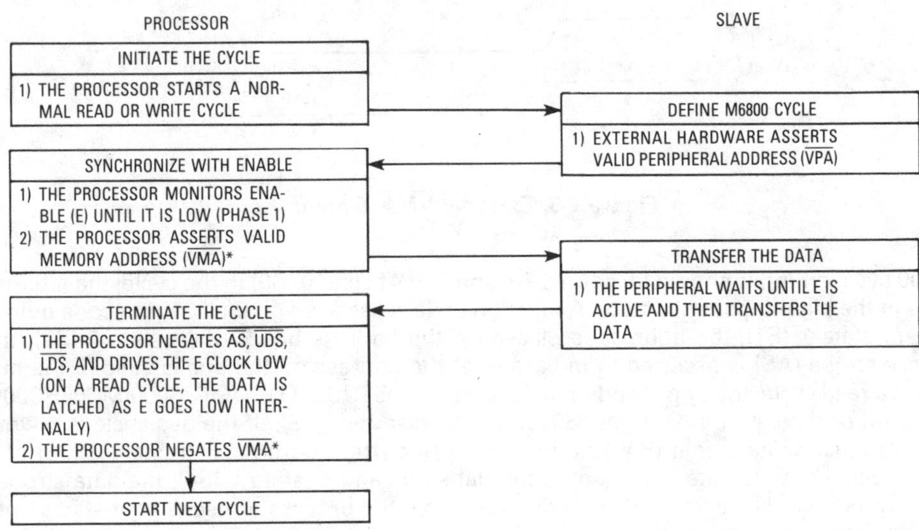

*For MC68008-based systems, $\overline{\text{VMA}}$ is supplied by external circuitry.

Figure 7-1. M6800 Data Transfer Flowchart

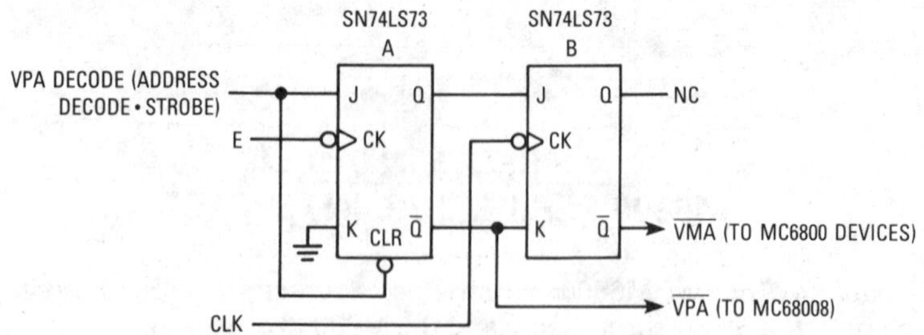

Figure 7-2. Example External $\overline{\text{VMA}}$ Circuit

address bus is a valid device address and that the processor is synchronized to the enable clock. The VPA decode input is an active high signal that is asserted when address strobe $\overline{\text{AS}}$ has been asserted and the address on the address bus is that of a peripheral device. The flip-flop on the left sets at the falling edge of E; the flip-flop on the right sets at the next fall of system clock, asserting $\overline{\text{VMA}}$. $\overline{\text{VMA}}$ remains asserted until the fall of system clock immediately following the negation of VPA decode. Figure 7-3 shows the timing for the $\overline{\text{VMA}}$ signal provided by this circuitry.

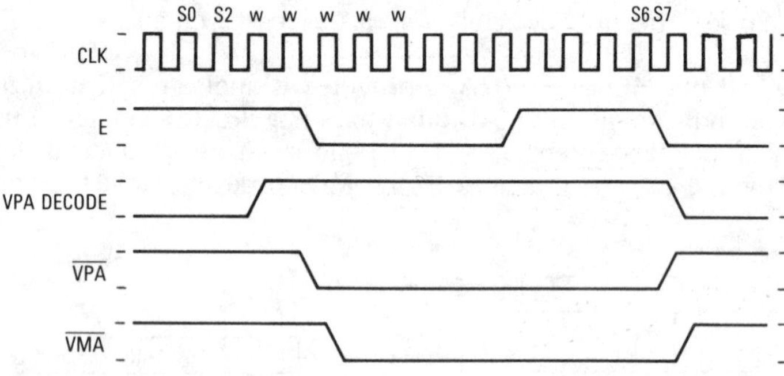

Figure 7-3. External $\overline{\text{VMA}}$ Timing

M6800 cycle timing is shown in Figures 7-4 and 7-5. At state 0 (S0) in the cycle, the address bus is in the high-impedance state. A function code is asserted on the function code output lines. In state 1 (S1), the address is placed on the address bus. During state 2 (S2), the address strobe ($\overline{\text{AS}}$) is asserted to indicate that the address on the bus is valid. If the bus cycle is a read cycle, the upper and/or lower data strobe ($\overline{\text{UDS}}$, $\overline{\text{LDS}}$) (MC68000/MC68HC000/MC68010) or data strobe ($\overline{\text{DS}}$) (MC68008) is also asserted in S2. If the bus cycle is a write cycle, the read/write signal (R/$\overline{\text{W}}$) is driven low (for write) during S2. In state 3 (S3) of a write cycle, the write data is placed on the data bus, and in state 4 (S4), the data strobes are asserted to indicate valid data on the bus. Next, the processor inserts wait states until it recognizes the assertion of $\overline{\text{VPA}}$.

The $\overline{\text{VPA}}$ input indicates to the processor that the address on the bus is the address of an M6800 device (or an area reserved for M6800 devices) and that the bus should conform

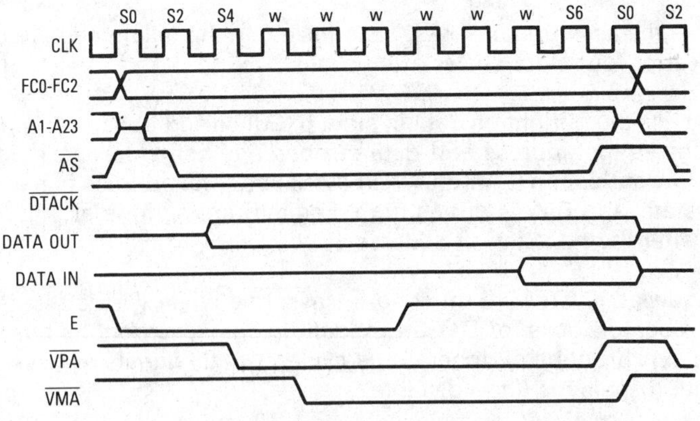

Figure 7-4. M6800 Peripheral Timing — Best Case

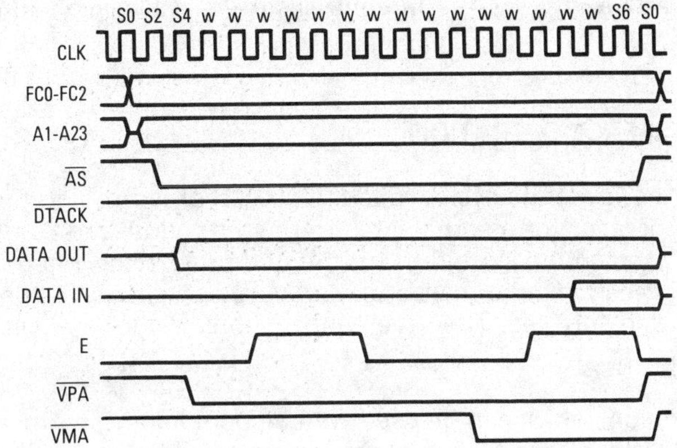

Figure 7-5. M6800 Peripheral Timing — Worst Case

to the phase 2 transfer characteristics of the M6800 bus. $\overline{\text{VPA}}$ is derived by decoding the address bus, conditioned by the address strobe ($\overline{\text{AS}}$).

After recognizing $\overline{\text{VPA}}$, the processor assures that enable (E) is low by waiting, if necessary, and subsequently asserts $\overline{\text{VMA}}$. $\overline{\text{VMA}}$ is then used as part of the chip select equation of the peripheral, to ensure correct timing for selection and deselection of the M6800 device. Once selected, the peripheral runs its cycle during the high portion of the E signal. Figure 7-4 shows the best case timing of an M6800 cycle, and Figure 7-5 shows the worst case timing. The cycle length is entirely dependent on the relationship of the assertion of VPA to the E clock.

When external circuitry asserts $\overline{\text{VPA}}$ as soon as possible following the assertion of $\overline{\text{AS}}$, the assertion of $\overline{\text{VPA}}$ is recognized on the falling edge of S4. In this case, no extra wait states are inserted (waiting for the assertion of $\overline{\text{VPA}}$). The only wait states inserted are those required to synchronize with the E clock. The synchronization delay is an integral number of system clock cycles within the following extremes:

1. Best Case — the assertion of $\overline{\text{VPA}}$ is recognized on the falling edge three clock cycles before E rises (or three clock cycles after E falls).

2. Worst Case — the assertion of $\overline{\text{VPA}}$ is recognized on the falling edge two clock cycles before E rises (or four clock cycles after E falls).

The processor latches the peripheral data in state 6 (S6) during a read cycle. For all cycles, the processor negates the address and data strobes one-half clock cycle later in state 7 (S7), and E goes low at this time. Another half clock later, the address bus is placed in the high-impedance state, and R/$\overline{\text{W}}$ is driven high. Logic in the peripheral must remove $\overline{\text{VPA}}$ within one clock after the negation of address strobe.

Data transfer acknowledge ($\overline{\text{DTACK}}$) must not be asserted while $\overline{\text{VPA}}$ is asserted. The state machine in the processor looks for $\overline{\text{DTACK}}$ to identify an asynchronous bus cycle and for $\overline{\text{VPA}}$ to identify a synchronous peripheral bus cycle. If both signals are asserted, the operation of the state machine is unpredictable.

To allow the processor to place its buses in the high-impedance state during DMA requests without inadvertently selecting the peripherals, $\overline{\text{VMA}}$ is active low for the M68000 Family of processors. The active low $\overline{\text{VMA}}$ is in contrast to the active high VMA signal of the M6800.

7.2 INTERRUPT INTERFACE OPERATION

During an interrupt acknowledge cycle while the processor is fetching the vector, $\overline{\text{VPA}}$ is asserted, and the processor (or external circuitry) asserts $\overline{\text{VMA}}$ and completes a normal M6800 read cycle as shown in Figure 7-6. For the interrupt vector, the processor uses an internally-generated vector number called an autovector. The autovector corresponds to the interrupt level being serviced. The seven autovectors are decimal vector numbers 25 through 31.

The autovector operation, which can be used with all peripherals, is similar to the normal interrupt acknowledge cycle. The autovector capability provides vectors for each of the six maskable interrupt levels and for the non maskable interrupt level. Whether the device supplies the vector number or the processor generates an autovector number, the interrupt service routine can be located anywhere within the supervisor program address space, because the user assigns the vectors in the vector table.

Since $\overline{\text{VMA}}$ is asserted during an autovector operation, care should be taken to prevent an unintended access to the device. An unintended access could occur if the peripheral address were on the address bus during the autovector operation.

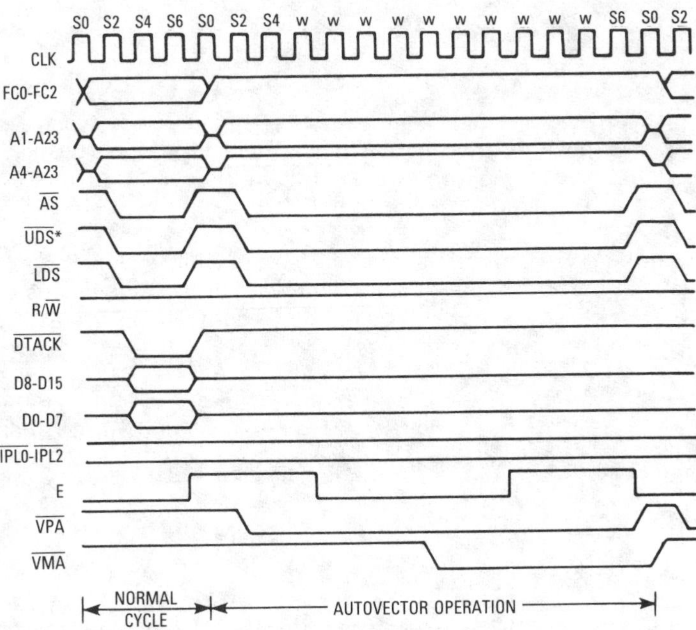

*Although UDS and LDs are asserted, no data is read from the bus during the autovector cycle. The vector number is generated internally.

Figure 7-6. Autovector Operation Timing Diagram

SECTION 8
MC68000 AND MC68HC000 INSTRUCTION EXECUTION TIMES

This section contains listings of the instruction execution times in terms of external clock (CLK) periods. In this data, it is assumed that both memory read and write cycles consist of four clock periods. A longer memory cycle causes the generation of wait states that must be added to the total instruction times.

The number of bus read and write cycles for each instruction is also included with the timing data. This data is shown as

n(r/w)

where
- n is the total number of clock periods
- r is the number of read cycles
- w is the number of write cycles

For example, a timing number shown as 18(3/1) means that the total number of clock periods is 18. Of the 18 clock periods, 12 are used for the three read cycles (four periods per cycle). Four additional clock periods are used for the single write cycle, for a total of 16 clock periods. The bus is idle for two clock periods during which the processor completes the internal operations required for the instruction.

NOTE

The total number of clock periods (n) includes instruction fetch and all applicable operand fetches and stores.

8.1 OPERAND EFFECTIVE ADDRESS CALCULATION TIMES

Table 8-1 lists the numbers of clock periods required to compute the effective addresses for instructions. The total includes fetching any extension words, computing the address, and fetching the memory operand. The total number of clock periods, the number of read cycles, and the number of write cycles (zero for all effective address calculations) are shown in the previously described format.

8.2 MOVE INSTRUCTION EXECUTION TIMES

Tables 8-2 and 8-3 list the numbers of clock periods for the move instructions. The totals include instruction fetch, operand reads, and operand writes. The total number of clock periods, the number of read cycles, and the number of write cycles are shown in the previously described format.

Table 8-1. Effective Address Calculation Times

Addressing Mode		Byte, Word	Long
	Register		
Dn	Data Register Direct	0(0/0)	0(0/0)
An	Address Register Direct	0(0/0)	0(0/0)
	Memory		
(An)	Address Register Indirect	4(1/0)	8(2/0)
(An)+	Address Register Indirect with Postincrement	4(1/0)	8(2/0)
−(An)	Address Register Indirect with Predecrement	6(1/0)	10(2/0)
(d_{16}, An)	Address Register Indirect with Displacement	8(2/0)	12(3/0)
(d_8, An, Xn)*	Address Register Indirect with Index	10(2/0)	14(3/0)
(xxx).W	Absolute Short	8(2/0)	12(3/0)
(xxx).L	Absolute Long	12(3/0)	16(4/0)
(d_8, PC)	Program Counter Indirect with Displacement	8(2/0)	12(3/0)
(d_{16}, PC, Xn)*	Program Counter Indirect with Index	10(2/0)	14(3/0)
#⟨data⟩	Immediate	4(1/0)	8(2/0)

*The size of the index register (Xn) does not affect execution time.

Table 8-2. Move Byte and Word Instruction Execution Times

Source	Destination								
	Dn	An	(An)	(An)+	−(An)	(d_{16}, An)	(d_8, An, Xn)*	(xxx).W	(xxx).L
Dn	4(1/0)	4(1/0)	8(1/1)	8(1/1)	8(1/1)	12(2/1)	14(2/1)	12(2/1)	16(3/1)
An	4(1/0)	4(1/0)	8(1/1)	8(1/1)	8(1/1)	12(2/1)	14(2/1)	12(2/1)	16(3/1)
(An)	8(2/0)	8(2/0)	12(2/1)	12(2/1)	12(2/1)	16(3/1)	18(3/1)	16(3/1)	20(4/1)
(An)+	8(2/0)	8(2/0)	12(2/1)	12(2/1)	12(2/1)	16(3/1)	18(3/1)	16(3/1)	20(4/1)
−(An)	10(2/0)	10(2/0)	14(2/1)	14(2/1)	14(2/1)	18(3/1)	20(3/1)	18(3/1)	22(4/1)
(d_{16}, An)	12(3/0)	12(3/0)	16(3/1)	16(3/1)	16(3/1)	20(4/1)	22(4/1)	20(4/1)	24(5/1)
(d_8, An, Xn)*	14(3/0)	14(3/0)	18(3/1)	18(3/1)	18(3/1)	22(4/1)	24(4/1)	22(4/1)	26(5/1)
(xxx).W	12(3/0)	12(3/0)	16(3/1)	16(3/1)	16(3/1)	20(4/1)	22(4/1)	20(4/1)	24(5/1)
(xxx).L	16(4/0)	16(4/0)	20(4/1)	20(4/1)	20(4/1)	24(5/1)	26(5/1)	24(5/1)	28(6/1)
(d_{16}, PC)	12(3/0)	12(3/0)	16(3/1)	16(3/1)	16(3/1)	20(4/1)	22(4/1)	20(4/1)	24(5/1)
(d_8, PC, Xn)*	14(3/0)	14(3/0)	18(3/1)	18(3/1)	18(3/1)	22(4/1)	24(4/1)	22(4/1)	26(5/1)
#⟨data⟩	8(2/0)	8(2/0)	12(2/1)	12(2/1)	12(2/1)	16(3/1)	18(3/1)	16(3/1)	20(4/1)

*The size of the index register (Xn) does not affect execution time.

Table 8-3. Move Long Instruction Execution Times

Source	Destination								
	Dn	An	(An)	(An)+	−(An)	(d_{16}, An)	(d_8, An, Xn)*	(xxx).W	(xxx).L
Dn	4(1/0)	4(1/0)	12(1/2)	12(1/2)	12(1/2)	16(2/2)	18(2/2)	16(2/2)	20(3/2)
An	4(1/0)	4(1/0)	12(1/2)	12(1/2)	12(1/2)	16(2/2)	18(2/2)	16(2/2)	20(3/2)
(An)	12(3/0)	12(3/0)	20(3/2)	20(3/2)	20(3/2)	24(4/2)	26(4/2)	24(4/2)	28(5/2)
(An)+	12(3/0)	12(3/0)	20(3/2)	20(3/2)	20(3/2)	24(4/2)	26(4/2)	24(4/2)	28(5/2)
−(An)	14(3/0)	14(3/0)	22(3/2)	22(3/2)	22(3/2)	26(4/2)	28(4/2)	26(4/2)	30(5/2)
(d_{16}, An)	16(4/0)	16(4/0)	24(4/2)	24(4/2)	24(4/2)	28(5/2)	30(5/2)	28(5/2)	32(6/2)
(d_8, An, Xn)*	18(4/0)	18(4/0)	26(4/2)	26(4/2)	26(4/2)	30(5/2)	32(5/2)	30(5/2)	34(6/2)
(xxx).W	16(4/0)	16(4/0)	24(4/2)	24(4/2)	24(4/2)	28(5/2)	30(5/2)	28(5/2)	32(6/2)
(xxx).L	20(5/0)	20(5/0)	28(5/2)	28(5/2)	28(5/2)	32(6/2)	34(6/2)	32(6/2)	36(7/2)
(d, PC)	16(4/0)	16(4/0)	24(4/2)	24(4/2)	24(4/2)	28(5/2)	30(5/2)	28(5/2)	32(5/2)
(d, PC, Xn)*	18(4/0)	18(4/0)	26(4/2)	26(4/2)	26(4/2)	30(5/2)	32(5/2)	30(5/2)	34(6/2)
#⟨data⟩	12(3/0)	12(3/0)	20(3/2)	20(3/2)	20(3/2)	24(4/2)	26(4/2)	24(4/2)	28(5/2)

*The size of the index register (Xn) does not affect execution time.

8.3 STANDARD INSTRUCTION EXECUTION TIMES

The numbers of clock periods shown in Table 8-4 indicate the times required to perform the operations, store the results, and read the next instruction. The total number of clock periods, the number of read cycles, and the number of write cycles are shown in the previously described format. The number of clock periods, the number of read cycles, and the number of write cycles, respectively, must be added to those of the effective address calculation where indicated by a plus sign (+).

In Table 8-4, the following notation applies:

- An - Address register operand
- Dn - Data register operand
- ea - An operand specified by an effective address
- M - Memory effective address operand

8

Table 8-4. Standard Instruction Execution Times

Instruction	Size	op<ea>, An†	op<ea>, Dn	op Dn, <M>
ADD/ADDA	Byte, Word	8(1/0)+	4(1/0)+	8(1/1)+
	Long	6(1/0)+ **	6(1/0)+ **	12(1/2)+
AND	Byte, Word	—	4(1/0)+	8(1/1)+
	Long	—	6(1/0)+ **	12(1/2)+
CMP/CMPA	Byte, Word	6(1/0)+	4(1/0)+	—
	Long	6(1/0)+	6(1/0)+	—
DIVS	—	—	158(1/0)+ *	—
DIVU	—	—	140(1/0)+ *	—
EOR	Byte, Word	—	4(1/0)***	8(1/1)+
	Long	—	8(1/0)***	12(1/2)+
MULS	—	—	70(1/0)+ *	—
MULU	—	—	70(1/0)+ *	—
OR	Byte, Word	—	4(1/0)+	8(1/1)+
	Long	—	6(1/0)+ **	12(1/2)+
SUB	Byte, Word	8(1/0)+	4(1/0)+	8(1/1)+
	Long	6(1/0)+ **	6(1/0)+ **	12(1/2)+

NOTES:

\+ add effective address calculation time

† word or long only

* indicates maximum basic value added to word effective address time.

** The base time of six clock periods is increased to eight if the effective address mode is register direct or immediate (effective address time should also be added).

*** Only available effective address mode is data register direct.

DIVS, DIVU — The divide algorithm used by the MC68000 provides less than 10% difference between the best and worst case timings.

MULS, MULU — The multiply algorithm requires 38+2n clocks where n is defined as:

MULU: n= the number of ones in the <ea>

MULS: n= concatanate the <ea> with a zero as the LSB; n is the resultant number of 10 or 01 patterns in the 17-bit source; i.e., worst case happens when the source is $5555.

8.4 IMMEDIATE INSTRUCTION EXECUTION TIMES

The numbers of clock periods shown in Table 8-5 include the times to fetch immediate operands, perform the operations, store the results, and read the next operation. The total number of clock periods, the number of read cycles, and the number of write cycles are shown in the previously described format. The number of clock periods, the number of read cycles, and the number of write cycles, respectively, must be added to those of the effective address calculation where indicated by a plus sign (+).

In Table 8-5, the following notation applies:

- # - Immediate operand
- Dn - Data register operand
- An - Address register operand
- M - Memory operand

8

Table 8-5. Immediate Instruction Execution Times

Instruction	Size	op #,Dn	op #,An	op #,M
ADDI	Byte, Word	**8**(2/0)	—	**12**(2/1)+
	Long	**16**(3/0)	—	**20**(3/2)+
ADDQ	Byte, Word	**4**(1/0)	**4**(1/0)*	**8**(1/1)+
	Long	**8**(1/0)	**8**(1/0)	**12**(1/2)+
ANDI	Byte, Word	**8**(2/0)	—	**12**(2/1)+
	Long	**14**(3/0)	—	**20**(3/2)+
CMPI	Byte, Word	**8**(2/0)	—	**8**(2/0)+
	Long	**14**(3/0)	—	**12**(3/0)+
EORI	Byte, Word	**8**(2/0)	—	**12**(2/1)+
	Long	**16**(3/0)	—	**20**(3/2)+
MOVEQ	Long	**4**(1/0)	—	—
ORI	Byte, Word	**8**(2/0)	—	**12**(2/1)+
	Long	**16**(3/0)	—	**20**(3/2)+
SUBI	Byte, Word	**8**(2/0)	—	**12**(2/1)+
	Long	**16**(3/0)	—	**20**(3/2)+
SUBQ	Byte, Word	**4**(1/0)	**8**(1/0)*	**8**(1/1)+
	Long	**8**(1/0)	**8**(1/0)	**12**(1/2)+

8.5 SINGLE OPERAND INSTRUCTION EXECUTION TIMES

Table 8-6 lists the timing data for the single operand instructions. The total number of clock periods, the number of read cycles, and the number of write cycles are shown in the previously described format. The number of clock periods, the number of read cycles, and the number of write cycles, respectively, must be added to those of the effective address calculation where indicated by a plus sign (+).

Table 8-6. Single Operand Instruction Execution Times

Instruction	Size	Register	Memory
CLR	Byte, Word	4(1/0)	8(1/1)+
	Long	6(1/0)	12(1/2)+
NBCD	Byte	6(1/0)	8(1/1)+
NEG	Byte, Word	4(1/0)	8(1/1)+
	Long	6(1/0)	12(1/2)+
NEGX	Byte, Word	4(1/0)	8(1/1)+
	Long	6(1/0)	12(1/2)+
NOT	Byte, Word	4(1/0)	8(1/1)+
	Long	6(1/0)	12(1/2)+
Scc	Byte, False	4(1/0)	8(1/1)+
	Byte, True	6(1/0)	8(1/1)+
TAS	Byte	4(1/0)	14(2/1)+
TST	Byte, Word	4(1/0)	4(1/0)+
	Long	4(1/0)	4(1/0)+

+ add effective address calculation time

8.6 SHIFT/ROTATE INSTRUCTION EXECUTION TIMES

Table 8-7 lists the timing data for the shift and rotate instructions. The total number of clock periods, the number of read cycles, and the number of write cycles are shown in the previously described format. The number of clock periods, the number of read cycles, and the number of write cycles, respectively, must be added to those of the effective address calculation where indicated by a plus sign (+).

Table 8-7. Shift/Rotate Instruction Execution Times

Instruction	Size	Register	Memory
ASR, ASL	Byte, Word	6 + 2n(1/0)	8(1/1)+
	Long	8 + 2n(1/0)	–
LSR, LSL	Byte, Word	6 + 2n(1/0)	8(1/1)+
	Long	8 + 2n(1/0)	–
ROR, ROL	Byte, Word	6 + 2n(1/0)	8(1/1)+
	Long	8 + 2n(1/0)	–
ROXR, ROXL	Byte, Word	6 + 2n(1/0)	8(1/1)+
	Long	8 + 2n(1/0)	–

+ add effective address calculation time for word operands

n is the shift count

8

8.7 BIT MANIPULATION INSTRUCTION EXECUTION TIMES

Table 8-8 lists the timing data for the bit manipulation instructions. The total number of clock periods, the number of read cycles, and the number of write cycles are shown in the previously described format. The number of clock periods, the number of read cycles, and the number of write cycles, respectively, must be added to those of the effective address calculation where indicated by a plus sign (+).

Table 8-8. Bit Manipulation Instruction Execution Times

Instruction	Size	Dynamic		Static	
		Register	Memory	Register	Memory
BCHG	Byte	—	8(1/1)+	—	12(2/1)+
	Long	8(1/0)*	—	12(2/0)*	—
BCLR	Byte	—	8(1/1)+	—	12(2/1)+
	Long	10(1/0)*	—	14(2/0)*	—
BSET	Byte	—	8(1/1)+	—	12(2/1)+
	Long	8(1/0)*	—	12(2/0)*	—
BTST	Byte	—	4(1/0)+	—	8(2/0)+
	Long	6(1/0)	—	10(2/0)	—

+ add effective address calculation time
*indicates maximum value; data addressing mode only

8

8.8 CONDITIONAL INSTRUCTION EXECUTION TIMES

Table 8-9 lists the timing data for the conditional instructions. The total number of clock periods, the number of read cycles, and the number of write cycles are shown in the previously described format.

Table 8-9. Conditional Instruction Execution Times

Instruction	Displacement	Branch Taken	Branch Not Taken
Bcc	Byte	10(2/0)	8(1/0)
	Word	10(2/0)	12(2/0)
BRA	Byte	10(2/0)	—
	Word	10(2/0)	—
BSR	Byte	18(2/2)	—
	Word	18(2/2)	—
DBcc	cc true	—	12(2/0)
	cc false, Count Not Expired	10(2/0)	—
	cc false, Counter Expired	—	14(3/0)

8.9 JMP, JSR, LEA, PEA, AND MOVEM INSTRUCTION EXECUTION TIMES

Table 8-10 lists the timing data for the jump (JMP), jump to subroutine (JSR), load effective address (LEA), push effective address (PEA), and move multiple registers (MOVEM) instructions. The total number of clock periods, the number of read cycles, and the number of write cycles are shown in the previously described format.

Table 8-10. JMP, JSR, LEA, PEA, and MOVEM Instruction Execution Times

Instruction	Size	(An)	(An)+	−(An)	(d_{16}, An)	(d_8, An, Xn)+	(xxx).W	(xxx).L	(d_{16} PC)	(d_8, PC, Xn)*
JMP	—	8(2/0)	—	—	10(2/0)	14(3/0)	10(2/0)	12(3/0)	10(2/0)	14(3/0)
JSR	—	16(2/2)	—	—	18(2/2)	22(2/2)	18(2/2)	20(3/2)	18(2/2)	22(2/2)
LEA	—	4(1/0)	—	—	8(2/0)	12(2/0)	8(2/0)	12(3/0)	8(2/0)	12(2/0)
PEA	—	12(1/2)	—	—	16(2/2)	20(2/2)	16(2/2)	20(3/2)	16(2/2)	20(2/2)
MOVEM M→R	Word	12+4n (3+n/0)	12+4n (3+n/0)	—	16+4n (4+n/0)	18+4n (4+n/0)	16+4n (4+n/0)	20+4n (5+n/0)	16+4n (4n/0)	18+4n (4+n/0)
	Long	12+8n (3+2n/0)	12+8n (3+2n/0)	—	16+8n (4+2n/0)	18+8n (4+2n/0)	16+8n (4+2n/0)	20+8n (5+2n/0)	16+8n (4+2n/0)	18+8n (4+2n/0)
MOVEM R→M	Word	8+4n (2/n)	—	8+4n (2/n)	12+4n (3/n)	14+4n (3/n)	12+4n (3/n)	16+4n (4/n)	—	—
	Long	8+8n (2/2n)	—	8+8n (2/2n)	12+8n (3/2n)	14+8n (3/2n)	12+8n (3/2n)	16+8n (4/2n)	—	—

n is the number of registers to move.
* The size of the index register (Xn) does not affect the instruction's execution time.

8.10 MULTI-PRECISION INSTRUCTION EXECUTION TIMES

Table 8-11 lists the timing data for multi-precision instructions. The number of clock periods includes the time to fetch both operands, perform the operations, store the results, and read the next instructions. The total number of clock periods, the number of read cycles, and the number of write cycles are shown in the previously described format.

The following notation applies in Table 8-11:

Dn - Data register operand
M - Memory operand

Table 8-11. Multi-Precision Instruction Execution Times

Instruction	Size	op Dn, Dn	op M, M
ADDX	Byte, Word	4(1/0)	18(3/1)
	Long	8(1/0)	30(5/2)
CMPM	Byte, Word	—	12(3/0)
	Long	—	20(5/0)
SUBX	Byte, Word	4(1/0)	18(3/1)
	Long	8(1/0)	30(5/2)
ABCD	Byte	6(1/0)	18(3/1)
SBCD	Byte	6(1/0)	18(3/1)

8

8.11 MISCELLANEOUS INSTRUCTION EXECUTION TIMES

Tables 8-12 and 8-13 list the timing data for miscellaneous instructions. The total number of clock periods, the number of read cycles, and the number of write cycles are shown in the previously described format. The number of clock periods, the number of read cycles, and the number of write cycles, respectively, must be added to those of the effective address calculation where indicated by a plus sign (+).

Table 8-12. Miscellaneous Instruction Execution Times

Instruction	Size	Register	Memory
ANDI to CCR	Byte	20(3/0)	–
ANDI to SR	Word	20(3/0)	–
CHK (No Trap)	–	10(1/0) +	–
EORI to CCR	Byte	20(3/0)	–
EORI to SR	Word	20(3/0)	–
ORI to CCR	Byte	20(3/0)	–
ORI to SR	Word	20(3/0)	–
MOVE from SR	–	6(1/0)	8(1/1) +
MOVE to CCR	–	12(1/0)	12(1/0) +
MOVE to SR	–	12(2/0)	12(2/0) +
EXG	–	6(1/0)	–
EXT	Word	4(1/0)	–
	Long	4(1/0)	–
LINK	–	16(2/2)	–
MOVE from USP	–	4(1/0)	–
MOVE to USP	–	4(1/0)	–
NOP	–	4(1/0)	–
RESET	–	132(1/0)	–
RTE	–	20(5/0)	–
RTR	–	20(5/0)	–
RTS	–	16(4/0)	–
STOP	–	4(0/0)	–
SWAP	–	4(1/0)	–
TRAPV	–	4(1/0)	–
UNLK	–	12(3/0)	–

+ add effective address calculation time

Table 8-13. Move Peripheral Instruction Execution Times

Instruction	Size	Register → Memory	Memory → Register
MOVEP	Word	16(2/2)	16(4/0)
	Long	24(2/4)	24(6/0)

8.12 EXCEPTION PROCESSING EXECUTION TIMES

Table 8-14 lists the timing data for exception processing. The numbers of clock periods include the times for all stacking, the vector fetch, and the fetch of the first instruction of the handler routine. The total number of clock periods, the number of read cycles, and the number of write cycles are shown in the previously described format. The number of clock periods, the number of read cycles, and the number of write cycles, respectively, must be added to those of the effective address calculation where indicated by a plus sign (+).

Table 8-14. Exception Processing Execution Times

Exception	Periods
Address Error	50(4/7)
Bus Error	50(4/7)
CHK Instruction	40(4/3) +
Divide by Zero	38(4/3) +
Illegal Instruction	34(4/3)
Interrupt	44(5/3) *
Privilege Violation	34(4/3)
$\overline{\text{RESET}}$ **	40(6/0)
Trace	34(4/3)
TRAP Instruction	34(4/3)
TRAPV Instruction	34(5/3)

+ add effective address calculation time

* The interrupt acknowledge cycle is assumed to take four clock periods.

** Indicates the time from when $\overline{\text{RESET}}$ and $\overline{\text{HALT}}$ are first sampled as negated to when instruction execution starts.

8

8

SECTION 9
MC68008 INSTRUCTION EXECUTION TIMES

This section contains listings of the instruction execution times in terms of external clock (CLK) periods. In this data, it is assumed that both memory read and write cycles consist of four clock periods. A longer memory cycle causes the generation of wait states that must be added to the total instruction times.

The number of bus read and write cycles for each instruction is also included with the timing data. This data is shown as

n(r/w)

where
  n is the total number of clock periods
  r is the number of read cycles
  w is the number of write cycles

For example, a timing number shown as 18(3/1) means that 18 clock periods are required to execute the instruction. Of the 18 clock periods, 12 are used for the three read cycles (four periods per cycle). Four additional clock periods are used for the single write cycle, for a total of 16 clock periods. The bus is idle for two clock periods during which the processor completes the internal operations required for the instruction.

NOTE

The total number of clock periods (n) includes instruction fetch and all applicable operand fetches and stores.

9.1 OPERAND EFFECTIVE ADDRESS CALCULATION TIMES

Table 9-1 lists the numbers of clock periods required to compute the effective addresses for instructions. The totals include fetching any extension words, computing the address, and fetching the memory operand. The total number of clock periods, the number of read cycles, and the number of write cycles (zero for all effective address calculations) are shown in the previously described format.

9.2 MOVE INSTRUCTION EXECUTION TIMES

Tables 9-2, 9-3, and 9-4 list the numbers of clock periods for the move instructions. The totals include instruction fetch, operand reads, and operand writes. The total number of clock periods, the number of read cycles, and the number of write cycles are shown in the previously described format.

Table 9-1. Effective Address Calculation Times

Addressing Mode		Byte	Word	Long
	Register			
Dn	Data Register Direct	0(0/0)	0(0/0)	0(0/0)
An	Address Register Direct	0(0/0)	0(0/0)	0(0/0)
	Memory			
(An)	Address Register Indirect	4(1/0)	8(2/0)	16(4/0)
(An)+	Address Register Indirect with Postincrement	4(1/0)	8(2/0)	16(4/0)
−(An)	Address Register Indirect with Predecrement	6(1/0)	10(2/0)	18(4/0)
(d_{16}, An)	Address Register Indirect with Displacement	12(3/0)	16(4/0)	24(6/0)
(d_8, An, Xn)*	Address Register Indirect with Index	14(3/0)	18(4/0)	26(6/0)
(xxx).W	Absolute Short	12(3/0)	16(4/0)	24(6/0)
(xxx).L	Absolute Long	20(5/0)	24(6/0)	32(8/0)
(d_{16}, PC)	Program Counter Indirect with Displacement	12(3/0)	16(3/0)	24(6/0)
(d_8, PC, Xn)*	Program Counter Indirect with Index	14(3/0)	18(4/0)	26(6/0)
#⟨data⟩	Immediate	8(2/0)	8(2/0)	16(4/0)

*The size of the index register (Xn) does not affect execution time.

Table 9-2. Move Byte Instruction Execution Times

Source	Destination								
	Dn	An	(An)	(An)+	−(An)	(d_{16}, An)	(d_8, An, Xn)*	(xxx).W	(xxx).L
Dn	8(2/0)	8(2/0)	12(2/1)	12(2/1)	12(2/1)	20(4/1)	22(4/1)	20(4/1)	28(6/1)
An	8(2/0)	8(2/0)	12(2/1)	12(2/1)	12(2/1)	20(4/1)	22(4/1)	20(4/1)	28(6/1)
(An)	12(3/0)	12(3/0)	16(3/1)	16(3/1)	16(3/1)	24(5/1)	26(5/1)	24(5/1)	32(7/1)
(An)+	12(3/0)	12(3/0)	16(3/1)	16(3/1)	16(3/1)	24(5/1)	26(5/1)	24(5/1)	32(7/1)
−(An)	14(3/0)	14(3/0)	18(3/1)	18(3/1)	18(3/1)	26(5/1)	28(5/1)	26(5/1)	34(7/1)
(d_{16}, An)	20(5/0)	20(5/0)	24(5/1)	24(5/1)	24(5/1)	32(7/1)	34(7/1)	32(7/1)	40(9/1)
(d_8, An, Xn)*	22(5/0)	22(5/0)	26(5/1)	26(5/1)	26(5/1)	34(7/1)	36(7/1)	34(7/1)	42(9/1)
(xxx).W	20(5/0)	20(5/0)	24(5/1)	24(5/1)	24(5/1)	32(7/1)	34(7/1)	32(7/1)	40(9/1)
(xxx).L	28(7/0)	28(7/0)	32(7/1)	32(7/1)	32(7/1)	40(9/1)	42(9/1)	40(9/1)	48(11/1)
(d_{16}, PC)	20(5/0)	20(5/0)	24(5/1)	24(5/1)	24(5/1)	32(7/1)	34(7/1)	32(7/1)	40(9/1)
(d_8, PC, Xn)*	22(5/0)	22(5/0)	26(5/1)	26(5/1)	26(5/1)	34(7/1)	36(7/1)	34(7/1)	42(9/1)
#⟨data⟩	16(4/0)	16(4/0)	20(4/1)	20(4/1)	20(4/1)	28(6/1)	30(6/1)	28(6/1)	36(8/1)

*The size of the index register (Xn) does not affect execution time.

Table 9-3. Move Word Instruction Execution Times

Source	Destination								
	Dn	An	(An)	(An)+	−(An)	(d_{16}, An)	(d_8, An, Xn)*	(xxx).W	(xxx).L
Dn	8(2/0)	8(2/0)	16(2/2)	16(2/2)	16(2/2)	24(4/2)	26(4/2)	24(4/2)	32(6/2)
An	8(2/0)	8(2/0)	16(2/2)	16(2/2)	16(2/2)	24(4/2)	26(4/2)	24(4/2)	32(6/2)
(An)	16(4/0)	16(4/0)	24(4/2)	24(4/2)	24(4/2)	32(6/2)	34(6/2)	32(6/2)	40(8/2)
(An)+	16(4/0)	16(4/0)	24(4/2)	24(4/2)	24(4/2)	32(6/2)	34(6/2)	32(6/2)	40(8/2)
−(An)	18(4/0)	18(4/0)	26(4/2)	26(4/2)	26(4/2)	34(6/2)	32(6/2)	34(6/2)	42(8/2)
(d_{16}, An)	24(6/0)	24(6/0)	32(6/2)	32(6/2)	32(6/2)	40(8/2)	42(8/2)	40(8/2)	48(10/2)
(d_8, An, Xn)*	26(6/0)	26(6/0)	34(6/2)	34(6/2)	34(6/2)	42(8/2)	44(8/2)	42(8/2)	50(10/2)
(xxx).W	24(6/0)	24(6/0)	32(6/2)	32(6/2)	32(6/2)	40(8/2)	42(8/2)	40(8/2)	48(10/2)
(xxx).L	32(8/0)	32(8/0)	40(8/2)	40(8/2)	40(8/2)	48(10/2)	50(10/2)	48(10/2)	56(12/2)
(d_{16}, PC)	24(6/0)	24(6/0)	32(6/2)	32(6/2)	32(6/2)	40(8/2)	42(8/2)	40(8/2)	48(10/2)
(d_8, PC, Xn)*	26(6/0)	26(6/0)	34(6/2)	34(6/2)	34(6/2)	42(8/2)	44(8/2)	42(8/2)	50(10/2)
#⟨data⟩	16(4/0)	16(4/0)	24(4/2)	24(4/2)	24(4/2)	32(6/2)	34(6/2)	32(6/2)	40(8/2)

*The size of the index register (Xn) does not affect execution time.

Table 9-4. Move Long Instruction Execution Times

Source	Destination								
	Dn	An	(An)	(An)+	−(An)	(d_{16}, An)	(d_8, An, Xn)*	(xxx).W	(xxx).L
Dn	8(2/0)	8(2/0)	24(2/4)	24(2/4)	24(2/4)	32(4/4)	34(4/4)	32(4/4)	40(6/4)
An	8(2/0)	8(2/0)	24(2/4)	24(2/4)	24(2/4)	32(4/4)	34(4/4)	32(4/4)	40(6/4)
(An)	24(6/0)	24(6/0)	40(6/4)	40(6/4)	40(6/4)	48(8/4)	50(8/4)	48(8/4)	56(10/4)
(An)+	24(6/0)	24(6/0)	40(6/4)	40(6/4)	40(6/4)	48(8/4)	50(8/4)	48(8/4)	56(10/4)
−(An)	26(6/0)	26(6/0)	42(6/4)	42(6/4)	42(6/4)	50(8/4)	52(8/4)	50(8/4)	58(10/4)
(d_{16}, An)	32(8/0)	32(8/0)	48(8/4)	48(8/4)	48(8/4)	56(10/4)	58(10/4)	56(10/4)	64(12/4)
(d_8, An, Xn)*	34(8/0)	34(8/0)	50(8/4)	50(8/4)	50(8/4)	58(10/4)	60(10/4)	58(10/4)	66(12/4)
(xxx).W	32(8/0)	32(8/0)	48(8/4)	48(8/4)	48(8/4)	56(10/4)	58(10/4)	56(10/4)	64(12/4)
(xxx).L	40(10/0)	40(10/0)	56(10/4)	56(10/4)	56(10/4)	64(12/4)	66(12/4)	64(12/4)	72(14/4)
(d_{16}, PC)	32(8/0)	32(8/0)	48(8/4)	48(8/4)	48(8/4)	56(10/4)	58(10/4)	56(10/4)	64(12/4)
(d_8, PC, Xn)*	34(8/0)	34(8/0)	50(8/4)	50(8/4)	50(8/4)	58(10/4)	60(10/4)	58(10/4)	66(12/4)
#<data>	24(6/0)	24(6/0)	40(6/4)	40(6/4)	40(6/4)	48(8/4)	50(8/4)	48(8/4)	56(10/4)

*The size of the index register (Xn) does not affect execution time.

9.3 STANDARD INSTRUCTION EXECUTION TIMES

The numbers of clock periods shown in Table 9-5 indicate the times required to perform the operations, store the results, and read the next instruction. The total number of clock periods, the number of read cycles, and the number of write cycles are shown in the previously described format. The number of clock periods, the number of read cycles, and the number of write cycles, respectively, must be added to those of the effective address calculation where indicated by a plus sign (+).

In Table 9-5, the following notation applies:

- An — Address register operand
- Dn — Data register operand
- ea — An operand specified by an effective address
- M — Memory effective address operand

Table 9-5. Standard Instruction Execution Times

Instruction	Size	op <ea>, An	op <ea>, Dn	op Dn, <M>
ADD/ ADDA	Byte	—	8(2/0) +	12(2/1) +
	Word	12(2/0) +	8(2/0) +	16(2/2) +
	Long	10(2/0) + **	10(2/0) + **	24(2/4) +
AND	Byte	—	8(2/0) +	12(2/1) +
	Word	—	8(2/0) +	16(2/2) +
	Long	—	10(2/0) + **	24(2/4) +
CMP/ CMPA	Byte	—	8(2/0) +	—
	Word	10(2/0) +	8(2/0) +	—
	Long	10(2/0) +	10(2/0) +	—
DIVS		—	162(2/0) + *	—
DIVU		—	144(2/0) + *	—
EOR	Byte	—	8(2/0) + ***	12(2/1) +
	Word	—	8(2/0) + ***	16(2/2) +
	Long	—	12(2/0) + ***	24(2/4) +
MULS		—	74(2/0) + *	—
MULU		—	74(2/0) + *	—
OR	Byte	—	8(2/0) +	12(2/1) +
	Word	—	8(2/0) +	16(2/2) +
	Long	—	10(2/0) + **	24(2/4) +
SUB	Byte	—	8(2/0) +	12(2/1) +
	Word	12(2/0) +	8(2/0) +	16(2/2) +
	Long	10(2/0) + **	10(2/0) + **	24(2/4) +

NOTES:

- \+ Add effective address calculation time
- * Indicates maximum base value added to word effective address time.
- ** The base time of 10 clock periods is increased to 12 if the effective address mode is register direct or immediate (effective address time should also be added).
- *** Only available effective address mode is data register direct

DIVS, DIVU — The divide algorithm used by the MC68008 provides less than 10% difference between the best and worst case timings.

MULS, MULU — The multiply algorithm requires 42 + 2n clocks where n is defined as:
MULS: n = tag the <ea> with a zero as the MSB; n is the resultant number of 10 or 01 patterns in the 17-bit source, i.e., worst case happens when the source is $5555.
MULU: n = the number of ones in the <ea>

9.4 IMMEDIATE INSTRUCTION EXECUTION TIMES

The numbers of clock periods shown in Table 9-6 include the times to fetch immediate operands, perform the operations, store the results, and read the next operation. The total number of clock periods, the number of read cycles, and the number of write cycles are shown in the previously described format. The number of clock periods, the number of read cycles, and the number of write cycles, respectively, must be added to those of the effective address calculation where indicated by a plus sign (+).

In Table 9-6, the following notation applies:

— Immediate operand
Dn — Data register operand
An — Address register operand
M — Memory operand

9

Table 9-6. Immediate Instruction Execution Times

Instruction	Size	op#, Dn	op#,An	op#, M
ADDI	Byte	16(4/0)	—	20(4/1)+
	Word	16(4/0)	—	24(4/2)+
	Long	28(6/0)	—	40(6/4)+
ADDQ	Byte	8(2/0)	—	12(2/1)+
	Word	8(2/0)	12(2/0)	16(2/2)+
	Long	12(2/0)	12(2/0)	24(2/4)+
ANDI	Byte	16(4/0)	—	20(4/1)+
	Word	16(4/0)	—	24(4/2)+
	Long	28(6/0)	—	40(6/4)+
CMPI	Byte	16(4/0)	—	16(4/0)+
	Word	16(4/0)	—	16(4/0)+
	Long	26(6/0)	—	24(6/0)+
EORI	Byte	16(4/0)	—	20(4/1)+
	Word	16(4/0)	—	24(4/2)+
	Long	28(6/0)	—	40(6/4)+
MOVEQ	Long	8(2/0)	—	—
ORI	Byte	16(4/0)	—	20(4/1)+
	Word	16(4/0)	—	24(4/2)+
	Long	28(6/0)	—	40(6/4)+
SUBI	Byte	16(4/0)	—	12(2/1)+
	Word	16(4/0)	—	16(2/2)+
	Long	28(6/0)	—	24(2/4)+
SUBQ	Byte	8(2/0)	—	20(4/1)+
	Word	8(2/0)	12(2/0)	24(4/2)+
	Long	12(2/0)	12(2/0)	40(6/4)+

+add effective address calculation time

9.5 SINGLE OPERAND INSTRUCTION EXECUTION TIMES

Table 9-7 lists the timing data for the single operand instructions. The total number of clock periods, the number of read cycles, and the number of write cycles are shown in the previously described format. The number of clock periods, the number of read cycles, and the number of write cycles, respectively, must be added to those of the effective address calculation where indicated by a plus sign (+).

9.6 SHIFT/ROTATE INSTRUCTION EXECUTION TIMES

Table 9-8 lists the timing data for the shift and rotate instructions. The total number of clock periods, the number of read cycles, and the number of write cycles are shown in the previously described format. The number of clock periods, the number of read cycles, and the number of write cycles, respectively, must be added to those of the effective address calculation where indicated by a plus sign (+).

Table 9-7. Single Operand Instruction Execution Times

Instruction	Size	Register	Memory
CLR	Byte	8(2/0)	12(2/1)+
	Word	8(2/0)	16(2/2)+
	Long	10(2/0)	24(2/4)+
NBCD	Byte	10(2/0)	12(2/1)+
NEG	Byte	8(2/0)	12(2/1)+
	Word	8(2/0)	16(2/2)+
	Long	10(2/0)	24(2/4)+
NEGX	Byte	8(2/0)	12(2/1)+
	Word	8(2/0)	16(2/2)+
	Long	10(2/0)	24(2/4)+
NOT	Byte	8(2/0)	12(2/1)+
	Word	8(2/0)	16(2/2)+
	Long	10(2/0)	24(2/4)+
Scc	Byte, False	8(2/0)	12(2/1)+
	Byte, True	10(2/0)	12(2/1)+
TAS	Byte	8(2/0)	14(2/1)+
TST	Byte	8(2/0)	8(2/0)+
	Word	8(2/0)	8(2/0)+
	Long	8(2/0)	8(2/0)+

+ add effective address calculation time.

Table 9-8. Shift/Rotate Instruction Execution Times

Instruction	Size	Register	Memory
ASR, ASL	Byte	10 + 2n(2/0)	–
	Word	10 + 2n(2/0)	16(2/2)+
	Long	12 + 2n(2/0)	–
LSR, LSL	Byte	10 + 2n(2/0)	–
	Word	10 + 2n(2/0)	16(2/2)+
	Long	12 + 2n(2/0)	–
ROR, ROL	Byte	10 + 2n(2/0)	–
	Word	10 + 2n(2/0)	16(2/2)+
	Long	12 + 2n(2/0)	–
ROXR, ROXL	Byte	10 + 2n(2/0)	–
	Word	10 + 2n(2/0)	16(2/2)+
	Long	12 + 2n(2/0)	–

+ add effective address calculation time for word operands
n is the shift count

9.7 BIT MANIPULATION INSTRUCTION EXECUTION TIMES

Table 9-9 lists the timing data for the bit manipulation instructions. The total number of clock periods, the number of read cycles, and the number of write cycles are shown in the previously described format. The number of clock periods, the number of read cycles, and the number of write cycles, respectively, must be added to those of the effective address calculation where indicated by a plus sign (+).

Table 9-9. Bit Manipulation Instruction Execution Times

Instruction	Size	Dynamic		Static	
		Register	Memory	Register	Memory
BCHG	Byte	—	12(2/1)+	—	20(4/1)+
	Long	12(2/0)*	—	20(4/0)*	—
BCLR	Byte	—	12(2/1)+	—	20(4/1)+
	Long	14(2/0)*	—	22(4/0)*	—
BSET	Byte	—	12(2/1)+	—	20(4/1)+
	Long	12(2/0)*	—	20(4/0)*	—
BTST	Byte	—	8(2/0)+	—	16(4/0)+
	Long	10(2/0)	—	18(4/0)	—

+ add effective address calculation time
* Indicates maximum value; data addressing mode only

9.8 CONDITIONAL INSTRUCTION EXECUTION TIMES

Table 9-10 lists the timing data for the conditional instructions. The total number of clock periods, the number of read cycles, and the number of write cycles are shown in the previously described format. The number of clock periods, the number of read cycles, and the number of write cycles, respectively, must be added to those of the effective address calculation where indicated by a plus sign (+).

Table 9-10. Conditional Instruction Execution Times

Instruction	Displacement	Trap or Branch Taken	Trap or Branch Not Taken
Bcc	Byte	18(4/0)	12(2/0)
	Word	18(4/0)	20(4/0)
BRA	Byte	18(4/0)	—
	Word	18(4/0)	—
BSR	Byte	34(4/4)	—
	Word	34(4/4)	—
DBcc	CC True	—	20(4/0)
	CC False	18(4/0)	26(6/0)
CHK	—	68(8/6)+*	14(2/0)+
TRAP	—	62(8/6)	—
TRAPV	—	66(10/6)	8(2/0)

+ add effective address calculation time for word operand
* indicates maximum base value

9.9 JMP, JSR, LEA, PEA, AND MOVEM INSTRUCTION EXECUTION TIMES

Table 9-11 lists the timing data for the jump (JMP), jump to subroutine (JSR), load effective address (LEA), push effective address (PEA), and move multiple registers (MOVEM) instructions. The total number of clock periods, the number of read cycles, and the number of write cycles are shown in the previously described format.

Table 9-11. JMP, JSR, LEA, PEA, and MOVEM Instruction Execution Times

Instruction	Size	(An)	(An)+	−(An)	(d_{16}, An)	(d_8, An, Xn)*	(xxx).W	(xxx).L	(d_{16} PC)	(d_8, PC, Xn)
JMP	—	**16**(4/0)	—	—	**18**(4/0)	**22**(4/0)	**18**(4/0)	**24**(6/0)	**18**(4/0)	**22**(4/0)
JSR	—	**32**(4/4)	—	—	**34**(4/4)	**38**(4/4)	**34**(4/4)	**40**(6/4)	**34**(4/4)	**32**(4/4)
LEA	—	**8**(2/0)	—	—	**16**(4/0)	**20**(4/0)	**16**(4/0)	**24**(6/0)	**16**(4/0)	**20**(4/0)
PEA	—	**24**(2/4)	—	—	**32**(4/4)	**36**(4/4)	**32**(4/4)	**40**(6/4)	**32**(4/4)	**36**(4/4)
MOVEM M→R	Word	**24+8n** (6+2n/0)	**24+8n** (6+2n/0)	— —	**32+8n** (8+2n/0)	**34+8n** (8+2n/0)	**32+8n** (10+n/0)	**40+8n** (10+2n/0)	**32+8n** (8+2n/0)	**34+8n** (8+2n/0)
	Long	**24+16n** (6+4n/0)	**24+16n** (6+4n/0)	— —	**32+16n** (8+4n/0)	**34+16n** (8+4n/0)	**32+16n** (8+4n/0)	**40+16n** (8+4n/0)	**32+16n** (8+4n/0)	**34+16n** (8+4n/0)
MOVEM R→M	Word	**16+8n** (4/2n)	— —	**16+8n** (4/2n)	**24+8n** (6/2n)	**26+8n** (6/2n)	**24+8n** (6/2n)	**32+8n** (8/2n)	—	—
	Long	**16+16n** (4/4n)	— —	**16+16n** (4/4n)	**24+16n** (6/4n)	**26+16n**	**24+16n** (8/4n)	**32+16n** (6/4n)	—	—

n is the number of registers to move.
* The size of the index register (Xn) does not affect the instruction's execution time.

9.10 MULTI-PRECISION INSTRUCTION EXECUTION TIMES

Table 9-12 lists the timing data for multi-precision instructions. The numbers of clock periods include the times to fetch both operands, perform the operations, store the results, and read the next instructions. The total number of clock periods, the number of read cycles, and the number of write cycles are shown in the previously described format.

The following notation applies in Table 9-12:

Dn — Data register operand
M — Memory operand

Table 9-12. Multi-Precision Instruction Execution Times

Instruction	Size	op Dn, Dn	op M, M
ADDX	Byte	**8**(2/0)	**22**(4/1)
	Word	**8**(2/0)	**50**(6/2)
	Long	**12**(2/0)	**58**(10/4)
CMPM	Byte	—	**16**(4/0)
	Word	—	**24**(6/0)
	Long	—	**40**(10/0)
SUBX	Byte	**8**(2/0)	**22**(4/1)
	Word	**8**(2/0)	**50**(6/2)
	Long	**12**(2/0)	**58**(10/4)
ABCD	Byte	**10**(2/0)	**20**(4/1)
SBCD	Byte	**10**(2/0)	**20**(4/1)

9.11 MISCELLANEOUS INSTRUCTION EXECUTION TIMES

Tables 9-13 and 9-14 list the timing data for miscellaneous instructions. The total number of clock periods, the number of read cycles, and the number of write cycles are shown in the previously described format. The number of clock periods, the number of read cycles, and the number of write cycles, respectively, must be added to those of the effective address calculation where indicated by a plus sign (+).

Table 9-13. Miscellaneous Instruction Execution Times

Instruction	Register	Memory
ANDI to CCR	32(6/0)	–
ANDI to SR	32(6/0)	–
EORI to CCR	32(6/0)	–
EORI to SR	32(6/0)	–
EXG	10(2/0)	–
EXT	8(2/0)	–
LINK	32(4/4)	–
MOVE to CCR	18(4/0)	18(4/0) +
MOVE to SR	18(4/0)	18(4/0) +
MOVE from SR	10(2/0)	16(2/2) +
MOVE to USP	8(2/0)	–
MOVE from USP	8(2/0)	–
NOP	8(2/0)	–
ORI to CCR	32(6/0)	–
ORI to SR	32(6/0)	–
RESET	136(2/0)	–
RTE	40(10/0)	–
RTR	40(10/0)	–
RTS	32(8/0)	–
STOP	4(0/0)	–
SWAP	8(2/0)	–
TRAPV (No Trap)	8(2/0)	–
UNLK	24(6/0)	–

+ add effective address calculation time for word operand

Table 9-14. Move Peripheral Instruction Execution Times

Instruction	Size	Register → Memory	Memory → Register
MOVEP	Word	24(4/2)	24(6/0)
	Long	32(4/4)	32(8/0)

+ add effective address calculation time

9.12 EXCEPTION PROCESSING EXECUTION TIMES

Table 9-15 lists the timing data for exception processing. The numbers of clock periods include the times for all stacking, the vector fetch, and the fetch of the first instruction of the handler routine. The total number of clock periods, the number of read cycles, and the number of write cycles are shown in the previously described format. The number of clock periods, the number of read cycles, and the number of write cycles, respectively, must be added to those of the effective address calculation where indicated by a plus sign (+).

Table 9-15. Exception Processing Execution Times

Exception	Periods
Address Error	**94**(8/14)
Bus Error	**94**(8/14)
CHK Instruction	**68**(8/6) +
Divide by Zero	**66**(8/6) +
Interrupt	**72**(9/6) *
Illegal Instruction	**62**(8/6)
Privileged Instruction	**62**(8/6)
$\overline{\text{RESET}}$ **	**64**(12/0)
Trace	**62**(8/6)
TRAP Instruction	**62**(8/6)
TRAPV Instruction	**66**(10/6)

+ add effective address calculation time

** Indicates the time from when $\overline{\text{RESET}}$ and $\overline{\text{HALT}}$ are first sampled as negated to when instruction execution starts.

9

SECTION 10
MC68010 INSTRUCTION EXECUTION TIMES

This section contains listings of the instruction execution times in terms of external clock (CLK) periods. In this data, it is assumed that both memory read and write cycles consist of four clock periods. A longer memory cycle causes the generation of wait states that must be added to the total instruction times.

The number of bus read and write cycles for each instruction is also included with the timing data. This data is shown as

n(r/w)

where
- n is the total number of clock periods
- r is the number of read cycles
- w is the number of write cycles

For example, a timing number shown as 18(3/1) means that 18 clock cycles are required to execute the instruction. Of the 18 clock periods, 12 are used for the three read cycles (four periods per cycle). Four additional clock periods are used for the single write cycle, for a total of 16 clock periods. The bus is idle for two clock periods during which the processor completes the internal operations required for the instructions.

NOTE

The total number of clock periods (n) includes instruction fetch and all applicable operand fetches and stores.

10.1 OPERAND EFFECTIVE ADDRESS CALCULATION TIMES

Table 10-1 lists the numbers of clock periods required to compute the effective addresses for instructions. The totals include fetching any extension words, computing the address, and fetching the memory operand. The total number of clock periods, the number of read cycles, and the number of write cycles (zero for all effective address calculations) are shown in the previously described format.

10.2 MOVE INSTRUCTION EXECUTION TIMES

Tables 10-2, 10-3, 10-4, and 10-5 list the numbers of clock periods for the move instructions. The totals include instruction fetch, operand reads, and operand writes. The total number of clock periods, the number of read cycles, and the number of write cycles are shown in the previously described format.

Table 10-1. Effective Address Calculation Times

Addressing Mode		Byte, Word		Long	
		Fetch	No Fetch	Fetch	No Fetch
	Register				
Dn	Data Register Direct	**0**(0/0)	—	**0**(0/0)	—
An	Address Register Direct	**0**(0/0)	—	**0**(0/0)	—
	Memory				
(An)	Address Register Indirect	**4**(1/0)	**2**(0/0)	**8**(2/0)	**2**(0/0)
(An)+	Address Register Indirect with Postincrement	**4**(1/0)	**4**(0/0)	**8**(2/0)	**4**(0/0)
−(An)	Address Register Indirect with Predecrement	**6**(1/0)	**4**(0/0)	**10**(2/0)	**4**(0/0)
(d_{16}, An)	Address Register Indirect with Displacement	**8**(2/0)	**4**(0/0)	**12**(3/0)	**4**(1/0)
(d_8, An, Xn)*	Address Register Indirect with Index	**10**(2/0)	**8**(1/0)	**14**(3/0)	**8**(1/0)
(xxx).W	Absolute Short	**8**(2/0)	**4**(1/0)	**12**(3/0)	**4**(1/0)
(xxx).L	Absolute Long	**12**(3/0)	**8**(2/0)	**16**(4/0)	8(2/0)
(d_{16}, PC)	Program Counter Indirect with Displacement	**8**(2/0)	—	**12**(3/0)	—
(d_8, PC, Xn)	Program Counter Indirect with Index	**10**(2/0)	—	**14**(3/0)	—
#⟨data⟩	Immediate	**4**(1/0)	—	**8**(2/0)	—

*The size of the index register (Xn) does not affect execution time.

Table 10-2. Move Byte and Word Instruction Execution Times

Source	Destination								
	Dn	An	(An)	(An)+	−(An)	(d_{16}, An)	(d_8, An, Xn)*	(xxx).W	(xxx).L
Dn	**4**(1/0)	**4**(1/0)	**8**(1/1)	**8**(1/1)	**8**(1/1)	**12**(2/1)	**14**(2/1)	**12**(2/1)	**16**(3/1)
An	**4**(1/0)	**4**(1/0)	**8**(1/1)	**8**(1/1)	**8**(1/1)	**12**(2/1)	**14**(2/1)	**12**(2/1)	**16**(3/1)
(An)	**8**(2/0)	**8**(2/0)	**12**(2/1)	**12**(2/1)	**12**(2/1)	**16**(3/1)	**18**(3/1)	**16**(3/1)	**20**(4/1)
(An)+	**8**(2/0)	**8**(2/0)	**12**(2/1)	**12**(2/1)	**12**(2/1)	**16**(3/1)	**18**(3/1)	**16**(3/1)	**20**(4/1)
−(An)	**10**(2/0)	**10**(2/0)	**14**(2/1)	**14**(2/1)	**14**(2/1)	**18**(3/1)	**20**(3/1)	**18**(3/1)	**22**(4/1)
(d_{16}, An)	**12**(3/0)	**12**(3/0)	**16**(3/1)	**16**(3/1)	**16**(3/1)	**20**(4/1)	**22**(4/1)	**20**(4/1)	**24**(5/1)
(d_8, An, Xn)*	**14**(3/0)	**14**(3/0)	**18**(3/1)	**18**(3/1)	**18**(3/1)	**22**(4/1)	**24**(4/1)	**22**(4/1)	**26**(5/1)
(xxx).W	**12**(3/0)	**12**(3/0)	**16**(3/1)	**16**(3/1)	**16**(3/1)	**20**(4/1)	**22**(4/1)	**20**(4/1)	**24**(5/1)
(xxx).L	**16**(4/0)	**16**(4/0)	**20**(4/1)	**20**(4/1)	**20**(4/1)	**24**(5/1)	**26**(5/1)	**24**(5/1)	**28**(6/1)
(d_{16}, PC)	**12**(3/0)	**12**(3/0)	**16**(3/1)	**16**(3/1)	**16**(3/1)	**20**(4/1)	**22**(4/1)	**20**(4/1)	**24**(5/1)
(d_8, PC, Xn)*	**14**(3/0)	**14**(3/0)	**18**(3/1)	**18**(3/1)	**18**(3/1)	**22**(4/1)	**24**(4/1)	**22**(4/1)	**26**(5/1)
#<data>	**8**(2/0)	**8**(2/0)	**12**(2/1)	**12**(2/1)	**12**(2/1)	**16**(3/1)	**18**(3/1)	**16**(3/1)	**20**(4/1)

*The size of the index register (Xn) does not affect execution time.

Table 10-3. Move Byte and Word Instruction Loop Mode Execution Times

	Loop Continued			Loop Terminated					
	Valid Count, cc False			Valid Count, cc True			Expired Count		
	Destination								
Source	(An)	(An)+	−(An)	(An)	(An)+	−(An)	(An)	(An)+	−(An)
Dn	**10**(0/1)	**10**(0/1)	—	**18**(2/1)	**18**(2/1)	—	**16**(2/1)	**16**(2/1)	—
An*	**10**(0/1)	**10**(0/1)	—	**18**(2/1)	**18**(2/1)	—	**16**(2/1)	**16**(2/1)	—
(An)	**14**(1/1)	**14**(1/1)	**16**(1/1)	**20**(3/1)	**20**(3/1)	**22**(3/1)	**18**(3/1)	**18**(3/1)	**20**(3/1)
(An)+	**14**(1/1)	**14**(1/1)	**16**(1/1)	**20**(3/1)	**20**(3/1)	**22**(3/1)	**18**(3/1)	**18**(3/1)	**20**(3/1)
−(An)	**16**(1/1)	**16**(1/1)	**18**(1/1)	**22**(3/1)	**22**(3/1)	**24**(3/1)	**20**(3/1)	**20**(3/1)	**22**(3/1)

*Word only.

Table 10-4. Move Long Instruction Execution Times

Source	Destination								
	Dn	An	(An)	(An)+	–(An)	(d_{16}, An)	(d_8, An, Xn)*	(xxx).W	(xxx).L
Dn	**4**(1/0)	**4**(1/0)	**12**(1/2)	**12**(1/2)	**14**(1/2)	**16**(2/2)	**18**(2/2)	**16**(2/2)	**20**(3/2)
An	**4**(1/0)	**4**(1/0)	**12**(1/2)	**12**(1/2)	**14**(1/2)	**16**(2/2)	**18**(2/2)	**16**(2/2)	**20**(3/2)
(An)	**12**(3/0)	**12**(3/0)	**20**(3/2)	**20**(3/2)	**20**(3/2)	**24**(4/2)	**26**(4/2)	**24**(4/2)	**28**(5/2)
(An)+	**12**(3/0)	**12**(3/0)	**20**(3/2)	**20**(3/2)	**20**(3/2)	**24**(4/2)	**26**(4/2)	**24**(4/2)	**28**(5/2)
–(An)	**14**(3/0)	**14**(3/0)	**22**(3/2)	**22**(3/2)	**22**(3/2)	**26**(4/2)	**28**(4/2)	**26**(4/2)	**30**(5/2)
(d_{16}, An)	**16**(4/0)	**16**(4/0)	**24**(4/2)	**24**(4/2)	**24**(4/2)	**28**(5/2)	**30**(5/2)	**28**(5/2)	**32**(6/2)
(d_8, An, Xn)*	**18**(4/0)	**18**(4/0)	**26**(4/2)	**26**(4/2)	**26**(4/2)	**30**(5/2)	**32**(5/2)	**30**(5/2)	**34**(6/2)
(xxx).W	**16**(4/0)	**16**(4/0)	**24**(4/2)	**24**(4/2)	**24**(4/2)	**28**(5/2)	**30**(5/2)	**28**(5/2)	**32**(6/2)
(xxx).L	**20**(5/0)	**20**(5/0)	**28**(5/2)	**28**(5/2)	**28**(5/2)	**32**(6/2)	**34**(6/2)	**32**(6/2)	**36**(7/2)
(d_{16}, PC)	**16**(4/0)	**16**(4/0)	**24**(4/2)	**24**(4/2)	**24**(4/2)	**28**(5/2)	**30**(5/2)	**28**(5/2)	**32**(5/2)
(d_8, PC, Xn)*	**18**(4/0)	**18**(4/0)	**26**(4/2)	**26**(4/2)	**26**(4/2)	**30**(5/2)	**32**(5/2)	**30**(5/2)	**34**(6/2)
#⟨data⟩	**12**(3/0)	**12**(3/0)	**20**(3/2)	**20**(3/2)	**20**(3/2)	**24**(4/2)	**26**(4/2)	**24**(4/2)	**28**(5/2)

*The size of the index register (Xn) does not affect execution time.

Table 10-5. Move Long Instruction Loop Mode Execution Times

	Loop Continued			Loop Terminated					
	Valid Count, cc False			Valid Count, cc True			Expired Count		
	Destination								
Source	(An)	(An)+	–(An)	(An)	(An)+	–(An)	(An)	(An)+	–(An)
Dn	**14**(0/2)	**14**(0/2)	—	**20**(2/2)	**20**(2/2)	—	**18**(2/2)	**18**(2/2)	—
An	**14**(0/2)	**14**(0/2)	—	**20**(2/2)	**20**(2/2)	—	**18**(2/2)	**18**(2/2)	—
(An)	**22**(2/2)	**22**(2/2)	**24**(2/2)	**28**(4/2)	**28**(4/2)	**30**(4/2)	**24**(4/2)	**24**(4/2)	**26**(4/2)
(An)+	**22**(2/2)	**22**(2/2)	**24**(2/2)	**28**(4/2)	**28**(4/2)	**30**(4/2)	**24**(4/2)	**24**(4/2)	**26**(4/2)
–(An)	**24**(2/2)	**24**(2/2)	**26**(2/2)	**30**(4/2)	**30**(4/2)	**32**(4/2)	**26**(4/2)	**26**(4/2)	**28**(4/2)

10.3 STANDARD INSTRUCTION EXECUTION TIMES

The numbers of clock periods shown in Tables 10-6 and 10-7 indicate the times required to perform the operations, store the results, and read the next instruction. The total number of clock periods, the number of read cycles, and the number of write cycles are shown in the previously described format. The number of clock periods, the number of read cycles, and the number of write cycles, respectively, must be added to those of the effective address calculation where indicated by a plus sign (+).

In Tables 10-6 and 10-7, the following notation applies:

An — Address register operand
Dn — Data register operand
ea — An operand specified by an effective address
M — Memory effective address operand

10.4 IMMEDIATE INSTRUCTION EXECUTION TIMES

The numbers of clock periods shown in Table 10-8 include the times to fetch immediate operands, perform the operations, store the results, and read the next operation. The total number of clock periods, the number of read cycles, and the number of write cycles are shown in the previously described format. The number of clock periods, the number of read cycles, and the number of write cycles, respectively, must be added to those of the effective address calculation where indicated by a plus sign (+).

Table 10-6. Standard Instruction Execution Times

Instruction	Size	op<ea>, An***	op<ea>, Dn	op Dn, <M>
ADD/ADDA	Byte, Word	8(1/0)+	4(1/0)+	8(1/1)+
	Long	6(1/0)+	6(1/0)+	12(1/2)+
AND	Byte, Word	–	4(1/0)+	8(1/1)+
	Long	–	6(1/0)+	12(1/2)+
CMP/CMPA	Byte, Word	6(1/0)+	4(1/0)+	–
	Long	6(1/0)+	6(1/0)+	–
DIVS	–	–	122(1/0)+	–
DIVU	–	–	108(1/0)+	–
EOR	Byte, Word	–	4(1/0)**	8(1/1)+
	Long	–	6(1/0)**	12(1/2)+
MULS	–	–	42(1/0)+*	–
MULU	–	–	40(1/0)+	–
OR	Byte, Word	–	4(1/0)+	8(1/1)+
	Long	–	6(1/0)+	12(1/2)+
SUB/SUBA	Byte, Word	8(1/0)+	4(1/0)+	8(1/1)+
	Long	6(1/0)+	6(1/0)+	12(1/2)+

NOTES:

\+ add effective address calculation time

* indicates maximum value

** only available addressing mode is data register direct

*** word or long only

Table 10-7. Standard Instruction Loop Mode Execution Times

		Loop Continued			Loop Terminated					
		Valid Count cc False			Valid Count cc True			Expired Count		
Instruction	Size	op <ea>, An*	op <ea>, Dn	op Dn, <ea>	op <ea>, An*	op <ea>, Dn	op Dn, <ea>	op <ea>, An*	op <ea>, Dn	op Dn, <ea>
ADD	Byte, Word	18(1/0)	16(1/0)	16(1/1)	24(3/0)	22(3/0)	22(3/1)	22(3/0)	20(3/0)	20(3/1)
	Long	22(2/0)	22(2/0)	24(2/2)	28(4/0)	28(4/0)	30(4/2)	26(4/0)	26(4/0)	28(4/2)
AND	Byte, Word	–	16(1/0)	16(1/1)	–	22(3/0)	22(3/1)	–	20(3/0)	20(3/1)
	Long	–	22(2/0)	24(2/2)	–	28(4/0)	30(4/2)	–	26(4/0)	28(4/2)
CMP	Byte, Word	12(1/0)	12(1/0)	–	18(3/0)	18(3/0)	–	16(3/0)	16(4/0)	–
	Long	18(2/0)	18(2/0)	–	24(4/0)	24(4/0)	–	20(4/0)	20(4/0)	–
EOR	Byte, Word	–	–	16(1/0)	–	–	22(3/1)	–	–	20(3/1)
	Long	–	–	24(2/2)	–	–	30(4/2)	–	–	28(4/2)
OR	Byte, Word	–	16(1/0)	16(1/0)	–	22(3/0)	22(3/1)	–	20(3/0)	20(3/1)
	Long	–	22(2/0)	24(2/2)	–	28(4/0)	30(4/2)	–	26(4/0)	28(4/2)
SUB	Byte, Word	18(1/0)	16(1/0)	16(1/1)	24(3/0)	22(3/0)	22(3/1)	22(3/0)	20(3/0)	20(3/1)
	Long	22(2/0)	20(2/0)	24(2/2)	28(4/0)	26(4/0)	30(4/2)	26(4/0)	24(4/0)	28(4/2)

*Word or long only.

<ea> may be (An), (An)+, or −(An) only. Add two clock periods to the table value if <ea> is −(An).

In Table 10-8, the following notation applies:

\# — Immediate operand
Dn — Data register operand
An — Address register operand
M — Memory operand

Table 10-8. Immediate Instruction Execution Times

Instruction	Size	op #,Dn	op #,An	op #,M
ADDI	Byte, Word	8(2/0)	—	12(2/1)+
	Long	14(3/0)	—	20(3/2)+
ADDQ	Byte, Word	4(1/0)	4(1/0)*	8(1/2)+
	Long	8(1/0)	8(1/1)	12(1/2)+
ANDI	Byte, Word	8(2/0)	—	12(2/1)+
	Long	14(3/0)	—	20(3/1)+
CMPI	Byte, Word	8(2/0)	—	8(2/0)+
	Long	12(3/0)	—	12(3/0)+
EORI	Byte, Word	8(2/0)	—	12(2/1)+
	Long	14(3/0)	—	20(3/2)+
MOVEQ	Long	4(1/0)	—	—
ORI	Byte, Word	8(2/0)	—	12(2/1)+
	Long	14(3/0)	—	20(3/2)+
SUBI	Byte, Word	8(2/0)	—	12(2/1)+
	Long	14(3/0)	—	20(3/2)+
SUBQ	Byte, Word	4(1/0)	4(1/0)*	8(1/1)+
	Long	8(1/0)	8(1/0)	12(1/2)+

+add effective address calculation time
*word only

10.5 SINGLE OPERAND INSTRUCTION EXECUTION TIMES

Tables 10-9, 10-10, and 10-11 list the timing data for the single operand instructions. The total number of clock periods, the number of read cycles, and the number of write cycles are shown in the previously described format. The number of clock periods, the number of read cycles, and the number of write cycles, respectively, must be added to those of the effective address calculation where indicated by a plus sign (+).

Table 10-9. Single Operand Instruction Execution Times

Instruction	Size	Register	Memory
NBCD	Byte	6(1/0)	8(1/1)+
NEG	Byte, Word	4(1/0)	8(1/1)+
	Long	6(1/0)	12(1/2)+
NEGX	Byte, Word	4(1/0)	8(1/1)+
	Long	6(1/0)	12(1/2)+
NOT	Byte, Word	4(1/0)	8(1/1)+
	Long	6(1/0)	12(1/2)+
Scc	Byte, False	4(1/0)	8(1/1)+ *
	Byte, True	4(1/0)	8(1/1)+ *
TAS	Byte	4(1/0)	14(2/1)+ *
TST	Byte, Word	4(1/0)	4(1/0)+
	Long	4(1/0)	4(1/0)+

+ add effective address calculation time
* Use non-fetching effective address calculation time.

Table 10-10. Clear Instruction Execution Times

	Size	Dn	An	(An)	(An)+	−(An)	(d_{16}, An)	(d_8, An, Xn)*	(xxx).W	(xxx).L
CLR	Byte, Word	4(1/0)	—	8(1/1)	8(1/1)	10(1/1)	12(2/1)	16(2/1)	12(2/1)	16(3/1)
	Long	6(1/0)	—	12(1/2)	12(1/2)	14(1/2)	16(2/2)	20(2/2)	16(2/2)	20(3/2)

*The size of the index register (Xn) does not affect execution time.

Table 10-11. Single Operand Instruction Loop Mode Execution Times

		Loop Continued			Loop Terminated					
		Valid Count, cc False			Valid Count, cc True			Expired Count		
Instruction	Size	(An)	(An)+	−(An)	(An)	(An)+	−(An)	(An)	(An)+	−(An)
CLR	Byte, Word	10(0/1)	10(0/1)	12(0/1)	18(2/1)	18(2/1)	20(2/0)	16(2/1)	16(2/1)	18(2/1)
	Long	14(0/2)	14(0/2)	16(0/2)	22(2/2)	22(2/2)	24(2/2)	20(2/2)	20(2/2)	22(2/2)
NBCD	Byte	18(1/1)	18(1/1)	20(1/1)	24(3/1)	24(3/1)	26(3/1)	22(3/1)	22(3/1)	24(3/1)
NEG	Byte, Word	16(1/1)	16(1/1)	18(2/2)	22(3/1)	22(3/1)	24(3/1)	20(3/1)	20(3/1)	22(3/1)
	Long	24(2/2)	24(2/2)	26(2/2)	30(4/2)	30(4/2)	32(4/2)	28(4/2)	28(4/2)	30(4/2)
NEGX	Byte, Word	16(1/1)	16(1/1)	18(2/2)	22(3/1)	22(3/1)	24(3/1)	20(3/1)	20(3/1)	22(3/1)
	Long	24(2/2)	24(2/2)	26(2/2)	30(4/2)	30(4/2)	32(4/2)	28(4/2)	28(4/2)	30(4/2)
NOT	Byte, Word	16(1/1)	16(1/1)	18(2/2)	22(3/1)	22(3/1)	24(3/1)	20(3/1)	20(3/1)	22(3/1)
	Long	24(2/2)	24(2/2)	26(2/2)	30(4/2)	30(4/2)	32(4/2)	28(4/2)	28(4/2)	30(4/2)
TST	Byte, Word	12(1/0)	12(1/0)	14(1/0)	18(3/0)	18(3/0)	20(3/0)	16(3/0)	16(3/0)	18(3/0)
	Long	18(2/0)	18(2/0)	20(2/0)	24(4/0)	24(4/0)	26(4/0)	20(4/0)	20(4/0)	22(4/0)

10.6 SHIFT/ROTATE INSTRUCTION EXECUTION TIMES

Tables 10-12 and 10-13 list the timing data for the shift and rotate instructions. The total number of clock periods, the number of read cycles, and the number of write cycles are shown in the previously described format. The number of clock periods, the number of read cycles, and the number of write cycles, respectively, must be added to those of the effective address calculation where indicated by a plus sign (+).

Table 10-12. Shift/Rotate Instruction Execution Times

Instruction	Size	Register	Memory*
ASR, ASL	Byte, Word	6 + 2n(1/0)	8(1/1) +
	Long	8 + 2n(1/0)	—
LSR, LSL	Byte, Word	6 + 2n(1/0)	8(1/1) +
	Long	8 + 2n(1/0)	—
ROR, ROL	Byte, Word	6 + 2n(1/0)	8(1/1) +
	Long	8 + 2n(1/0)	—
ROXR, ROXL	Byte, Word	6 + 2n(1/0)	8(1/1) +
	Long	8 + 2n(1/0)	—

+ add effective address calculation time
n is the shift or rotate count
* word only

Table 10-13. Shift/Rotate Instruction Loop Mode Execution Times

		Loop Continued			Loop Terminated					
		Valid Count, cc False			Valid Count, cc True			Expired Count		
Instruction	Size	(An)	(An)+	−(An)	(An)	(An)+	−(An)	(An)	(An)+	−(An)
ASR, ASL	Word	18(1/1)	18(1/1)	20(1/1)	24(3/1)	24(3/1)	26(3/1)	22(3/1)	22(3/1)	24(3/1)
LSR, LSL	Word	18(1/1)	18(1/1)	20(1/1)	24(3/1)	24(3/1)	26(3/1)	22(3/1)	22(3/1)	24(3/1)
ROR, ROL	Word	18(1/1)	18(1/1)	20(1/1)	24(3/1)	24(3/1)	26(3/1)	22(3/1)	22(3/1)	24(3/1)
ROXR, ROXL	Word	18(1/1)	18(1/1)	20(1/1)	24(3/1)	24(3/1)	26(3/1)	22(3/1)	22(3/1)	24(3/1)

10.7 BIT MANIPULATION INSTRUCTION EXECUTION TIMES

Table 10-14 lists the timing data for the bit manipulation instructions. The total number of clock periods, the number of read cycles, and the number of write cycles are shown in the previously described format. The number of clock periods, the number of read cycles, and the number of write cycles, respectively, must be added to those of the effective address calculation where indicated by a plus sign (+).

Table 10-14. Bit Manipulation Instruction Execution Times

Instruction	Size	Dynamic		Static	
		Register	Memory	Register	Memory
BCHG	Byte	–	8(1/1)+	–	12(2/1)+
	Long	8(1/0)*	–	12(2/0)*	–
BCLR	Byte	–	10(1/1)+	–	14(2/1)+
	Long	10(1/0)*	–	14(2/0)*	–
BSET	Byte	–	8(1/1)+	–	12(2/1)+
	Long	8(1/0)*	–	12(2/0)*	–
BTST	Byte	–	4(1/0)+	–	8(2/0)+
	Long	6(1/0)*	–	10(2/0)	–

+add effective address calculation time
*indicates maximum value

10

10.8 CONDITIONAL INSTRUCTION EXECUTION TIMES

Table 10-15 lists the timing data for the conditional instructions. The total number of clock periods, the number of read cycles, and the number of write cycles are shown in the previously described format.

Table 10-15. Conditional Instruction Execution Times

Instruction	Displacement	Branch Taken	Branch Not Taken
Bcc	Byte	10(2/0)	6(1/0)
	Word	10(2/0)	10(2/0)
BRA	Byte	10(2/0)	–
	Word	10(2/0)	–
BSR	Byte	18(2/2)	–
	Word	18(2/2)	–
DBcc	cc true	–	10(2/0)
	cc false	10(2/0)	16(3/0)

10.9 JMP, JSR, LEA, PEA, AND MOVEM INSTRUCTION EXECUTION TIMES

Table 10-16 lists the timing data for the jump (JMP), jump to subroutine (JSR), load effective address (LEA), push effective address (PEA), and move multiple registers (MOVEM) instructions. The total number of clock periods, the number of read cycles, and the number of write cycles are shown in the previously described format.

Table 10-6. JMP, JSR, LEA, PEA, MOVES, and MOVEM Instruction Execution Times

Instruction	Size	(An)	(An)+	−(An)	(d_{16}, An)	(d_8, An, Xn)+	(xxx).W	(xxx).L	(d_8 PC)	(d_{16}, PC, Xn)*
JMP	—	8(2/0)	—	—	10(2/0)	14(3/0)	10(2/0)	12(3/0)	10(2/0)	14(3/0)
JSR	—	16(2/2)	—	—	18(2/2)	22(2/2)	18(2/2)	20(3/2)	18(2/2)	22(2/2)
LEA	—	4(1/0)	—	—	8(2/0)	12(2/0)	8(2/0)	12(3/0)	8(2/0)	12(2/0)
PEA	—	12(1/2)	—	—	16(2/2)	20(2/2)	16(2/2)	20(3/2)	16(2/2)	20(2/2)
MOVEM M→R	Word	12+4n (3+n/0)	12+4n (3+n/0)	—	16+4n (4+n/0)	18+4n (4+n/0)	16+4n (4+n/0)	20+4n (5+n/0)	16+4n (4+n/0)	18+4n (4+n/0)
	Long	24+8n (3+2n/0)	12+8n (3+2n/0)	—	16+8n (4+2n/0)	18+8n (4+2n/0)	16+8n (4+2n/0)	20+8n (5+2n/0)	16+8n (4+2n/0)	18+8n (4+2n/0)
MOVEM R→M	Word	8+4n (2/n)	—	8+4n (2/n)	12+4n (3/n)	14+4n (3/n)	12+4n (3/n)	16+4n (4/n)	—	—
	Long	8+8n (2/2n)	—	8+8n (2/2n)	12+8n (3/2n)	14+8n (3/2n)	12+8n (3/2n)	16+8n (4/2n)	—	—
MOVES M→R	Byte/Word	18(3/0)	20(3/0)	20(3/0)	20(4/0)	24(4/0)	20(4/0)	24(5/0)		
	Long	22(4/0)	24(4/0)	24(4/0)	24(5/0)	28(5/0)	24(5/0)	28(6/0)		
MOVES R→M	Byte/Word	18(2/1)	20(2/1)	20(2/1)	20(3/1)	24(3/1)	20(3/1)	24(4/1)		
	Long	22(2/2)	24(2/2)	24(2/2)	24(3/2)	28(3/2)	24(3/2)	28(4/2)		

n is the number of registers to move.

*The size of the index register (Xn) does not affect the instruction's execution time.

10

10.10 MULTI-PRECISION INSTRUCTION EXECUTION TIMES

Table 10-17 lists the timing data for multi-precision instructions. The numbers of clock periods include the times to fetch both operands, perform the operations, store the results, and read the next instructions. The total number of clock periods, the number of read cycles, and the number of write cycles are shown in the previously described format. The following notation applies in Table 8-11:

Dn — Data register operand
M — Memory operand

Table 10-17. Multi-Precision Instruction Execution Times

		Non-Looped		Loop Mode: Continued	Loop Mode: Terminated	
				Valid Count, cc False	Valid Count, cc True	Expired Count
Instruction	Size	op Dn, Dn	op M, M*			
ADDX	Byte, Word	4(1/0)	18(3/10)	22(2/1)	28(4/1)	26(4/1)
	Long	6(1/0)	30(5/2)	32(4/2)	38(6/2)	36(6/2)
CMPM	Byte, Word	–	12(3/0)	14(2/0)	20(4/0)	18(4/0)
	Long	–	20(5/0)	24(4/0)	30(6/0)	26(6/0)
SUBX	Byte, Word	4(1/0)	18(3/1)	22(2/1)	28(4/1)	26(4/1)
	Long	6(1/0)	30(5/2)	32(4/2)	38(6/2)	36(6/2)
ABCD	Byte	6(1/0)	18(3/1)	24(2/1)	30(4/1)	28(4/1)
SBCD	Byte	6(1/0)	18(3/1)	24(2/1)	30(4/1)	28(4/1)

* Source and destination ea is (An)+ for CMPM and −(An) for all others.

10.11 MISCELLANEOUS INSTRUCTION EXECUTION TIMES

Table 10-18 lists the timing data for miscellaneous instructions. The total number of clock periods, the number of read cycles, and the number of write cycles are shown in the previously described format. The number of clock periods, the number of read cycles, and the number of write cycles, respectively, must be added to those of the effective address calculation where indicated by a plus sign (+).

Table 10-18. Miscellaneous Instruction Execution Times

Instruction	Size	Register	Memory	Register → Destination**	Source** → Register
ANDI to CCR	–	16(2/0)	–	–	–
ANDI to SR	–	16(2/0)	–	–	–
CHK	–	8(1/0)+	–	–	–
EORI to CCR	–	16(2/0)	–	–	–
EORI to SR	–	16(2/0)	–	–	–
EXG	–	6(1/0)	–	–	–
EXT	Word	4(1/0)	–	–	–
	Long	4(1/0)	–	–	–
LINK	–	16(2/2)	–	–	–
MOVE from CCR	–	4(1/0)	8(1/1)+*	–	–
MOVE to CCR	–	12(2/0)	12(2/0)+	–	–
MOVE from SR	–	4(1/0)	8(1/1)+*	–	–
MOVE to SR	–	12(2/0)	12(2/0)+	–	–
MOVE from USP	–	6(1/0)	–	–	–
MOVE to USP	–	6(1/0)	–	–	–
MOVEC	–	–	–	10(2/0)	12(2/0)
MOVEP	Word	–	–	16(2/2)	16(4/0)
	Long	–	–	24(2/4)	24(6/0)
NOP	–	4(1/0)	–	–	–
ORI to CCR	–	16(2/0)	–	–	–
ORI to SR	–	16(2/0)	–	–	–
RESET	–	130(1/0)	–	–	–
RTD	–	16(4/0)	–	–	–
RTE	Short	24(6/0)	–	–	–
	Long, Retry Read	112(27/10)	–	–	–
	Long, Retry Write	112(26/1)	–	–	–
	Long, No Retry	110(26/0)	–	–	–
RTR	–	20(5/0)	–	–	–
RTS	–	16(4/0)	–	–	–
STOP	–	4(0/0)	–	–	–
SWAP	–	4(1/0)	–	–	–
TRAPV	–	4(1/0)	–	–	–
UNLK	–	12(3/0)	–	–	–

\+ add effective address calculation time.

* use non-fetching effective address calculation time.

** Source or destination is a memory location for the MOVEP instruction and a control register for the MOVEC instruction.

10.12 EXCEPTION PROCESSING EXECUTION TIMES

Table 10-19 lists the timing data for exception processing. The numbers of clock periods include the times for all stacking, the vector fetch, and the fetch of the first instruction of the handler routine. The total number of clock periods, the number of read cycles, and the number of write cycles are shown in the previously described format. The number of clock periods, the number of read cycles, and the number of write cycles, respectively, must be added to those of the effective address calculation where indicated by a plus sign (+).

Table 10-19. Exception Processing Execution Times

Exception	
Address Error	**126**(4/26)
Breakpoint Instruction*	**42**(5/4)
Bus Error	**126**(4/26)
CHK Instruction**	**44**(5/4) +
Divide By Zero	**42**(5/4) +
Illegal Instruction	**38**(5/4)
Interrupt*	**46**(5/4)
MOVEC, Illegal Control Register**	**46**(5/4)
Privilege Violation	**38**(5/4)
Reset***	**40**(6/0)
RTE, Illegal Format	**50**(7/4)
RTE, Illegal Revision	**70**(12/4)
Trace	**38**(4/4)
TRAP Instruction	**38**(4/4)
TRAPV Instruction	**38**(5/4)

+ add effective address calculation time.

*The interrupt acknowledge and breakpoint cycles are assumed to take four clock periods.

**Indicates maximum value.

***Indicates the time from when $\overline{RESET}$ and $\overline{HALT}$ are first sampled as negated to when instruction execution starts.

SECTION 11
MC68000 ELECTRICAL SPECIFICATIONS

The electrical specifications for the MC68000 microprocessor are shown in this section.

11.1 MAXIMUM RATINGS

Rating	Symbol	Value	Unit
Supply Voltage	V_{CC}	−0.3 to +7.0	V
Input Voltage	V_{in}	−0.3 to +7.0	V
Operating Temperature Range MC68000 MC68000C	T_A	T_L to T_H 0 to 70 −40 to 85	°C
Storage Temperature	T_{stg}	−55 to 150	°C

The device contains circuitry to protect the inputs against damage due to high static voltages or electric fields; however, normal precautions should be taken to avoid application of voltages higher than maximum-rated voltages to these high-impedance circuits. Tying unused inputs to the appropriate logic voltage level (e.g., either GND or V_{CC}) enhances reliability of operation.

11.2 THERMAL CHARACTERISTICS

Characteristic	Symbol	Value	Symbol	Value	Rating
Thermal Resistance (Still Air)	θ_{JA}		θ_{JC}		°C/W
Ceramic, Type L/LC		30		15*	
Ceramic, Type R/RC		33		15	
Plastic, Type P		30		15*	
Plastic, Type FN		45*		25*	

*Estimated

11.3 POWER CONSIDERATIONS

The average die-junction temperature, T_J, in °C can be obtained from:

$$T_J = T_A + (P_D \cdot \theta_{JA}) \quad (1)$$

where:

T_A = Ambient Temperature, °C
θ_{JA} = Package Thermal Resistance, Junction-to-Ambient, °C/W
P_D = $P_{INT} + P_{I/O}$
P_{INT} = $I_{CC} \times V_{CC}$, Watts — Chip Internal Power
$P_{I/O}$ = Power Dissipation on Input and Output Pins — User Determined

For most applications $P_{I/O} < P_{INT}$ and can be neglected.

An appropriate relationship between P_D and T_J (if $P_{I/O}$ is neglected) is:

$$P_D = K \div (T_J + 273\ °C) \quad (2)$$

Solving equations (1) and (2) for K gives:

$$K = P_D \cdot (T_A + 273°C) + \theta_{JA} \cdot P_D^2 \quad (3)$$

where K is a constant pertaining to the particular part. K can be determined from equation (3) by measuring P_D (at thermal equilibrium) for a known T_A. Using this value of K, the values of P_D and T_J can be obtained by solving equations (1) and (2) iteratively for any value of T_A.

11

The curve shown in Figure 11-1 gives the graphic solution to the above equations for the specified power dissipation of 1.5 watts over the ambient temperature range of −55 °C to 125 °C using a maximum θ_{JA} of 45 °C/W. Ambient temperature is that of the still air surrounding the device. Lower values of θ_{JA} cause the curve to shift downward slightly; for instance, for θ_{JA} of 40 °/W, the curve is just below 1.4 watts at 25 °C.

The total thermal resistance of a package (θ_{JA}) can be separated into two components, θ_{JC} and θ_{CA}, representing the barrier to heat flow from the semiconductor junction to the package (case) surface (θ_{JC}) and from the case to the outside ambient air (θ_{CA}). These terms are related by the equation:

$$\theta_{JA} = \theta_{JC} + \theta_{CA}$$

θ_{JC} is device related and cannot be influenced by the user. However, θ_{CA} is user dependent and can be minimized by such thermal management techniques as heat sinks, ambient air cooling, and thermal convection. Thus, good thermal management on the part of the user can significantly reduce θ_{CA} so that θ_{JA} approximately equals θ_{JC}. Substitution of θ_{JC} for θ_{JA} in equation 1 results in a lower semiconductor junction temperature.

Table 11-1 summarizes maximum power dissipation and average junction temperature for the curve drawn in Figure 11-1, using the minimum and maximum values of ambient temperature for different packages and substituting θ_{JC} for θ_{JA} (assuming good thermal management). Table 11-2 provides the maximum power dissipation and average junction temperature assuming that no thermal management is applied (i.e., still air).

NOTE

Since the power dissipation curve shown in Figure 11-1 is negatively sloped, power dissipation declines as ambient temperature increases. Therefore, maximum power dissipation occurs at the lowest rated ambient temperature, but the highest average junction temperature occurs at the maximum ambient temperature where *power diissipation is lowest.*

Values for thermal resistance presented in this manual, unless estimated, were derived using the procedure described in Motorola Reliability Report 7843, "Thermal Resistance Measurement Method for MC68XXX Microcomponent Devices", and are provided for design purposes only. Thermal measurements are complex and dependent on procedure and setup. User-derived values for thermal resistance may differ.

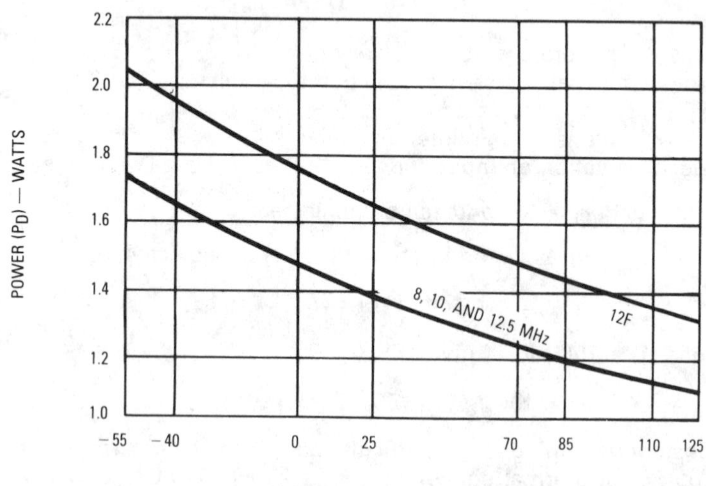

Figure 11-1. MC68000 Power Dissipation(P_D) vs Ambient Temperature (T_A)

Table 11-1. MC68000 Power Dissipation and Junction Temperature vs Temperature ($\theta_{JC} = \theta_{JA}$)

Package	T_A Range	θ_{JC} (°C/W)	P_D (W) @ T_A Min.	T_J (°C) @ T_A Min.	P_D (W) @ T_A Max.	T_J (°C) @ T_A Max.
L/LC	0°C to 70°C −40°C to 85°C 0°C to 85°C	15 15 15	1.5 1.7 1.5	23 −14 23	1.2 1.2 1.2	88 103 103
P	0°C to 70°C	15	1.5	23	1.2	88
R/RC	0°C to 70°C −40°C to 85°C 0°C to 85°C	15 15 15	1.5 1.7 1.5	23 −14 23	1.2 1.2 1.2	88 103 103
FN	0°C to 70°C	25	1.5	38	1.2	101

NOTE: Table does not include values for the MC68000 12F.

Table 11-2. MC68000 Power Dissipation and Junction Temperature vs Temperature ($\theta_{JC} \neq \theta_{JA}$)

Package	T_A Range	θ_{JA} (°C/W)	P_D (W) @ T_A Min.	T_J (°C) @ T_A Min.	P_D (W) @ T_A Max.	T_J (°C) @ T_A Max.
L/LC	0°C to 70°C −40°C to 85°C 0°C to 85°C	30 30 30	1.5 1.7 1.5	23 −14 23	1.2 1.2 1.2	88 103 103
P	0°C to 70°C	30	1.5	23	1.2	88
R/RC	0°C to 70°C −40°C to 85°C 0°C to 85°C	33 33 33	1.5 1.7 1.5	23 −14 23	1.2 1.2 1.2	88 103 103
FN	0°C to 70°C	40	1.5	38	1.2	101

NOTE: Table does not include values for the MC68000 12F.

11

11.4 DC ELECTRICAL CHARACTERISTICS

(V_{CC} = 5.0 Vdc ± 5%; GND = 0 Vdc; $T_A = T_L$ to T_H)

Characteristic		Symbol	Min	Max	Unit
Input High Voltage		V_{IH}	2.0	V_{CC}	V
Input Low Voltage		V_{IL}	GND −0.3	0.8	V
Input Leakage Current @ 5.25 V	$\overline{BERR}$, $\overline{BGACK}$, $\overline{BR}$, $\overline{DTACK}$, CLK, $\overline{IPL0}$-$\overline{IPL2}$, $\overline{VPA}$ $\overline{HALT}$, $\overline{RESET}$	I_{IN}	— —	2.5 20	μA
Three-State (Off State) Input Current @ 2.4 V/0.4 V	$\overline{AS}$, A1-A23, D0-D15, FC0-FC2, $\overline{LDS}$, R/$\overline{W}$, $\overline{UDS}$, $\overline{VMA}$	I_{TSI}	—	20	μA
Output High Voltage (I_{OH} = −400 μA) (I_{OH} = −400 μA)	E* E, $\overline{AS}$, A1-A23, $\overline{BG}$, D0-D15, FC0-FC2, $\overline{LDS}$, R/$\overline{W}$, $\overline{UDS}$, $\overline{VMA}$	V_{OH}	V_{CC}−0.75 2.4	— 2.4	V
Output Low Voltage (I_{OL} = 1.6 mA) (I_{OL} = 3.2 mA) (I_{OL} = 5.0 mA) (I_{OL} = 5.3 mA)	 $\overline{HALT}$ A1-A23, $\overline{BG}$, FC0-FC2 $\overline{RESET}$ E, $\overline{AS}$, D0-D15, $\overline{LDS}$, R/$\overline{W}$, $\overline{UDS}$, $\overline{VMA}$	V_{OL}	 — — — —	 0.5 0.5 0.5 0.5	V
Power Dissipation (see **11.3 POWER CONSIDERATIONS**)		P_D***	—	—	W
Capacitance (V_{in} = 0 V, T_A = 25°C, Frequency = 1 MHz)**		C_{in}	—	20.0	pF
Load Capacitance	$\overline{HALT}$ All Others	C_L	— —	70 130	pF

*With external pullup resistor of 1.1 KΩ.
**Capacitance is periodically sampled rather than 100% tested.
***During normal operation instantaneous V_{CC} current requirements may be as high as 1.5 A.

11.5 AC ELECTRICAL SPECIFICATIONS — CLOCK TIMING

Num.	Characteristic	Symbol	8 MHz*		10 MHz*		12.5 MHz*		16.67 MHz '12F'		Unit
			Min	Max	Min	Max	Min	Max	Min	Max	
	Frequency of Operation	f	4.0	8.0	4.0	10.0	4.0	12.5	8.0	16.7	MHz
1	Cycle Time	t_{cyc}	125	250	100	250	80	250	60	125	ns
2,3	Clock Pulse Width (Measured from 1.5 V to 1.5 V for 12F)	t_{CL} t_{CH}	55 55	125 125	45 45	125 125	35 35	125 125	27 27	62.5 62.5	ns
4,5	Clock Rise and Fall Times	t_{Cr} t_{Cf}	— —	10 10	— —	10 10	— —	5 5	— —	5 5	ns

*These specifications represent an improvement over previously published specifications for the 8-, 10-, and 12.5-MHz MC68000 and are valid only for product bearing date codes of 8827 and later.

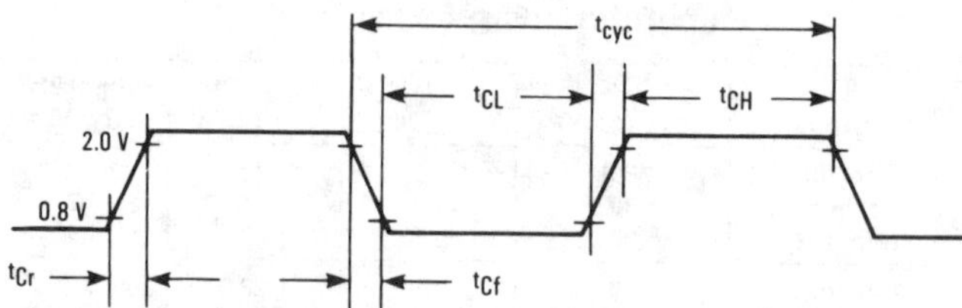

NOTE: Timing measurements are referenced to and from a low voltage of 0.8 volt and high a voltage of 2.0 volts, unless otherwise noted. The voltage swing through this range should start outside and pass through the range such that the rise or fall will be linear between 0.8 volt and 2.0 volts.

Figure 11-2. MC68000 Clock Input Timing Diagram

11.6 AC ELECTRICAL SPECIFICATION DEFINITIONS

The AC specifications presented consist of output delays, input setup and hold times, and signal skew times. All signals are specified relative to an appropriate edge of the clock and possibly to one or more other signals.

The measurement of the AC specifications is defined by the waveforms shown in Figure 11-3. In order to test the parameters guaranteed by Motorola, inputs must be driven to the voltage levels specified in the figure. Outputs are specified with minimum and/or maximum limits, as appropriate, and are measured as shown in Figure 11-3. Inputs are specified with minimum setup and hold times, and are measured as shown. Finally, the measurement for signal-to-signal specifications are also shown.

NOTE

The testing levels used to verify conformance to the AC specifications does not affect the guaranteed DC operation of the device as specified in the DC electrical characteristics.

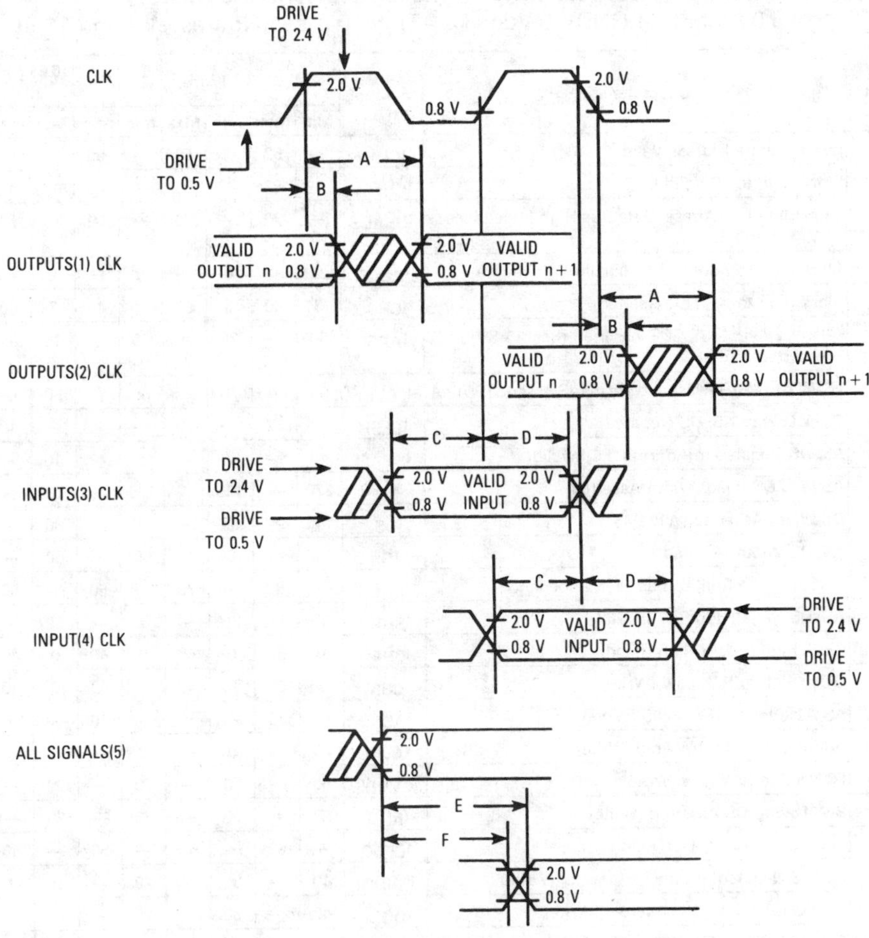

NOTES:

1. This output timing is applicable to all parameters specified relative to the rising edge of the clock.
2. This output timing is applicable to all parameters specified relative to the falling edge of the clock.
3. This input timing is applicable to all parameters specified relative to the rising edge of the clock.
4. This input timing is applicable to all parameters specified relative to the falling edge of the clock.
5. This timing is applicable to all parameters specified relative to the assertion/negation of another signal.

LEGEND:

A. Maximum output delay specification.
B. Minimum output hold time.
C. Minimum input setup time specification.
D. Minimum input hold time specification.
E. Signal valid to signal valid specification (maximum or minimum).
F. Signal valid to signal invalid specification (maximum or minimum).

Figure 11-3. Drive Levels and Test Points for AC Specifications

11

11.7 AC ELECTRICAL SPECIFICATIONS — READ AND WRITE CYCLES

(V_{CC} = 5.0 Vdc ± 5%; GND = 0 Vdc; T_A = T_L to T_H; see Figures 11-4 and 11-5)

Num.	Characteristic	Symbol	8 MHz*		10 MHz*		12.5 MHz*		16.67 MHz '12F'		Unit
			Min	Max	Min	Max	Min	Max	Min	Max	
6	Clock Low to Address Valid	t_{CLAV}	—	62	—	50	—	50	—	50	ns
6A	Clock High to FC Valid	t_{CHFCV}	—	62	—	50	—	45	—	45	ns
7	Clock High to Address, Data Bus High Impedance (Maximum)	t_{CHADZ}	—	80	—	70	—	60	—	50	ns
8	Clock High to Address, FC Invalid (Minimum)	t_{CHAFI}	0	—	0	—	0	—	0	—	ns
9[1]	Clock High to $\overline{AS}$, $\overline{DS}$ Asserted	t_{CHSL}	3	60	3	50	3	40	3	40	ns
11[2]	Address Valid to $\overline{AS}$, $\overline{DS}$ Asserted (Read)/$\overline{AS}$ Asserted (Write)	t_{AVSL}	30	—	20	—	15	—	15	—	ns
11A[2]	FC Valid to $\overline{AS}$, $\overline{DS}$ Asserted (Read)/$\overline{AS}$ Asserted (Write)	t_{FCVSL}	90	—	70	—	60	—	30	—	ns
12[1]	Clock Low to $\overline{AS}$, $\overline{DS}$ Negated	t_{CLSH}	—	62	—	50	—	40	—	40	ns
13[2]	$\overline{AS}$, $\overline{DS}$ Negated to Address, FC Invalid	t_{SHAFI}	40	—	30	—	20	—	10	—	ns
14[2]	$\overline{AS}$ (and $\overline{DS}$ Read) Width Asserted	t_{SL}	270	—	195	—	160	—	120	—	ns
14A	$\overline{DS}$ Width Asserted (Write)	t_{DSL}	140	—	95	—	80	—	60	—	ns
15[2]	$\overline{AS}$, $\overline{DS}$ Width Negated	t_{SH}	150	—	105	—	65	—	60	—	ns
16	Clock High to Control Bus High Impedance	t_{CHCZ}	—	80	—	70	—	60	—	50	ns
17[2]	$\overline{AS}$, $\overline{DS}$ Negated to R/$\overline{W}$ Invalid	t_{SHRH}	40	—	30	—	20	—	10	—	ns
18[1]	Clock High to R/$\overline{W}$ High (Read)	t_{CHRH}	0	55	0	45	0	40	0	40	ns
20[1]	Clock High to R/$\overline{W}$ Low (Write)	t_{CHRL}	0	55	0	45	0	40	0	40	ns
20A[2,6]	$\overline{AS}$ Asserted to R/$\overline{W}$ Valid (Write)	t_{ASRV}	—	10	—	10	—	10	—	10	ns
21[2]	Address Valid to R/$\overline{W}$ Low (Write)	t_{AVRL}	20	—	0	—	0	—	0	—	ns
21A[2]	FC Valid to R/$\overline{W}$ Low (Write)	t_{FCVRL}	60	—	50	—	30	—	20	—	ns
22[2]	R/$\overline{W}$ Low to $\overline{DS}$ Asserted (Write)	t_{RLSL}	80	—	50	—	30	—	20	—	ns
23	Clock Low to Data-Out Valid (Write)	t_{CLDO}	—	62	—	50	—	50	—	50	ns
25[2]	$\overline{AS}$, $\overline{DS}$ Negated to Data-Out Invalid (Write)	t_{SHDOI}	40	—	30	—	20	—	15	—	ns
26[2]	Data-Out Valid to $\overline{DS}$ Asserted (Write)	t_{DOSL}	40	—	30	—	20	—	15	—	ns
27[5]	Data-In Valid to Clock Low (Setup Time on Read)	t_{DICL}	10	—	10	—	10	—	7	—	ns
28[2]	$\overline{AS}$, $\overline{DS}$ Negated to $\overline{DTACK}$ Negated (Asynchronous Hold)	t_{SHDAH}	0	240	0	190	0	150	0	110	ns
29	$\overline{AS}$, $\overline{DS}$ Negated to Data-In Invalid (Hold Time on Read)	t_{SHDII}	0	—	0	—	0	—	0	—	ns
29A	$\overline{AS}$, $\overline{DS}$ Negated to Data-In High Impedance	t_{SHDZ}	—	187	—	150	—	120	—	90	ns
30	$\overline{AS}$, $\overline{DS}$ Negated to $\overline{BERR}$ Negated	t_{SHBEH}	0	—	0	—	0	—	0	—	ns
31[2,5]	$\overline{DTACK}$ Asserted to Data-In Valid (Setup Time)	t_{DALDI}	—	90	—	65	—	50	—	40	ns
32	$\overline{HALT}$ and $\overline{RESET}$ Input Transition Time	$t_{RHr,f}$	0	200	0	200	0	200	0	150	ns
33	Clock High to $\overline{BG}$ Asserted	t_{CHGL}	—	62	—	50	—	40	—	40	ns
34	Clock High to $\overline{BG}$ Negated	t_{CHGH}	—	62	—	50	—	40	—	40	ns
35	$\overline{BR}$ Asserted to $\overline{BG}$ Asserted	t_{BRLGL}	1.5	3.5	1.5	3.5	1.5	3.5	1.5	3.5	Clks
36[7]	$\overline{BR}$ Negated to $\overline{BG}$ Negated	t_{BRHGH}	1.5	3.5	1.5	3.5	1.5	3.5	1.5	3.5	Clks
37	$\overline{BGACK}$ Asserted to $\overline{BG}$ Negated	t_{GALGH}	1.5	3.5	1.5	3.5	1.5	3.5	1.5	3.5	Clks
37A[8]	$\overline{BGACK}$ Asserted to $\overline{BR}$ Negated	t_{GALBRH}	20	1.5 Clks	20	1.5 Clks	20	1.5 Clks	10	1.5 Clks	ns
38	$\overline{BG}$ Asserted to Control, Address, Data Bus High Impedance ($\overline{AS}$ Negated)	t_{GLZ}	—	80	—	70	—	60	—	50	ns

11.7 AC ELECTRICAL SPECIFICATIONS — READ AND WRITE CYCLES (Continued)

Num.	Characteristic	Symbol	8 MHz*		10 MHz*		12.5 MHz*		16.67 MHz '12F'		Unit
			Min	Max	Min	Max	Min	Max	Min	Max	
39	BG Width Negated	t_{GH}	1.5	—	1.5	—	1.5	—	1.5	—	Clks
40	Clock Low to VMA Asserted	t_{CLVML}	—	70	—	70	—	70	—	50	ns
41	Clock Low to E Transition	t_{CLET}	—	55	—	45	—	35	—	35	ns
42	E Output Rise and Fall Time	$t_{Er,f}$	—	15	—	15	—	15	—	15	ns
43	VMA Asserted to E High	t_{VMLEH}	200	—	150	—	90	—	80	—	ns
44	AS, DS Negated to VPA Negated	t_{SHVPH}	0	120	0	90	0	70	0	50	ns
45	E Low to Control, Address Bus Invalid (Address Hold Time)	t_{ELCAI}	30	—	10	—	10	—	10	—	ns
46	BGACK Width Low	t_{GAL}	1.5	—	1.5	—	1.5	—	1.5	—	Clks
47[5]	Asynchronous Input Setup Time	t_{ASI}	10	—	10	—	10	—	10	—	ns
48[2,3]	BERR Asserted to DTACK Asserted	t_{BELDAL}	20	—	20	—	20	—	10	—	ns
49[9]	AS, DS, Negated to E Low	t_{SHEL}	−70	70	−55	55	−45	45	−35	35	ns
50	E Width High	t_{EH}	450	—	350	—	280	—	220	—	ns
51	E Width Low	t_{EL}	700	—	550	—	440	—	340	—	ns
53	Data-Out Hold from Clock High	t_{CHDOI}	0	—	0	—	0	—	0	—	ns
54	E Low to Data-Out Invalid	t_{ELDOI}	30	—	20	—	15	—	10	—	ns
55	R/W Asserted to Data Bus Impedance Change	t_{RLDBD}	30	—	20	—	10	—	0	—	ns
56[4]	HALT/RESET Pulse Width	t_{HRPW}	10	—	10	—	10	—	10	—	Clks
57	BGACK Negated to AS, DS, R/W Driven	t_{GASD}	1.5	—	1.5	—	1.5	—	1.5	—	Clks
57A	BGACK Negated to FC, VMA Driven	t_{GAFD}	1	—	1	—	1	—	1	—	Clks
58[7]	BR Negated to AS, DS, R/W Driven	t_{RHSD}	1.5	—	1.5	—	1.5	—	1.5	—	Clks
58A[7]	BR Negated to FC, VMA Driven	t_{RHFD}	1	—	1	—	1	—	1	—	Clks

*These specifications represent improvement over previously published specifications for the 8-, 10-, and 12.5-MHz MC68000 and are valid only for product bearing date codes of 8827 and later.

NOTES:

1. For a loading capacitance of less than or equal to 50 picofarads, subtract 5 nanoseconds from the value given in the maximum columns.
2. Actual value depends on clock period.
3. If #47 is satisfied for both DTACK and BERR, #48 may be ignored. In the absence of DTACK, BERR is an asynchronous input using the asynchronous input setup time (#47).
4. For power-up, the MC68000 must be held in the reset state for 100 milliseconds to allow stabilization of on-chip circuitry. After the system is powered up, #56 refers to the minimum pulse width required to reset the processor.
5. If the asynchronous input setup time (#47) requirement is satisfied for DTACK, the DTACK-asserted to data setup time (#31) requirement can be ignored. The data must only satisfy the data-in to clock low setup time (#27) for the following clock cycle.
6. When AS and R/W are equally loaded (±20%), subtract 5 nanoseconds from the values given in these columns.
7. The processor will negate BG and begin driving the bus again if external arbitration logic negates BR before asserting BGACK.
8. The minimum value must be met to guarantee proper operation. If the maximum value is exceeded, BG may be re-asserted.
9. The falling edge of S6 triggers both the negation of the strobes (AS and xDS) and the falling edge of E. Either of these events can occur first, depending upon the loading on each signal. Specification #49 indicates the absolute maximum skew that will occur between the rising edge of the strobes and the falling edge of the E clock.

These waveforms should only be referenced in regard to the edge-to-edge measurement of the timing specifications. They are not intended as a functional description of the input and output signals. Refer to other functional descriptions and their related diagrams for device operation.

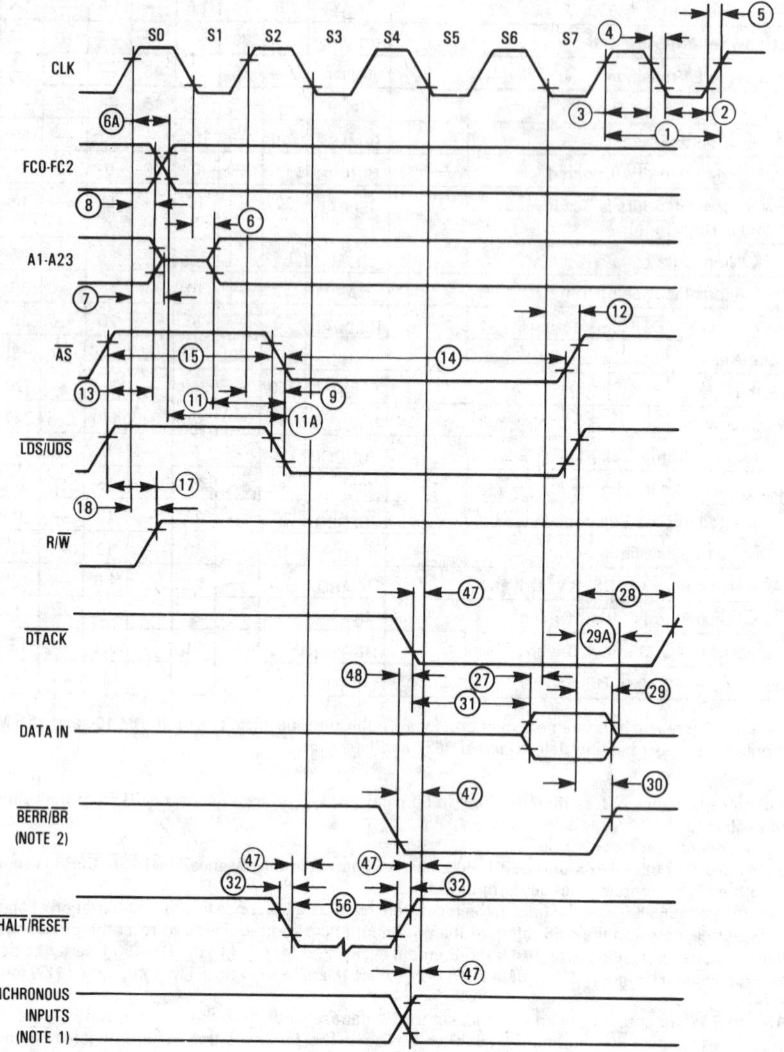

11

NOTES:

1. Setup time for the asynchronous inputs IPL0-IPL2 and VPA (#47) guarantees their recognition at the next falling edge of the clock.
2. BR need fall at this time only in order to insure being recognized at the end of the bus cycle.
3. Timing measurements are referenced to and from a low voltage of 0.8 volt and a high voltage of 2.0 volts, unless otherwise noted. The voltage swing through this range should start outside and pass through the range such that the rise or fall is linear between 0.8 volt and 2.0 volts.

Figure 11-4. MC68000 Read-Cycle Timing Diagram

These waveforms should only be referenced in regard to the edge-to-edge measurement of the timing specifications. They are not intended as a functional description of the input and output signals. Refer to other functional descriptions and their related diagrams for device operation.

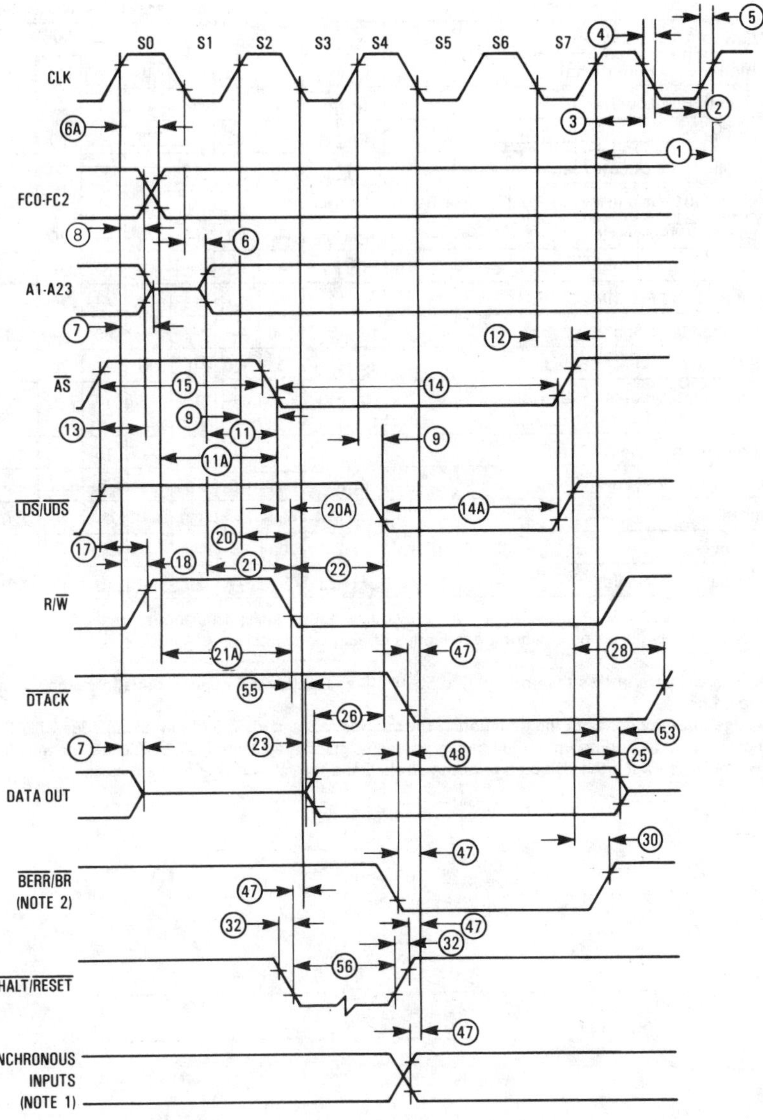

NOTES:

1. Timing measurements are referenced to and from a low voltage of 0.8 volt and a high voltage of 2.0 volts, unless otherwise noted. The voltage swing through this range should start outside and pass through the range such that the rise or fall is linear between 0.8 and 2.0 volts.
2. Because of loading variations, R/$\overline{W}$ may be valid after $\overline{AS}$ even though both are initiated by the rising edge of S2 (specification #20A).

Figure 11-5. MC68000 Write-Cycle Timing Diagram

11

11.8 AC ELECTRICAL SPECIFICATIONS — MC68000 TO M6800 PERIPHERAL CYCLES

(V_{CC} = 5.0 Vdc ± 5%; GND = 0 Vdc; $T_A = T_L$ to T_H; see Figures 11-6 and 11-7)

Num.	Characteristic	Symbol	8 MHz*		10 MHz*		12.5 MHz*		16.67 MHz '12F'		Unit
			Min	Max	Min	Max	Min	Max	Min	Max	
12[1]	Clock Low to $\overline{AS}$, $\overline{DS}$ Negated	t_{CLSH}	—	62	—	50	—	40	—	40	ns
18[1]	Clock High to R/$\overline{W}$ High (Read)	t_{CHRH}	0	55	0	45	0	40	0	40	ns
20[1]	Clock High to R/$\overline{W}$ Low (Write)	t_{CHRL}	0	55	0	45	0	40	0	40	ns
23	Clock Low to Data-Out Valid (Write)	t_{CLDO}	—	62	—	50	—	50	—	50	ns
27	Data-In Valid to Clock Low (Setup Time of Read)	t_{DICL}	10	—	10	—	10	—	7	—	ns
29	$\overline{AS}$, $\overline{DS}$ Negated to Data-In Invalid (Hold Time on Read)	t_{SHDII}	0	—	0	—	0	—	0	—	ns
40	Clock Low to $\overline{VMA}$ Asserted	t_{CLVML}	—	70	—	70	—	70	—	50	ns
41	Clock Low to E Transition	t_{CLET}	—	55	—	45	—	35	—	35	ns
42	E Output Rise and Fall Time	$t_{Er,f}$	—	15	—	15	—	15	—	15	ns
43	$\overline{VMA}$ Asserted to E High	t_{VMLEH}	200	—	150	—	90	—	80	—	ns
44	$\overline{AS}$, $\overline{DS}$ Negated to $\overline{VPA}$ Negated	t_{SHVPH}	0	120	0	90	0	70	0	50	ns
45	E Low to Control, Address Bus Invalid (Address Hold Time)	t_{ELCAI}	30	—	10	—	10	—	10	—	ns
47	Asynchronous Input Setup Time	t_{ASI}	10	—	10	—	10	—	10	—	ns
49[2]	$\overline{AS}$, $\overline{DS}$, Negated to E Low	t_{SHEL}	−70	70	−55	55	−45	45	−35	35	ns
50	E Width High	t_{EH}	450	—	350	—	280	—	220	—	ns
51	E Width Low	t_{EL}	700	—	550	—	440	—	340	—	ns
54	E Low to Data-Out Invalid	t_{ELDOI}	30	—	20	—	15	—	10	—	ns

*These specifications represent an improvement over previously published specifications for the 8-, 10-, and 12.5-MHz MC68000 and are valid only for product bearing date codes of 8827 and later.

NOTES:

1. For a loading capacitance of less than or equal to 50 picofarads, subtract 5 nanoseconds from the value given in the maximum columns.
2. The falling edge of S6 trigger both the negation of the strobes ($\overline{AS}$ and $\overline{xDS}$) and the falling edge of E. Either of these events can occur first, depending upon the loading on each signal. Specification #49 indicates the absolute maximum skew that will occur between the rising edge of the strobes and the falling edge of the E clock.

These waveforms should only be referenced in regard to the edge-to-edge measurement of the timing specifications. They are not intended as a functional description of the input and output signals. Refer to other functional descriptions and their related diagrams for device operation.

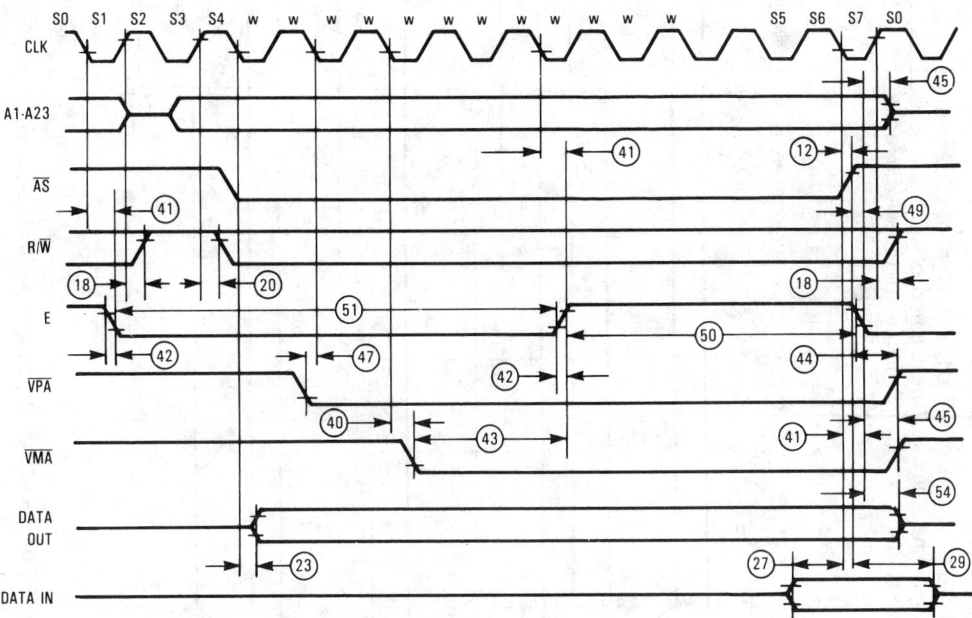

NOTE: This timing diagram is included for those who wish to design their own circuit to generate $\overline{\text{VMA}}$. It shows the best case possibly attainable.

Figure 11-6. MC68000 to M6800 Peripheral Timing Diagram (Best Case)

11

These waveforms should only be referenced in regard to the edge-to-edge measurement of the timing specifications. They are not intended as a functional description of the input and output signals. Refer to other functional descriptions and their related diagrams for device operation.

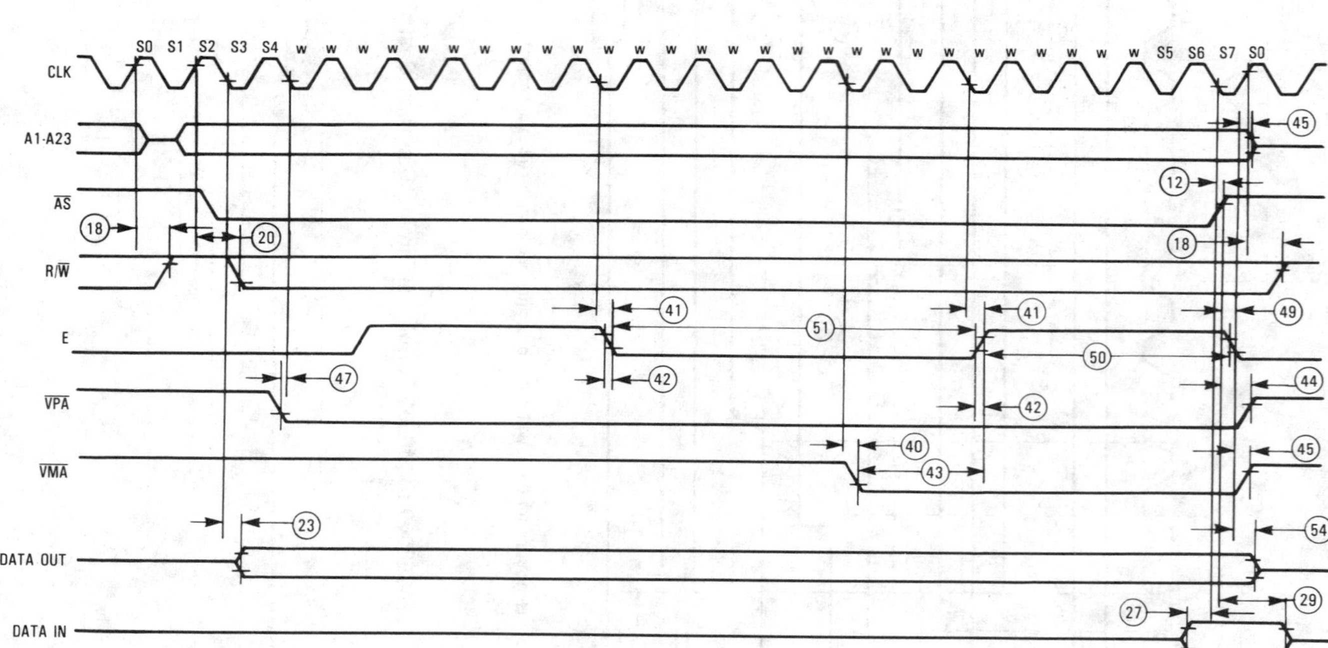

NOTE: This timing diagram is included for those who wish to design their own circuit to generate $\overline{VMA}$. It shows the worst case possibly attainable

Figure 11-7. MC68000 to M6800 Peripheal Timing Diagram (Worst Case)

11.9 AC ELECTRICAL SPECIFICATIONS — BUS ARBITRATION

(V_{CC} = 5.0 Vdc ± 5%; GND = 0 Vdc; T_A = T_L to T_H; see Figure 11-8)

Num.	Characteristic	Symbol	8 MHz*		10 MHz*		12.5 MHz*		16.67 MHz '12F'		Unit
			Min	Max	Min	Max	Min	Max	Min	Max	
7	Clock High to Address, Data Bus High Impedance (Maximum)	t_{CHADZ}	—	80	—	70	—	60	—	50	ns
16	Clock High to Control Bus High Impedance	t_{CHCZ}	—	80	—	70	—	60	—	50	ns
33	Clock High to $\overline{BG}$ Asserted	t_{CHGL}	—	62	—	50	—	40	—	40	ns
34	Clock High to $\overline{BG}$ Negated	t_{CHGH}	—	62	—	50	—	40	—	40	ns
35	$\overline{BR}$ Asserted to $\overline{BG}$ Asserted	t_{BRLGL}	1.5	3.5	1.5	3.5	1.5	3.5	1.5	3.5	Clks
36[1]	$\overline{BR}$ Negated to $\overline{BG}$ Negated	t_{BRHGH}	1.5	3.5	1.5	3.5	1.5	3.5	1.5	3.5	Clks
37	$\overline{BGACK}$ Asserted to $\overline{BG}$ Negated	t_{GALGH}	1.5	3.5	1.5	3.5	1.5	3.5	1.5	3.5	Clks
37A[2]	$\overline{BGACK}$ Asserted to $\overline{BR}$ Negated	t_{GALBRH}	20	1.5 Clks	20	1.5 Clks	20	1.5 Clks	10	1.5 Clks	ns
38	$\overline{BG}$ Asserted to Control, Address, Data Bus High Impedance ($\overline{AS}$ Negated)	t_{GLZ}	—	80	—	70	—	60	—	50	ns
39	$\overline{BG}$ Width Negated	t_{GH}	1.5	—	1.5	—	1.5	—	1.5	—	Clks
46	$\overline{BGACK}$ Width Low	t_{GAL}	1.5	—	1.5	—	1.5	—	1.5	—	Clks
47	Asynchronous Input Setup Time	t_{ASI}	10	—	10	—	10	—	10	—	ns
57	$\overline{BGACK}$ Negated to $\overline{AS}$, $\overline{DS}$, R/$\overline{W}$ Driven	t_{GASD}	1.5	—	1.5	—	1.5	—	1.5	—	Clks
57A	$\overline{BGACK}$ Negated to FC, $\overline{VMA}$ Driven	t_{GAFD}	1	—	1	—	1	—	1	—	Clks
58[1]	$\overline{BR}$ Negated to $\overline{AS}$, $\overline{DS}$, R/$\overline{W}$ Driven	t_{RHSD}	1.5	—	1.5	—	1.5	—	1.5	—	Clks
58A[1]	$\overline{BR}$ Negated to FC, $\overline{VMA}$ Driven	t_{RHFD}	1	—	1	—	1	—	1	—	Clks

*These specifications represent an improvement over previously published specifications for the 8-, 10-, and 12.5-MHz MC68000 and are valid only for product bearing date codes of 8827 and later.

NOTES:

1. The processor will negate $\overline{BG}$ and begin driving the bus again if external arbitration logic negates $\overline{BR}$ before asserting $\overline{BGACK}$.
2. The minimum value must be met to guarantee proper operation. If the maximum value is exceeded, $\overline{BG}$ may be re-asserted.

These waveforms should only be referenced in regard to the edge-to-edge measurement of the timing specifications. They are not intended as a functional description of the input and output signals. Refer to other functional descriptions and their related diagrams for device operation.

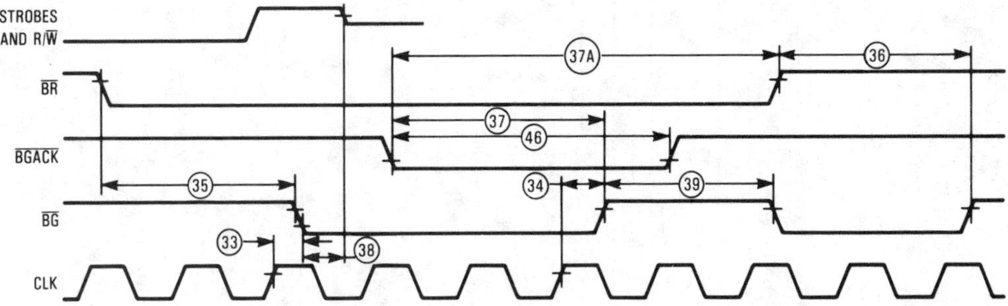

NOTE: Setup time to the clock (#47) for the asynchronous inputs $\overline{BERR}$, $\overline{BGACK}$, $\overline{BR}$, $\overline{DTACK}$, $\overline{IPL0}$-$\overline{IPL2}$ and $\overline{VPA}$ guarantees their recognition at the next falling edge of the clock.

Figure 11-8. MC68000 Bus Arbitration Timing Diagram

SECTION 12
MC68HC000 ELECTRICAL SPECIFICATIONS

The electrical specifications for the MC68HC000 microprocessor are shown in this section. The MC68HC000 microprocessor can be interchanged with the MC68000 microprocessor for the same clock frequency. The lower power dissipation of the MC68HC000 is the only difference between these two microprocessors.

12.1 MAXIMUM RATINGS

Rating	Symbol	Value	Unit
Supply Voltage	V_{CC}	−0.3 to +6.5	V
Input Voltage	V_{in}	−0.3 to +6.5	V
Operating Temperature Range MC68HC000	T_A	T_L to T_H 0 to 70	°C
Storage Temperature	T_{stg}	−55 to +150	°C

This device contains circuitry to protect the inputs against damage due to high static voltages or electric fields; however, it is advised that normal precautions be taken to avoid application of any voltage higher than maximum-rated voltages to this high-impedance circuit. Reliability of operation is enhanced if unused inputs are tied to the appropriate logic voltage level (e.g., either GND or V_{CC}).

12.2 THERMAL CHARACTERISTICS

Characteristic	Symbol	Value	Symbol	Value	Rating
Thermal Resistance (Still Air)	θ_{JA}		θ_{JC}		°C/W
Ceramic, Type L/LC		30		15*	
Ceramic, Type R/RC		33		15	
Plastic, Type P		30		15*	
Plastic, Type FN		45*		25*	

*Estimated

12.3 CMOS CONSIDERATIONS

The MC68HC000, with its significantly lower power consumption, has other considerations. The CMOS cell is basically composed of two complementary transistors (a P channel and an N channel), and only one transistor is turned on while the cell is in the steady state. The active P-channel transistor sources current when the output is a logic high and presents a high impedance when the output is a logic low. Thus, the overall result is extremely low power consumption because no power is lost through the active P-channel transistor. Also, since only one transistor is turned on during the steady state, power consumption is determined by leakage currents.

Because the basic CMOS cell is composed of two complementary transistors, a virtual semiconductor controlled rectifier (SCR) may be formed when an input exceeds the supply voltage. The SCR that is formed by this high input causes the device to become latched in a mode that may result in excessive current drain and eventual destruction of the device. Although the MC68HC000 is implemented with input protection diodes, care should be exercised to ensure that the maximum input voltage specification is not exceeded. Some systems may require that the CMOS circuitry be isolated from voltage transients; others may require no additional circuitry.

The MC68HC000, implemented in CMOS, is applicable to designs to which the following considerations are relevant:

1. The MC68HC000 completely satisfies the input/output drive requirements of CMOS logic devices.
2. The HCMOS MC68HC000 provides an order of magnitude reduction in power dissipation when compared to the HMOS MC68000. However, the MC68HC000 does not offer a "power down" mode. The minimum operating frequency of the MC68HC000 is 4 MHz.

12.4 DC ELECTRICAL CHARACTERISTICS

(V_{CC}=5.0 Vdc±5%; GND=0 Vdc; T_A=T_L to T_H)

Characteristic		Symbol	Min	Max	Unit
Input High Voltage		V_{IH}	2.0	V_{CC}	V
Input Low Voltage		V_{IL}	GND−0.3	0.8	V
Input Leakage Current @ 5.25 V	BERR, BGACK, BR, DTACK, CLK, IPL0-IPL2, VPA HALT, RESET	I_{in}	— —	2.5 20	μA
Three-State (Off State) Input Current @ 2.4 V/0.4 V	AS, A1-A23, D0-D15, FC0-FC2, LDS, R/W, UDS, VMA	I_{TSI}	—	20	μA
Output High Voltage (I_{OH}=−400 μA)	E, AS, A1-A23, BG, D0-D15, FC0-FC2, LDS, R/W, UDS, VMA	V_{OH}	V_{CC} −0.75	—	V
Output Low Voltage (I_{OL}=1.6 mA) (I_{OL}=3.2 mA) (I_{OL}=5.0 mA) (I_{OL}=5.3 mA)	 HALT A1-A23, BG, FC0-FC2 RESET E, AS, D0-D15, LDS, R/W, UDS, VMA	V_{OL}	 — — — —	 0.5 0.5 0.5 0.5	V
Current Dissipation*	f=8 MHz f=10 MHz f=12.5 MHz f=16.67 MHz	I_D	— — —	25 30 35 50	mA
Power Dissipation	f=8 MHz f=10 MHz f=12.5 MHz	P_D	— — —	0.13 0.16 0.19 0.26	W
Capacitance (V_{in}=0 V, T_A=25°C, Frequency=1 MHz)**		C_{in}	—	20.0	pF
Load Capacitance	HALT All Others	C_L	— —	70 130	pF

*Currents listed are with no loading.
**Capacitance is periodically sampled rather than 100% tested.

12.5 AC ELECTRICAL SPECIFICATIONS — CLOCK TIMING

Num.	Characteristic	8 MHz*		10 MHz*		12.5 MHz*		16.67 MHz '12F'		16 MHz		Unit
		Min	Max	Min	Max	Min	Max	Min	Max	Min	Max	
	Frequency of Operation	4.0	8.0	4.0	10.0	4.0	12.5	8.0	16.7	8.0	16.7	MHz
1	Cycle Time	125	250	100	250	80	250	60	125	60	125	ns
2,3	Clock Pulse Width (Measured from 1.5 V to 1.5 V for 12F)	55 55	125 125	45 45	125 125	35 35	125 125	27 27	62.5 62.5	27 27	62.5 62.5	ns
4,5	Clock Rise and Fall Times	— —	10 10	— —	10 10	— —	5 5	— —	5 5	— —	5 5	ns

*These specifications represent an improvement over previously published specifications for the 8-, 10-, and 12.5-MHz MC68HC000 and are valid only for product bearing date codes of 8827 and later.

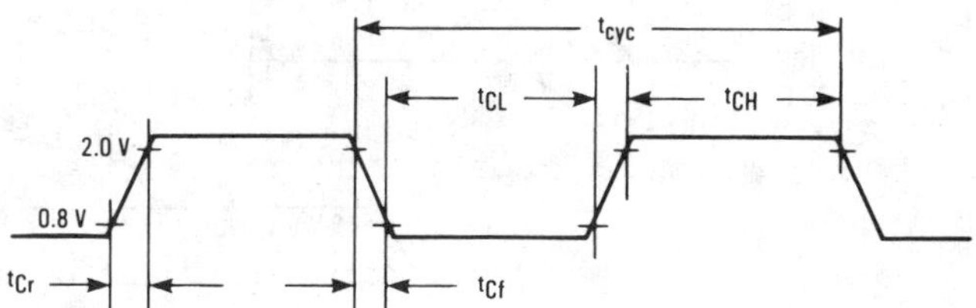

NOTE: Timing measurements are referenced to and from a low voltage of 0.8 volt and high a voltage of 2.0 volts, unless otherwise noted. The voltage swing through this range should start outside and pass through the range such that the rise or fall will be linear between 0.8 volt and 2.0 volts.

Figure 12-1. MC68HC000 Clock Input Timing Diagram

12

12.6 AC ELECTRICAL SPECIFICATION DEFINITIONS

The AC specifications presented consist of output delays, input setup and hold times, and signal skew times. All signals are specified relative to an appropriate edge of the clock and possibly to one or more other signals.

The measurement of the AC specifications is defined by the waveforms shown in Figure 12-2. In order to test the parameters guaranteed by Motorola, inputs must be driven to the voltage levels specified in that figure. Outputs are specified with minimum and/or maximum limits, as appropriate, and are measured as shown in Figure 12-2. Inputs are specified with minimum setup and hold times, and are measured as shown. Finally, the measurement for signal-to-signal specifications is also shown.

NOTE

The testing levels used to verify conformance to the AC specifications does not affect the guaranteed DC operation of the device as specified in the DC electrical characteristics.

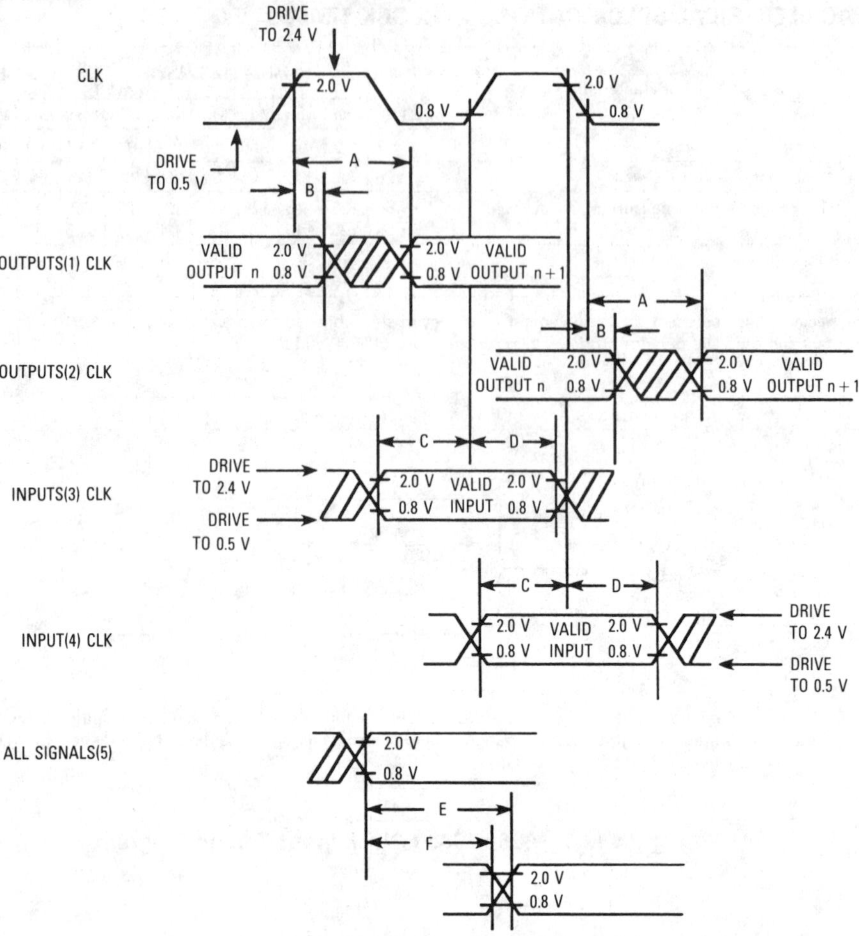

NOTES:

1. This output timing is applicable to all parameters specified relative to the rising edge of the clock.
2. This output timing is applicable to all parameters specified relative to the falling edge of the clock.
3. This input timing is applicable to all parameters specified relative to the rising edge of the clock.
4. This input timing is applicable to all parameters specified relative to the falling edge of the clock.
5. This timing is applicable to all parameters specified relative to the assertion/negation of another signal.

LEGEND:

A. Maximum output delay specification.
B. Minimum output hold time.
C. Minimum input setup time specification.
D. Minimum input hold time specification.
E. Signal valid to signal valid specification (maximum or minimum).
F. Signal valid to signal invalid specification (maximum or minimum).

Figure 12-2. Drive Levels and Test Points for AC Specifications

12.7 AC ELECTRICAL SPECIFICATIONS — READ AND WRITE CYCLES

(V_{CC} = 5.0 Vdc ± 5%; GND = 0 Vdc; $T_A = T_L$ to T_H; see Figures 12-3 and 12-4)

Num.	Characteristic	8 MHz*		10 MHz*		12.5 MHz*		16.67 MHz '12F'		16 MHz		Unit
		Min	Max	Min	Max	Min	Max	Min	Max	Min	Max	
6	Clock Low to Address Valid	—	62	—	50	—	50	—	50	—	30	ns
6A	Clock High to FC Valid	—	62	—	50	—	45	—	45	0	30	ns
7	Clock High to Address, Data Bus High Impedance (Maximum)	—	80	—	70	—	60	—	50	—	50	ns
8	Clock High to Address, FC Invalid (Minimum)	0	—	0	—	0	—	0	—	0	—	ns
9[1]	Clock High to $\overline{AS}$, $\overline{DS}$ Asserted	3	60	3	50	3	40	3	40	3	30	ns
11[2]	Address Valid to $\overline{AS}$, $\overline{DS}$ Asserted (Read)/$\overline{AS}$ Asserted (Write)	30	—	20	—	15	—	15	—	15	—	ns
11A[2]	FC Valid to $\overline{AS}$, $\overline{DS}$ Asserted (Read)/$\overline{AS}$ Asserted (Write)	90	—	70	—	60	—	30	—	45	—	ns
12[1]	Clock Low to $\overline{AS}$, $\overline{DS}$ Negated	—	62	—	50	—	40	—	40	3	30	ns
13[2]	$\overline{AS}$, $\overline{DS}$ Negated to Address, FC Invalid	40	—	30	—	20	—	10	—	15	—	ns
14[2]	$\overline{AS}$ (and $\overline{DS}$ Read) Width Asserted	270	—	195	—	160	—	120	—	120	—	ns
14A	$\overline{DS}$ Width Asserted (Write)	140	—	95	—	80	—	60	—	60	—	ns
15[2]	$\overline{AS}$, $\overline{DS}$ Width Negated	150	—	105	—	65	—	60	—	60	—	ns
16	Clock High to Control Bus High Impedance	—	80	—	70	—	60	—	50	—	50	ns
17[2]	$\overline{AS}$, $\overline{DS}$ Negated to R/$\overline{W}$ Invalid	40	—	30	—	20	—	10	—	15	—	ns
18[1]	Clock High to R/$\overline{W}$ High (Read)	0	55	0	45	0	40	0	40	0	30	ns
20[1]	Clock High to R/$\overline{W}$ Low (Write)	0	55	0	45	0	40	0	40	0	30	ns
20A[2,6]	$\overline{AS}$ Asserted to R/$\overline{W}$ Valid (Write)	—	10	—	10	—	10	—	10	—	10	ns
21[2]	Address Valid to R/$\overline{W}$ Low (Write)	20	—	0	—	0	—	0	—	0	—	ns
21A[2]	FC Valid to R/$\overline{W}$ Low (Write)	60	—	50	—	30	—	20	—	30	—	ns
22[2]	R/$\overline{W}$ Low to $\overline{DS}$ Asserted (Write)	80	—	50	—	30	—	20	—	30	—	ns
23	Clock Low to Data-Out Valid (Write)	—	62	—	50	—	50	—	50	—	30	ns
25[2]	$\overline{AS}$, $\overline{DS}$ Negated to Data-Out Invalid (Write)	40	—	30	—	20	—	15	—	15	—	ns
26[2]	Data-Out Valid to $\overline{DS}$ Asserted (Write)	40	—	30	—	20	—	15	—	15	—	ns
27[5]	Data-In Valid to Clock Low (Setup Time on Read)	10	—	10	—	10	—	7	—	5	—	ns
28[2]	$\overline{AS}$, $\overline{DS}$ Negated to $\overline{DTACK}$ Negated (Asynchronous Hold)	0	240	0	190	0	150	0	110	0	110	ns
29	$\overline{AS}$, $\overline{DS}$ Negated to Data-In Invalid (Hold Time on Read)	0	—	0	—	0	—	0	—	0	—	ns
29A	$\overline{AS}$, $\overline{DS}$ Negated to Data-In High Impedance	—	187	—	150	—	120	—	90	—	90	ns
30	$\overline{AS}$, $\overline{DS}$ Negated to $\overline{BERR}$ Negated	0	—	0	—	0	—	0	—	0	—	ns
31[2,5]	$\overline{DTACK}$ Asserted to Data-In Valid (Setup Time)	—	90	—	65	—	50	—	40	—	50	ns
32	$\overline{HALT}$ and $\overline{RESET}$ Input Transition Time	0	200	0	200	0	200	0	150	—	150	ns
33	Clock High to $\overline{BG}$ Asserted	—	62	—	50	—	40	—	40	0	30	ns
34	Clock High to $\overline{BG}$ Negated	—	62	—	50	—	40	—	40	0	30	ns
35	$\overline{BR}$ Asserted to $\overline{BG}$ Asserted	1.5	3.5	1.5	3.5	1.5	3.5	1.5	3.5	1.5	3.5	Clks
36[7]	$\overline{BR}$ Negated to $\overline{BG}$ Negated	1.5	3.5	1.5	3.5	1.5	3.5	1.5	3.5	1.5	3.5	Clks

12.7 AC ELECTRICAL SPECIFICATIONS — READ AND WRITE CYCLES (Continued)

Num.	Characteristic	8 MHz*		10 MHz*		12.5 MHz*		16.67 MHz '12F'		16 MHz		Unit
		Min	Max	Min	Max	Min	Max	Min	Max	Min	Max	
37	BGACK Asserted to BG Negated	1.5	3.5	1.5	3.5	1.5	3.5	1.5	3.5	1.5	3.5	Clks
37A[8]	BGACK Asserted to BR Negated	20	1.5 Clks	20	1.5 Clks	20	1.5 Clks	10	1.5 Clks	10	1.5 Clks	ns
38	BG Asserted to Control, Address, Data Bus High Impedance (AS Negated)	—	80	—	70	—	60	—	50	—	50	ns
39	BG Width Negated	1.5	—	1.5	—	1.5	—	1.5	—	1.5	—	Clks
40	Clock Low to VMA Asserted	—	70	—	70	—	70	—	50	—	50	ns
41	Clock Low to E Transition	—	55	—	45	—	35	—	35	—	35	ns
42	E Output Rise and Fall Time	—	15	—	15	—	15	—	15	—	15	ns
43	VMA Asserted to E High	200	—	150	—	90	—	80	—	80	—	ns
44	AS, DS Negated to VPA Negated	0	120	0	90	0	70	0	50	0	50	ns
45	E Low to Control, Address Bus Invalid (Address Hold Time)	30	—	10	—	10	—	10	—	10	—	ns
46	BGACK Width Low	1.5	—	1.5	—	1.5	—	1.5	—	1.5	—	Clks
47[5]	Asynchronous Input Setup Time	10	—	10	—	10	—	10	—	5	—	ns
48[2,3]	BERR Asserted to DTACK Asserted	20	—	20	—	20	—	10	—	10	—	ns
49[9]	AS, DS, Negated to E Low	−70	70	−55	55	−45	45	−35	35	−35	35	ns
50	E Width High	450	—	350	—	280	—	220	—	220	—	ns
51	E Width Low	700	—	550	—	440	—	340	—	340	—	ns
53	Data-Out Hold from Clock High	0	—	0	—	0	—	0	—	0	—	ns
54	E Low to Data-Out Invalid	30	—	20	—	15	—	10	—	10	—	ns
55	R/W Asserted to Data Bus Impedance Change	30	—	20	—	10	—	0	—	0	—	ns
56[4]	HALT/RESET Pulse Width	10	—	10	—	10	—	10	—	10	—	Clks
57	BGACK Negated to AS, DS, R/W Driven	1.5	—	1.5	—	1.5	—	1.5	—	1.5	—	Clks
57A	BGACK Negated to FC, VMA Driven	1	—	1	—	1	—	1	—	1	—	Clks
58[7]	BR Negated to AS, DS, R/W Driven	1.5	—	1.5	—	1.5	—	1.5	—	1.5	—	Clks
58A[7]	BR Negated to FC, VMA Driven	1	—	1	—	1	—	1	—	1	—	Clks

*These specifications represent improvement over previously published specifications for the 8-, 10-, and 12.5-MHz MC68HC000 and are valid only for product bearing date codes of 8827 and later.

NOTES:

1. For a loading capacitance of less than or equal to 50 picofarads, subtract 5 nanoseconds from the value given in the maximum columns.
2. Actual value depends on clock period.
3. If #47 is satisfied for both DTACK and BERR, #48 may be ignored. In the absence of DTACK, BERR is an asynchronous input using the asynchronous input setup time (#47).
4. For power-up, the MC68HC000 must be held in the reset state for 100 milliseconds to allow stabilization of on-chip circuitry. After the system is powered up, #56 refers to the minimum pulse width required to reset the processor.
5. If the asynchronous input setup time (#47) requirement is satisfied for DTACK, the DTACK-asserted to data setup time (#31) requirement can be ignored. The data must only satisfy the data-in to clock low setup time (#27) for the following clock cycle.
6. When AS and R/W are equally loaded (±20%), subtract 5 nanoseconds from the values given in these columns.
7. The processor will negate BG and begin driving the bus again if external arbitration logic negates BR before asserting BGACK.
8. The minimum value must be met to guarantee proper operation. If the maximum value is exceeded, BG may be re-asserted.
9. The falling edge of S6 triggers both the negation of the strobes (AS and xDS) and the falling edge of E. Either of these events can occur first, depending upon the loading on each signal. Specification #49 indicates the absolute maximum skew that will occur between the rising edge of the strobes and the falling edge of the E clock.

These waveforms should only be referenced in regard to the edge-to-edge measurement of the timing specifications. They are not intended as a functional description of the input and output signals. Refer to other functional descriptions and their related diagrams for device operation.

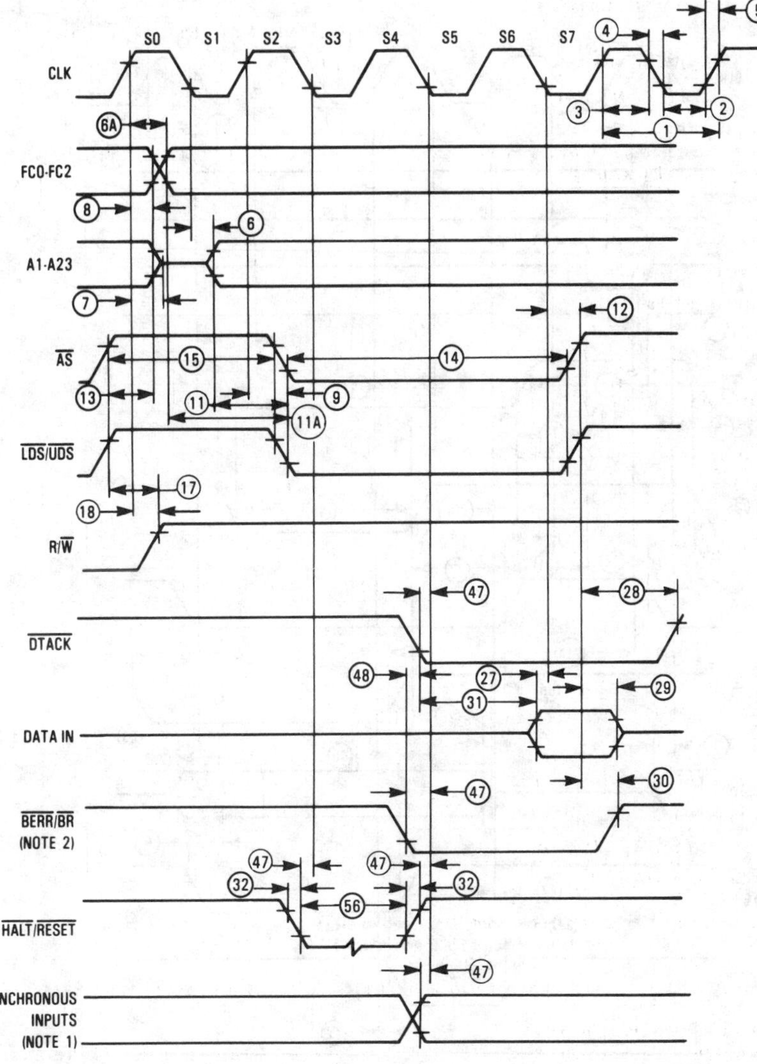

12

NOTES:

1. Setup time for the asynchronous inputs IPL0-IPL2 and VPA (#47) guarantees their recognition at the next falling edge of the clock.
2. BR need fall at this time only in order to insure being recognized at the end of the bus cycle.
3. Timing measurements are referenced to and from a low voltage of 0.8 volt and a high voltage of 2.0 volts, unless otherwise noted. The voltage swing through this range should start outside and pass through the range such that the rise or fall is linear between 0.8 volt and 2.0 volts.

Figure 12-3. MC68HC000 Read-Cycle Timing Diagram

These waveforms should only be referenced in regard to the edge-to-edge measurement of the timing specifications. They are not intended as a functional description of the input and output signals. Refer to other functional descriptions and their related diagrams for device operation.

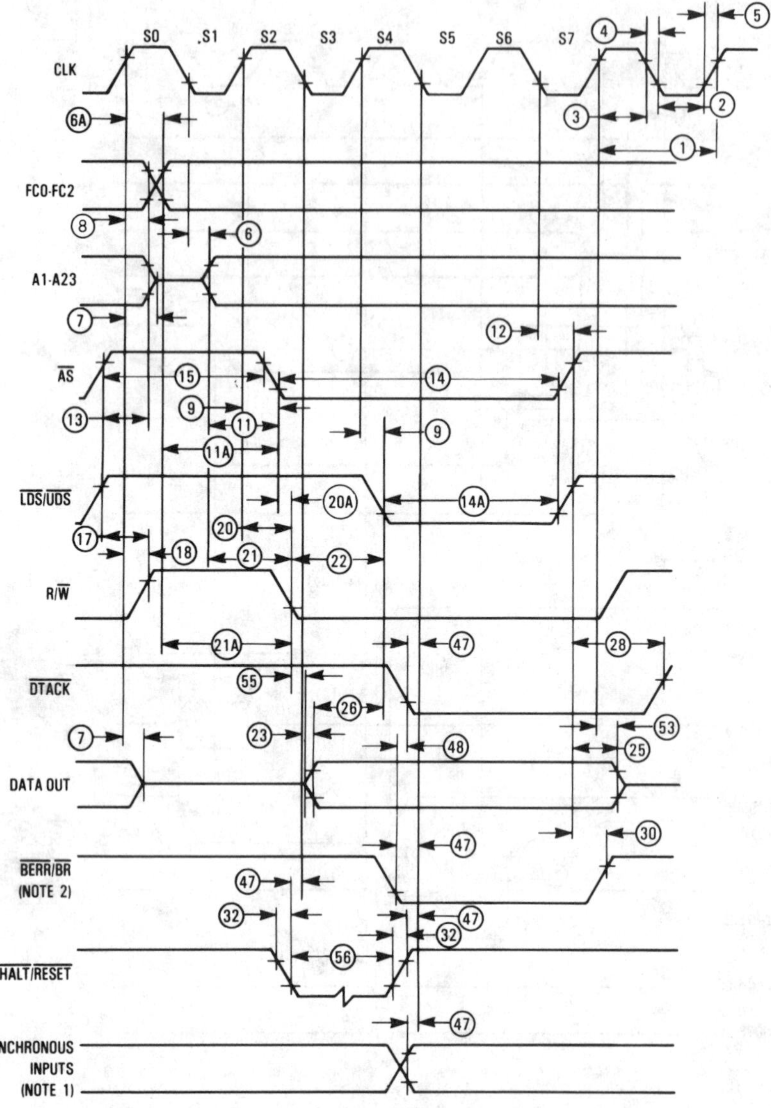

NOTES:

1. Timing measurements are referenced to and from a low voltage of 0.8 volt and a high voltage of 2.0 volts, unless otherwise noted. The voltage swing through this range should start outside and pass through the range such that the rise or fall is linear between 0.8 volt and 2.0 volts.
2. Because of loading variations, R/$\overline{\text{W}}$ may be valid after $\overline{\text{AS}}$ even though both are initiated by the rising edge of S2 (specification #20A).

Figure 12-4. MC68HC000 Write-Cycle Timing Diagram

12.8 AC ELECTRICAL SPECIFICATIONS — MC68HC000 TO M6800 PERIPHERAL CYCLES

(V_{CC}=5.0 Vdc±5%; GND=0 Vdc; T_A=T_L to T_H; see Figures 12-5 and 12-6)

Num.	Characteristic	8 MHz*		10 MHz*		12.5 MHz*		16.67 MHz '12F'		16 MHz		Unit
		Min	Max	Min	Max	Min	Max	Min	Max	Min	Max	
12[1]	Clock Low to $\overline{AS}$, $\overline{DS}$ Negated	—	62	—	50	—	40	—	40	3	30	ns
18[1]	Clock High to R/$\overline{W}$ High (Read)	0	55	0	45	0	40	0	40	0	30	ns
20[1]	Clock High to R/$\overline{W}$ Low (Write)	0	55	0	45	0	40	0	40	0	30	ns
23	Clock Low to Data-Out Valid (Write)	—	62	—	50	—	50	—	50	—	30	ns
27	Data-In Valid to Clock Low (Setup Time of Read)	10	—	10	—	10	—	7	—	5	—	ns
29	$\overline{AS}$, $\overline{DS}$ Negated to Data-In Invalid (Hold Time on Read)	0	—	0	—	0	—	0	—	0	—	ns
40	Clock Low to $\overline{VMA}$ Asserted	—	70	—	70	—	70	—	50	—	50	ns
41	Clock Low to E Transition	—	55	—	45	—	35	—	35	—	35	ns
42	E Output Rise and Fall Time	—	15	—	15	—	15	—	15	—	15	ns
43	$\overline{VMA}$ Asserted to E High	200	—	150	—	90	—	80	—	80	—	ns
44	$\overline{AS}$, $\overline{DS}$ Negated to $\overline{VPA}$ Negated	0	120	0	90	0	70	0	50	0	50	ns
45	E Low to Control, Address Bus Invalid (Address Hold Time)	30	—	10	—	10	—	10	—	10	—	ns
47	Asynchronous Input Setup Time	10	—	10	—	10	—	10	—	5	—	ns
49[2]	$\overline{AS}$, $\overline{DS}$, Negated to E Low	−70	70	−55	55	−45	45	−35	35	−35	35	ns
50	E Width High	450	—	350	—	280	—	220	—	220	—	ns
51	E Width Low	700	—	550	—	440	—	340	—	340	—	ns
54	E Low to Data-Out Invalid	30	—	20	—	15	—	10	—	10	—	ns

*These specifications represent an improvement over previously published specifications for the 8-, 10-, and 12.5-MHz MC68HC000 and are valid only for product bearing date codes of 8827 and later.

NOTES:

1. For a loading capacitance of less than or equal to 50 picofarads, subtract 5 nanoseconds from the value given in the maximum columns.
2. The falling edge of S6 trigger both the negation of the strobes ($\overline{AS}$ and x$\overline{DS}$) and the falling edge of E. Either of these events can occur first, depending upon the loading on each signal. Specification #49 indicates the absolute maximum skew that will occur between the rising edge of the strobes and the falling edge of the E clock.

12

These waveforms should only be referenced in regard to the edge-to-edge measurement of the timing specifications. They are not intended as a functional description of the input and output signals. Refer to other functional descriptions and their related diagrams for device operation.

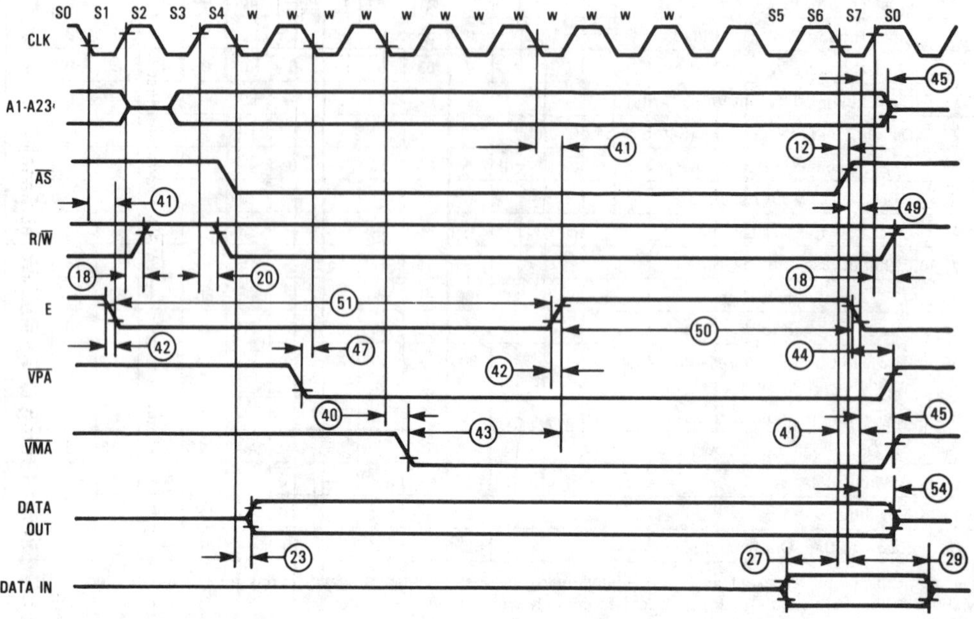

12

NOTE: This timing diagram is included for those who wish to design their own circuit to generate $\overline{VMA}$. It shows the best case possibly attainable.

Figure 12-5. MC68HC000 to M6800 Peripheral Timing Diagram (Best Case)

These waveforms should only be referenced in regard to the edge-to-edge measurement of the timing specifications. They are not intended as a functional description of the input and output signals. Refer to other functional descriptions and their related diagrams for device operation.

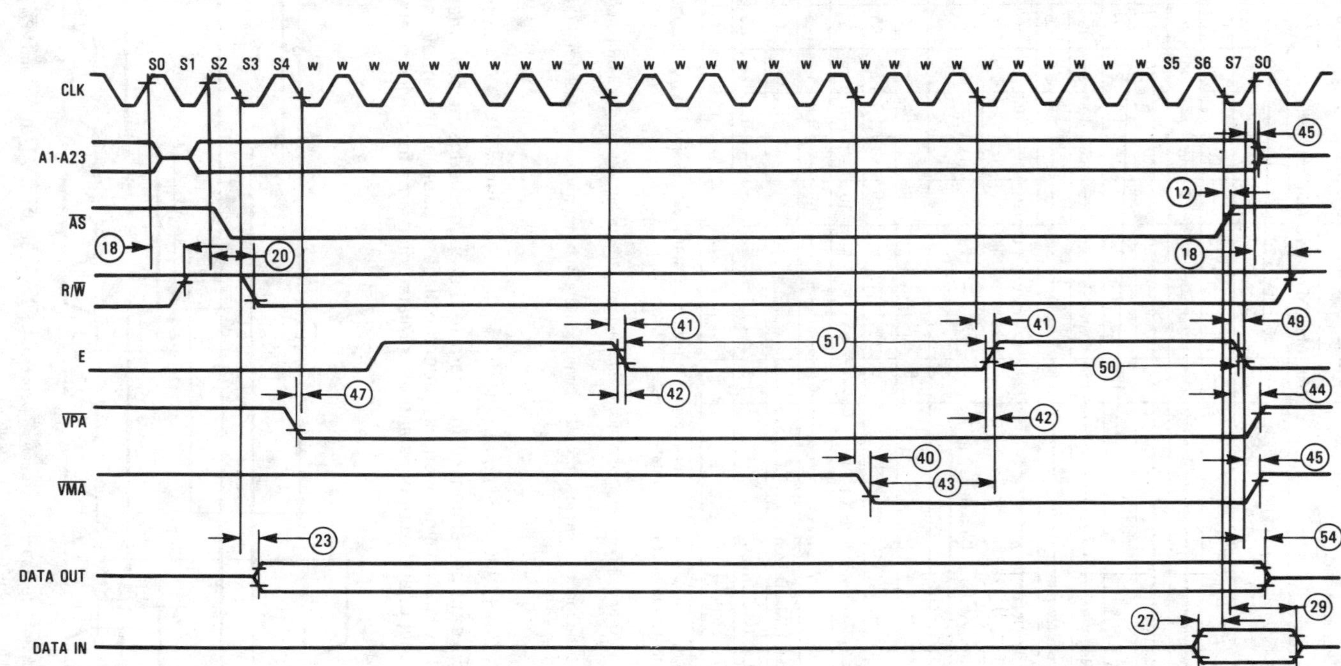

NOTE: This timing diagram is included for those who wish to design their own circuit to generate $\overline{VMA}$. It shows the worst case possibly attainable.

Figure 12-6. MC68HC000 to M6800 Peripheral Timing Diagram (Worst Case)

12

12.9 AC ELECTRICAL SPECIFICATIONS — BUS ARBITRATION

(V_{CC}=5.0 Vdc+5%; GND=0 Vdc; T_A=T_L to T_H; see Figure 12-7)

Num.	Characteristic	8 MHz*		10 MHz*		12.5 MHz*		16.67 MHz '12F'		16 MHz		Unit
		Min	Max	Min	Max	Min	Max	Min	Max	Min	Max	
7	Clock High to Address, Data Bus High Impedance (Maximum)	—	80	—	70	—	60	—	50	—	50	ns
16	Clock High to Control Bus High Impedance	—	80	—	70	—	60	—	50	—	50	ns
33	Clock High to $\overline{\mathrm{BG}}$ Asserted	—	62	—	50	—	40	—	40	0	30	ns
34	Clock High to $\overline{\mathrm{BG}}$ Negated	—	62	—	50	—	40	—	40	0	30	ns
35	$\overline{\mathrm{BR}}$ Asserted to $\overline{\mathrm{BG}}$ Asserted	1.5	3.5	1.5	3.5	1.5	3.5	1.5	3.5	1.5	3.5	Clks
36[1]	$\overline{\mathrm{BR}}$ Negated to $\overline{\mathrm{BG}}$ Negated	1.5	3.5	1.5	3.5	1.5	3.5	1.5	3.5	1.5	3.5	Clks
37	$\overline{\mathrm{BGACK}}$ Asserted to $\overline{\mathrm{BG}}$ Negated	1.5	3.5	1.5	3.5	1.5	3.5	1.5	3.5	1.5	3.5	Clks
37A[2]	$\overline{\mathrm{BGACK}}$ Asserted to $\overline{\mathrm{BR}}$ Negated	20	1.5 Clks	20	1.5 Clks	20	1.5 Clks	10	1.5 Clks	10	1.5 Clks	ns
38	$\overline{\mathrm{BG}}$ Asserted to Control, Address, Data Bus High Impedance ($\overline{\mathrm{AS}}$ Negated)	—	80	—	70	—	60	—	50	—	50	ns
39	$\overline{\mathrm{BG}}$ Width Negated	1.5	—	1.5	—	1.5	—	1.5	—	1.5	—	Clks
46	$\overline{\mathrm{BGACK}}$ Width Low	1.5	—	1.5	—	1.5	—	1.5	—	1.5	—	Clks
47	Asynchronous Input Setup Time	10	—	10	—	10	—	10	—	5	—	ns
57	$\overline{\mathrm{BGACK}}$ Negated to $\overline{\mathrm{AS}}$, $\overline{\mathrm{DS}}$, R/$\overline{\mathrm{W}}$ Driven	1.5	—	1.5	—	1.5	—	1.5	—	1.5	—	Clks
57A	$\overline{\mathrm{BGACK}}$ Negated to FC, $\overline{\mathrm{VMA}}$ Driven	1	—	1	—	1	—	1	—	1	—	Clks
58[1]	$\overline{\mathrm{BR}}$ Negated to $\overline{\mathrm{AS}}$, $\overline{\mathrm{DS}}$, R/$\overline{\mathrm{W}}$ Driven	1.5	—	1.5	—	1.5	—	1.5	—	1.5	—	Clks
58A[1]	$\overline{\mathrm{BR}}$ Negated to FC, $\overline{\mathrm{VMA}}$ Driven	1	—	1	—	1	—	1	—	1	—	Clks

*These specifications represent an improvement over previously published specifications for the 8-, 10-, and 12.5-MHz MC68HC000 and are valid only for product bearing date codes of 8827 and later.

NOTES:

1. The processor will negate $\overline{\mathrm{BG}}$ and begin driving the bus again if external arbitration logic negates $\overline{\mathrm{BR}}$ before asserting $\overline{\mathrm{BGACK}}$.
2. The minimum value must be met to guarantee proper operation. If the maximum value is exceeded, $\overline{\mathrm{BG}}$ may be re-asserted.

These waveforms should only be referenced in regard to the edge-to-edge measurement of the timing specifications. They are not intended as a functional description of the input and output signals. Refer to other functional descriptions and their related diagrams for device operation.

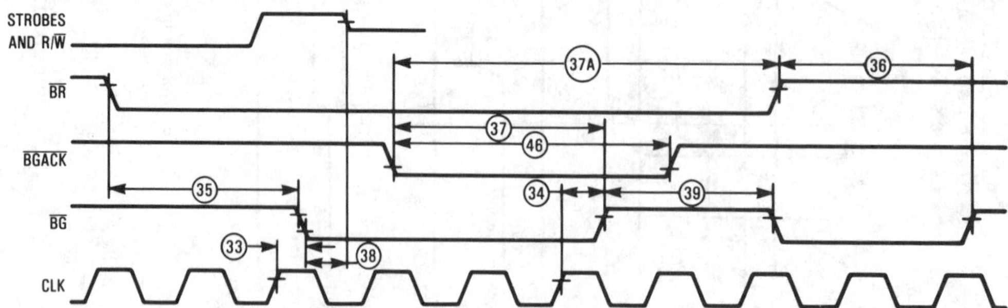

NOTE: Setup time to the clock (#47) for the asynchronous inputs $\overline{\mathrm{BERR}}$, $\overline{\mathrm{BGACK}}$, $\overline{\mathrm{BR}}$, $\overline{\mathrm{DTACK}}$, $\overline{\mathrm{IPL0}}$-$\overline{\mathrm{IPL2}}$ and $\overline{\mathrm{VPA}}$ guarantees their recognition at the next falling edge of the clock.

Figure 12-7. MC68HC000 Bus Arbitration Timing Diagram

SECTION 13
MC68008 ELECTRICAL SPECIFICATIONS

The electrical specifications for the MC68008 microprocessor are shown in this section.

13.1 MAXIMUM RATINGS

Rating	Symbol	Value	Unit
Supply Voltage	V_{CC}	−0.3 to +7.0	V
Input Voltage	V_{in}	−0.3 to +7.0	V
Operating Temperature Range MC68008 MC68008C	T_A	T_L to T_H 0 to 70 −40 to 85	°C
Storage Temperature	T_{stg}	−55 to 150	°C

The device contains circuitry to protect the inputs against damage due to high static voltages or electric fields; however, normal precautions should be taken to avoid application of voltages higher than maximum-rated voltages to these high-impedance circuits. Tying unused inputs to the appropriate logic voltage level (e.g., either GND or V_{CC}) enhances reliability of operation.

13.2 THERMAL CHARACTERISTICS

Characteristic	Symbol	Value	Symbol	Value	Rating
Thermal Resistance (Still Air)	θ_{JA}		θ_{JC}		°C/W
Ceramic, Type L/LC		30		15*	
Ceramic, Type R/RC		33		15	
Plastic, Type P		30		15*	
Plastic, Type FN		45*		25*	

*Estimated

13.3 POWER CONSIDERATIONS

The average die-junction temperature, T_J, in °C can be obtained from:

$$T_J = T_A + (P_D \cdot \theta_{JA}) \qquad (1)$$

where:

T_A = Ambient Temperature, °C
θ_{JA} = Package Thermal Resistance, Junction-to-Ambient, °C/W
P_D = $P_{INT} + P_{I/O}$
P_{INT} = $I_{CC} \times V_{CC}$, Watts — Chip Internal Power
$P_{I/O}$ = Power Dissipation on Input and Output Pins — User Determined

For most applications $P_{I/O} < P_{INT}$ and can be neglected.

An apropriate relationship between $P_D$and T_J (if $P_{I/O}$ is neglected) is:

$$P_D = K \div (T_J + 273\ °C) \qquad (2)$$

Solving equations (1) and (2) for K gives:

$$K = P_D \cdot (T_A + 273°C) + \theta_{JA} \cdot P_D^2 \qquad (3)$$

where K is a constant pertaining to the particular part. K can be determined from equation (3) by measuring P_D (at thermal equilibrium) for a known T_A. Using this value of K, the

13

values of P_D and T_J can be obtained by solving equations (1) and (2) iteratively for any value of T_A.

The curve shown in Figure 13-1 gives the graphic solution to the above equations for the specified power dissipation of 1.5 watts over the ambient temperature range of −55 °C to 125 °C using a maximum θ_{JA} of 45 °C/W. Ambient temperature is that of the still air surrounding the device. Lower values of θ_{JA} cause the curve to shift downward slightly; for instance, for θ_{JA} of 40 °/W, the curve is just below 1.4 watts at 25 °C.

The total thermal resistance of a package (θ_{JA}) can be separated into two components, θ_{JC} and θ_{CA}, representing the barrier to heat flow from the semiconductor junction to the package (case) surface (θ_{JC}) and from the case to the outside ambient air (θ_{CA}). These terms are related by the equation:

$$\theta_{JA} = \theta_{JC} + \theta_{CA} \qquad (4)$$

θ_{JC} is device related and cannot be influenced by the user. However, θ_{CA} is user dependent and can be minimized by such thermal management techniques as heat sinks, ambient air cooling, and thermal convection. Thus, good thermal management on the part of the user can significantly reduce θ_{CA} so that θ_{JA} approximately equals θ_{JC}. Substitution of θ_{JC} for θ_{JA} in equation 1 results in a lower semiconductor junction temperature.

Table 13-1 summarizes maximum power dissipation and average junction temperature for the curve drawn in Figure 13-1, using the minimum and maximum values of ambient temperature for different packages and substituting θ_{JC} for θ_{JA} (assuming good thermal management). Table 13-2 provides the maximum power dissipation and average junction temperature for the MC68000 assuming that no thermal management is applied (i.e., still air).

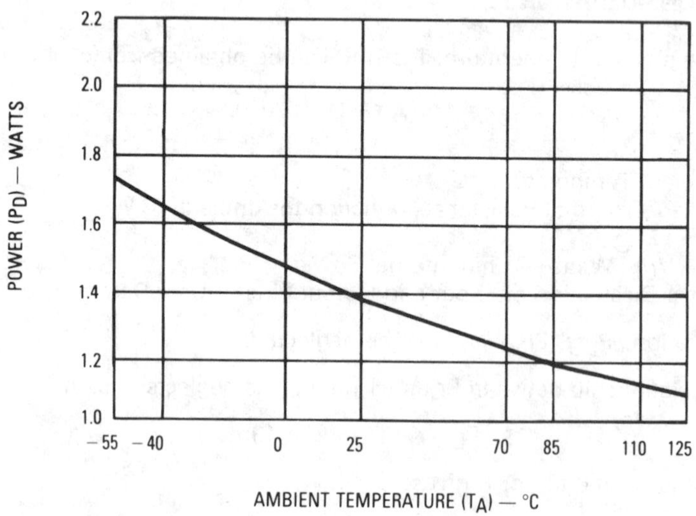

Figure 13-1. MC68008 Power Dissipation (P_D) vs Ambient Temperature(T_A)

Table 13-1. MC68008 Power Dissipation and Junction Temperature vs Temperature ($\theta_{JC} = \theta_{JA}$)

Package	T_A Range	θ_{JC} (°C/W)	P_D (W) @ T_A Min.	T_J (°C) @ T_A Min.	P_D (W) @ T_A Max.	T_J (°C) @ T_A Max.
LC	0°C to 70°C −40°C to 85°C 0°C to 85°C	15 15 15	1.5 1.7 1.5	23 −14 23	1.2 1.2 1.2	88 103 103
P	0°C to 70°C	20	1.5	30	1.2	95
FN	0°C to 70°C	30	1.5	45	1.3	108

Table 13-2. MC68008 Power Dissipation and Junction Temperature vs Temperature ($\theta_{JC} \neq \theta_{JA}$)

Package	T_A Range	θ_{JA} (°C/W)	P_D (W) @ T_A Min.	T_J (°C) @ T_A Min.	P_D (W) @ T_A Max.	T_J (°C) @ T_A Max.
LC	0°C to 70°C −40°C to 85°C 0°C to 85°C	40 40 40	1.5 1.7 1.5	60 −27 60	1.2 1.2 1.2	121 134 134
P	0°C to 70°C	40	1.5	60	1.2	121
FN	0°C to 70°C	50	1.5	75	1.3	134

NOTE

Since the power dissipation curve shown in Figure 13-1 is negatively sloped, power dissipation declines as ambient temperature increases. Therefore, maximum power dissipation occurs at the lowest rated ambient temperature, but the highest average junction temperature occurs at the maximum ambient temperature where *power dissipation is lowest.*

13

Values for thermal resistance presented in this manual, unless estimated, were derived using the procedure described in Motorola Reliability Report 7843, *Thermal Resistance Measurement Method for MC68XXX Microcomponent Devices*, and are provided for design purposes only. Thermal measurements are complex and dependent on procedure and setup. User-derived values for thermal resistance may differ.

13.4 DC ELECTRICAL CHARACTERISTICS
(V_{CC} = 5.0 Vdc ± 5%; GND = 0 Vdc; $T_A = T_L$ to T_H)

Characteristic		Symbol	Min	Max	Unit
Input High Voltage		V_{IH}	2.0	V_{CC}	V
Input Low Voltage		V_{IL}	GND −0.3	0.8	V
Input Leakage Current @ 5.25 V	$\overline{BERR}$, $\overline{BGACK}$, $\overline{BR}$, $\overline{DTACK}$, CLK, $\overline{IPL0}/\overline{IPL2}$, $\overline{VPA}$	I_{IN}	—	2.5	μA
	$\overline{HALT}$, $\overline{RESET}$		—	20	
Three-State (Off State) Input Current @ 2.4 V/0.4 V	$\overline{AS}$, A0-A18, A20, A21, D0-D7, FC0-FC2, $\overline{DS}$, R/$\overline{W}$, $\overline{VMA}$	I_{TSI}	—	20	μA
Output High Voltage (I_{OH} = −400 μA)	E*	V_{OH}	V_{CC}−0.75	—	V
(I_{OH} = −400 μA)	E, $\overline{AS}$, A0-A19, A20, A21, $\overline{BG}$, D0-D7, FC0-FC2, $\overline{DS}$, R/$\overline{W}$, $\overline{VMA}$		2.4	2.4	
Output Low Voltage		V_{OL}			V
(I_{OL} = 1.6 mA)	$\overline{HALT}$		—	0.5	
(I_{OL} = 3.2 mA)	A0-A19, A20, A21, FC0-FC2		—	0.5	
(I_{OL} = 5.0 mA)	$\overline{RESET}$		—	0.5	
(I_{OL} = 5.3 mA)	E, $\overline{AS}$, D0-D7, $\overline{DS}$, R/$\overline{W}$, $\overline{VMA}$		—	0.5	
Power Dissipation (see **13.3 POWER CONSIDERATIONS**)		P_D***	—	—	W
Capacitance (V_{in} = 0 V, T_A = 25°C, Frequency = 1 MHz)**		C_{in}	—	20.0	pF
Load Capacitance	$\overline{HALT}$	C_L	—	70	pF
	All Others		—	130	

*With external pullup resistor of 1.1K Ω.
**Capacitance is periodically sampled rather than 100% tested.
***During normal operation instantaneous V_{CC} current requirements may be as high as 1.5 A.

13.5 AC ELECTRICAL SPECIFICATIONS — CLOCK TIMING

Num.	Characteristic	Symbol	8 MHz*		10 MHz*		Unit
			Min	Max	Min	Max	
	Frequency of Operation	f	2.0	8.0	2.0	10.0	MHz
1	Clock Period	t_{cyc}	125	500	100	500	ns
2,3	Clock Pulse Width	t_{CL}, t_{CH}	55	250	45	250	ns
4,5	Clock Rise and Fall Times	t_{Cr}, t_{Cf}	—	10	—	10	ns

*These specifications represent an improvement over previously published specifications for the 8- and 10-MHz MC68008 and are valid only for product bearing date codes of 8827 and later.

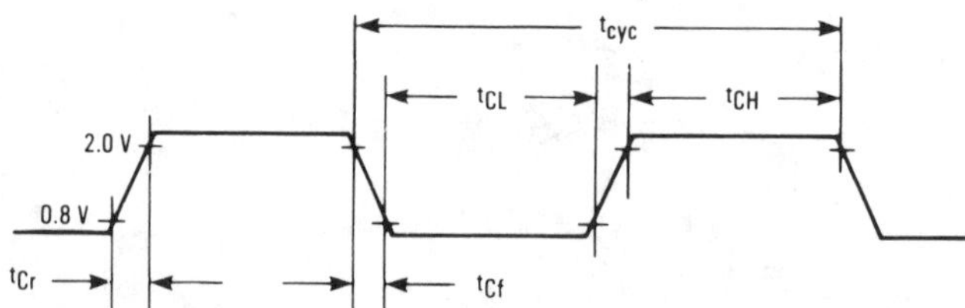

NOTE: Timing measurements are referenced to and from a low voltage of 0.8 volt and high a voltage 2.0 volts, unless otherwise noted. The voltage swing through this range should stat outside and pass through the range such that the rise or fall will be linear between 0.8 volt and 2.0 volts.

Figure 13-2. MC68008 Clock Input Timing Diagram

13.6 AC ELECTRICAL SPECIFICATION DEFINITIONS

The AC specifications presented consist of output delays, input setup and hold times, and signal skew times. All signals are specified relative to an appropriate edge of the clock and possibly to one or more other signals.

The measurement of the AC specifications is defined by the waveforms shown in Figure 13-3. In order to test the parameters guaranteed by Motorola, inputs must be driven to the voltage levels specified in this figure. Outputs are specified with minimum and/or maximum limits, as appropriate, and are measured as shown in Figure 13-3. Inputs are specified with minimum setup and hold times, and are measured as shown. Finally, the measurement for signal-to-signal specifications are also shown.

NOTES

The testing levels used to verify conformance to the AC specifications does not affect the guaranteed DC operation of the device as specified in the DC electrical characteristics.

13

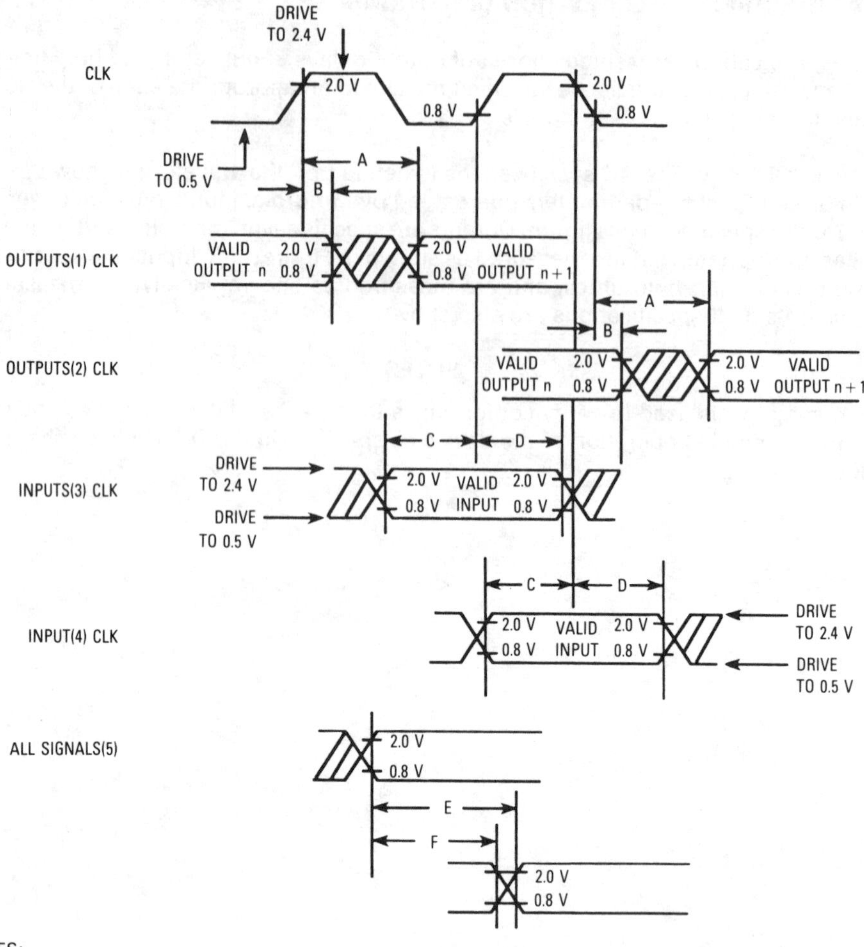

NOTES:

1. This output timing is applicable to all parameters specified relative to the rising edge of the clock.
2. This output timing is applicable to all parameters specified relative to the falling edge of the clock.
3. This input timing is applicable to all parameters specified relative to the rising edge of the clock.
4. This input timing is applicable to all parameters specified relative to the falling edge of the clock.
5. This timing is applicable to all parameters specified relative to the assertion/negation of another signal.

LEGEND:

A. Maximum output delay specification.
B. Minimum output hold time.
C. Minimum input setup time specification.
D. Minimum input hold time specification.
E. Signal valid to signal valid specification (maximum or minimum).
F. Signal valid to signal invalid specification (maximum or minimum).

Figure 13-3. Drive Levels and Test Points for AC Specifications

13

13.7 AC ELECTRICAL SPECIFICATIONS — READ AND WRITE CYCLES

(V_{CC} = 5.0 Vdc ± 5%; GND = 0 Vdc; $T_A = T_L$ to T_H; see Figures 13-4 and 13-5)

Num.	Characteristic	Symbol	8 MHz* Min	8 MHz* Max	10 MHz* Min	10 MHz* Max	Unit
6	Clock Low to Address Valid	t_{CLAV}	—	62	—	50	ns
6A	Clock High to FC Valid	t_{CHFCV}	—	62	—	50	ns
7	Clock High to Address, Data Bus High Impedance (Maximum)	t_{CHADZ}	—	80	—	70	ns
8	Clock High to Address, FC Invalid (Minimum)	t_{CHAFI}	0	—	0	—	ns
9[1]	Clock High to $\overline{AS}$, $\overline{DS}$ Asserted	t_{CHSL}	3	60	3	50	ns
11[2]	Address Valid to $\overline{AS}$, $\overline{DS}$ Asserted (Read)/$\overline{AS}$ Asserted (Write)	t_{AVSL}	30	—	20	—	ns
11A[2]	FC Valid to $\overline{AS}$, $\overline{DS}$ Asserted (Read)/$\overline{AS}$ Asserted (Write)	t_{FCVSL}	90	—	70	—	ns
12[1]	Clock Low to $\overline{AS}$, $\overline{DS}$ Negated	t_{CLSH}	—	62	—	50	ns
13[2]	$\overline{AS}$, $\overline{DS}$ Negated to Address, FC Invalid	t_{SHAFI}	40	—	30	—	ns
14[2]	$\overline{AS}$ (and $\overline{DS}$ Read) Width Asserted	t_{SL}	270	—	195	—	ns
14A[2]	$\overline{DS}$ Width Asserted (Write)	t_{DSL}	140	—	95	—	ns
15[2]	$\overline{AS}$, $\overline{DS}$ Width Negated	t_{SH}	150	—	105	—	ns
16	Clock High to Control Bus High Impedance	t_{CHCZ}	—	80	—	70	ns
17[2]	$\overline{AS}$, $\overline{DS}$ Negated to R/$\overline{W}$ Invalid	t_{SHRH}	40	—	30	—	ns
18[1]	Clock High to R/$\overline{W}$ High (Read)	t_{CHRH}	0	55	0	45	ns
20[1]	Clock High to R/$\overline{W}$ Low (Write)	t_{CHRL}	0	55	0	45	ns
20A[2, 6]	$\overline{AS}$ Asserted to R/$\overline{W}$ Valid (Write)	t_{ASRV}	—	10	—	10	ns
21[2]	Address Valid to R/$\overline{W}$ Low (Write)	t_{AVRL}	20	—	0	—	ns
21A[2]	FC Valid to R/$\overline{W}$ Low (Write)	t_{FCVRL}	60	—	50	—	ns
22[2]	R/$\overline{W}$Low to $\overline{DS}$ Asserted (Write)	t_{RLSL}	80	—	50	—	ns
23	Clock Low to Data-Out Valid (Write)	t_{CLDO}	—	62	—	50	ns
25[2]	$\overline{AS}$, $\overline{DS}$ Negated to Data-Out Invalid (Write)	t_{SHDOI}	50	—	30	—	ns
26[2]	Data-Out Valid to $\overline{DS}$ Asserted (Write)	t_{DOSL}	40	—	30	—	ns
27[5]	Data-In Valid to Clock Low (Setup Time of Read)	t_{DICL}	10	—	10	—	ns
28[2]	$\overline{AS}$, $\overline{DS}$ Negated to $\overline{DTACK}$ Negated (Asynchronous Hold)	t_{SHDAH}	0	245	0	190	ns
29	$\overline{AS}$, $\overline{DS}$ Negated to Data-In Invalid (Hold Time on Read)	t_{SHDII}	0	—	0	—	ns
29A	$\overline{AS}$, $\overline{DS}$ Negated to Data In High Impedance	t_{SHDZ}	—	187	—	150	ns
30	$\overline{AS}$, $\overline{DS}$ Negated to $\overline{BERR}$ Negated	t_{SHBEH}	0	—	0	—	ns
31[2, 5]	$\overline{DTACK}$ Asserted to Data In Valid (Setup Time)	t_{DALDI}	—	90	—	65	ns
32	$\overline{HALT}$ and $\overline{RESET}$ Input Transition Time	$t_{RHr,f}$	0	200	0	200	ns
33	Clock High to $\overline{BG}$ Asserted	t_{CHGL}	—	62	—	50	ns
34	Clock High to $\overline{BG}$ Negated	t_{CHGH}	—	62	—	50	ns
35	$\overline{BR}$ Asserted to $\overline{BG}$ Asserted	t_{BRLGL}	1.5	3.5	1.5	3.5	Clks
36[7]	$\overline{BR}$ Negated to $\overline{BG}$ Negated	t_{BRHGH}	1.5	3.5	1.5	3.5	Clks
37	$\overline{BGACK}$ Asserted to $\overline{BG}$ Negated (52-Pin Version Only)	t_{GALGH}	1.5	3.5	1.5	3.5	Clks
37A[8]	$\overline{BGACK}$ Asserted to $\overline{BR}$ Negated (52-Pin Version Only)	t_{GALBRH}	20	1.5 Clks	20	1.5 Clks	ns
38	$\overline{BG}$ Asserted to Control, Address, Data Bus High Impedance ($\overline{AS}$ Negated)	t_{GLZ}	—	80	—	70	ns
39	$\overline{BG}$ Width Negated	t_{GH}	1.5	—	1.5	—	Clks
41	Clock Low to E Transition	t_{CLET}	—	50	—	45	ns
42	E Output Rise and Fall Time	$t_{Er,f}$	—	15	—	15	ns
44	$\overline{AS}$, $\overline{DS}$ Negated to $\overline{VPA}$ Negated	t_{SHVPH}	0	120	0	90	ns
45	E Low to Control, Address Bus Invalid (Address Hold Time)	t_{ELCAI}	30	—	10	—	ns

13.7 AC ELECTRICAL SPECIFICATIONS — READ AND WRITE CYCLES (Continued)

Num.	Characteristic	Symbol	8 MHz*		10 MHz*		Unit
			Min	Max	Min	Max	
46	$\overline{\text{BGACK}}$ Width Low (52-Pin Version Only)	t_{GAL}	1.5	—	1.5	—	Clks
47[5]	Asynchronous Input Setup Time	t_{ASI}	10	—	10	—	ns
48[2, 3]	$\overline{\text{DTACK}}$ Asserted to $\overline{\text{BERR}}$ Asserted	t_{BELDAL}	20	—	20	—	ns
49[9]	$\overline{\text{AS}}$, $\overline{\text{DS}}$, Negated to E Low	t_{SHEL}	−70	70	−55	55	ns
50	E Width High	t_{EH}	450	—	350	—	ns
51	E Width Low	t_{EL}	700	—	550	—	ns
53	Data-Out Hold from Clock High	t_{CHDOI}	0	—	0	—	ns
54	E Low to Data-Out Invalid	t_{ELDOI}	30	—	20	—	ns
55	R/$\overline{\text{W}}$ Asserted to Data Bus Impedance Change	t_{RLDBD}	30	—	20	—	ns
56[4]	$\overline{\text{HALT}}$/$\overline{\text{RESET}}$ Pulse Width	t_{HRPW}	10	—	10	—	Clks
57	$\overline{\text{BGACK}}$ Negated to $\overline{\text{AS}}$, $\overline{\text{DS}}$, R/$\overline{\text{W}}$ Driven (52-Pin Version Only)	t_{GASD}	1.5	—	1.5	—	Clks
57A	$\overline{\text{BGACK}}$ Negated to FC, $\overline{\text{VMA}}$ Driven (52-Pin Version Only)	t_{GAFD}	1	—	1	—	Clks
58[7]	$\overline{\text{BR}}$ Negated to $\overline{\text{AS}}$, $\overline{\text{DS}}$, R/$\overline{\text{W}}$ Driven	t_{RHSD}	1.5	—	1.5	—	Clks
58A[7]	$\overline{\text{BR}}$ Negated to FC, $\overline{\text{VMA}}$ Driven	t_{RHFD}	1	—	1	—	Clks

*These specifications represent an improvement over previously published specifications for the 8- and 10-MHz MC68008 and are valid only for product bearing date codes of 8827 and later.

NOTES:

1. For a loading capacitance of less than or equal to 50 picofarads, subtract 5 nanoseconds from the value given in the maximum columns.
2. Actual value depends on clock period.
3. If #47 is satisfied for both $\overline{\text{DTACK}}$ and $\overline{\text{BERR}}$, #48 may be ignored. In the absence of $\overline{\text{DTACK}}$, $\overline{\text{BERR}}$ is an asynchronous input using the asynchronous input setup time (#47).
4. For power-up, the MC68008 must be held in the $\overline{\text{RESET}}$ state for 100 milliseconds to allow stabilization of on-chip circuitry. After the system is powered up, #56 refers to the minimum pulse width required to reset the processor.
5. If the asynchronous input setup time (#47) requirement is satisfied for $\overline{\text{DTACK}}$, the $\overline{\text{DTACK}}$-asserted to data setup time (#31) requirement can be ignored. The data must only satisfy the data-in to clock low setup time (#27) for the following clock cycle.
6. When $\overline{\text{AS}}$ and R/$\overline{\text{W}}$ are equally loaded (±20%), subtract 5 nanoseconds from the values given in these columns.
7. The processor will negate $\overline{\text{BG}}$ and begin driving the bus again if external arbitration logic negates $\overline{\text{BR}}$ before asserting $\overline{\text{BGACK}}$.
8. The minimum value must be met to guarantee power operation. If the maximum value is exceeded, $\overline{\text{BG}}$ may be reasserted.
9. The falling edge of S6 triggers both the negation of the strobes ($\overline{\text{AS}}$ and $\overline{\text{xDS}}$) and the falling edge of E. Either of these events can occur first, depending upon the loading on each signal. Specification #49 indicates the absolute maximum skew that will occur between the rising edge of the strobes and the falling edge of the E clock.

These waveforms should only be referenced to the edge-to-edge measurement of the timing specifications. They are not intended as a functional description of the input and output signals. Refer to other functional descriptions and their related diagrams for device operation.

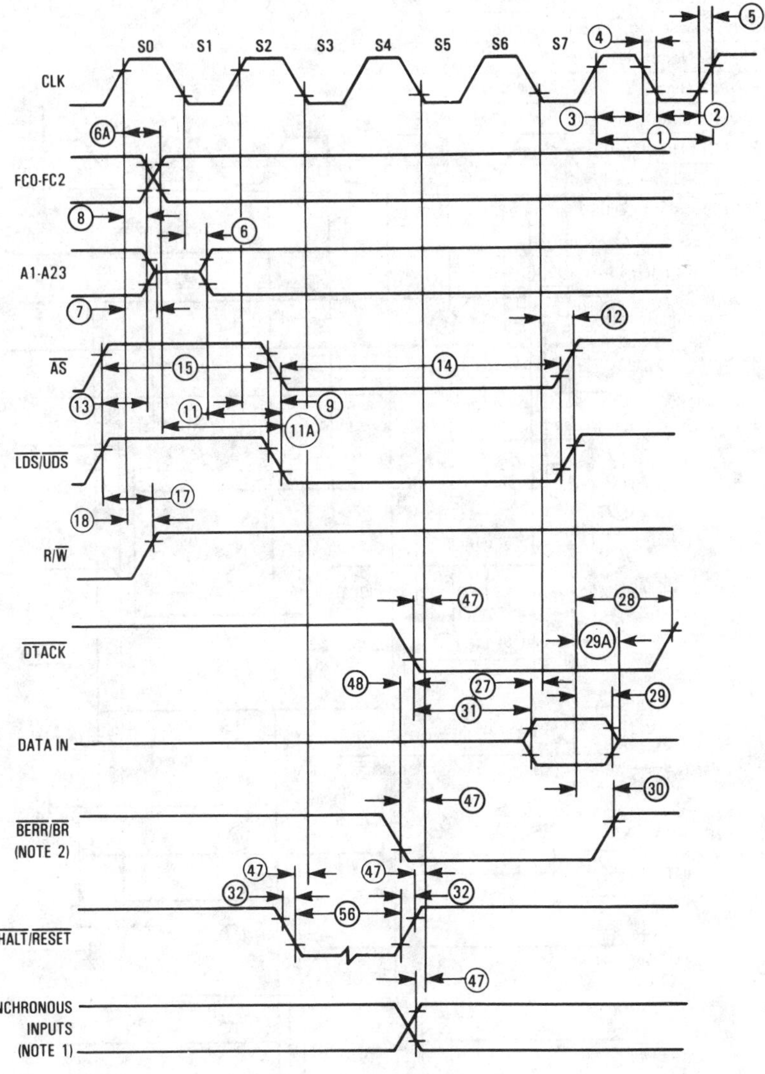

NOTES:

1. Setup time for the asynchronous inputs $\overline{IPL0}/\overline{IPL2}$, $\overline{IPL1}$, and $\overline{VPA}$ (#47) guarantees their recognition at the next falling edge of the clock.
2. $\overline{BR}$ need fall at this time only in order to insure being recognized at the end of this bus cycle.
3. Timing measurements are referenced to and from a low-voltage of 0.8 volts and a high voltage of 2.0 volts, unless otherwise noted.

Figure 13-4. MC68008 Read-Cycle Timing Diagram

13

These waveforms should only be referenced to the edge-to-edge measurement of the timing specifications. They are not intended as a functional description of the input and output signals. Refer to other functional descriptions and their related diagrams for device operation.

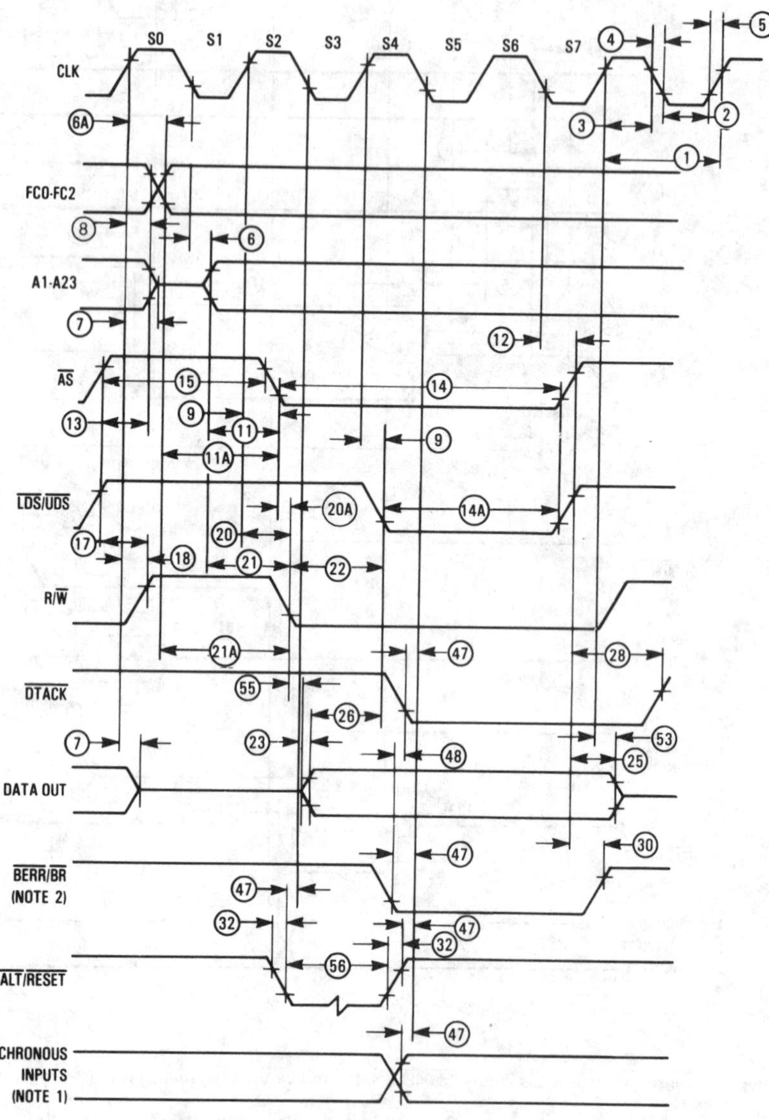

Figure 13-5. MC68008 Write-Cycle Timing Diagram

13

13.8 AC ELECTRICAL SPECIFICATIONS — MC68008 TO M6800 PERIPHERAL CYCLES

(V_{CC}=5.0 Vdc±5%; GND=0 Vdc; T_A=T_L to T_H; see Figures 13-6 and 13-7)

Num.	Characteristic	Symbol	8 MHz*		10 MHz*		Unit
			Min	Max	Min	Max	
12[1]	Clock Low to $\overline{AS}$, $\overline{DS}$ Negated	t_{CLSH}	—	62	—	50	ns
18[1]	Clock High to R/$\overline{W}$ High (Read)	t_{CHRH}	0	55	0	45	ns
20[1]	Clock High to R/$\overline{W}$ Low (Write)	t_{CHRL}	0	55	0	45	ns
23	Clock Low to Data-Out Valid (Write)	t_{CLDO}	—	62	—	50	ns
27	Data-In Valid to Clock Low (Setup Time of Read)	t_{DICL}	10	—	10	—	ns
29	$\overline{AS}$, $\overline{DS}$ Negated to Data-In Invalid (Hold Time on Read)	t_{SHDII}	0	—	0	—	ns
41	Clock Low to E Transition	t_{CLET}	—	55	—	45	ns
42	E Output Rise and Fall Time	$t_{Er,f}$	—	15	—	15	ns
44	$\overline{AS}$, $\overline{DS}$ Negated to VPA Negated	t_{SHVPH}	0	120	0	90	ns
45	E Low to Control, Address Bus Invalid (Address Hold Time)	t_{ELCAI}	30	—	10	—	ns
47	Asynchronous Input Setup Time	t_{ASI}	10	—	10	—	ns
49[2]	$\overline{AS}$, $\overline{DS}$, Negated to E Low	t_{SHEL}	−70	70	−55	55	ns
50	E Width High	t_{EH}	450	—	350	—	ns
51	E Width Low	t_{EL}	700	—	550	—	ns
54	E Low to Data-Out Invalid	t_{ELDOI}	30	—	20	—	ns

*These specifications represent an improvement over previously published specifications for the 8- and 10-MHz MC68008 and are valid only for product bearing date codes of 8827 and later.

NOTES:

1. For a loading capacitance of less or equal to 50 picofarads, subtract 5 nanoseconds from the value given in the maximum columns.
2. The falling edge of S6 triggers both the negation of the strobes ($\overline{AS}$ and $\overline{xDS}$) and the falling edge of E. Either of these events can occur first, depending upon the loading on each signal. Specification #49 indicates the absolute maximum skew that will occur between the rising edge of the strobes and the falling edge of the E clock.

These waveforms should only be referenced to the edge-to-edge measurement of the timing specifications. They are not intended as a functional description of the input and output signals. Refer to other functional descriptions and their related diagrams for device operation.

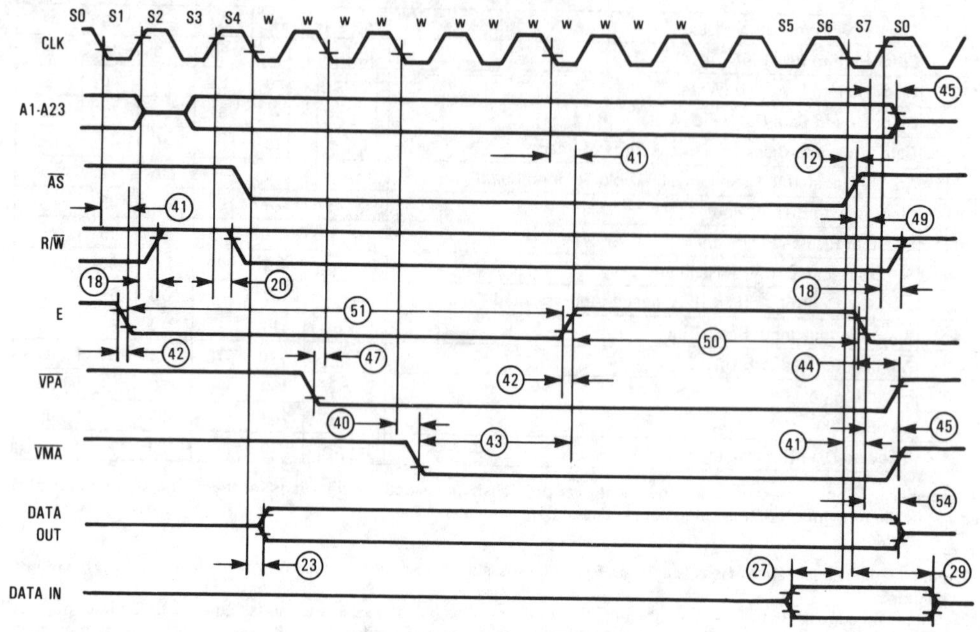

NOTE: This timing diagram is included for those who wish to design their own circuit to generate $\overline{\text{VMA}}$. It shows the best case possibly attainable.

13

Figure 13-6. MC68008 to M6800 Peripheral Timing Diagram (Best Case)

These waveforms should only be referenced to the edge-to-edge measurement of the timing specifications. They are not intended as a functional description of the input and output signals. Refer to other functional descriptions and their related diagrams for device operation.

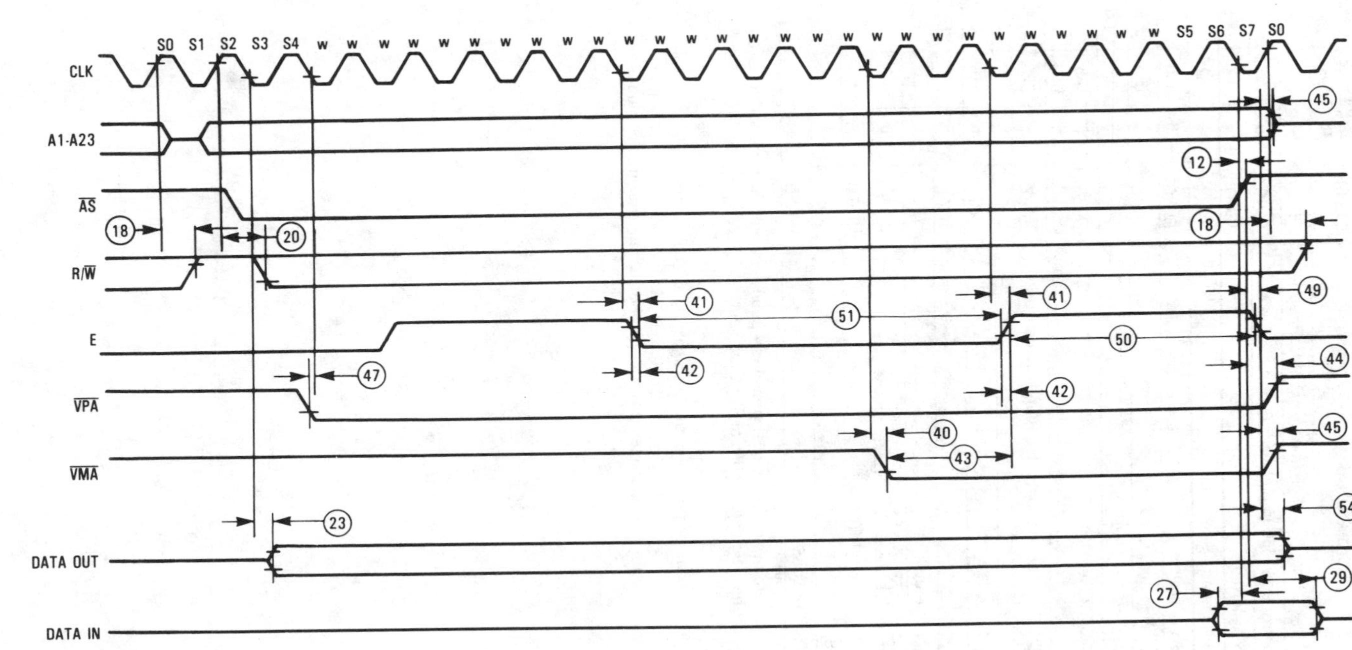

NOTE: This timing diagram is included for those who wish to design their own circuit to generate $\overline{VMA}$. It shows the worst case possibly attainable

Figure 13-7. MC68008 to M6800 Peripheral Timing Diagram (Worst Case)

13

13.9 AC ELECTRICAL SPECIFICATIONS — BUS ARBITRATION

(V_{CC}=5.0 Vdc±5%; GND=0 Vdc; T_A=T_L to T_H; see Figures 13-8, 13-9, and 13-10)

Num	Characteristic	Symbol	8 MHz*		10 MHz*		Unit
			Min	Max	Min	Max	
7	Clock High to Address, Data Bus High Impedance (Maximum)	t_{CHADZ}	—	80	—	70	ns
16	Clock High to Control Bus High Impedance	t_{CHCZ}	—	80	—	70	ns
33	Clock High to $\overline{BG}$ Asserted	t_{CHGL}	—	62	—	50	ns
34	Clock High to $\overline{BG}$ Negated	t_{CHGH}	—	62	—	50	ns
35	$\overline{BR}$ Asserted to $\overline{BG}$ Asserted	t_{BRLGL}	1.5	3.5	1.5	3.5	Clks
36[1]	$\overline{BR}$ Negated to $\overline{BG}$ Negated	t_{BRHGH}	1.5	3.5	1.5	3.5	Clks
37	$\overline{BGACK}$ Asserted to $\overline{BG}$ Negated	t_{GALGH}	1.5	3.5	1.5	3.5	Clks
37A[2]	$\overline{BGACK}$ Asserted to $\overline{BR}$ Negated	t_{GALBRH}	20	1.5 Clks	20	1.5 Clks	ns
38	$\overline{BG}$ Asserted to Control, Address, Data Bus High Impedance ($\overline{AS}$ Negated)	t_{GLZ}	—	80	—	70	ns
39	$\overline{BG}$ Width Negated	t_{GH}	1.5	—	1.5	—	Clks
46	$\overline{BGACK}$ Width Low	t_{GAL}	1.5	—	1.5	—	Clks
47	Asynchronous Input Setup Time	t_{ASI}	10	—	10	—	ns
57	$\overline{BGACK}$ Negated to $\overline{AS}$, $\overline{DS}$, R/$\overline{W}$ Driven	t_{GASD}	1.5	—	1.5	—	Clks
57A	$\overline{BGACK}$ Negated to FC, $\overline{VMA}$ Driven	t_{GAFD}	1	—	1	—	Clks
58[1]	$\overline{BR}$ Negated to $\overline{AS}$, $\overline{DS}$, R/$\overline{W}$ Driven	t_{RHSD}	1.5	—	1.5	—	Clks
58A[1]	$\overline{BR}$ Negated to FC, $\overline{VMA}$ Driven	t_{RHFD}	1	—	1	—	Clks

*These specifications represent an improvement over previously published specifications for the 8- and 10-MHz MC68008 and are valid only for product bearing dates codes of 8827 and later.

NOTES:

1. The processor will negate $\overline{BG}$ and begin driving the bus again if external arbitration logic negates $\overline{BR}$ before asserting $\overline{BGACK}$.
2. The minimum value must be met to guarantee proper operation. If the maximum value is exceeded, $\overline{BG}$ may be reasserted.

13

These waveforms should only be referenced to the edge-to-edge measurement of the timing specifications. They are not intended as a functional description of the input and output signals. Refer to other functional descriptions and their related diagrams for device operation.

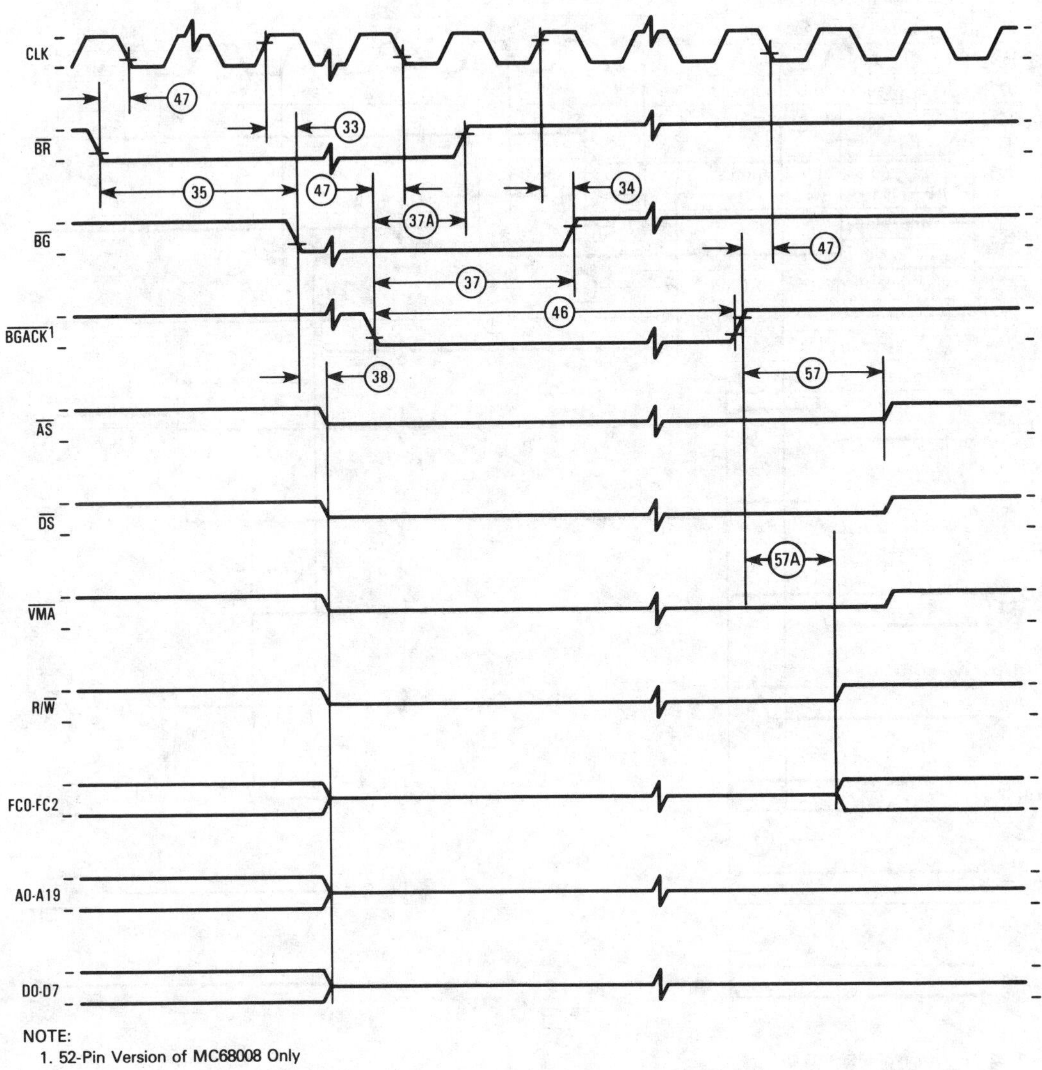

Figure 13-8. MC68008 Bus Arbitration Timing — Idle Bus Case (52-pin Version Only)

13

These waveforms should only be referenced to the edge-to-edge measurement of the timing specifications. They are not intended as a functional description of the input and output signals. Refer to other functional descriptions and their related diagrams for device operation.

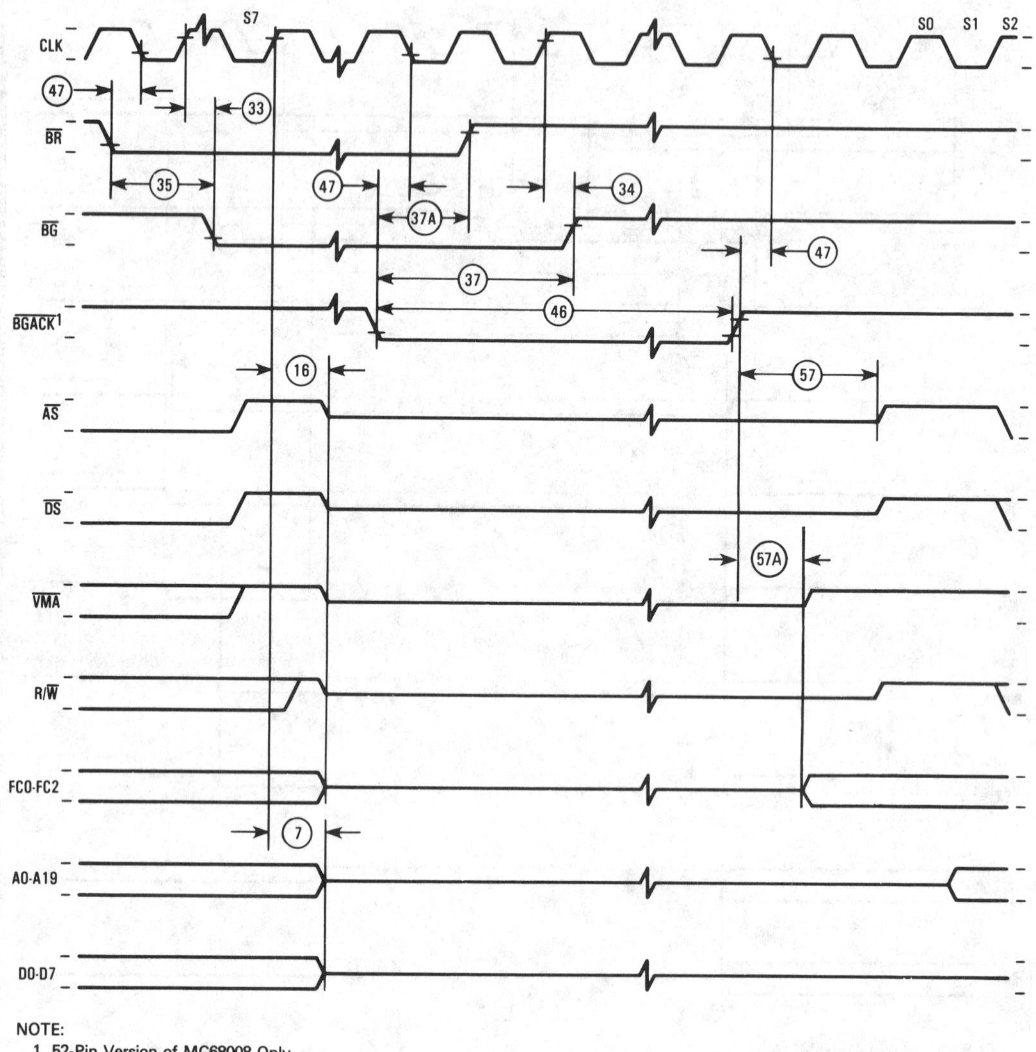

NOTE:
1. 52-Pin Version of MC68008 Only

Figure 13-9. MC68008 Bus Arbitration Timing — Active Bus Case (52-pin Version Only)

13

These waveforms should only be referenced to the edge-to-edge measurement of the timing specifications. They are not intended as a functional description of the input and output signals. Refer to other functional descriptions and their related diagrams for device operation.

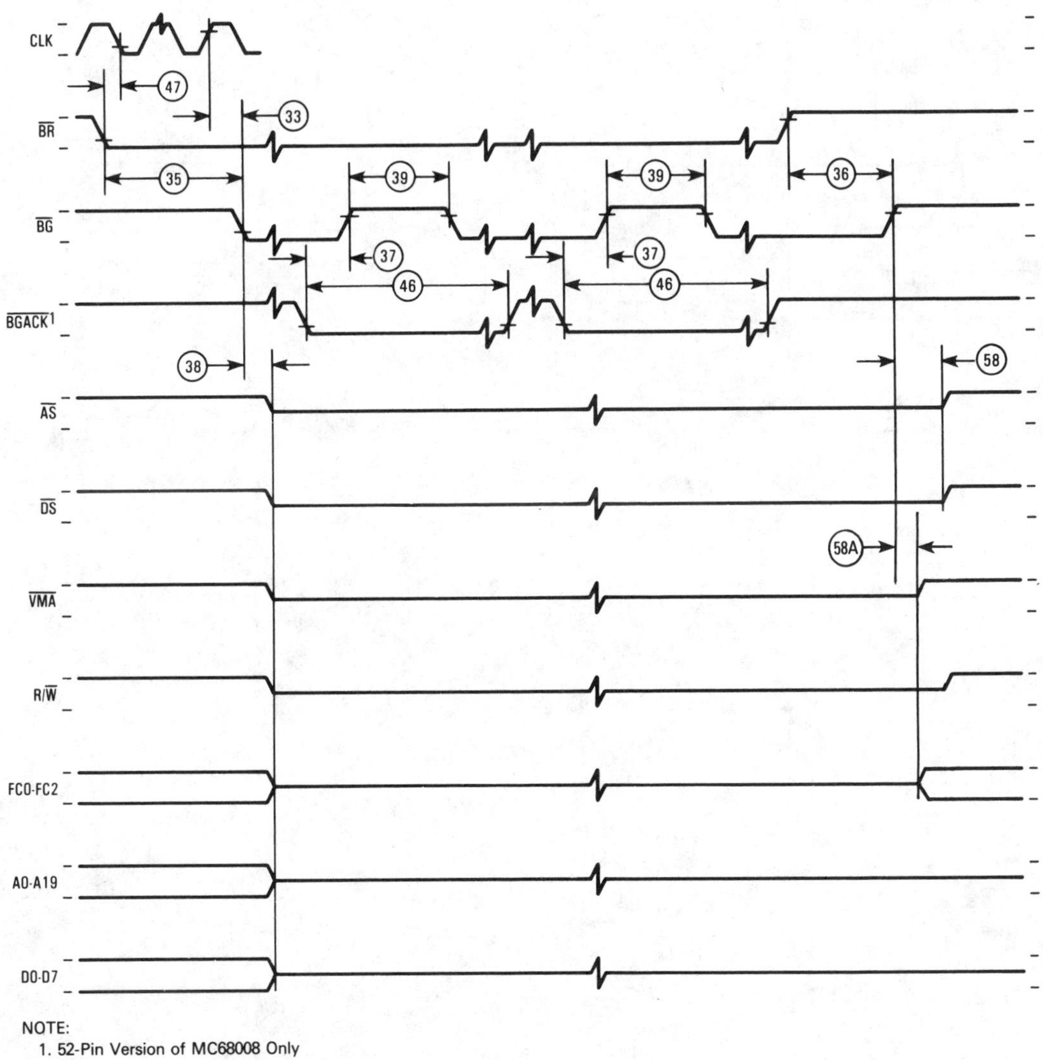

NOTE:
1. 52-Pin Version of MC68008 Only

Figure 13-10. MC68008 Bus Arbitration Timing — Multiple Bus Requests (52-pin Version)

13

13

SECTION 14
MC68010 ELECTRICAL SPECIFICATIONS

The electrical specifications for the MC68010 microprocessor are shown in this section.

14.1 MAXIMUM RATINGS

Rating	Symbol	Value	Unit
Supply Voltage	V_{CC}	−0.3 to +7.0	V
Input Voltage	V_{in}	−0.3 to +7.0	V
Operating Temperature Range MC68010 MC68010C	T_A	T_L to T_H 0 to 70 −40 to +85	°C
Storage Temperature	T_{stg}	−55 to +150	°C

The device contains circuitry to protect the inputs against damage due to high static voltages or electric fields; however, normal precautions should be taken to avoid application of voltages higher than maximum-rated voltages to these high-impedance circuits. Tying unused inputs to the appropriate logic voltage level (e.g., either GND or V_{CC}) enhances reliability of operation.

14.2 THERMAL CHARACTERISTICS

Characteristic	Symbol	Value	Symbol	Value	Rating
Thermal Resistance (Still Air)	θ_{JA}		θ_{JC}		°C/W
Ceramic, Type L/LC		30		15*	
Ceramic, Type R/RC		33		15	
Plastic, Type P		30		15*	
Plastic, Type FN		45*		25*	

*Estimated

14.3 POWER CONSIDERATIONS

The average die-junction temperature T_J in °C can be obtained from:

$$T_J = T_A + (P_D \cdot \theta_{JA}) \quad (1)$$

where:

T_A = Ambient Temperature, °C

θ_{JA} = Package Thermal Resistance, Junction-to-Ambient, °C/W

P_D = $P_{INT} + P_{I/O}$

P_{INT} = $I_{CC} \times V_{CC}$, Watts — Chip Internal Power

$P_{I/O}$ = Power Dissipation on Input and Output Pins — User Determined

For most applications $P_{I/O} < P_{INT}$ and can be neglected. An appropriate relationship between P_D and T_J (if $P_{I/O}$ is neglected) is:

$$P_D = K/(T_J + 273\ °C) \quad (2)$$

Solving equations (1) and (2) for K gives:

$$K = P_D \cdot (T_A + 273°C) + \theta_{JA} \cdot {P_D}^2 \quad (3)$$

where K is a constant pertaining to the particular part. K can be determined from equation (3) by measuring P_D (at thermal equilibrium) for a known T_A. Using this value of K, the values of P_D and T_J can be obtained by solving equations (1) and (2) iteratively for any value of T_A.

14

The curve shown in Figure 14-1 provides the graphic solution to these equations for the specified power dissipation of 1.5 watts over the ambient temperature range of −55 °C to +125 °C using a maximum θ_{JA} of 45 °C/W. Ambient temperature is that of the still air surrounding the device. Lower values of θ_{JA} cause the curve to shift downward slightly; for instance, for θ_{JA} of 40 °/W, the curve is just below 1.4 watts at 25 °C.

The total thermal resistance of a package (θ_{JA}) can be separated into two components, θ_{JC} and θ_{CA}, representing the barrier to heat flow from the semiconductor junction to the package (case) surface (θ_{JC}) and from the case to the outside ambient air θ_{CA}). These terms are related by the equation:

$$\theta_{JA} = \theta_{JC} + \theta_{CA} \quad (4)$$

Variable θ_{JC} is device related and cannot be influenced by the user. However, θ_{CA} is user dependent and can be minimized by heat sinks, ambient air cooling, thermal convection, and other thermal management techniques. Thus, good thermal management on the part of the user can significantly reduce θ_{CA} so that θ_{JA} approximately equals θ_{JC}. Substitution of θ_{JC} for θ_{JA} in equation 1 results in a lower semiconductor junction temperature.

For the MC68010 microprocessor, Table 14-1 summarizes maximum power dissipation and average junction temperature for the curve drawn in Figure 14-1, using the minimum and maximum values of ambient temperature for different packages and substituting θ_{JC} for θ_{JA} (assuming good thermal management). Table 14-2 provides the maximum power dissipation and average junction temperature for the MC68010 assuming that no thermal management is applied (i.e., still air).

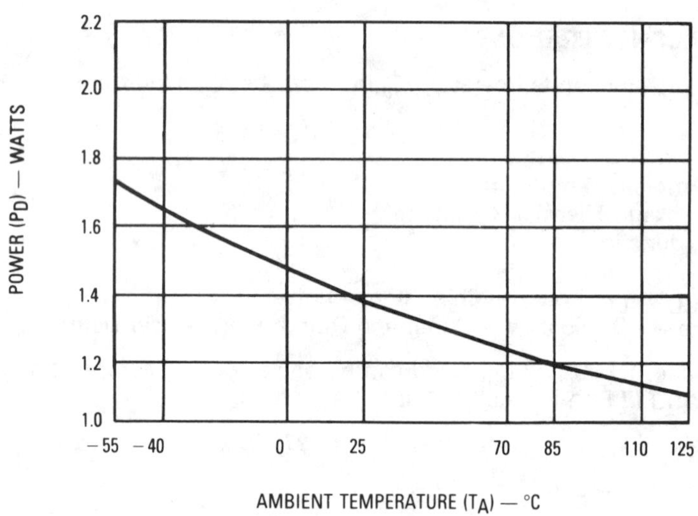

Figure 14-1. MC68010 Power Dissipation (P_D) vs Ambient Temperature (T_A)

Table 14-1. MC68010 Power Dissipation and Junction Temperature vs Temperature ($\theta_{JC} = \theta_{JA}$)

Package	T_A Range	θ_{JC} (°C/W)	P_D (W) @ T_A Min	T_J (°C) @ T_A Min	P_D (W) @ T_A Max	T_J (°C) @ T_A Max
L/LC	0°C to 70°C	15	1.5	23	1.2	88
	−40°C to +85°C	15	1.7	−14	1.2	103
	0°C to 85°C	15	1.5	23	1.2	103
P	0°C to 70°C	15	1.5	23	1.2	88
R/RC	0°C to 70°C	15	1.5	23	1.2	88
	−40°C to +85°C	15	1.7	−14	1.2	103
	0°C to 85°C	15	1.5	23	1.2	103
FN	0°C to 70°C	25	1.5	38	1.2	101

Table 14-2. MC68010 Power Dissipation and Junction Temperature vs Temperature ($\theta_{JC} \neq \theta_{JA}$)

Package	T_A Range	θ_{JA} (°C/W)	P_D (W) @ T_A Min	T_J (°C) @ T_A Min	P_D (W) @ T_A Max	T_J (°C) @ T_A Max
L/LC	0°C to 70°C	30	1.5	23	1.2	88
	−40°C to +85°C	30	1.7	−14	1.2	103
	0°C to 85°C	30	1.5	23	1.2	103
P	0°C to 70°C	30	1.5	23	1.2	88
R/RC	0°C to 70°C	33	1.5	23	1.2	88
	−40°C to +85°C	33	1.7	−14	1.2	103
	0°C to 85°C	33	1.5	23	1.2	103
FN	0°C to 70°C	40	1.5	38	1.2	101

NOTE

Since the power dissipation curve shown in Figure 14-1 is negatively sloped, power dissipation declines as ambient temperature increases. Therefore, maximum power dissipation occurs at the lowest rated ambient temperature, but the highest average junction temperature occurs at the maximum ambient temperature where *power dissipation is lowest.*

Values for thermal resistance presented in this manual, unless estimated, were derived using the procedure described in Motorola Reliability Report 7843, *Thermal Resistance Measurement Method for MC68XXX Microcomponent Devices*, and are provided for design purposes only. Thermal measurements are complex and dependent on procedure and setup. User-derived values for thermal resistance may differ.

14.4 DC ELECTRICAL CHARACTERISTICS
(V_{CC} = 5.0 Vdc ± 5%; GND = 0 Vdc; $T_A = T_L$ to T_H)

Characteristics		Symbol	Min	Max	Unit
Input High Voltage		V_{IH}	2.0	V_{CC}	V
Input Low Voltage		V_{IL}	GND −0.3	0.8	V
Input Leakage Current @ 5.25 V	$\overline{\text{BERR}}$, $\overline{\text{BGACK}}$, $\overline{\text{BR}}$, $\overline{\text{DTACK}}$, CLK, $\overline{\text{IPL0}}$-$\overline{\text{IPL2}}$, $\overline{\text{VPA}}$ $\overline{\text{HALT}}$, $\overline{\text{RESET}}$	I_{IN}	— —	2.5 20	µA
Three-State (Off State) Input Current @ 2.4V/0.4 V	$\overline{\text{AS}}$, A1-A23, D0-D15, FC0-FC2, $\overline{\text{LDS}}$, R/$\overline{\text{W}}$, $\overline{\text{UDS}}$, $\overline{\text{VMA}}$	I_{TSI}	—	20	µA
Output High Voltage (I_{OH} = −400 µA) (I_{OH} = −400 µA)	E* E, $\overline{\text{AS}}$, A1-A23, $\overline{\text{BG}}$, D0-D15, FC0-FC2, $\overline{\text{LDS}}$, R/$\overline{\text{W}}$, $\overline{\text{UDS}}$, $\overline{\text{VMA}}$	V_{OH}	V_{CC} −0.75 2.4	— 2.4	V
Output Low Voltage (I_{OL} = 1.6 mA) (I_{OL} = 3.2 mA) (I_{OL} = 5.0 mA) (I_{OL} = 5.3 mA)	 $\overline{\text{HALT}}$ A1-A23, $\overline{\text{BG}}$, FC0-FC2 $\overline{\text{RESET}}$ E, $\overline{\text{AS}}$, D0-D15, $\overline{\text{LDS}}$, R/$\overline{\text{W}}$, $\overline{\text{UDS}}$, $\overline{\text{VMA}}$	V_{OL}	 — — — —	 0.5 0.5 0.5 0.5	V
Power Dissipation (see **14.3 POWER CONSIDERATIONS**)		P_D***	—	—	W
Capacitance (V_{in} = 0 V, T_A = 25°C, Frequency = 1 MHz)**		C_{in}	—	20.0	pF
Load Capacitance	$\overline{\text{HALT}}$ All Others	C_L	— —	70 130	pF

*With external pullup resistor of 1.1K Ω.
**Capacitance is periodically sampled rather than 100% tested.
***During normal operation instantaneous V_{CC} current requirements may be as high as 1.5 A.

14.5 AC ELECTRICAL SPECIFICATIONS — CLOCK TIMING

Num.	Characteristic	Symbol	8 MHz*		10 MHz*		12.5 MHz*		Unit
			Min	Max	Min	Mat	Min	Max	
	Frequency of Operation	f	4	8	4	10	4	12.5	MHz
1	Clock Period	t_{cyc}	125	250	100	250	80	250	ns
2,3	Clock Pulse Measured from 1.5 V to 1.5 V	t_{CL}, t_{CH}	55	125	45	125	35	125	ns
4,5	Clock Rise and Fall Times	t_{Cr}, t_{Cf}	—	10	—	10	—	5	ns

*These specifications represent an improvement over previously published specifications for the 8-, 10-, and 12.5-MHz MC68010 and are valid only for product bearing date codes of 8827 and later.

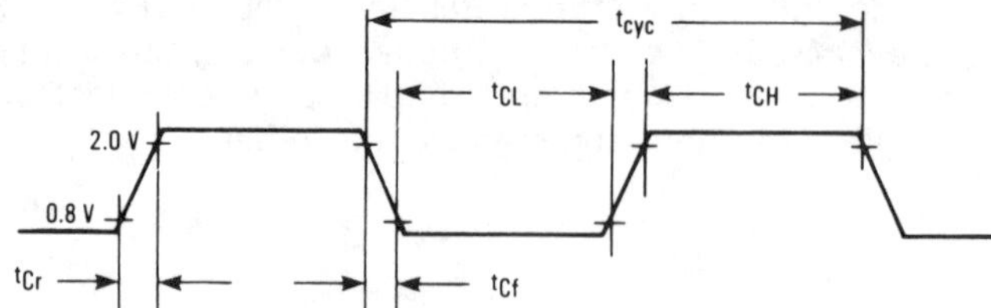

NOTE: Timing measurements are referenced to and from a low voltage of 0.8 volt and high a voltage 2.0 volts, unless otherwise noted. The voltage swing through this range should stat outside and pass through the range such that the rise or fall will be linear between 0.8 volt and 2.0 volts.

Figure 14-2. MC68010 Clock Input Timing Diagram

14.6 AC ELECTRICAL SPECIFICATION DEFINITIONS

The AC specifications presented consist of output delays, input setup and hold times, and signal skew times. All signals are specified relative to an appropriate edge of the clock and possibly to one or more other signals.

The measurement of the AC specifications is defined by the waveforms shown in Figure 14-3. In order to test the parameters guaranteed by Motorola, inputs must be driven to the voltage levels specified in this figure. Outputs are specified with minimum and/or maximum limits, as appropriate, and are measured as shown in Figure 14-3. Inputs are specified with minimum setup and hold times, and are measured as shown. Finally, the measurement for signal-to-signal specifications are also shown.

NOTE

The testing levels used to verify conformance to the AC specifications does not affect the guaranteed DC operation of the device as specified in the DC electrical characteristics.

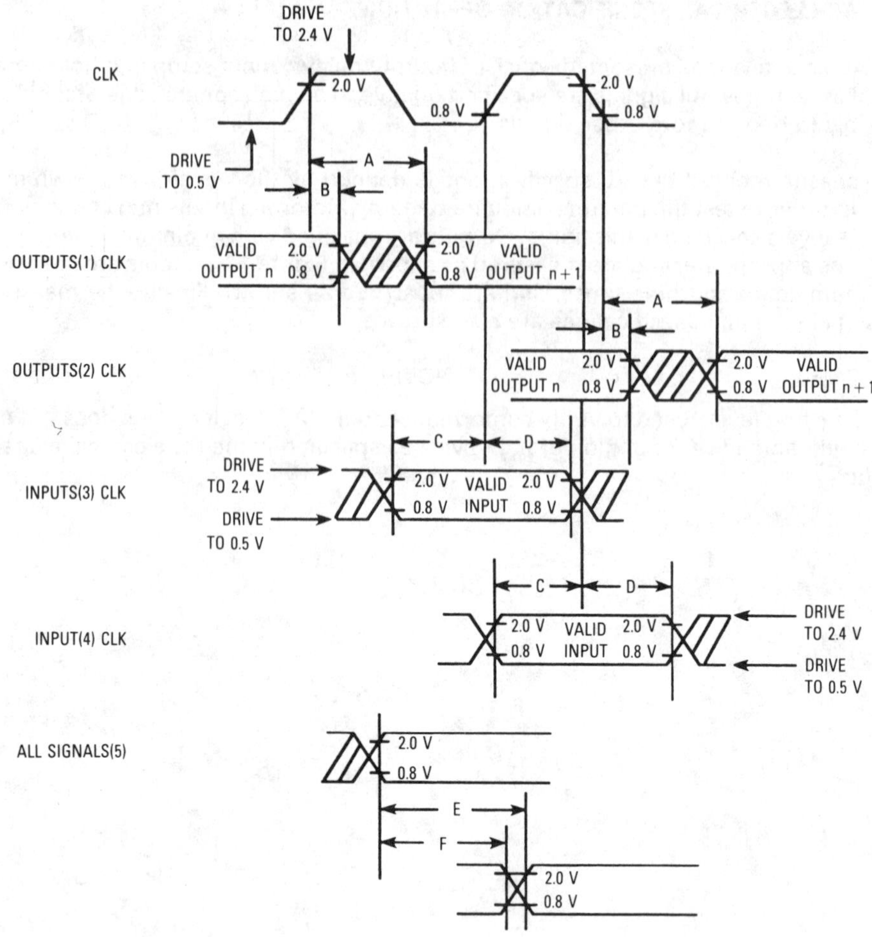

NOTES:

1. This output timing is applicable to all parameters specified relative to the rising edge of the clock.
2. This output timing is applicable to all parameters specified relative to the falling edge of the clock.
3. This input timing is applicable to all parameters specified relative to the rising edge of the clock.
4. This input timing is applicable to all parameters specified relative to the falling edge of the clock.
5. This timing is applicable to all parameters specified relative to the assertion/negation of another signal.

LEGEND:

A. Maximum output delay specification.
B. Minimum output hold time.
C. Minimum input setup time specification.
D. Minimum input hold time specification.
E. Signal valid to signal valid specification (maximum or minimum).
F. Signal valid to signal invalid specification (maximum or minimum).

Figure 14-3. Drive Levels and Test Points for AC Specifications

14.7 AC ELECTRICAL SPECIFICATIONS — READ AND WRITE CYCLES

(V_{CC} = 5.0 Vdc ± 5%; GND = 0 Vdc; T_A = T_L to T_H; see Figures 14-4 and 14-5)

Num.	Characteristic	Symbol	8 MHz*		10 MHz*		12.5 MHz*		Unit
			Min	Max	Min	Mat	Min	Max	
6	Clock Low to Address Valid	t_{CLAV}	—	62	—	50	—	50	ns
6A	Clock High to FC Valid	t_{CHFCV}	—	62	—	50	—	45	ns
7	Clock High to Address, Data Bus High Impedance (Maximum)	t_{CHADZ}	—	80	—	70	—	60	ns
8	Clock High to Address, FC Invalid (Minimum)	t_{CHAFI}	0	—	0	—	0	—	ns
9[1]	Clock High to $\overline{AS}$, $\overline{DS}$ Asserted	t_{CHSL}	3	60	3	50	3	40	ns
11[2]	Address Valid to $\overline{AS}$, $\overline{DS}$ Asserted (Read)/$\overline{AS}$ Asserted (Write)	t_{AVSL}	30	—	20	—	15	—	ns
11A[2]	FC Valid to $\overline{AS}$, $\overline{DS}$ Asserted (Read)/$\overline{AS}$ Asserted (Write)	t_{FCVSL}	90	—	70	—	60	—	ns
12[1]	Clock Low to $\overline{AS}$, $\overline{DS}$ Negated	t_{CLSH}	—	62	—	50	—	40	ns
13[2]	$\overline{AS}$, $\overline{DS}$ Negated to Address, FC Invalid	t_{SHAFI}	40	—	30	—	20	—	ns
14[2]	$\overline{AS}$ (and $\overline{DS}$ Read) Width Asserted	t_{SL}	270	—	195	—	160	—	ns
14A[2]	$\overline{DS}$ Width Asserted (Write)	t_{DSL}	140	—	95	—	80	—	ns
15[2]	$\overline{AS}$, $\overline{DS}$ Width Negated	t_{SH}	150	—	105	—	65	—	ns
16	Clock High to Control Bus High Impedance	t_{CHCZ}	—	80	—	70	—	60	ns
17[2]	$\overline{AS}$, $\overline{DS}$ Negated to R/$\overline{W}$ Invalid	t_{SHRH}	40	—	30	—	20	—	ns
18[1]	Clock High to R/$\overline{W}$ High (Read)	t_{CHRH}	0	55	0	45	0	40	ns
20[1]	Clock High to R/$\overline{W}$ Low (Write)	t_{CHRL}	0	55	0	45	0	40	ns
20A[2, 6]	$\overline{AS}$ Asserted to R/$\overline{W}$ Valid (Write)	t_{ASRV}	—	10	—	10	—	10	ns
21[2]	Address Valid to R/$\overline{W}$ Low (Write)	t_{AVRL}	20	—	0	—	0	—	ns
21A[2]	FC Valid to R/$\overline{W}$ Low (Write)	t_{FCVRL}	60	—	50	—	30	—	ns
22[2]	R/$\overline{W}$ Low to $\overline{DS}$ Asserted (Write)	t_{RLSL}	80	—	50	—	30	—	ns
23	Clock Low to Data-Out Valid (Write)	t_{CLDO}	—	62	—	50	—	50	ns
25[2]	$\overline{AS}$, $\overline{DS}$ Negated to Data-Out Invalid (Write)	t_{SHDOI}	40	—	30	—	20	—	ns
26[2]	Data-Out Valid to $\overline{DS}$ Asserted (Write)	t_{DOSL}	40	—	30	—	20	—	ns
27[5]	Data-In Valid to Clock Low (Setup Time of Read)	t_{DICL}	10	—	10	—	10	—	ns
27A[5]	Late $\overline{BERR}$ Asserted to Clock Low (Setup Time)	t_{BELCL}	45	—	45	—	45	—	ns
28[2]	$\overline{AS}$, $\overline{DS}$ Negated to $\overline{DTACK}$ Negated (Asynchronous Hold)	t_{SHDAH}	0	240	0	190	0	150	ns
29	$\overline{AS}$, $\overline{DS}$ Negated to Data-In Invalid (Hold Time on Read)	t_{SHDII}	0	—	0	—	0	—	ns
29A	$\overline{AS}$, $\overline{DS}$ Negated to Data In High Impedance	t_{SHDZ}	—	187	—	150	—	120	ns
30	$\overline{AS}$, $\overline{DS}$ Negated to $\overline{BERR}$ Negated	t_{SHBEH}	0	—	0	—	0	—	ns
31[2, 5]	$\overline{DTACK}$ Asserted to Data-In Valid (Setup Time)	t_{DALDI}	—	90	—	65	—	50	ns
32	$\overline{HALT}$ and $\overline{RESET}$ Input Transition Time	$t_{RHr,f}$	0	200	0	200	0	200	ns
33	Clock High to $\overline{BG}$ Asserted	t_{CHGL}	—	62	—	50	—	40	ns
34	Clock High to $\overline{BG}$ Negated	t_{CHGH}	—	62	—	50	—	40	ns
35	$\overline{BR}$ Asserted to $\overline{BG}$ Asserted	t_{BRLGL}	1.5	3.5	1.5	3.5	1.5	3.5	Clks
36[7]	$\overline{BR}$ Negated to $\overline{BG}$ Negated	t_{BRHGH}	1.5	3.5	1.5	3.5	1.5	3.5	Clks
37	$\overline{BGACK}$ Asserted to $\overline{BG}$ Negated	t_{GALGH}	1.5	3.5	1.5	3.5	1.5	3.5	Clks
37A[8]	$\overline{BGACK}$ Asserted to $\overline{BR}$ Negated	t_{GALBRH}	20	1.5 Clks	20	1.5 Clks	20	1.5 Clks	ns

14.7 AC ELECTRICAL SPECIFICATIONS — READ AND WRITE CYCLES (Continued)

Num.	Characteristic	Symbol	8 MHz*		10 MHz*		12.5 MHz*		Unit
			Min	Max	Min	Mat	Min	Max	
38	BG Asserted to Control, Address, Data Bus High Impedance (AS Negated)	t_{GLZ}	—	80	—	70	—	60	ns
39	BG Width Negated	t_{GH}	1.5	—	1.5	—	1.5	—	Clks
40	Clock Low to VMA Asserted	t_{CLVML}	—	70	—	70	—	70	ns
41	Clock Low to E Transition	t_{CLET}	—	55	—	45	—	35	ns
42	E Output Rise and Fall Time	$t_{Er,f}$	—	15	—	15	—	15	ns
43	VMA Asserted to E High	t_{VMLEH}	200	—	150	—	90	—	ns
44	AS, DS Negated to VPA Negated	t_{SHVPH}	0	120	0	90	0	70	ns
45	E Low to Control, Address Bus Invalid (Address Hold Time)	t_{ELCAI}	30	—	10	—	10	—	ns
46	BGACK Width Low	t_{GAL}	1.5	—	1.5	—	1.5	—	Clks
47[5]	Asynchronous Input Setup Time	t_{ASI}	10	—	10	—	10	—	ns
48[2,3,5]	DTACK Asserted to BERR Asserted	t_{DALBEL}	—	80	—	55	—	35	ns
49[9]	AS, DS, Negated to E Low	t_{SHEL}	−70	70	−55	55	−45	45	ns
50	E Width High	t_{EH}	450	—	350	—	280	—	ns
51	E Width Low	t_{EL}	700	—	550	—	440	—	ns
53	Data-Out Hold from Clock High	t_{CHDOI}	0	—	0	—	0	—	ns
54	E Low to Data-Out Invalid	t_{ELDOI}	30	—	20	—	15	—	ns
55	R/W Asserted to Data Bus Impedance Change	t_{RLDBD}	30	—	20	—	10	—	ns
56[4]	HALT/RESET Pulse Width	t_{HRPW}	10	—	10	—	10	—	Clks
57	BGACK Negated to AS, DS, R/W Driven	t_{GASD}	1.5	—	1.5	—	1.5	—	Clks
57A	BGACK Negated to FC, VMA Driven	t_{GAFD}	1	—	1	—	1	—	Clks
58[7]	BR Negated to AS, DS, R/W Driven	t_{RHSD}	1.5	—	1.5	—	1.5	—	Clks
58A[7]	BR Negated to FC, VMA Driven	t_{RHFD}	1	—	1	—	1	—	Clks

*These specifications represent an improvement over previously published specifications for the 8-, 10-, and 12.5-MHz MC68010 and are valid only for product bearing date codes of 8827 and later.

NOTES:

1. For a loading capacitance of less than or equal to 50 picofarads, subtract 5 nanoseconds from the value given in the maximum columns.
2. Actual value depends on clock period.
3. In the absence of DTACK, BERR is an asynchronous input using the asynchronous input setup time (#47).
4. For power up, the MC68010 must be held in the RESET state for 100 milliseconds to allow stabilization of on-chip circuitry. After the system is powered up, #56 refers to the minimum pulse width required to reset the processor.
5. If the asynchronous input setup time (#47) requirement is satisfied for DTACK, the DTACK-asserted to data setup time (#31) and DTACK-asserted to BERR-asserted setup time (#48) requirements can be ignored. The data must only satisfy the data-in to clock low setup time (#27) for the following clock cycle, and BERR must only satisfy the late-BERR-asserted to clock-low setup time (#27A) for the following clock cycle.
6. When AS and R/W are equally loaded (±20%), subtract 5 nanoseconds from the values given in these columns.
7. The processor will negate BG and begin driving the bus again if external arbitration logic negates BR before asserting BGACK.
8. The minimum value must be met to guarantee proper operation. If the maximum value is exceeded, BG may be reasserted.
9. The falling edge of S6 triggers both the negation of the strobes (AS and xDS) and the falling edge of E. Either of these events can occur first, depending upon the loading on each signal. Specification #49 indicates the absolute maximum skew that will occur between the rising edge of the strobes and the falling edge of the E clock.

These waveforms should only be referenced in regard to the edge-to-edge measurement of the timing specifications. They are not intended as a functional description of the input and output signals. Refer to other functional descriptions and their related diagrams for device operation.

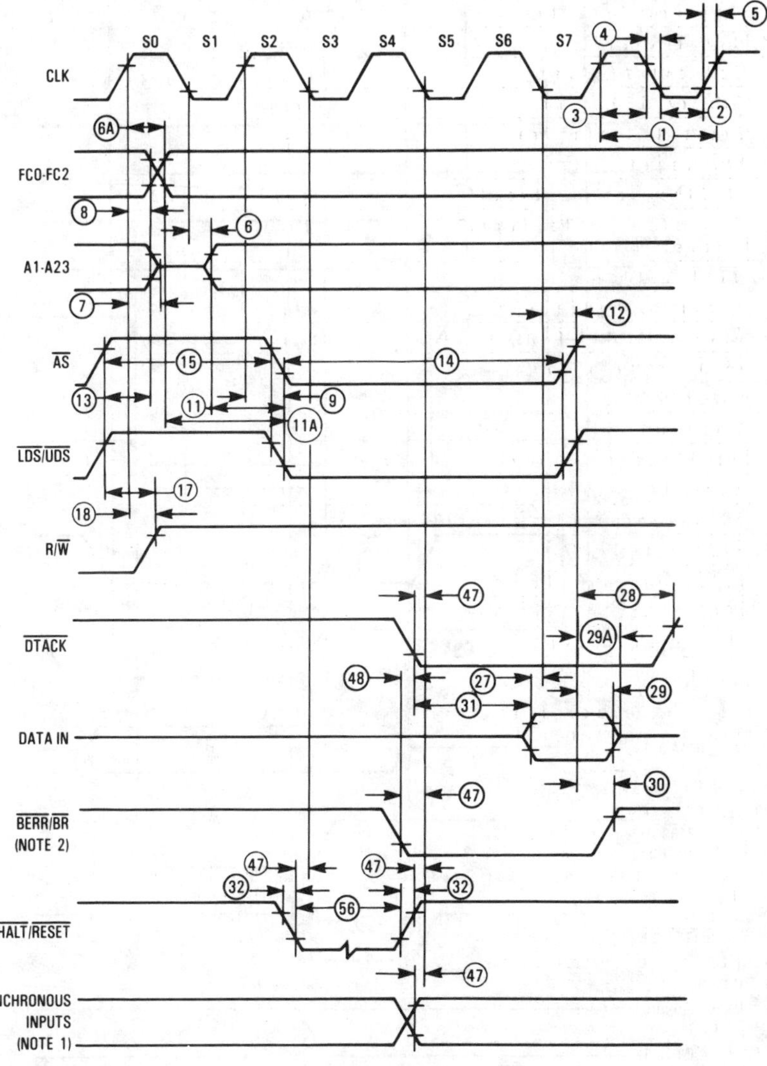

NOTES:

1. Setup time for the asynchronous inputs $\overline{IPL0}$-$\overline{IPL2}$ and $\overline{VPA}$ guarantees their recognition at the next falling edge of the clock.
2. $\overline{BR}$ need fall at this time only in order to insure being recognized at the end of this bus cycle.
3. Timing measurements are referenced to and from a low voltage of 0.8 volts and a high voltages of 2.0 volts, unless otherwise noted.
4. The timing for the first falling edge (47) of $\overline{BERR}$ are for $\overline{BERR}$ without $\overline{DTACK}$, the timings for the second falling edge (27A and 48) are for $\overline{BERR}$ with $\overline{DTACK}$.

Figure 14-4. MC68010 Read-Cycle Timing Diagram

These waveforms should only be referenced in regard to the edge-to-edge measurement of the timing specifications. They are not intended as a functional description of the input and output signals. Refer to other functional descriptions and their related diagrams for device operation.

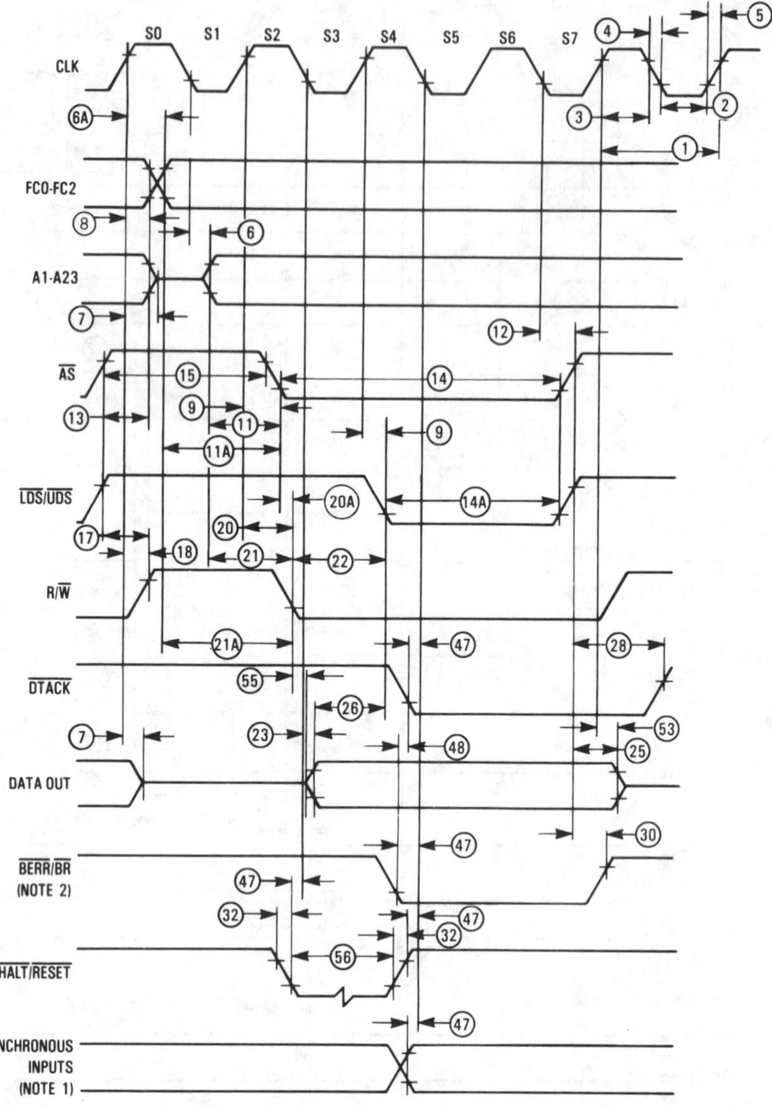

NOTES:

1. Timing measuremets are referenced to and from a low voltage of 0.8 volts and a high voltage of 2.0 volts, unless otherwise noted.
2. Because of loading variations, R/W may be valid after AS even though both are initiated by the rising edge of S2 (Specification 20A).
3. The timing for the first falling edge (47) of BERR are for BERR without DTACK, the timings for the second falling edge (27A and 48) are for BERR with DTACK.

Figure 14-5. MC68010 Write-Cycle Timing Diagram

14

14.8 AC ELECTRICAL SPECIFICATIONS — MC68010 TO M6800 PERIPHERAL CYCLES

(V_{CC}=5.0 Vdc±5%; GND=0 Vdc; T_A=T_L to T_H, see Figures 14-6 and 14-7)

Num.	Characteristic	Symbol	8 MHz*		10 MHz*		12.5 MHz*		Unit
			Min	Max	Min	Max	Min	Max	
12[1]	Clock Low to $\overline{AS}$, $\overline{DS}$ Negated	t_{CLSH}	—	62	—	50	—	40	ns
18[1]	Clock High to R/$\overline{W}$ High (Read)	t_{CHRH}	0	55	0	45	0	40	ns
20[1]	Clock High to R/$\overline{W}$ Low (Write)	t_{CHRL}	0	55	0	45	0	40	ns
23	Clock Low to Data-Out Valid (Write)	t_{CLDO}	—	62	—	50	—	50	ns
27	Data-In Valid to Clock Low (Setup Time of Read)	t_{DICL}	10	—	10	—	10	—	ns
29	$\overline{AS}$, $\overline{DS}$ Negated to Data-In Invalid (Hold Time on Read)	t_{SHDII}	0	—	0	—	0	—	ns
40	Clock Low to $\overline{VMA}$ Asserted	t_{CLVML}	—	70	—	70	—	70	ns
41	Clock Low to E Transition	t_{CLET}	—	55	—	45	—	35	ns
42	E Output Rise and Fall Time	$t_{Er,f}$	—	15	—	15	—	15	ns
43	$\overline{VMA}$ Asserted to E High	t_{VMLEH}	200	—	150	—	90	—	ns
44	$\overline{AS}$, $\overline{DS}$ Negated to $\overline{VPA}$ Negated	t_{SHVPH}	0	120	0	90	0	70	ns
45	E Low to Control, Address Bus Invalid (Address Hold Time)	t_{ELCAI}	30	—	10	—	10	—	ns
47	Asynchronous Input Setup Time	t_{ASI}	10	—	10	—	10	—	ns
49[2]	$\overline{AS}$, $\overline{DS}$, Negated to E Low	t_{SHEL}	−70	70	−55	55	−45	45	ns
50	E Width High	t_{EH}	450	—	350	—	280	—	ns
51	E Width Low	t_{EL}	700	—	550	—	440	—	ns
54	E Low to Data-Out Invalid	t_{ELDOI}	30	—	20	—	15	—	ns

*These specifications represent an improvement over previously published specifications for the 8-, 10-, and 12.5-MHz MC68010 and are valid only for product bearing date codes of 8827 and later.

NOTES:

1. For a loading capacitance of less than or equal to 50 picofarads, subtract 5 nanoseconds from the value given in the maximum columns.
2. The falling edge of S6 triggers both the negation of the strobes ($\overline{AS}$ and x$\overline{DS}$) and the falling edge of E. Either of these events can occur first, depending upon the loading on each signal. Specification #49 indicates the absolute maximum skew that will occur between the rising edge of the strobes and the falling edge of the E clock.

These waveforms should only be referenced in regard to the edge-to-edge measurement of the timing specifications. They are not intended as a functional description of the input and output signals. Refer to other functional descriptions and their related diagrams for device operation.

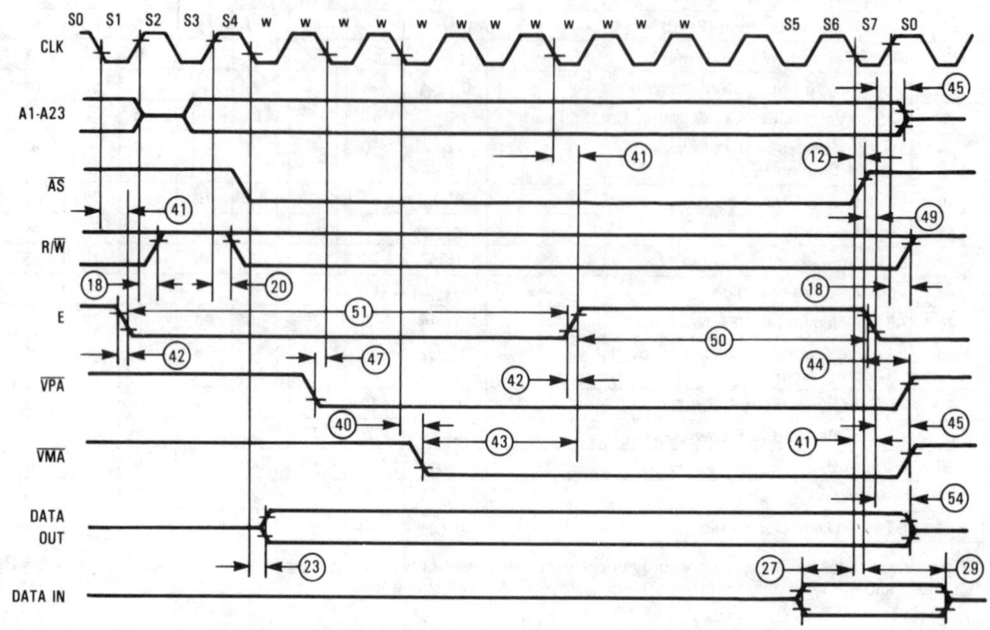

NOTE: This timing diagram is included for those who wish to design their own circuit to generate $\overline{VMA}$. It shows the best case possibly attainable.

Figure 14-6. MC68010 to M6800 Peripheral Timing Diagram (Best Case)

14

These waveforms should only be referenced in regard to the edge-to-edge measurement of the timing specifications. They are not intended as a functional description of the input and output signals. Refer to other functional descriptions and their related diagrams for device operation.

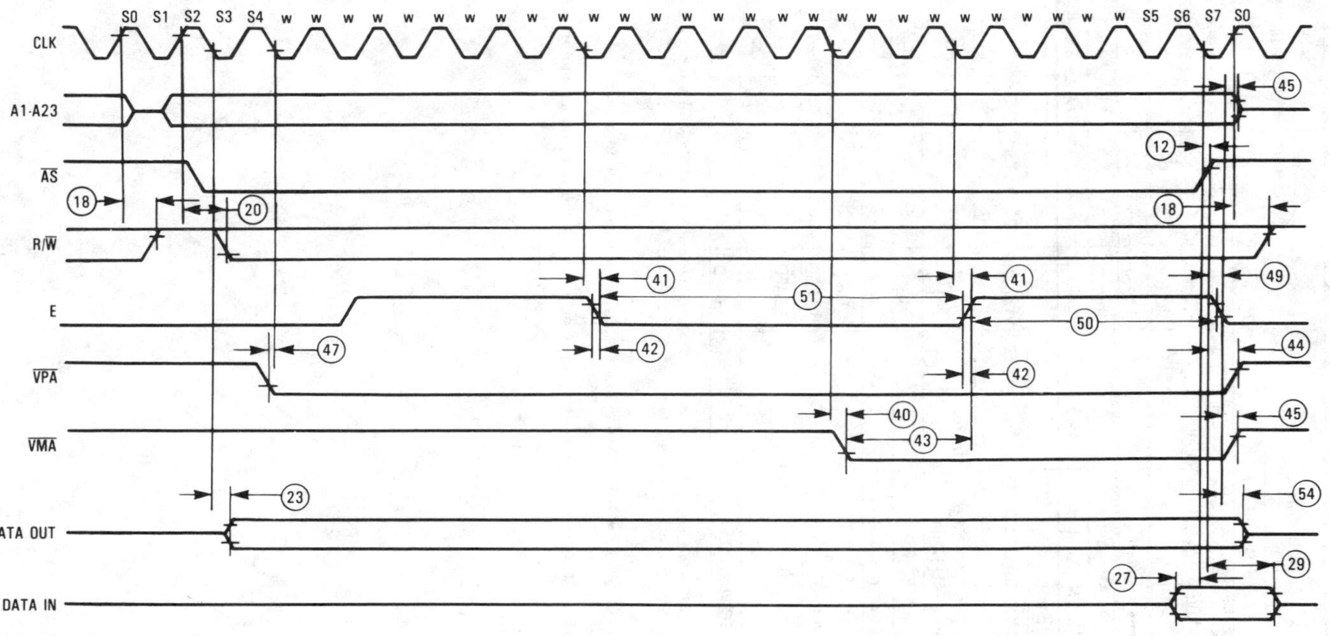

NOTE: This timing diagram is included for those who wish to design their own circuit to generate $\overline{VMA}$. It shows the worst case possibly attainable.

Figure 14-7. MC68010 to M6800 Peripheral Timing Diagram (Worst Case)

14

14.9 AC ELECTRICAL SPECIFICATIONS — BUS ARBITRATION

(V_{CC}=5.0 Vdc±5%; GND=0 Vdc; $T_A=T_L$ to T_H; see Figures 14-8, 14-9, and 14-10)

Num.	Characteristic	Symbol	8 MHz*		10 MHz*		12.5 MHz*		Unit
			Min	Max	Min	Max	Min	Max	
7	Clock High to Address, Data Bus High Impedance (Maximum)	t_{CHADZ}	—	80	—	70	—	60	ns
16	Clock High to Control Bus High Impedance	t_{CHCZ}	—	80	—	70	—	60	ns
33	Clock High to $\overline{BG}$ Asserted	t_{CHGL}	—	62	—	50	—	40	ns
34	Clock High to $\overline{BG}$ Negated	t_{CHGH}	—	62	—	50	—	40	ns
35	$\overline{BR}$ Asserted to $\overline{BG}$ Asserted	t_{BRLGL}	1.5	3.5	1.5	3.5	1.5	3.5	Clks
36[1]	$\overline{BR}$ Negated to $\overline{BG}$ Negated	t_{BRHGH}	1.5	3.5	1.5	3.5	1.5	3.5	Clks
37	$\overline{BGACK}$ Asserted to $\overline{BG}$ Negated	t_{GALGH}	1.5	3.5	1.5	3.5	1.5	3.5	Clks
37A[2]	$\overline{BGACK}$ Asserted to $\overline{BR}$ Negated	t_{GALBRH}	20	1.5 Clks	20	1.5 Clks	20	1.5 Clks	ns
38	$\overline{BG}$ Asserted to Control, Address, Data Bus High Impedance ($\overline{AS}$ Negated)	t_{GLZ}	—	80	—	70	—	60	ns
39	$\overline{BG}$ Width Negated	t_{GH}	1.5	—	1.5	—	1.5	—	Clks
46	$\overline{BGACK}$ Width Low	t_{GAL}	1.5	—	1.5	—	1.5	—	Clks
47	Asynchronous Input Setup Time	t_{ASI}	10	—	10	—	10	—	ns
57	$\overline{BGACK}$ Negated to $\overline{AS}$, $\overline{DS}$, R/$\overline{W}$ Driven	t_{GASD}	1.5	—	1.5	—	1.5	—	Clks
57A	$\overline{BGACK}$ Negated to FC, $\overline{VMA}$ Driven	t_{GAFD}	1	—	1	—	1	—	Clks
58[1]	$\overline{BR}$ Negated to $\overline{AS}$, $\overline{DS}$, R/$\overline{W}$ Driven	t_{RHSD}	1.5	—	1.5	—	1.5	—	Clks
58A[1]	BR Negated to FC, $\overline{VMA}$ Driven	t_{RHFD}	1	—	1	—	1	—	Clks

*These specifications represent an improvement over previously published specifications for the 8-, 10-, and 12.5-MHz MC68010 and are valid only for product bearing date codes of 8827 and later.

NOTES:

1. The processor will negate $\overline{BG}$ and begin driving the bus again if external arbitration logic negates $\overline{BR}$ before asserting $\overline{BGACK}$.
2. The minimum value must be met to guarantee proper operation. If the maximum value is exceeded, $\overline{BG}$ may be reasserted.

These waveforms should only be referenced in regard to the edge-to-edge measurement of the timing specifications. They are not intended as a functional description of the input and output signals. Refer to other functional descriptions and their related diagrams for device operation.

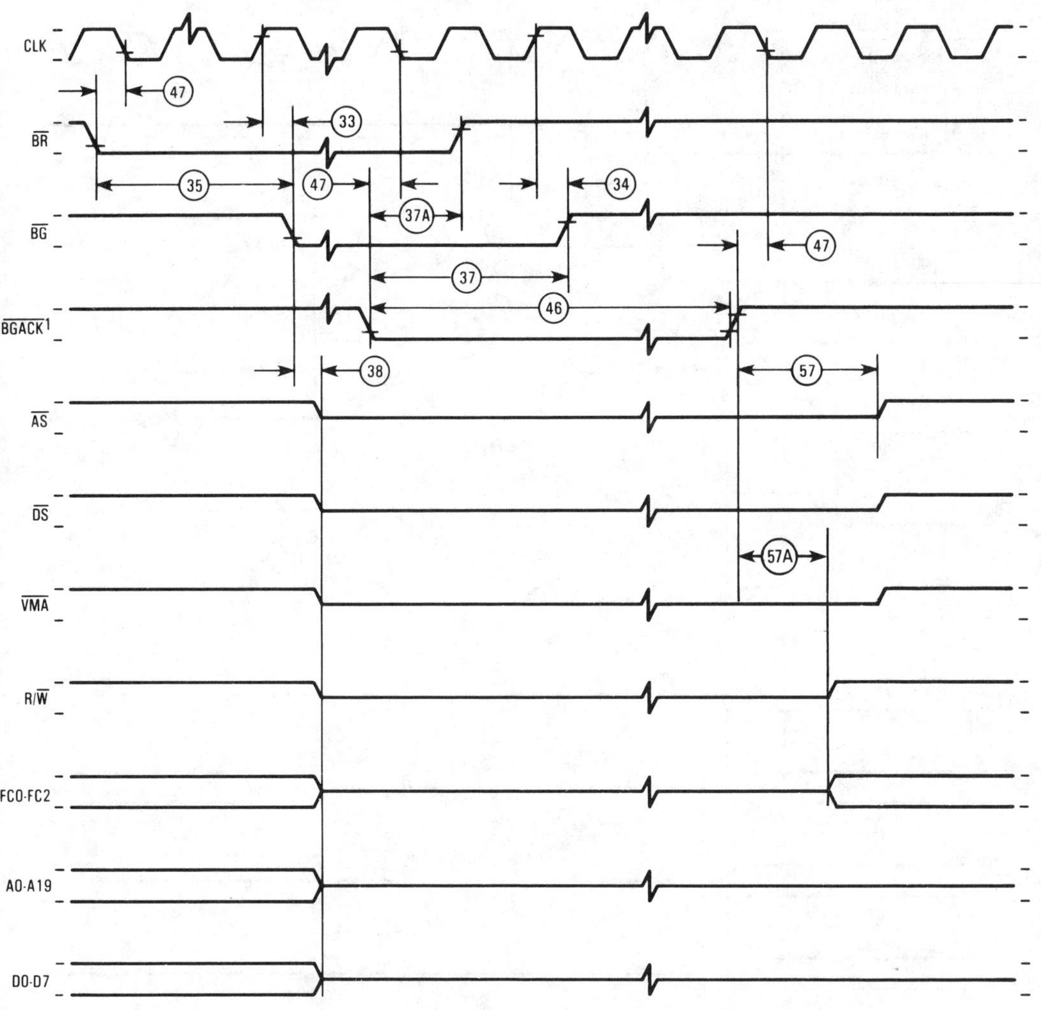

NOTES:

1. Setup time for the asynchronous inputs $\overline{BGACK}$ and $\overline{BR}$ (#47) guarantees their recognition at the next falling edge of the clock.
2. Waveform measurements for all inputs and outputs are specified at: logic high = 2.0 volts, logic low = 0.8 volt.

Figure 14-8. MC68010 Bus Arbitration Timing — Idle Bus Case

14

These waveforms should only be referenced in regard to the edge-to-edge measurement of the timing specifications. They are not intended as a functional description of the input and output signals. Refer to other functional descriptions and their related diagrams for device operation.

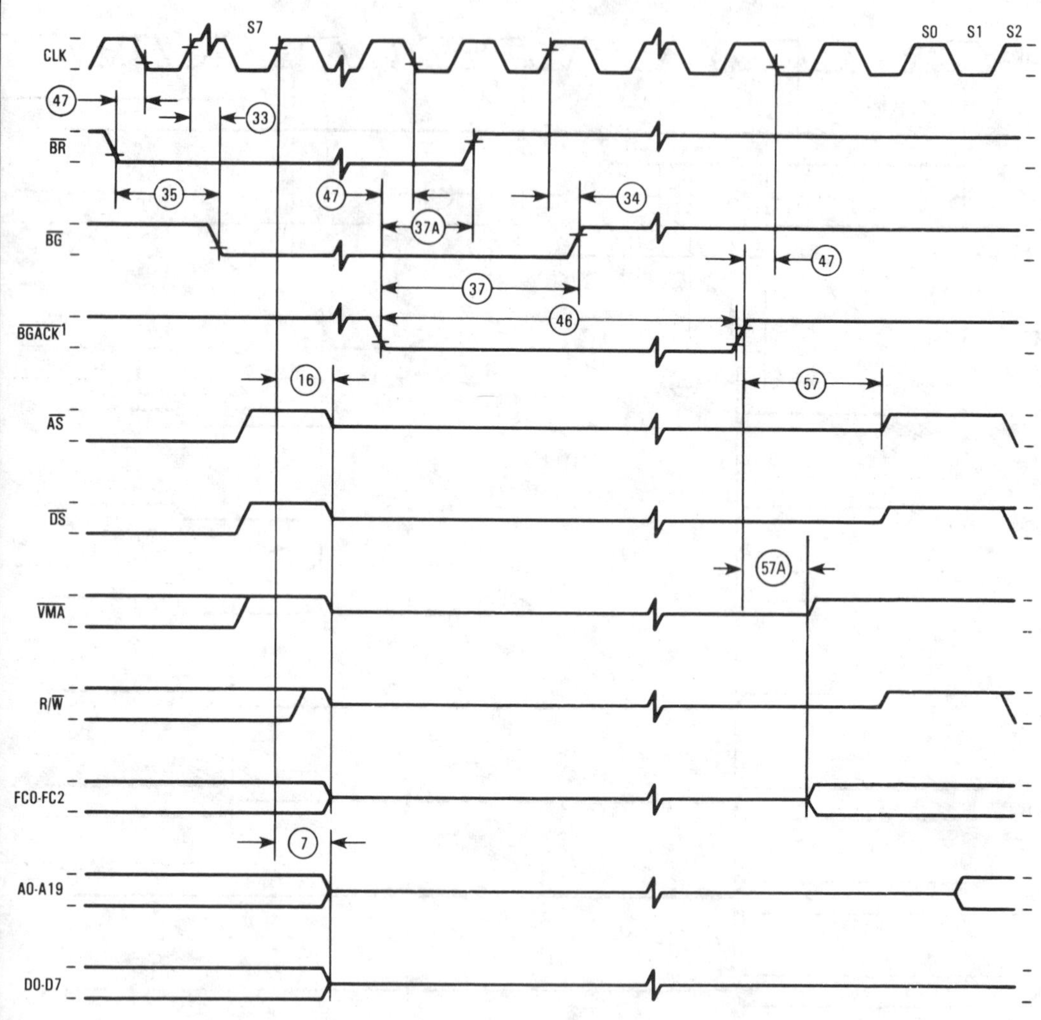

NOTES:

1. Setup time for the asynchronous inputs $\overline{BGACK}$ and $\overline{BR}$ (#47) guarantees their recognition at the next falling edge of the clock.
2. Waveform measurements for all inputs and outputs are specified at: logic high = 2.0 volts, logic low = 0.8 volt.

Figure 14-9. MC68010 Bus Arbitration Timing — Active Bus Case

14

These waveforms should only be referenced in regard to the edge-to-edge measurement of the timing specifications. They are not intended as a functional description of the input and output signals. Refer to other functional descriptions and their related diagrams for device operation.

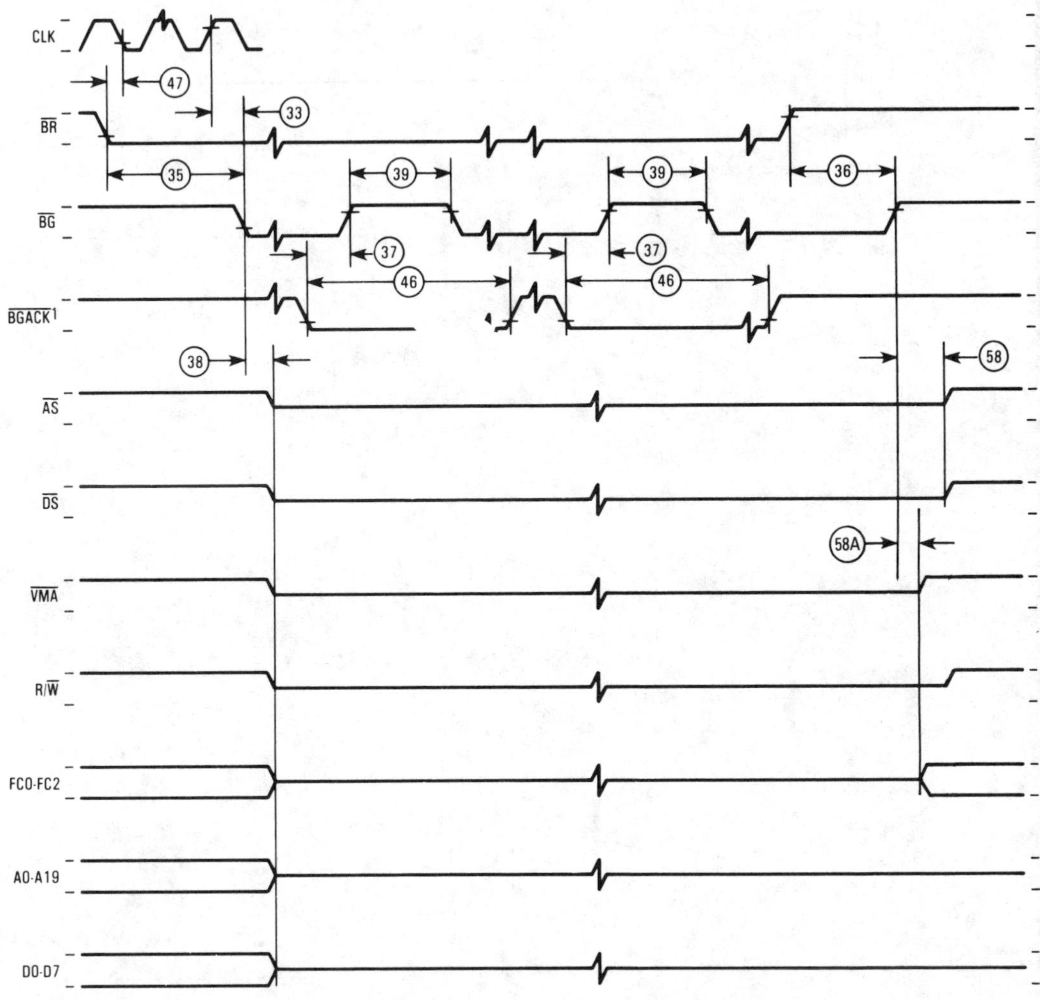

NOTES:

1. Setup time for the asynchronous inputs BGACK and BR (#47) guarantees their recognition at the next falling edge of the clock.
2. Waveform measurements for all inputs and outputs are specified at: logic high = 2.0 volts, logic low = 0.8 volt.

Figure 14-10. MC68010 Bus Arbitration Timing — Multiple Bus Requests

14

SECTION 15
ORDERING INFORMATION

Table 15-1 lists the standard ordering information for the M68000 Family. The microprocessors described in this manual are emphasized.

Table 15-1. M68000 Family Ordering Information

Device	Package Designation						Operating Frequency						
	L	LC	P	R	RC	FN	8	10	12	16	20	25	33
MC68000	√	√	√	√	√	√	√	√	√	√			
MC68HC00	√	√	√	√	√	√	√	√	√	√			
MC68008	√		√			√	√	√					
MC68010	√	√	√	√	√	√	√	√	√				
MC68020					√				√	√	√	√	√
MC68030					√					√	√	√	√
MC68230		√	√			√	√	√					
MC68440	√	√	√	√	√	√	√	√					
MC68442					√	√	√	√					
MC68450	√	√		√	√		√	√					
MC68605				√	√	√		√	√	√			
MC68606				√	√	√			√	√			
MC68652	√		√										
MC68661			√										
MC2681	√		√			√							
MC68681	√		√			√							
MC68824*				√	√	√		√	√	√			
MC68851					√				√	√	√		
MC68881					√				√	√	√	√	
MC68882					√					√	√	√	√
MC68901		√	√			√							

NOTE: Consult Factory for Products Requiring Extended Operating Temperatures or Special Processing.

The following example shows how the Motorola order numbers are constructed.

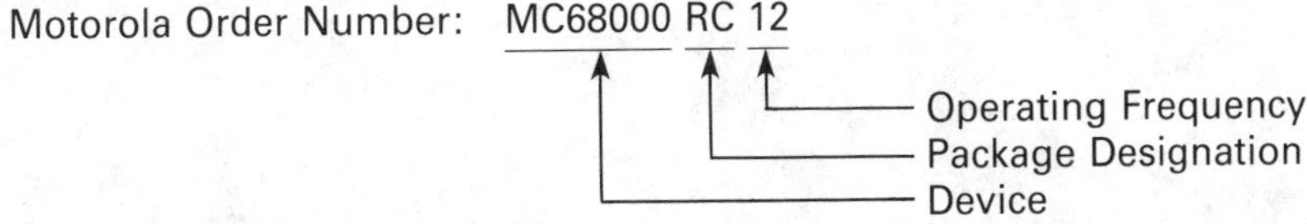

SECTION 16
MECHANICAL DATA

This section provides pin assignments and package dimensions for the devices described in this manual.

16.1 PIN ASSIGNMENTS

64-PIN DUAL-IN-LINE PACKAGE
MC68000, MC68HC000, MC68010
L, LC, P Suffixes

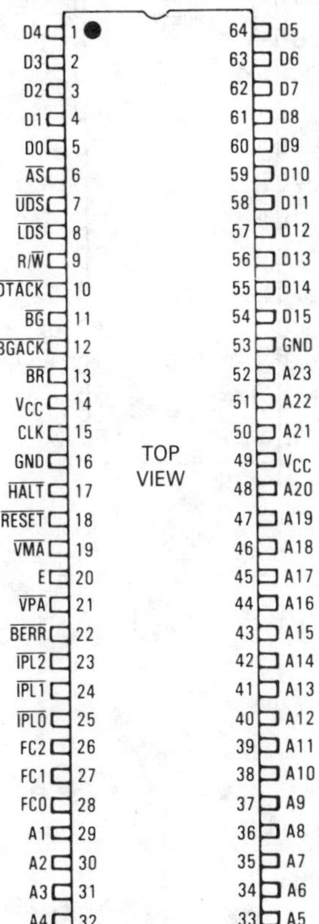

68-TERMINAL PIN GRID ARRAY
MC68000, MC68HC000, MC68010
R, RC Suffixes

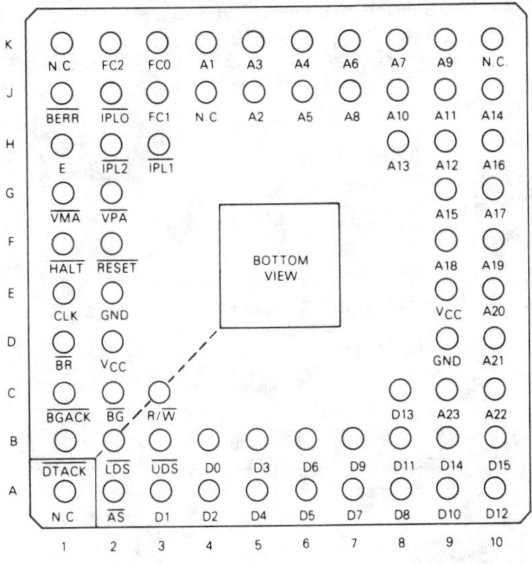

68-LEAD QUAD PACK
MC68000, MC68HC000, MC68010
FN Suffix

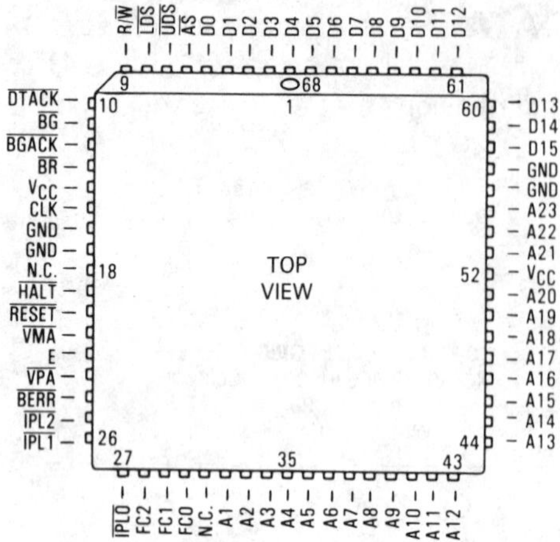

48-PIN DUAL-IN-LINE
MC68008 Only
LC, P Suffixes

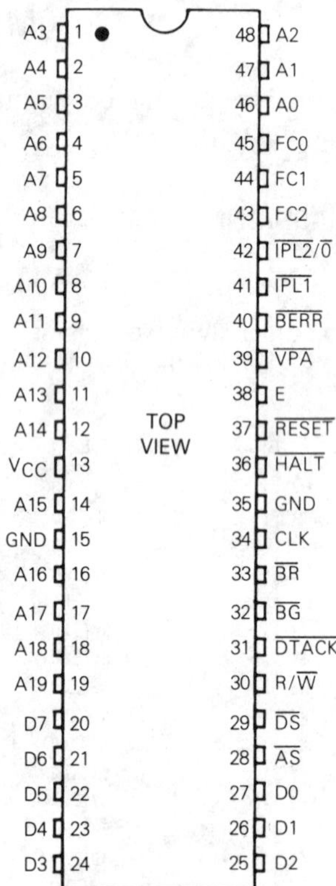

52-LEAD QUAD MC68008
MC68008 Only
FN Suffix

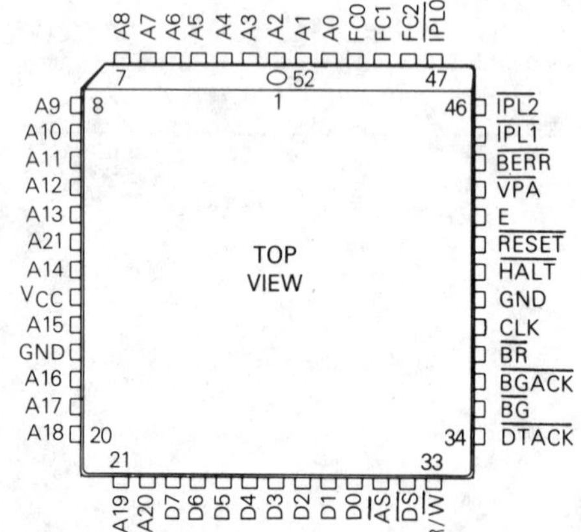

16.2 PACKAGE DIMENSIONS

MC68000, MC68HC000, and MC68010

L SUFFIX
CASE 746-01
CERAMIC PACKAGE

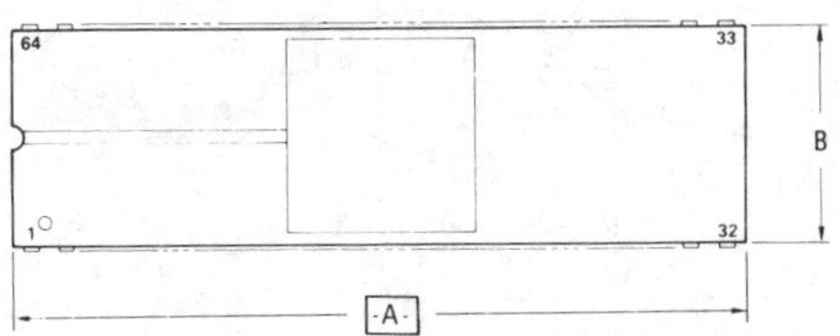

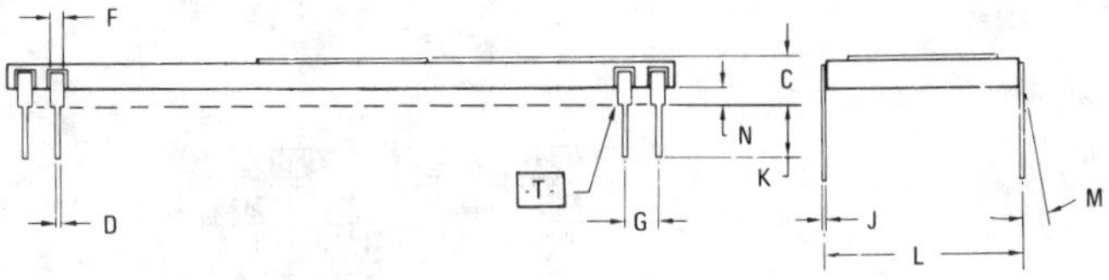

NOTES:
1. DIMENSION -A- IS DATUM.
2. POSITIONAL TOLERANCE FOR LEADS:
   ⊕ 0.25 (0.010) Ⓜ T A Ⓜ
3. -T- IS SEATING PLANE.
4. DIMENSION "L" TO CENTER OF LEADS WHEN FORMED PARALLEL.
5. DIMENSIONING AND TOLERANCING PER ANSI Y14.5, 1973.

DIM	MILLIMETERS		INCHES	
	MIN	MAX	MIN	MAX
A	80.52	82.04	3.170	3.230
B	22.25	22.96	0.876	0.904
C	3.05	4.32	0.120	0.170
D	0.38	0.53	0.015	0.021
F	0.76	1.40	0.030	0.055
G	2.54 BSC		0.100 BSC	
J	0.20	0.33	0.008	0.013
K	2.54	4.19	0.100	0.165
L	22.61	23.11	0.890	0.910
M	–	10°	–	10°
N	1.02	1.52	0.040	0.060

P SUFFIX
CASE 754-01
PLASTIC PACKAGE

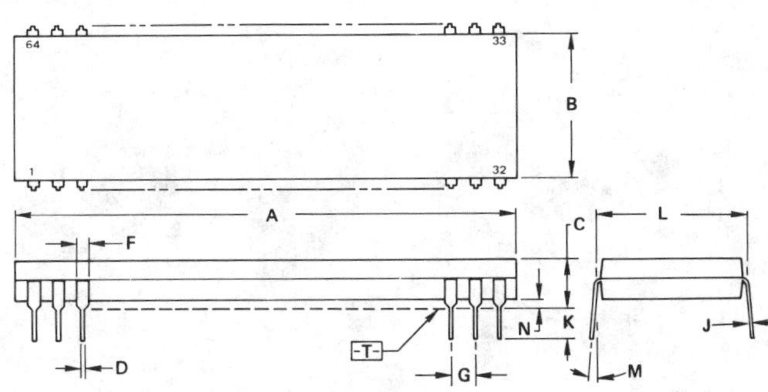

NOTES:
1. DIMENSIONS A AND B ARE DATUMS.
2. -T- IS SEATING PLANE.
3. POSITIONAL TOLERANCE FOR LEADS (DIMENSION D):
   ⊕ Ø 0.25 (0.010) Ⓜ T A Ⓜ B Ⓜ
4. DIMENSION L TO CENTER OF LEADS WHEN FORMED PARALLEL.
5. DIMENSION B DOES NOT INCLUDE MOLD FLASH.
6. DIMENSIONING AND TOLERANCING PER ANSI Y14.5, 1973.

16

DIM	MILLIMETERS		INCHES	
	MIN	MAX	MIN	MAX
A	81.16	81.91	3.195	3.225
B	20.17	20.57	0.790	0.810
C	4.83	5.84	0.190	0.230
D	0.33	0.53	0.013	0.021
F	1.27	1.77	0.050	0.070
G	2.54 BSC		0.100 BSC	
J	0.20	0.38	0.008	0.015
K	3.05	3.55	0.120	0.140
L	22.86 BSC		0.900 BSC	
M	0°	15°	0°	15°
N	0.51	1.01	0.020	0.040

RC SUFFIX
CASE 765A-05
PIN GRID ARRAY

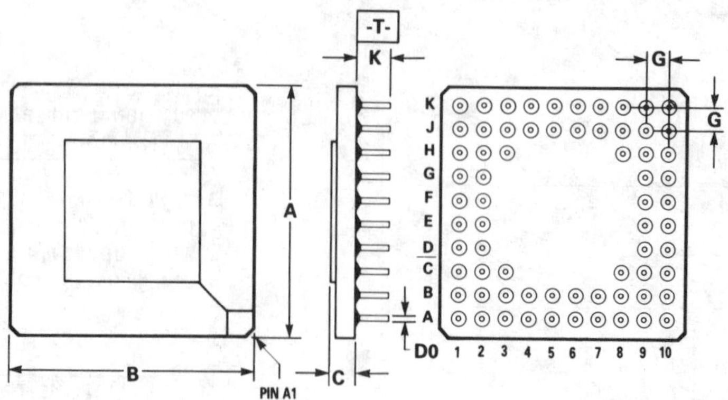

NOTES:
1. DIMENSIONS A AND B ARE DATUMS AND -T- IS DATUM SURFACE.
2. POSITIONAL TOLERANCE FOR LEADS (68 PLACES): ⌖ | ϕ 0.13 (0.005) Ⓜ | T | A Ⓢ | B Ⓢ
3. DIMENSIONING AND TOLERANCING PER ANSI Y14.5M, 1982.
4. CONTROLLING DIMENSION: INCH.

DIM	MILLIMETERS		INCHES	
	MIN	MAX	MIN	MAX
A	26.67	27.17	1.050	1.070
B	26.67	27.17	1.050	1.070
C	2.09	2.59	0.082	0.102
D	0.43	0.50	0.017	0.020
G	2.54 BSC		0.100 BSC	
K	4.32	4.82	0.170	0.190

R SUFFIX
PIN GRID ARRAY
WITH STANDOFF
(Dimensions essentially those of
Case 765A-05.)

16

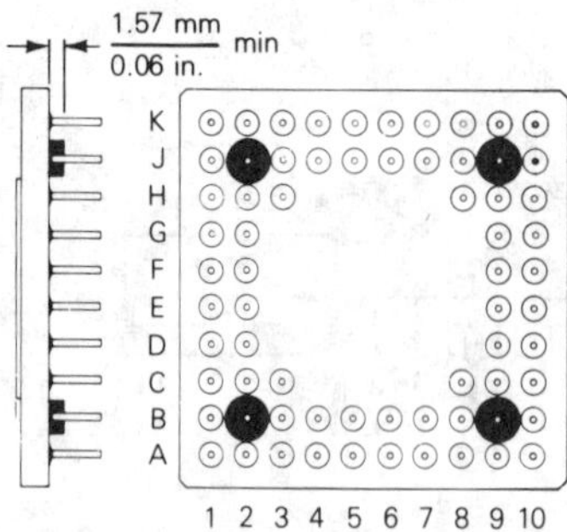

FN SUFFIX
CASE 779-02
QUAD PACK

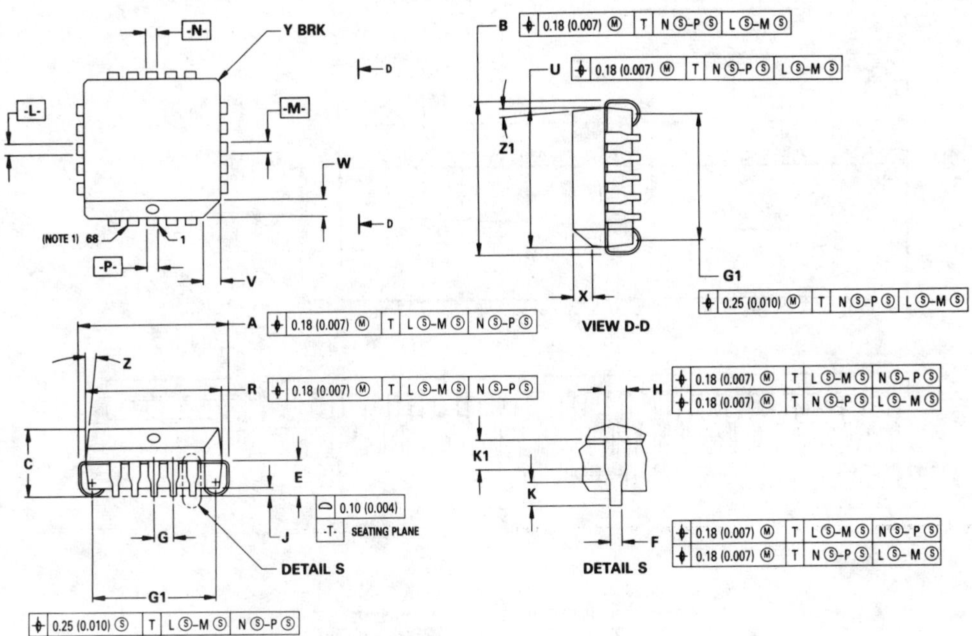

DIM	MILLIMETERS		INCHES	
	MIN	MAX	MIN	MAX
A	25.02	25.27	0.985	0.995
B	25.02	25.27	0.985	0.995
C	4.20	4.57	0.165	0.180
E	2.29	2.79	0.090	0.110
F	0.33	0.48	0.013	0.019
G	1.27 BSC		0.050 BSC	
H	0.66	0.81	0.026	0.032
J	0.51	—	0.020	—
K	0.64	—	0.025	—
R	24.13	24.28	0.950	0.956
U	24.13	24.28	0.950	0.956
V	1.07	1.21	0.042	0.048
W	1.07	1.21	0.042	0.048
X	1.07	1.42	0.042	0.056
Y	—	0.50	—	0.020
Z	2°	10°	2°	10°
G1	23.12	23.62	0.910	0.930
K1	1.02	—	0.040	—
Z1	2°	10°	2°	10°

NOTES:

1. DUE TO SPACE LIMITATION, CASE 779-02 SHALL BE REPRESENTED BY A GENERAL (SMALLER) CASE OUTLINE DRAWING RATHER THAN SHOWING ALL 68 LEADS.
2. DATUMS -L-, -M-, -N-, AND -P- DETERMINED WHERE TOP OF LEAD SHOULDER EXIT PLASTIC BODY AT MOLD PARTING LINE.
3. DIM G1, TRUE POSITION TO BE MEASURED AT DATUM -T-, SEATING PLANE.
4. DIM R AND U DO NOT INCLUDE MOLD PROTRUSION. ALLOWABLE MOLD PROTRUSION IS 0.25 (0.010) PER SIDE.
5. DIMENSIONING AND TOLERANCING PER ANSI Y14.5M, 1982.
6. CONTROLLING DIMENSION: INCH.

P SUFFIX
PLASTIC
CASE 767-02

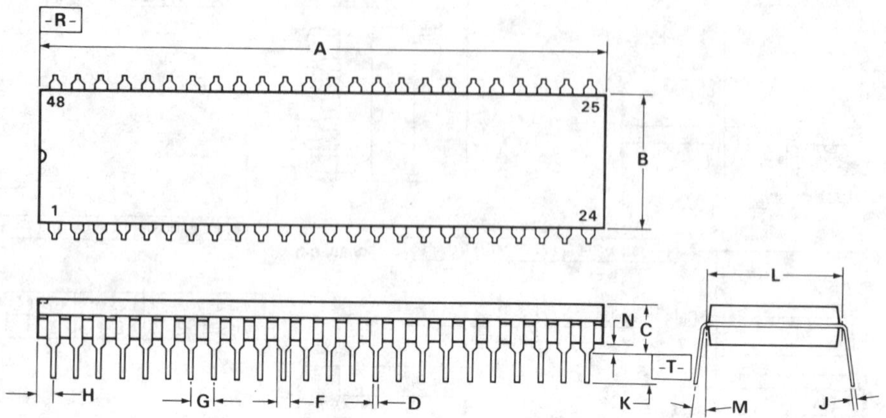

NOTES:
1. -R- IS END OF PACKAGE DATUM PLANE. -T- IS BOTH A DATUM AND SEATING PLANE.
2. POSITIONAL TOLERANCE FOR LEADS 1 AND 48:
   | ⌖ | 0.51 (0.020) | T | B Ⓜ | R |
   POSITIONAL TOLERANCE FOR LEAD PATTERN:
   | ⌖ | 0.25 (0.010) | T | B Ⓜ |
3. DIMENSION B DOES NOT INCLUDE MOLD FLASH.
4. DIMENSION L IS TO CENTER OF LEADS WHEN FORMED PARALLEL.
5. DIMENSIONING AND TOLERANCING PER ANSI Y14.5, 1982.
6. CONTROLLING DIMENSION: INCH.

16

	MILLIMETERS		INCHES	
DIM	MIN	MAX	MIN	MAX
A	61.34	62.10	2.415	2.445
B	13.72	14.22	0.540	0.560
C	3.94	5.08	0.155	0.200
D	0.36	0.55	0.014	0.022
F	1.02	1.52	0.040	0.060
G	2.54 BSC		0.100 BSC	
H	1.79 BSC		0.070 BSC	
J	0.20	0.38	0.008	0.015
K	2.92	3.42	0.115	0.135
L	15.24 BSC		0.600 BSC	
M	0°	15°	0°	15°
N	0.51	1.01	0.020	0.040

L SUFFIX
CERAMIC
CASE 740-03

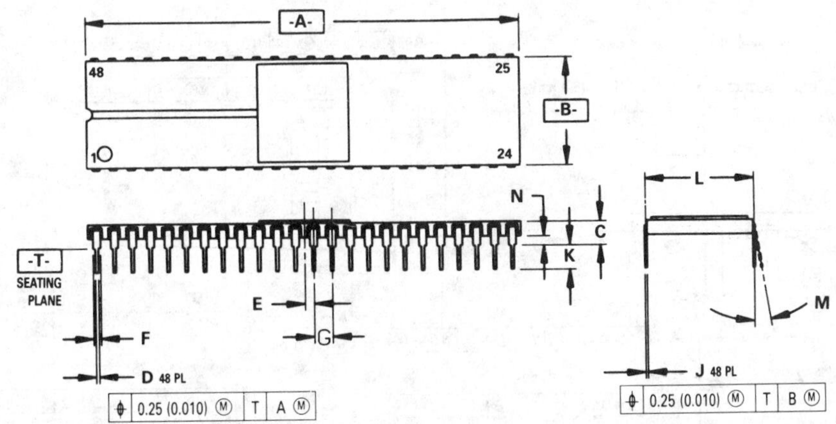

NOTES:
1. DIMENSIONING AND TOLERANCING PER ANSI Y14.5M, 1982.
2. CONTROLLING DIMENSION: INCH.
3. DIM L TO CENTER OF LEAD WHEN FORMED PARALLEL.

DIM	MILLIMETERS		INCHES	
	MIN	MAX	MIN	MAX
A	60.36	61.56	2.376	2.424
B	14.64	15.34	0.576	0.604
C	3.05	4.31	0.120	0.170
D	0.381	0.533	0.015	0.021
E	1.27 BSC		0.050 BSC	
F	0.762	1.397	0.030	0.055
G	2.54 BSC		0.100 BSC	
J	0.204	0.330	0.008	0.013
K	2.54	4.19	0.100	0.165
L	15.24 BSC		0.600 BSC	
M	0°	10°	0°	10°
N	1.016	1.524	0.040	0.060

FN SUFFIX
CASE 778-02
QUAD PACK

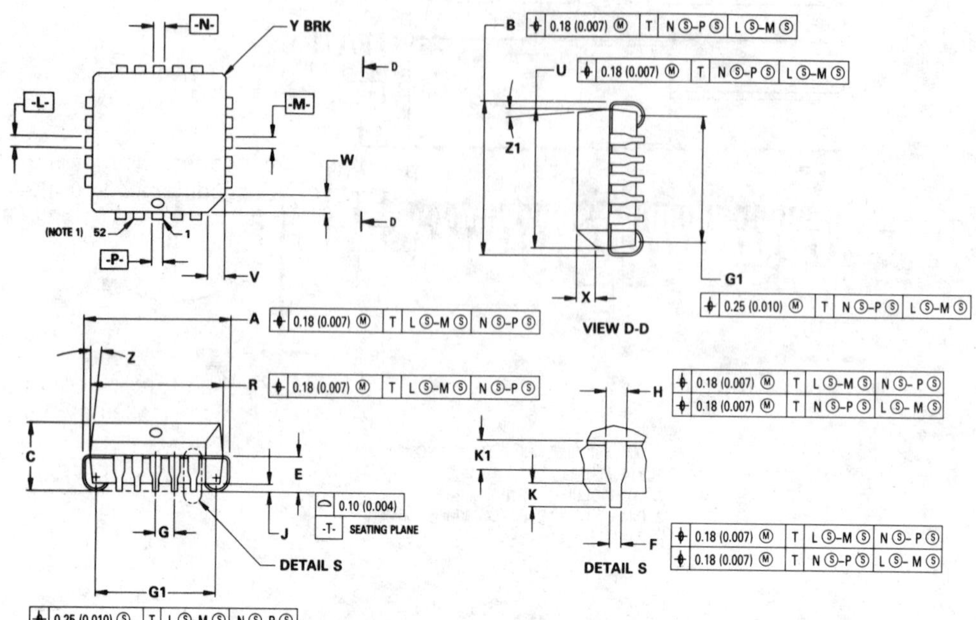

DIM	MILLIMETERS		INCHES	
	MIN	MAX	MIN	MAX
A	19.94	20.19	0.785	0.795
B	19.94	20.19	0.785	0.795
C	4.20	4.57	0.165	0.180
E	2.29	2.79	0.090	0.110
F	0.33	0.48	0.013	0.019
G	1.27 BSC		0.050 BSC	
H	0.66	0.81	0.026	0.032
J	0.51	—	0.020	—
K	0.64	—	0.025	—
R	19.05	19.20	0.750	0.756
U	19.05	19.20	0.750	0.756
V	1.07	1.21	0.042	0.048
W	1.07	1.21	0.042	0.048
X	1.07	1.42	0.042	0.056
Y	—	0.50	—	0.020
Z	2°	10°	2°	10°
G1	18.04	18.54	0.710	0.730
K1	1.02	—	0.040	—
Z1	2°	10°	2°	10°

NOTES:

1. DUE TO SPACE LIMITATION, CASE 778-02 SHALL BE REPRESENTED BY A GENERAL (SMALLER) CASE OUTLINE DRAWING RATHER THAN SHOWING ALL 52 LEADS.
2. DATUMS -L-, -M-, -N-, AND -P- DETERMINED WHERE TOP OF LEAD SHOULDER EXIT PLASTIC BODY AT MOLD PARTING LINE.
3. DIM G1, TRUE POSITION TO BE MEASURED AT DATUM -T-, SEATING PLANE.
4. DIM R AND U DO NOT INCLUDE MOLD PROTRUSION. ALLOWABLE MOLD PROTRUSION IS 0.25 (0.010) PER SIDE.
5. DIMENSIONING AND TOLERANCING PER ANSI Y14.5M, 1982.
6. CONTROLLING DIMENSION: INCH.

APPENDIX A
CONDITION CODE COMPUTATION

A.1 INTRODUCTION

This appendix provides a discussion of the development of condition codes, the meaning of each bit, the computing of each bit, and the representation of the condition code in the instruction set details.

Two criteria were used in developing the condition codes:
- Consistency – across instructions, uses, and instances
- Meaningful Results – no change unless it provides useful information

Consistency across instructions means instructions that are special cases of more general instructions affect the condition codes in the same way. Consistency across uses means that conditional instructions test the condition codes similarly and provide the same results whether the condition codes are set by a compare, test, or move instruction. Consistency across instances means that all instances of an instruction affect the condition codes in the same way. The tests used for the conditional instructions and the code computations are listed in Table A-2.

A.2 CONDITION CODE REGISTER

The condition code register portion of the status register contains the following five bits:

X - Extend
N - Negative
Z - Zero
V - Overflow
C - Carry

The X bit is an operand for multiprecision computations. The next four bits are true condition code bits in that they reflect the condition of the result of a processor operation. The carry bit (C) and the multiprecision operand extend bit (X) are separate in the M68000 Family to simplify the programming model.

A

A.3 CONDITION CODE REGISTER NOTATION

In **APPENDIX B INSTRUCTION SET DETAILS**, the effect of the instruction on the condition codes is shown in the following form:

Condition Codes:

X	N	Z	V	C

where

X (extend) Transparent to data movement. When affected by arithmetic operations, it is set the same as the C bit.

N (negative) Set if the most significant bit of the result is set. Cleared otherwise.
Z (zero) Set if the result equals zero. Cleared otherwise.
V (overflow) Set if there was arithmetic overflow. This implies that the result is not representable in the operand size. Cleared otherwise.
C (carry) Set if a carry is generated out of the most significant bit of the operands for an addition. Also, set if a borrow is generated in a subtraction. Cleared otherwise.

The notation that is used in the condition code register representation is as follows:

- * set according to the result of the operation
- —not affected by the operation
- 0 cleared
- 1 set
- U undefined after the operation

A.4 CONDITION CODE COMPUTATION

Most operations compute a result from a source operand and a destination operand and store the result in the destination location. Unary operations compute a result from a destination operand and store the result in the destination location. Table A-1 lists condition code computations used by all instructions.

A.5 CONDITIONAL TESTS

Table A-2 lists the condition names, encodings, and tests for the condition branch and set instructions. The test associated with each condition is a logical formula based on the current state of the condition codes. If this formula evaluates to one, the condition succeeds, or is true. If the formula evaluates to zero, the condition is unsuccessful, or false. For example, the true (T) condition always succeeds, and the equal (EQ) condition succeeds only if the Z condition code bit is currently set.

Table A-1. Condition Code Computations

Operations	X	N	Z	V	C	Special Definition
ABCD	*	U	?	U	?	C = Decimal Carry $Z = Z \land \overline{Rm} \land \ldots \land \overline{R0}$
ADD, ADDI, ADDQ	*	*	*	?	?	$V = Sm \land Dm \land \overline{Rm} \lor \overline{Sm} \land \overline{Dm} \land Rm$ $C = Sm \land Dm \lor \overline{Rm} \land Dm \lor Sm \land \overline{Rm}$
ADDX	*	*	?	?	?	$V = Sm \land Dm \land \overline{Rm} \lor \overline{Sm} \land \overline{Dm} \land Rm$ $C = Sm \land Dm \lor \overline{Rm} \land Dm \lor Sm \land \overline{Rm}$ $Z = Z \land \overline{Rm} \land \ldots \land \overline{R0}$
AND, ANDI, EOR, EORI, MOVEQ, MOVE, OR, ORI, CLR, EXT, NOT, TAS, TST	—	*	*	0	0	
CHK	—	*	U	U	U	
CHK2, CMP2	—	U	?	U	?	$Z = (R = LB) \lor (R = UB)$ $C = (LB <= UB) \land (IR < LB) \lor (R > UB)) \lor (UB < LB) \land (R > UB) \land (R < LB)$
SUB, SUBI, SUBQ	*	*	*	?	?	$V = \overline{Sm} \land Dm \land \overline{Rm} \lor Sm \land \overline{Dm} \land Rm$ $C = Sm \land \overline{Dm} \lor Rm \land \overline{Dm} \lor Sm \land Rm$
SUBX	*	*	?	?	?	$V = \overline{Sm} \land Dm \land \overline{Rm} \lor Sm \land \overline{Dm} \land Rm$ $C = Sm \land \overline{Dm} \lor Rm \land \overline{Dm} \lor Sm \land Rm$ $Z = Z \land \overline{Rm} \land \ldots \land \overline{R0}$

Table A-1. Condition Code Computations (Continued)

Operations	X	N	Z	V	C	Special Definition
CAS, CAS2, CMP, CAMPI, CMPM	—	*	*	?	?	$V = \overline{Sm} \wedge Dm \wedge \overline{Rm} \vee Sm \wedge \overline{Dm} \wedge Rm$ $C = Sm \wedge \overline{Dm} \vee Rm \wedge \overline{Dm} \vee Sm \wedge Rm$
DIVS, DUVI	—	*	*	?	0	V = Division Overflow
MULS, MULU	—	*	*	0	0	V = Multiplication Overflow
SBCD, NBCD	*	U	?	U	?	C = Decimal Borrow $Z = Z \wedge \overline{Rm} \wedge \ldots \wedge \overline{Ro}$
NEG	*	*	*	?	?	$V = Dm \wedge Rm$ $C = Dm \vee Rm$
NEGX	*	*	?	?	?	$V = Dm \wedge Rm$ $C = Dm \vee Rm$ $Z = Z \wedge \overline{Rm} \wedge \ldots \wedge \overline{R0}$
BTST, BCHG, BSET, BCLR	—	—	?	—	—	$Z = \overline{Dn}$
BFTST, BFCHG, BFSET, BFCLR	—	?	?	0	0	$N = Dm$ $Z = \overline{Dm} \wedge \overline{DM-1} \wedge \ldots \wedge \overline{D0}$
BFEXTS, BFEXTU, BFFFO	—	?	?	0	0	$N = Sm$ $Z = \overline{Sm} \wedge \overline{Sm-1} \wedge \ldots \wedge \overline{S0}$
BFINS	—	?	?	0	0	$N = Dm$ $Z = \overline{Dm} \wedge \overline{DM-1} \wedge \ldots \wedge \overline{D0}$
ASL	*	*	*	?	?	$V = Dm \wedge (\overline{Dm-1} \vee \ldots \vee \overline{Dm-r}) \vee \overline{Dm} \wedge$ $(DM-1 \vee \ldots \vee Dm-r)$ $C = \overline{Dm-r+1}$
ASL (R=0)	—	*	*	0	0	
LSL, ROXL	*	*	*	0	?	$C = Dm-r+1$
LSR (r=0)	—	*	*	0	0	
ROXL (r=0)	—	*	*	0	?	C=X
ROL	—	*	*	0	?	$C=Dm-r+1$
ROL (r=0)	—	*	*	0	0	
ASR, LSR, ROXR	*	*	*	0	?	$C=Dr-1$
ASR, LSR (r=0)	—	*	*	0	0	
ROXR (r=0)	—	*	*	0	?	C=X
ROR	—	*	*	0	?	$C = Dr-1$
ROR (r=0)	—	*	*	0	0	

— = Not Affected
U = Undefined, Result Meaningless
? = Other — See Special Definition
* = General Case
  X = C
  N = Rm
  $Z = \overline{Rm} \wedge \ldots \wedge \overline{R0}$
Sm = Source Operand — Most Significant Bit
Dm = Destination Operand — Most Significant Bit

Rm = Result Operand — Most Significant Bit
R = Register Tested
n = Bit Number
r = Shift Count
LB = Lower bound
UB = Upper Bound
$\wedge$ = Boolean AND
$\vee$ = Boolean OR
$\overline{Rm}$ = NOT Rm

A

Table A-2. Conditional Tests

Mnemonic	Condition	Encoding	Test
T*	True	0000	1
F*	False	0001	0
HI	High	0010	$\overline{C} \cdot \overline{Z}$
LS	Low or Same	0011	$C + Z$
CC(HS)	Carry Clear	0100	$\overline{C}$
CS(LO)	Carry Set	0101	C
NE	Not Equal	0110	$\overline{Z}$
EQ	Equal	0111	Z
VC	Overflow Clear	1000	$\overline{V}$
VS	Overflow Set	1001	V
PL	Plus	1010	$\overline{N}$
MI	Minus	1011	N
GE	Greater or Equal	1100	$N \cdot V + \overline{N} \cdot \overline{V}$
LT	Less Than	1101	$N \cdot \overline{V} + \overline{N} \cdot V$
GT	Greater Than	1110	$N \cdot V \cdot \overline{Z} + \overline{N} \cdot \overline{V} \cdot \overline{Z}$
LE	Less or Equal	1111	$Z + N \cdot \overline{V} + \overline{N} \cdot V$

• = Boolean AND
\+ = Boolean OR
$\overline{N}$ = Boolean NOT N

*Not available for the Bcc instruction.

A

APPENDIX B
INSTRUCTION SET DETAILS

This appendix contains detailed information about each instruction in the M68000 instruction set. Instruction descriptions are arranged in alphabetical order with the mnemonic heading set in large bold type for easy reference.

B.1 ADDRESSING CATEGORIES

Effective address modes can be categorized by the ways in which they are used. The following classifications are used in the instruction definitions.

Data	If an effective address mode is used to refer to data operands, it is considered a data addressing effective address mode.
Memory	If an effective address mode is used to refer to memory operands, it is considered a memory addressing effective address mode.
Alterable	If an effective address mode is used to refer to alterable (writeable) operands, it is considered an alterable addressing effective address mode.
Control	If an effective address mode is used to refer to memory operands without associated sizes, it is considered a control addressing effective address mode.

Table B-1 shows the categories of each of the effective address modes.

Table B-1. Effective Address Mode Categories

Address Modes	Mode	Register	Data	Memory	Control	Alterable	Assembler Syntax
Data Register Direct	000	reg. no.	X	—	—	X	Dn
Address Register Direct	001	reg. no.	—	—	—	X	An
Address Register Indirect	010	reg. no.	X	X	X	X	(An)
Address Register Indirect with Postincrement	011	reg. no.	X	X	—	X	(An)+
Address Register Indirect with Predecrement	100	reg. no.	X	X	—	X	−(An)
Address Register Indirect with Displacement	101	reg. no.	X	X	X	X	(d_{16},An) or D_{16}(An)
Address Register Indirect with Index	110	reg. no.	X	X	X	X	(d_8,An,Xn) or d_8(An,Xn)
Absolute Short	111	000	X	X	X	X	(xxx).W
Absolute Long	111	001	X	X	X	X	(xxx).L
Program Counter Indirect with Displacement	111	010	X	X	X	—	(d_{16},PC) or d_{16}(PC)
Program Counter Indirect with Index	111	011	X	X	X	—	d_8,PC,Xn) or d_8(PC,Xn)
Immediate	111	100	X	X	—	—	#<data>

These categories can be combined to define additional, more restrictive classifications. For example, the instruction descriptions use such classifications as memory alterable and data alterable. Memory alterable memory refers to addressing modes that are both alterable and memory addresses. Data alterable refers to addressing modes that are both data and alterable.

B.2 INSTRUCTION DESCRIPTION

The instruction descriptions in this section contain detailed information about the instructions. The format of these descriptions is shown in Figure B-1.

B.3 OPERATION DESCRIPTION DEFINITIONS

The following notation is used in the instruction descriptions.

OPERANDS

An	—Address register
Dn	—Data register
Rn	—Any data or address register
PC	—Program counter
SR	—Status register
CCR	—Condition codes (low-order byte of status)
SSP	—Supervisor stack pointer
USP	—User stack pointer
SP	—Active stack pointer (equivalent to A7)
X	—Extend operand condition code
N	—Negative condition code
Z	—Zero condition code
V	—Overflow condition code
C	—Carry condition code
Immediate data	—Immediate data from the instruction
d	—Address displacement
Source	—Source contents
Destination	—Destination contents
Vector	—Location of exception vector
ea	—Any valid effective address

SUBFIELDS AND QUALIFIERS

⟨bit⟩ of ⟨operand⟩	Selects a single bit of the operand
(⟨operand⟩)	The contents of the referenced location
⟨operand⟩$_{10}$	The operand is binary coded decimal; operations are to be performed in decimal
(⟨address register⟩) –(⟨address register⟩) (⟨address register⟩)+	The register indirect operator, which indicates that the operand register points to the memory location of the instruction operand
#xxx or #⟨data⟩	Immediate data operand from the instruction

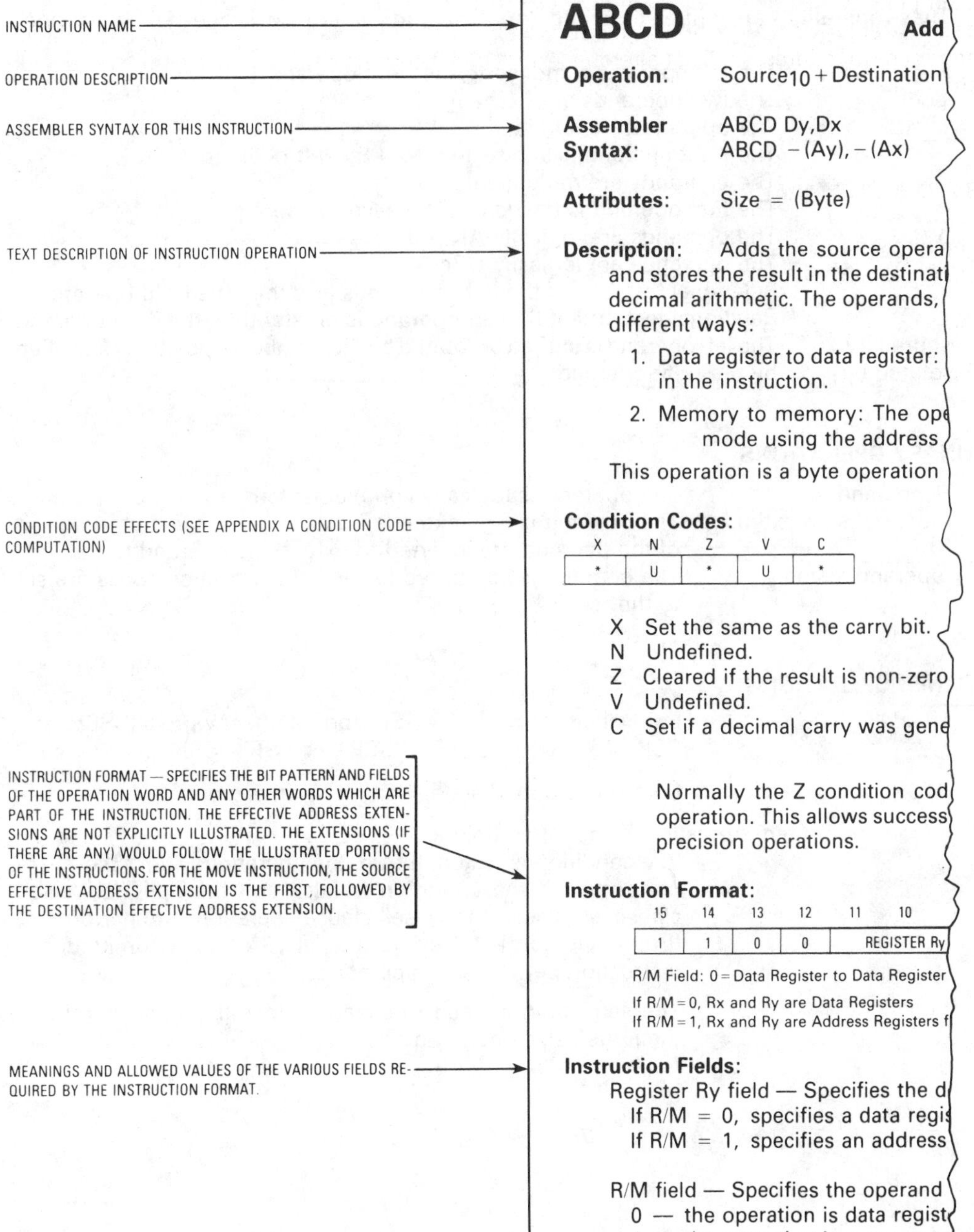

INSTRUCTION NAME
OPERATION DESCRIPTION
ASSEMBLER SYNTAX FOR THIS INSTRUCTION
TEXT DESCRIPTION OF INSTRUCTION OPERATION
CONDITION CODE EFFECTS (SEE APPENDIX A CONDITION CODE COMPUTATION)
INSTRUCTION FORMAT — SPECIFIES THE BIT PATTERN AND FIELDS OF THE OPERATION WORD AND ANY OTHER WORDS WHICH ARE PART OF THE INSTRUCTION. THE EFFECTIVE ADDRESS EXTENSIONS ARE NOT EXPLICITLY ILLUSTRATED. THE EXTENSIONS (IF THERE ARE ANY) WOULD FOLLOW THE ILLUSTRATED PORTIONS OF THE INSTRUCTIONS. FOR THE MOVE INSTRUCTION, THE SOURCE EFFECTIVE ADDRESS EXTENSION IS THE FIRST, FOLLOWED BY THE DESTINATION EFFECTIVE ADDRESS EXTENSION.
MEANINGS AND ALLOWED VALUES OF THE VARIOUS FIELDS REQUIRED BY THE INSTRUCTION FORMAT.
ABCD
Add
Operation: Source10 + Destination
Assembler Syntax: ABCD Dy,Dx
ABCD –(Ay),–(Ax)
Attributes: Size = (Byte)
Description: Adds the source opera
and stores the result in the destinat
decimal arithmetic. The operands,
different ways:
1. Data register to data register:
in the instruction.
2. Memory to memory: The op
mode using the address
This operation is a byte operation
Condition Codes:
X N Z V C
* U * U *
X Set the same as the carry bit.
N Undefined.
Z Cleared if the result is non-zero
V Undefined.
C Set if a decimal carry was gene
Normally the Z condition cod
operation. This allows success
precision operations.
Instruction Format:
15 14 13 12 11 10
1 1 0 0 REGISTER Ry
R/M Field: 0 = Data Register to Data Register
If R/M = 0, Rx and Ry are Data Registers
If R/M = 1, Rx and Ry are Address Registers f
Instruction Fields:
Register Ry field — Specifies the d
If R/M = 0, specifies a data regi
If R/M = 1, specifies an address
R/M field — Specifies the operand
0 — the operation is data regist
1 — the operation is memory to

Figure B-1. Instruction Description Format

B

BINARY OPERATIONS

These operations are written ⟨operand⟩ ⟨op⟩ ⟨operand⟩, where ⟨op⟩ is one of the following:

→	The left operand is moved to the right operand
↔	The two operands are exchanged
+	The operands are added
−	The right operand is subtracted from the left operand
*	The operands are multiplied
/	The first operand is divided by the second operand
Λ	The operands are logically ANDed
V	The operands are logically ORed
<	Relational test, true if the left operand is less than the right operand
>	Relational test, true if the left operand is greater than the right operand
shifted by rotated by	The left operand is shifted or rotated by the number of positions specified by the right operand

UNARY OPERATIONS

~⟨operand⟩	The operand is logically complemented
⟨operand⟩sign extended	The operand is sign extended; bits equal to the high-order bit of the operand are inserted to extend the operand to the left
⟨operand⟩tested	The operand is compared to zero; the condition codes are set to the result.

OTHER OPERATIONS

TRAP	Equivalent to: SSP - 2 → SSP; format/offset word → (SSP); SSP - 4 → SSP; PC → (SSP); SSP - 2 → ; SR → (SSP); (vector) → PC
STOP	Enter the stopped state, waiting for interrupts

if ⟨condition⟩ then ⟨operations⟩ else ⟨operations⟩;

The condition is tested. If true, the operations after "then" are performed. If the condition is false and the optional "else" clause is present, the "else" clause operations are performed. If the condition is false and the "else" clause is omitted, the instruction performs no operation.

The semicolon is used to separate operations and terminate the if/then/else operation.

ABCD — Add Decimal with Extend

ABCD

Operation: $Source_{10} + Destination_{10} + X \rightarrow Destination$

Assembler Syntax: ABCD Dy,Dx
ABCD −(Ay),−(Ax)

Attributes: Size = (Byte)

Description: Adds the source operand to the destination operand along with the extend bit, and stores the result in the destination location. The addition is performed using binary coded decimal arithmetic. The operands, which are packed BCD numbers, can be addressed in two different ways:

1. Data register to data register: The operands are contained in the data registers specified in the instruction.
2. Memory to memory: The operands are addressed with the predecrement addressing mode using the address registers specified in the instruction.

This operation is a byte operation only.

Condition Codes:

X	N	Z	V	C
*	U	*	U	*

X Set the same as the carry bit.
N Undefined
Z Cleared if the result is non-zero. Unchanged otherwise.
V Undefined
C Set if a decimal carry was generated. Cleared otherwise.

NOTE

Normally the Z condition code bit is set via programming before the start of an operation. This allows successful tests for zero results upon completion of multiple-precision operations.

Instruction Format:

15	14	13	12	11	10	9	8	7	6	5	4	3	2	1	0
1	1	0	0	REGISTER Rx			1	0	0	0	0	R/M	REGISTER Ry		

Instruction Fields:

Register Rx field — Specifies the destination register:
If R/M = 0, specifies a data register
If R/M = 1, specifies an address register for the predecrement addressing mode

R/M field — Specifies the operand addressing mode:
0 — the operation is data register to data register
1 — the operation is memory to memory

Register Ry field — Specifies the source register:
If R/M = 0, specifies a data register
If R/M = 1, specifies an address register for the predecrement addressing mode

B

Operation: Source + Destination ➧ Destination

Assembler Syntax: ADD ⟨ea⟩,Dn
ADD Dn,⟨ea⟩

Attributes: Size = (Byte, Word, Long)

Description: Adds the source operand to the destination operand using binary addition, and stores the result in the destination location. The size of the operation may be specified as byte, word, or long. The mode of the instruction indicates which operand is the source and which is the destination as well as the operand size.

Condition Codes:

X	N	Z	V	C
*	*	*	*	*

X Set the same as the carry bit.
N Set if the result is negative. Cleared otherwise.
Z Set if the result is zero. Cleared otherwise.
V Set if an overflow is generated. Cleared otherwise.
C Set if a carry is generated. Cleared otherwise.

Instruction Format:

15	14	13	12	11	10	9	8	7	6	5	4	3	2	1	0
1	1	0	1	REGISTER			OP-MODE			EFFECTIVE ADDRESS					
										MODE			REGISTER		

Instruction Fields:

Register field — Specifies any of the eight data registers.

Op-Mode field —

Byte	Word	Long	Operation
000	001	010	⟨ea⟩ + ⟨Dn⟩ ➧ ⟨n⟩
100	101	110	⟨Dn⟩ + ⟨ea⟩ ➧ ⟨ea⟩

B

Effective Address Field — Determines addressing mode:

a. If the location specified is a source operand, all addressing modes are allowed as shown:

Addressing Mode	Mode	Register
Dn	000	reg. number:Dn
An*	001	reg. number:An
(An)	010	reg. number:An
(An)+	011	reg. number:An
−(An)	100	reg. number:An
(d_{16},An)	101	reg. number:An
(d_8,An,Xn)	110	reg. number:An

Addressing Mode	Mode	Register
(xxx).W	111	000
(xxx).L	111	001
#⟨data⟩	111	100
(d_{16},PC)	111	010
(d_8,PC,Xn)	111	011

*Word and Long only.

b. If the location specified is a destination operand, only memory alterable addressing modes are allowed as shown:

Addressing Mode	Mode	Register
Dn	—	—
An	—	—
(An)	010	reg. number:An
(An)+	011	reg. number:An
−(An)	100	reg. number:An
(d_{16},An)	101	reg. number:An
(d_8,An,Xn)	110	reg. number:An

Addressing Mode	Mode	Register
(xxx).W	111	000
(xxx).L	111	001
#⟨data⟩	—	—
(d_{16},PC)	—	—
(d_8,PC,Xn)	—	—

Notes:

1. The Dn mode is used when the destination is a data register; the destination ⟨ea⟩ mode is invalid for a data register.
2. ADDA is used when the destination is an address register. ADDI and ADDQ are used when the source is immediate data. Most assemblers automatically make this distinction.

Operation: Source + Destination ➧ Destination

Assembler Syntax: ADDA ⟨ea⟩, An

Attributes: Size = (Word, Long)

Description: Adds the source operand to the destination address register, and stores the result in the address register. The size of the operation may be specified as word or long. The entire destination address register is used regardless of the operation size.

Condition Codes:
Not affected

Instruction Format:

15	14	13	12	11	10	9	8	7	6	5	4	3	2	1	0
1	1	0	1	REGISTER			OP-MODE			EFFECTIVE ADDRESS MODE			EFFECTIVE ADDRESS REGISTER		

Op-Mode Field:

Word	Long	Operation
011	111	(⟨ea⟩) + (⟨An⟩) ➧ ⟨An⟩

Instruction Fields:

Register field — Specifies any of the eight address registers. This is always the destination.

Op-Mode field — Specifies the size of the operation:

011 — Word operation. The source operand is sign-extended to a long operand and the operation is performed on the address register using all 32 bits.

111 — Long operation.

Effective Address field — Specifies the source operand. All addressing modes are allowed as shown:

Addressing Mode	Mode	Register
Dn	000	reg. number:Dn
An	001	reg. number:An
(An)	010	reg. number:An
(An)+	011	reg. number:An
−(An)	100	reg. number:An
(d_{16},An)	101	reg. number:An
(d_8,An,Xn)	110	reg. number:An

Addressing Mode	Mode	Register
(xxx).W	111	000
(xxx).L	111	001
#⟨data⟩	111	100
(d_{16},PC)	111	010
(d_8,PC,Xn)	111	011

B

ADDI — Add Immediate — ADDI

Operation: Immediate Data + Destination ➧ Destination

Assembler Syntax: ADDI #⟨data⟩,⟨ea⟩

Attributes: Size = (Byte, Word, Long)

Description: Adds the immediate data to the destination operand, and stores the result in the destination location. The size of the operation may be specified as byte, word, or long. The size of the immediate data matches the operation size.

Condition Codes:

X	N	Z	V	C
*	*	*	*	*

X Set the same as the carry bit.
N Set if the result is negative. Cleared otherwise.
Z Set if the result is zero. Cleared otherwise.
V Set if an overflow is generated. Cleared otherwise.
C Set if a carry is generated. Cleared otherwise.

Instruction Format:

15	14	13	12	11	10	9	8	7	6	5	4	3	2	1	0
0	0	0	0	0	1	1	0	SIZE		EFFECTIVE ADDRESS MODE			EFFECTIVE ADDRESS REGISTER		
WORD DATA (16 BITS)								BYTE DATA (8 BITS)							
LONG DATA (32 BITS)															

Instruction Fields:

Size field — Specifies the size of the operation:
- 00 — Byte operation
- 01 — Word operation
- 10 — Long operation

Effective Address field — Specifies the destination operand
Only data alterable addressing modes are allowed as shown:

Addressing Mode	Mode	Register
Dn	000	reg. number:Dn
An	—	—
(An)	010	reg. number:An
(An)+	011	reg. number:An
−(An)	100	reg. number:An
(d_{16},An)	101	reg. number:An
(d_8,An,Xn)	110	reg. number:An

Addressing Mode	Mode	Register
(xxx).W	111	000
(xxx).L	111	001
#⟨data⟩	—	—
(d_{16},PC)	—	—
(d_8,PC,Xn)	—	—

Immediate field — (Data immediately following the instruction):
If size = 00, the data is the low order byte of the immediate word
If size = 01, the data is the entire immediate word
If size = 10, the data is the next two immediate words

ADDQ — Add Quick

Operation: Immediate Data + Destination ➧ Destination

Assembler Syntax: ADDQ #⟨data⟩,⟨ea⟩

Attributes: Size = (Byte, Word, Long)

Description: Adds an immediate value of 1 to 8 to the operand at the destination location. The size of the operation may be specified as byte, word, or long. Word and long operations are also allowed on the address registers. When adding to address registers, the condition codes are not altered, and the entire destination address register is used regardless of the operation size.

Condition Codes:

X	N	Z	V	C
*	*	*	*	*

X Set the same as the carry bit.
N Set if the result is negative. Cleared otherwise.
Z Set if the result is zero. Cleared otherwise.
V Set if an overflow occurs. Cleared otherwise.
C Set if a carry occurs. Cleared otherwise.

The condition codes are not affected when the destination is an address register.

Instruction Format:

15	14	13	12	11	10	9	8	7	6	5	4	3	2	1	0
0	1	0	1	DATA			0	SIZE		EFFECTIVE ADDRESS					
										MODE			REGISTER		

Instruction Fields:

Data field — Three bits of immediate data, 0-7 (with the immediate value 0 representing a value of 8).

Size field — Specifies the size of the operation:
- 00 — Byte operation
- 01 — Word operation
- 10 — Long operation

B

Effective Address field — Specifies the destination location
Only alterable addressing modes are allowed as shown:

Addressing Mode	Mode	Register
Dn	000	reg. number:Dn
An*	001	reg. number:An
(An)	010	reg. number:An
(An)+	011	reg. number:An
−(An)	100	reg. number:An
(d_{16},An)	101	reg. number:An
(d_8,An,Xn)	110	reg. number:An

Addressing Mode	Mode	Register
(xxx).W	111	000
(xxx).L	111	001
#⟨data⟩	—	—
(d_{16},PC)	—	—
(d_8,PC,Xn)	—	—

*Word and Long only.

B

ADDX — Add Extended — ADDX

Operation: Source + Destination + X → Destination

Assembler Syntax: ADDX Dy,Dx
ADDX −(Ay),−(Ax)

Attributes: Size = (Byte, Word, Long)

Description: Adds the source operand to the destination operand along with the extend bit and stores the result in the destination location. The operands can be addressed in two different ways:

1. Data register to data register: The data registers specified in the instruction contain the operands.
2. Memory to memory: The address registers specified in the instruction address the operands using the predecrement addressing mode.

The size of the operation can be specified as byte, word, or long.

Condition Codes:

X	N	Z	V	C
*	*	*	*	*

X Set the same as the carry bit.
N Set if the result is negative. Cleared otherwise.
Z Cleared if the result is non-zero. Unchanged otherwise.
V Set if an overflow occurs. Cleared otherwise.
C Set if a carry is generated. Cleared otherwise.

NOTE

Normally the Z condition code bit is set via programming before the start of an operation. This allows successful tests for zero results upon completion of multiple-precision operations.

Instruction Format:

15	14	13	12	11	10	9	8	7	6	5	4	3	2	1	0
1	1	0	1	REGISTER Rx			1	SIZE		0	0	R/M	REGISTER Ry		

B

Instruction Fields:

Register Rx field — Specifies the destination register:
- If R/M = 0, specifies a data register
- If R/M = 1, specifies an address register for the predecrement addressing mode

Size field — Specifies the size of the operation:
- 00 — Byte operation
- 01 — Word operation
- 10 — Long operation

R/M field — Specifies the operand address mode:
- 0 — The operation is data register to data register
- 1 — The operation is memory to memory

Register Ry field — Specifies the source register:
- If R/M = 0, specifies a data register
- If R/M = 1, specifies an address register for the predecrement addressing mode

AND — And Logical

Operation: SourceΛDestination ➧ Destination

Assembler Syntax: AND ⟨ea⟩,Dn
AND Dn,⟨ea⟩

Attributes: Size = (Byte, Word, Long)

Description: Performs an AND operation of the source operand with the destination operand and stores the result in the destination location. The size of the operation can be specified as byte, word, or long. The contents of an address register may not be used as an operand.

Condition Codes:

X	N	Z	V	C
—	*	*	0	0

X Not affected
N Set if the most-significant bit of the result is set. Cleared otherwise.
Z Set if the result is zero. Cleared otherwise.
V Always cleared
C Always cleared

Instruction Format:

15	14	13	12	11	10	9	8	7	6	5	4	3	2	1	0
1	1	0	0	REGISTER			OP-MODE			EFFECTIVE ADDRESS MODE			EFFECTIVE ADDRESS REGISTER		

Instruction Fields:

Register field — Specifies any of the eight data registers
Op-Mode field —

Byte	Word	Long	Operation
000	001	010	(⟨ea⟩)Λ(⟨Dn⟩) ➧ Dn
100	101	110	(⟨Dn⟩)Λ(⟨ea⟩) ➧ ea

B

Effective Address field — Determines addressing mode:

If the location specified is a source operand only data addressing modes are allowed as shown:

Addressing Mode	Mode	Register	Addressing Mode	Mode	Register
Dn	000	reg. number:Dn	(xxx).W	111	000
An	—	—	(xxx).L	111	001
(An)	010	reg. number:An	#⟨data⟩	111	100
(An)+	011	reg. number:An			
−(An)	100	reg. number:An			
(d_{16},An)	101	reg. number:An	(d_{16},PC)	111	010
(d_8,An,Xn)	110	reg. number:An	(d_8,PC,Xn)	111	011

If the location specified is a destination operand only memory alterable addressing modes are allowed as shown:

Addressing Mode	Mode	Register	Addressing Mode	Mode	Register
Dn	—	—	(xxx).W	111	000
An	—	—	(xxx).L	111	001
(An)	010	reg. number:An	#⟨data⟩	—	—
(An)+	011	reg. number:An			
−(An)	100	reg. number:An			
(d_{16},An)	101	reg. number:An	(d_{16},PC)	—	—
(d_8,An,Xn)	110	reg. number:An	(d_8,PC,Xn)	—	—

Notes:

1. The Dn mode is used when the destination is a data register; the destination ⟨ea⟩ mode is invalid for a data register.
2. Most assemblers use ANDI when the source is immediate data.

B

ANDI — AND Immediate — ANDI

Operation: Immediate Data Λ Destination → Destination

Assembler Syntax: ANDI #⟨data⟩,⟨ea⟩

Attributes: Size = (Byte, Word, Long)

Description: Performs an AND operation of the immediate data with the destination operand and stores the result in the destination location. The size of the operation can be specified as byte, word, or long. The size of the immediate data matches the operation size.

Condition Codes:

X	N	Z	V	C
—	*	*	0	0

X Not affected
N Set if the most-significant bit of the result is set. Cleared otherwise.
Z Set if the result is zero. Cleared otherwise.
V Always cleared
C Always cleared

Instruction Format:

15	14	13	12	11	10	9	8	7	6	5	4	3	2	1	0
										EFFECTIVE ADDRESS					
0	0	0	0	0	0	1	0	SIZE		MODE			REGISTER		
WORD DATA (16 BITS)								BYTE DATA (8 BITS)							
LONG DATA (32 BITS)															

Instruction Fields:

Size field — Specifies the size of the operation:
- 00 — Byte operation
- 01 — Word operation
- 10 — Long operation

B

Effective Address field — Specifies the destination operand
Only data alterable addressing modes are allowed as shown:

Addressing Mode	Mode	Register
Dn	000	reg. number:Dn
An	—	—
(An)	010	reg. number:An
(An)+	011	reg. number:An
−(An)	100	reg. number:An
(d_{16},An)	101	reg. number:An
(d_8,An,Xn)	110	reg. number:An

Addressing Mode	Mode	Register
(xxx).W	111	000
(xxx).L	111	001
#⟨data⟩	—	—
(d_{16},PC)	—	—
(d_8,PC,Xn)	—	—

Immediate field — (Data immediately following the instruction):
If size = 00, the data is the low order byte of the immediate word
If size = 01, the data is the entire immediate word
If size = 10, the data is the next two immediate words

B

ANDI to CCR

AND Immediate to Condition Codes

ANDI to CCR

Operation: Source$\wedge$CCR → CCR

Assembler Syntax: ANDI #⟨data⟩,CCR

Attributes: Size = (Byte)

Description: Performs an AND operation of the immediate operand with the condition codes and stores the result in the low-order byte of the status register.

Condition Codes:

X	N	Z	V	C
*	*	*	*	*

X Cleared if bit 4 of immediate operand is zero. Unchanged otherwise.
N Cleared if bit 3 of immediate operand is zero. Unchanged otherwise.
Z Cleared if bit 2 of immediate operand is zero. Unchanged otherwise.
V Cleared if bit 1 of immediate operand is zero. Unchanged otherwise.
C Cleared if bit 0 of immediate operand is zero. Unchanged otherwise.

Instruction Format:

15	14	13	12	11	10	9	8	7	6	5	4	3	2	1	0
0	0	0	0	0	0	1	0	0	0	1	1	1	1	0	0
0	0	0	0	0	0	0	0	BYTE DATA (8 BITS)							

B

ANDI to SR

AND Immediate to the Status Register
(Privileged Instruction)

ANDI to SR

Operation: If supervisor state
then Source∧SR → SR
else TRAP

Assembler Syntax: ANDI #⟨data⟩,SR

Attributes: Size = (Word)

Description: Performs an AND operation of the immediate operand with the contents of the status register and stores the result in the status register. All implemented bits of the status register are affected.

Condition Codes:

X	N	Z	V	C
*	*	*	*	*

X Cleared if bit 4 of immediate operand is zero. Unchanged otherwise.
N Cleared if bit 3 of immediate operand is zero. Unchanged otherwise.
Z Cleared if bit 2 of immediate operand is zero. Unchanged otherwise.
V Cleared if bit 1 of immediate operand is zero. Unchanged otherwise.
C Cleared if bit 0 of immediate operand is zero. Unchanged otherwise.

Instruction Format:

15	14	13	12	11	10	9	8	7	6	5	4	3	2	1	0
0	0	0	0	0	0	1	0	0	1	1	1	1	1	0	0
WORD DATA (16 BITS)															

B

Operation: Destination Shifted by ⟨count⟩ ▸ Destination

Assembler Syntax:
ASd Dx,Dy
ASd #⟨data⟩,Dy
ASd ⟨ea⟩
where d is direction, L or R

Attributes: Size = (Byte, Word, Long)

Description: Arithmetically shifts the bits of the operand in the direction (L or R) specified. The carry bit receives the last bit shifted out of the operand. The shift count for the shifting of a register may be specified in two different ways:

1. Immediate — The shift count is specified in the instruction (shift range, 1-8).
2. Register — The shift count is the value in the data register specified in instruction modulo 64.

The size of the operation can be specified as byte, word, or long. An operand in memory can be shifted one bit only, and the operand size is restricted to a word.

For ASL, the operand is shifted left; the number of positions shifted is the shift count. Bits shifted out of the high-order bit go to both the carry and the extend bits; zeros are shifted into the low-order bit. The overflow bit indicates if any sign changes occur during the shift.

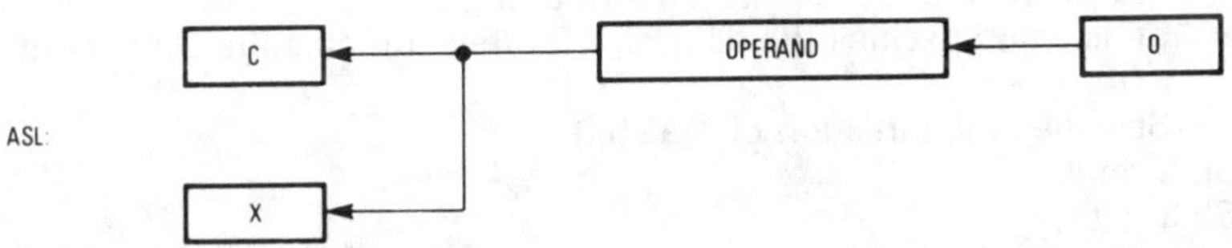

For ASR, the operand is shifted right; the number of positions shifted is the shift count. Bits shifted out of the low-order bit go to both the carry and the extend bits; the sign-bit (MSB) is shifted into the high-order bit.

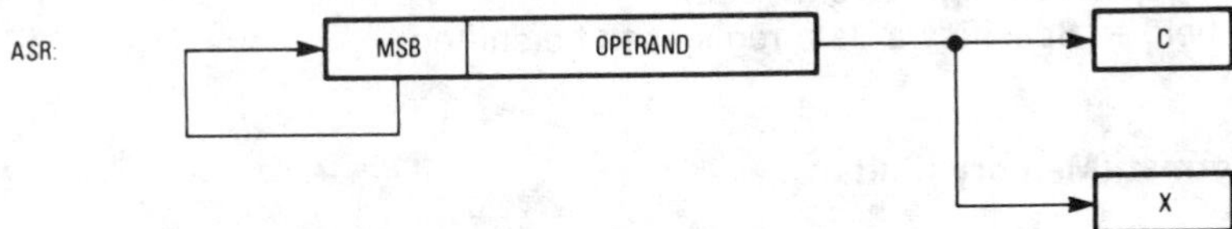

B

Condition Codes:

X	N	Z	V	C
*	*	*	*	*

X Set according to the last bit shifted out of the operand. Unaffected for a shift count of zero.
N Set if the most-significant bit of the result is set. Cleared otherwise.
Z Set if the result is zero. Cleared otherwise.
V Set if the most significant bit is changed at any time during the shift operation. Cleared otherwise.
C Set according to the last bit shifted out of the operand. Cleared for a shift count of zero.

Instruction Format (Register Shifts):

15	14	13	12	11	10	9	8	7	6	5	4	3	2	1	0
1	1	1	0	COUNT/REGISTER			dr	SIZE		i/r	0	0	REGISTER		

Instruction Fields (Register Shifts):

Count/Register field — Specifies shift count or register that contains the shift count:
- If i/r = 0, this field contains the shift count. The values 1-7 represent counts of 1-7; value of zero represents a count of 8.
- If i/r = 1, this field specifies the data register that contains the shift count (modulo 64).

dr field — Specifies the direction of the shift:
- 0 — Shift right
- 1 — Shift left

Size field — Specifies the size of the operation:
- 00 — Byte operation
- 01 — Word operation
- 10 — Long operation

i/r field:
- If i/r = 0, specifies immediate shift count
- If i/r = 1, specifies register shift count

Register field — Specifies a data register to be shifted

Instruction Format (Memory Shifts):

B

15	14	13	12	11	10	9	8	7	6	5	4	3	2	1	0
										EFFECTIVE ADDRESS					
1	1	1	0	0	0	0	dr	1	1	MODE			REGISTER		

Instruction Fields (Memory Shifts):

dr field — Specifies the direction of the shift:
- 0 — Shift right
- 1 — Shift left

Effective Address field — Specifies the operand to be shifted

Only memory alterable addressing modes are allowed as shown:

Addressing Mode	Mode	Register
Dn	—	—
An	—	—
(An)	010	reg. number:An
(An)+	011	reg. number:An
−(An)	100	reg. number:An
(d_{16},An)	101	reg. number:An
(d_8,An,Xn)	110	reg. number:An

Addressing Mode	Mode	Register
(xxx).W	111	000
(xxx).L	111	001
#⟨data⟩	—	—
(d_{16},PC)	—	—
(d_8,PC,Xn)	—	—

B

Operation: If (condition true) then PC+d ➧ PC

Assembler Syntax: Bcc ⟨label⟩

Attributes: Size = (Byte, Word)

Description: If the specified condition is true, program execution continues at location (PC)+displacement. The PC contains the address of the instruction word of the Bcc instruction plus two. The displacement is a twos complement integer that represents the relative distance in bytes from the current PC to the destination PC. If the 8-bit displacement field in the instruction word is zero, a 16-bit displacement (the word immediately following the instruction) is used. Condition code cc specifies one of the following conditions:

CC	carry clear	0100	$\overline{C}$	LS	low or same	0011	$C+Z$
CS	carry set	0101	C	LT	less than	1101	$N\cdot\overline{V}+\overline{N}\cdot V$
EQ	equal	0111	Z	MI	minus	1011	N
GE	greater or equal	1100	$N\cdot V+\overline{N}\cdot\overline{V}$	NE	not equal	0110	$\overline{Z}$
GT	greater than	1110	$N\cdot V\cdot\overline{Z}+\overline{N}\cdot\overline{V}\cdot\overline{Z}$	PL	plus	1010	$\overline{N}$
HI	high	0010	$\overline{C}\cdot\overline{Z}$	VC	overflow clear	1000	$\overline{V}$
LE	less or equal	1111	$Z+N\cdot\overline{V}+\overline{N}\cdot V$	VS	overflow set	1001	V

Condition Codes:
Not affected

Instruction Format:

15	14	13	12	11	10	9	8	7	6	5	4	3	2	1	0
0	1	1	0	CONDITION				8-BIT DISPLACEMENT							
16-BIT DISPLACEMENT IF 8-BIT DISPLACEMENT = $00															

Instruction Fields:

Condition field — The binary code for one of the conditions listed in the table.

8-Bit Displacement field — Twos complement integer specifying the number of bytes between the branch instruction and the next instruction to be executed if the condition is met.

16-Bit Displacement field — Used for the displacement when the 8-bit displacement field contains $00.

B

NOTE

A branch to the immediately following instruction automatically uses the 16-bit displacement format because the 8-bit displacement field contains $00 (zero offset).

Operation: ~(⟨number⟩ of Destination) ➧ Z;
~(⟨number⟩ of Destination) ➧ ⟨bit number⟩ of Destination

Assembler Syntax: BCHG Dn,⟨ea⟩
BCHG #⟨data⟩,⟨ea⟩

Attributes: Size = (Byte, Long)

Description: Tests a bit in the destination operand and sets the Z condition code appropriately, then inverts the specified bit in the destination. When the destination is a data register, any of the 32 bits can be specified by the modulo 32-bit number. When the destination is a memory location, the operation is a byte operation, and the bit number is modulo 8. In all cases, bit zero refers to the least-significant bit. The bit number for this operation may be specified in either of two ways:

1. Immediate — The bit number is specified in a second word of the instruction.
2. Register — The specified data register contains the bit number.

Condition Codes:

X	N	Z	V	C
—	—	*	—	—

X Not affected
N Not affected
Z Set if the bit tested is zero. Cleared otherwise.
V Not affected
C Not affected

Instruction Format (Bit Number Dynamic, specified in a register):

15	14	13	12	11	10	9	8	7	6	5	4	3	2	1	0
										EFFECTIVE ADDRESS					
										MODE			REGISTER		
0	0	0	0	REGISTER			1	0	1						

Instruction Fields (Bit Number Dynamic):

Register field — Specifies the data register that contains the bit number

Effective Address field — Specifies the destination location. Only data alterable addressing modes are allowed as shown:

Addressing Mode	Mode	Register
Dn*	000	reg. number:Dn
An	—	—
(An)	010	reg. number:An
(An)+	011	reg. number:An
–(An)	100	reg. number:An
(d_{16},An)	101	reg. number:An
(d_8,An,Xn)	110	reg. number:An

Addressing Mode	Mode	Register
(xxx).W	111	000
(xxx).L	111	001
#⟨data⟩	—	—
(d_{16},PC)	—	—
(d_8,PC,Xn)	—	—

*Long only; all others are byte only.

B

Instruction Format (Bit Number Static, specified as immediate data):

15	14	13	12	11	10	9	8	7	6	5	4	3	2	1	0
0	0	0	0	1	0	0	0	0	1	EFFECTIVE ADDRESS MODE			EFFECTIVE ADDRESS REGISTER		
0	0	0	0	0	0	0	0	BIT NUMBER							

Instruction Fields (Bit Number Static):

Effective Address field — Specifies the destination location

Only data alterable addressing modes are allowed as shown:

Addressing Mode	Mode	Register
Dn*	000	reg. number:Dn
An	—	—
(An)	010	reg. number:An
(An)+	011	reg. number:An
−(An)	100	reg. number:An
(d_{16},An)	101	reg. number:An
(d_8,An,Xn)	110	reg. number:An

*Long only; all others are byte only.

Addressing Mode	Mode	Register
(xxx).W	111	000
(xxx).L	111	001
#⟨data⟩	—	—
(d_{16},PC)	—	—
(d_8,PC,Xn)	—	—

Bit Number field — Specifies the bit number

B

BCLR — Test a Bit and Clear

BCLR

Operation: ~(⟨bit number⟩ of Destination) ➧ Z;
0 ➧ ⟨bit number⟩ of Destination

Assembler Syntax: BCLR Dn,⟨ea⟩
BCLR #⟨data⟩,⟨ea⟩

Attributes: Size = (Byte, Long)

Description: Tests a bit in the destination operand and sets the Z condition code appropriately, then clears the specified bit in the destination. When a data register is the destination, any of the 32 bits can be specified by a modulo 32-bit number. When a memory location is the destination, the operation is a byte operation, and the bit number is modulo 8. In all cases, bit zero refers to the least-significant bit. The bit number for this operation can be specified in either of two ways:

1. Immediate — The bit number is specified in a second word of the instruction.
2. Register — The specified data register contains the bit number.

Condition Codes:

X	N	Z	V	C
—	—	*	—	—

X Not affected
N Not affected
Z Set if the bit tested is zero. Cleared otherwise.
V Not affected
C Not affected

Instruction Format (Bit Number Dynamic, specified in a register):

15	14	13	12	11	10	9	8	7	6	5	4	3	2	1	0
										EFFECTIVE ADDRESS					
0	0	0	0	REGISTER			1	1	0	MODE			REGISTER		

Instruction Fields (Bit Number Dynamic):

Register field — Specifies the data register that contains the bit number

B

Effective Address field — Specifies the destination location
Only data alterable addressing modes are allowed as shown:

Addressing Mode	Mode	Register
Dn*	000	reg. number:Dn
An	—	—
(An)	010	reg. number:An
(An)+	011	reg. number:An
−(An)	100	reg. number:An
(d_{16},An)	101	reg. number:An
(d_8,An,Xn)	110	reg. number:An

*Long only; all others are byte only.

Addressing Mode	Mode	Register
(xxx).W	111	000
(xxx).L	111	001
#⟨data⟩	—	—
(d_{16},PC)	—	—
(d_8,PC,Xn)	—	—

Instruction Format (Bit Number Static, specified as immediate data):

15	14	13	12	11	10	9	8	7	6	5	4	3	2	1	0
0	0	0	0	1	0	0	0	1	0	EFFECTIVE ADDRESS					
										MODE			REGISTER		
0	0	0	0	0	0	0	0	BIT NUMBER							

Instruction Fields (Bit Number Static):

Effective Address field — Specifies the destination location
Only data alterable addressing modes are allowed as shown:

Addressing Mode	Mode	Register
Dn*	000	reg. number:Dn
An	—	—
(An)	010	reg. number:An
(An)+	011	reg. number:An
−(An)	100	reg. number:An
(d_{16},An)	101	reg. number:An
(d_8,An,Xn)	110	reg. number:An

*Long only; all others are byte only.

Addressing Mode	Mode	Register
(xxx).W	111	000
(xxx).L	111	001
#⟨data⟩	—	—
(d_{16},PC)	—	—
(d_8,PC,Xn)	—	—

Bit Number field — Specifies the bit number

Operation: Execute breakpoint acknowledge bus cycle;
Trap as illegal instruction

Assembler Syntax: BKPT #⟨data⟩

Attributes: Unsized

Description: This instruction is used to support the program breakpoint function for debug monitors and real-time hardware emulators, and the operation will be dependent on the implementation. Execution of this instruction will cause the MC68010 to run a breakpoint acknowledge bus cycle (all function codes driven high) and zeros on all address lines.

Whether the breakpoint acknowledge bus cycle is terminated with $\overline{DTACK}$, $\overline{BERR}$, or $\overline{VPA}$, the processor always takes an illegal instruction exception. During exception processing, a debug monitor can distinguish eight different software breakpoints by decoding the field in the BKPT instruction.

For the MC68000, MC68HC000, and MC68008, this instruction causes an illegal instruction exception but does not run the breakpoint acknowledge bus cycle.

Condition Codes:
Not affected

Instruction Format:

15	14	13	12	11	10	9	8	7	6	5	4	3	2	1	0
0	1	0	0	1	0	0	0	0	1	0	0	1	VECTOR		

Instruction Fields:
Vector field — Contains the immediate data, a value in the range of 0-7. This is the breakpoint number.

B

Operation: PC + d ➧ PC

Assembler Syntax: BRA ⟨label⟩

Attributes: Size = (Byte, Word)

Description: Program execution continues at location (PC) + displacement. The PC contains the address of the instruction word of the BRA instruction plus two. The displacement is a twos complement integer that represents the relative distance in bytes from the current PC to the destination PC. If the 8-bit displacement field in the instruction word is zero, a 16-bit displacement (the word immediately following the instruction) is used.

Condition Codes:
Not affected

Instruction Format:

15	14	13	12	11	10	9	8	7	6	5	4	3	2	1	0
0	1	1	0	0	0	0	0	8-BIT DISPLACEMENT							
16-BIT DISPLACEMENT IF 8-BIT DISPLACEMENT = $00															

Instruction Fields:

8-Bit Displacement field — Twos complement integer specifying the number of bytes between the branch instruction and the next instruction to be executed.

16-Bit Displacement field — Used for a larger displacement when the 8-bit displacement is equal to $00.

NOTE

A branch to the immediately following instruction automatically uses the 16-bit displacement format because the 8-bit displacement field contains $00 (zero offset).

B

Operation: ~(⟨bit number⟩ of Destination) → Z;
1 → ⟨bit number⟩ of Destination

Assembler Syntax: BSET Dn,⟨ea⟩
BSET #⟨data⟩,⟨ea⟩

Attributes: Size = (Byte, Long)

Description: Tests a bit in the destination operand and sets the Z condition code appropriately. Then sets the specified bit in the destination operand. When a data register is the destination, any of the 32 bits can be specified by a modulo 32-bit number. When a memory location is the destination, the operation is a byte operation, and the bit number is modulo 8. In all cases, bit zero refers to the least-significant bit. The bit number for this operation can be specified in either of two ways:

1. Immediate — The bit number is specified in the second word of the instruction.
2. Register — The specified data register contains the bit number.

Condition Codes:

X	N	Z	V	C
—	—	*	—	—

X Not affected
N Not affected
Z Set if the bit tested is zero. Cleared otherwise.
V Not affected
C Not affected

Instruction Format (Bit Number Dynamic, specified in a register):

15	14	13	12	11	10	9	8	7	6	5	4	3	2	1	0
										EFFECTIVE ADDRESS					
0	0	0	0	REGISTER			1	1	1	MODE			REGISTER		

B

Instruction Fields (Bit Number Dynamic):

Register field — Specifies the data register that contains the bit number

Effective Address field — Specifies the destination location. Only data alterable addressing modes are allowed as shown:

Addressing Mode	Mode	Register
Dn*	000	reg. number:Dn
An	—	—
(An)	010	reg. number:An
(An)+	011	reg. number:An
−(An)	100	reg. number:An
(d_{16},An)	101	reg. number:An
(d_8,An,Xn)	110	reg. number:An

Addressing Mode	Mode	Register
(xxx).W	111	000
(xxx).L	111	001
#⟨data⟩	—	—
(d_{16},PC)	—	—
(d_8,PC,Xn)	—	—

*Long only; all others are byte only.

Instruction Format (Bit Number Static, specified as immediate data):

15	14	13	12	11	10	9	8	7	6	5	4	3	2	1	0
0	0	0	0	1	0	0	0	1	1	EFFECTIVE ADDRESS MODE			EFFECTIVE ADDRESS REGISTER		
0	0	0	0	0	0	0	BIT NUMBER								

Instruction Fields (Bit Number Static):

Effective Address field — Specifies the destination location. Only data alterable addressing modes are allowed as shown:

Addressing Mode	Mode	Register
Dn*	000	reg. number:Dn
An	—	—
(An)	010	reg. number:An
(An)+	011	reg. number:An
−(An)	100	reg. number:An
(d_{16},An)	101	reg. number:An
(d_8,An,Xn)	110	reg. number:An

Addressing Mode	Mode	Register
(xxx).W	111	000
(xxx).L	111	001
#⟨data⟩	—	—
(d_{16},PC)	—	—
(d_8,PC,Xn)	—	—

*Long only; all others are byte only.

Bit Number field — Specifies the bit number

Operation: SP – 4 ➧ SP; PC ➧ (SP); PC + d ➧ PC

Assembler Syntax: BSR ⟨label⟩

Attributes: Size = (Byte, Word)

Description: Pushes the long word address of the instruction immediately following the BSR instruction onto the system stack. The PC contains the address of the instruction word plus two. Program execution then continues at location (PC) + displacement. The displacement is a twos complement integer that represents the relative distance in bytes from the current PC to the destination PC. If the 8-bit displacement field in the instruction word is zero, a 16-bit displacement (the word immediately following the instruction) is used.

Condition Codes:
Not affected

Instruction Format:

15	14	13	12	11	10	9	8	7	6	5	4	3	2	1	0
0	1	1	0	0	0	0	1	8-BIT DISPLACEMENT							
16-BIT DISPLACEMENT IF 8-BIT DISPLACEMENT = $00															

Instruction Fields:

8-Bit Displacement field — Twos complement integer specifying the number of bytes between the branch instruction and the next instruction to be executed

16-Bit Displacement field — Used for a larger displacement when the 8-bit displacement is equal to $00

NOTE

A branch to the immediately following instruction automatically uses the 16-bit displacement format because the 8-bit displacement field contains $00 (zero offset).

BTST — Test a Bit — BTST

Operation: −(⟨bit number⟩ of Destination) → Z;

Assembler Syntax:
BTST Dn,⟨ea⟩
BTST #⟨data⟩,⟨ea⟩

Attributes: Size = (Byte, Long)

Description: Tests a bit in the destination operand and sets the Z condition code appropriately. When a data register is the destination, any of the 32 bits can be specified by a modulo 32 bit number. When a memory location is the destination, the operation is a byte operation, and the bit number is modulo 8. In all cases, bit zero refers to the least significant bit. The bit number for this operation can be specified in either of two ways:

1. Immediate — The bit number is specified in a second word of the instruction.
2. Register — The specified data register contains the bit number.

Condition Codes:

X	N	Z	V	C
—	—	*	—	—

X Not affected
N Not affected
Z Set if the bit tested is zero. Cleared otherwise.
V Not affected
C Not affected

Instruction Format (Bit Number Dynamic, specified in a register):

15	14	13	12	11	10	9	8	7	6	5	4	3	2	1	0
0	0	0	0	REGISTER			1	0	0	EFFECTIVE ADDRESS					
										MODE			REGISTER		

Instruction Fields (Bit Number Dynamic):

Register field — Specifies the data register that contains the bit number

Effective Address field — Specifies the destination location. Only data addressing modes are allowed as shown:

Addressing Mode	Mode	Register
Dn*	000	reg. number:Dn
An	—	—
(An)	010	reg. number:An
(An)+	011	reg. number:An
−(An)	100	reg. number:An
(d_{16},An)	101	reg. number:An
(d_8,An,Xn)	110	reg. number:An

Addressing Mode	Mode	Register
(xxx).W	111	000
(xxx).L	111	001
#⟨data⟩	111	100
(d_{16},PC)	111	010
(d_8,PC,Xn)	111	011

*Long only; all others are byte only.

Instruction Format (Bit Number Static, specified as immediate data):

15	14	13	12	11	10	9	8	7	6	5	4	3	2	1	0
0	0	0	0	1	0	0	0	0	0	EFFECTIVE ADDRESS MODE			EFFECTIVE ADDRESS REGISTER		
0	0	0	0	0	0	0	0	BIT NUMBER							

Instruction Fields (Bit Number Static):

Effective Address field — Specifies the destination location. Only data addressing modes are allowed as shown:

Addressing Mode	Mode	Register
Dn	000	reg. number:Dn
An	—	—
(An)	010	reg. number:An
(An)+	011	reg. number:An
−(An)	100	reg. number:An
(d_{16},An)	101	reg. number:An
(d_8,An,Xn)	110	reg. number:An

Addressing Mode	Mode	Register
(xxx).W	111	000
(xxx).L	111	001
#⟨data⟩	—	—
(d_{16},PC)	111	010
(d_8,PC,Xn)	111	011

Bit Number field — Specifies the bit number

CHK Check Register Against Bounds

Operation: If Dn < 0 or Dn > Source then TRAP

Assembler Syntax: CHK ⟨ea⟩,Dn

Attributes: Size = (Word)

Description: Compares the value in the data register specified in the instruction to zero and to the upper bound (effective address operand). The upper bound is a twos complement integer. If the register value is less than zero or greater than the upper bound, a CHK instruction exception, vector number 6, occurs.

Condition Codes:

X	N	Z	V	C
—	*	U	U	U

X Not affected
N Set if Dn < 0; cleared if Dn > effective address operand. Undefined otherwise.
Z Undefined
V Undefined
C Undefined

Instruction Format:

15	14	13	12	11	10	9	8	7	6	5	4	3	2	1	0
0	1	0	0	REGISTER			1	1	0	EFFECTIVE ADDRESS					
										MODE			REGISTER		

Instruction Fields:

Register field — Specifies the data register that contains the value to be checked

Effective Address field — Specifies the upper bound operand. Only data addressing modes are allowed as shown:

Addressing Mode	Mode	Register
Dn	000	reg. number:Dn
An	—	—
(An)	010	reg. number:An
(An)+	011	reg. number:An
−(An)	100	reg. number:An
(d_{16},An)	101	reg. number:An
(d_8,An,Xn)	110	reg. number:An

Addressing Mode	Mode	Register
(xxx).W	111	000
(xxx).L	111	001
#⟨data⟩	111	100
(d_{16},PC)	111	010
(d_8,PC,Xn)	111	011

CLR — Clear an Operand

CLR

Operation: 0 ➧ Destination

Assembler Syntax: CLR ⟨ea⟩

Attributes: Size = (Byte, Word, Long)

Description: Clears the destination operand to zero. The size of the operation may be specified as byte, word, or long.

Condition Codes:

X	N	Z	V	C
—	0	1	0	0

X Not affected
N Always cleared
Z Always set
V Always cleared
C Always cleared

Instruction Format:

15	14	13	12	11	10	9	8	7	6	5	4	3	2	1	0
0	1	0	0	0	0	1	0	SIZE		EFFECTIVE ADDRESS MODE			EFFECTIVE ADDRESS REGISTER		

Instruction Fields:

Size field — Specifies the size of the operation
- 00 — Byte operation
- 01 — Word operation
- 10 — Long operation

Effective Address field — Specifies the destination location. Only data alterable addressing modes are allowed as shown:

Addressing Mode	Mode	Register
Dn	000	reg. number:Dn
An	—	—
(An)	010	reg. number:An
(An)+	011	reg. number:An
−(An)	100	reg. number:An
(d_{16},An)	101	reg. number:An
(d_8,An,Xn)	110	reg. number:An

Addressing Mode	Mode	Register
(xxx).W	111	000
(xxx).L	111	001
#⟨data⟩	—	—
(d_{16},PC)	—	—
(d_8,PC,Xn)	—	—

NOTE

In the MC68000, MC68HC000, and MC68008 a memory destination is read before it is cleared.

B

Operation: Destination — Source ▶ cc

Assembler Syntax: CMP ⟨ea⟩, Dn

Attributes: Size = (Byte, Word, Long)

Description: Subtracts the source operand from the destination data register and sets the condition codes according to the result; the data register is not changed. The size of the operation can be byte, word, or long.

Condition Codes:

X	N	Z	V	C
—	*	*	*	*

X Not affected
N Set if the result is negative. Cleared otherwise.
Z Set if the result is zero. Cleared otherwise.
V Set if an overflow occurs. Cleared otherwise.
C Set if a borrow occurs. Cleared otherwise.

Instruction Format:

15	14	13	12	11	10	9	8	7	6	5	4	3	2	1	0
1	0	1	1	REGISTER			OP-MODE			EFFECTIVE ADDRESS					
										MODE			REGISTER		

Instruction Fields:

Register field — Specifies the destination data register

Op-Mode field —

Byte	Word	Long	Operation
000	001	010	(⟨Dn⟩) − (⟨ea⟩)

B

Effective Address field — Specifies the source operand. All addressing modes are allowed as shown:

Addressing Mode	Mode	Register
Dn	000	reg. number:Dn
An*	001	reg. number:An
(An)	010	reg. number:An
(An)+	011	reg. number:An
−(An)	100	reg. number:An
(d_{16},An)	101	reg. number:An
(d_8,An,Xn)	110	reg. number:An

*Word and Long only.

Addressing Mode	Mode	Register
(xxx).W	111	000
(xxx).L	111	001
#⟨data⟩	111	100
(d_{16},PC)	111	010
(d_8,PC,Xn)	111	011

NOTE

CMPA is used when the destination is an address register. CMPI is used when the source is immediate data. CMPM is used for memory to memory compares. Most assemblers automatically make the distinction.

B

Operation: Destination − Source

Assembler Syntax: CMPA ⟨ea⟩, An

Attributes: Size = (Word, Long)

Description: Subtracts the source operand from the destination address register and sets the condition codes according to the result; the address register is not changed. The size of the operation can be specified as word or long. Word length source operands are sign extended to 32-bits for comparison.

Condition Codes:

X	N	Z	V	C
—	*	*	*	*

X Not affected
N Set if the result is negative. Cleared otherwise.
Z Set if the result is zero. Cleared otherwise.
V Set if an overflow is generated. Cleared otherwise.
C Set if a borrow is generated. Cleared otherwise.

Instruction Format:

15	14	13	12	11	10	9	8	7	6	5	4	3	2	1	0
1	0	1	1	REGISTER			OP-MODE			EFFECTIVE ADDRESS MODE			EFFECTIVE ADDRESS REGISTER		

Op-Mode Field:
Word **Long** **Operation**

Instruction Fields:
Register field — Specifies the destination address register
Op-Mode field — Specifies the size of the operation:
011 — Word operation. The source operand is sign-extended to a long operand and the operation is performed on the address register using all 32 bits.
111 — Long operation

B

Effective Address field — Specifies the source operand. All addressing modes are allowed as shown:

Addressing Mode	Mode	Register
Dn	000	reg. number:Dn
An	001	reg. number:An
(An)	010	reg. number:An
(An)+	011	reg. number:An
−(An)	100	reg. number:An
(d_{16},An)	101	reg. number:An
(d_8,An,Xn)	110	reg. number:An

Addressing Mode	Mode	Register
(xxx).W	111	000
(xxx).L	111	001
#⟨data⟩	111	100
(d_{16},PC)	111	010
(d_8,PC,Xn)	111	011

CMPI — Compare Immediate

Operation: Destination − Immediate Data

Assembler Syntax: CMPI #<data>,<ea>

Attributes: Size = (Byte, Word, Long)

Description: Subtracts the immediate data from the destination operand and sets the condition codes according to the result; the destination location is not changed. The size of the operation may be specified as byte, word, or long. The size of the immediate data matches the operation size.

Condition Codes:

X	N	Z	V	C
—	*	*	*	*

X Not affected
N Set if the result is negative. Cleared otherwise.
Z Set if the result is zero. Cleared otherwise.
V Set if an overflow occurs. Cleared otherwise.
C Set if a borrow occurs. Cleared otherwise.

Instruction Format:

15	14	13	12	11	10	9	8	7	6	5	4	3	2	1	0
0	0	0	0	1	1	0	0	SIZE		EFFECTIVE ADDRESS MODE			EFFECTIVE ADDRESS REGISTER		
WORD DATA (16 BITS)								BYTE DATA (8 BITS)							
LONG DATA (32 BITS)															

Instruction Fields:

Size field — Specifies the size of the operation:
- 00 — Byte operation
- 01 — Word operation
- 10 — Long operation

B

Effective Address field — Specifies the destination operand. Only data addressing modes are allowed as shown:

Addressing Mode	Mode	Register
Dn	000	reg. number:Dn
An	—	—
(An)	010	reg. number:An
(An)+	011	reg. number:An
−(An)	100	reg. number:An
(d_{16},An)	101	reg. number:An
(d_8,An,Xn)	110	reg. number:An

Addressing Mode	Mode	Register
(xxx).W	111	000
(xxx).L	111	001
#⟨data⟩	—	—
(d_{16},PC)	111	010
(d_8,PC,Xn)	111	011

Immediate field — (Data immediately following the instruction):
If size = 00, the data is the low order byte of the immediate word
If size = 01, the data is the entire immediate word
If size = 10, the data is the next two immediate words

B

Operation: Destination — Source ♦ cc

Assembler Syntax: CMPM (Ay)+,(Ax)+

Attributes: Size = (Byte, Word, Long)

Description: Subtracts the source operand from the destination operand and sets the condition codes according to the results; the destination location is not changed. The operands are always addressed with the postincrement addressing mode, using the address registers specified in the instruction. The size of the operation may be specified as byte, word, or long.

Condition Codes:

X	N	Z	V	C
—	*	*	*	*

X Not affected
N Set if the result is negative. Cleared otherwise.
Z Set if the result is zero. Cleared otherwise.
V Set if an overflow is generated. Cleared otherwise.
C Set if a borrow is generated. Cleared otherwise.

Instruction Format:

15	14	13	12	11	10	9	8	7	6	5	4	3	2	1	0
1	0	1	1	REGISTER Ax			1	SIZE		0	0	1	REGISTER Ay		

Instruction Fields:

Register Ax field — (always the destination) Specifies an address register in the postincrement addressing mode

Size field — Specifies the size of the operation:
- 00 — Byte operation
- 01 — Word operation
- 10 — Long operation

Register Ay field — (always the source) Specifies an address register in the postincrement addressing mode

B

DBcc — Test Condition, Decrement, and Branch

Operation: If condition false then (Dn − 1 ➧ Dn;
If Dn ≠ −1 then PC+d ➧ PC)

Assembler Syntax: DBcc Dn,⟨label⟩

Attributes: Size = (Word)

Description: Controls a loop of instructions. The parameters are: a condition code, a data register (counter), and a displacement value. The instruction first tests the condition (for termination); if it is true, no operation is performed. If the termination condition is not true, the low-order 16 bits of the counter data register are decremented by one. If the result is −1, execution continues with the next instruction. If the result is not equal to −1, execution continues at the location indicated by the current value of the PC plus the sign-extended 16-bit displacement. The value in the PC is the address of the instruction word of the DBcc instruction plus two. The displacement is a twos complement integer that represents the relative distance in bytes from the current PC to the destination PC.

Condition code cc specifies one of the following conditions:

CC	carry clear	0100	$\overline{C}$	LS	low or same	0011	$C+Z$
CS	carry set	0101	C	LT	less than	1101	$N\cdot\overline{V}+\overline{N}\cdot V$
EQ	equal	0111	Z	MI	minus	1011	N
F	never equal	0001	0	NE	not equal	0110	$\overline{Z}$
GE	greater or equal	1100	$N\cdot V+\overline{N}\cdot\overline{V}$	PL	plus	1010	$\overline{N}$
GT	greater than	1110	$N\cdot V\cdot\overline{Z}+\overline{N}\cdot\overline{V}\cdot\overline{Z}$	T	always true	0000	1
HI	high	0010	$\overline{C}\cdot\overline{Z}$	VC	overflow clear	1000	$\overline{V}$
LE	less or equal	1111	$Z+N\cdot\overline{V}+\overline{N}\cdot V$	VS	overflow set	1001	V

Condition Codes:
Not affected

Instruction Format:

15	14	13	12	11	10	9	8	7	6	5	4	3	2	1	0
0	1	0	1	CONDITION				1	1	0	0	1	REGISTER		
DISPLACEMENT (16 BITS)															

B

Instruction Fields:

Condition field — The binary code for one of the conditions listed in the table
Register field — Specifies the data register used as the counter
Displacement field — Specifies the number of bytes to branch

Notes:

1. The terminating condition is similar to the UNTIL loop clauses of high-level languages. For example: DBMI can be stated as "decrement and branch until minus".
2. Most assemblers accept DBRA for DBF for use when only a count terminates the loop (no condition is tested).
3. A program can enter a loop at the beginning or by branching to the trailing DBcc instruction. Entering the loop at the beginning is useful for indexed addressing modes and dynamically specified bit operations. In this case, the control index count must be one less than the desired number of loop executions. However, when entering a loop by branching directly to the trailing DBcc instruction, the control count should equal the loop execution count. In this case, if a zero count occurs, the DBcc instruction does not branch, and the main loop is not executed.

Operation: Destination/Source ➧ Destination

Assembler Syntax: DIVS.W ⟨ea⟩,Dn 32/16 ➧ 16r:16q

Attributes: Size = (Word)

Description: Divides the signed destination operand by the signed source operand and stores the signed result in the destination. The instruction divides a long word by a word. The result is a quotient in the lower word (least-significant 16 bits) and the remainder is in the upper word (most-significant 16 bits) of the result. The sign of the remainder is the same as the sign of the dividend.

Two special conditions may arise during the operation:

1. Division by zero causes a trap
2. Overflow may be detected and set before the instruction completes. If the instruction detects an overflow, it sets the overflow condition code, and the operands are unaffected.

Condition Codes:

X	N	Z	V	C
—	*	*	*	0

X Not affected
N Set if the quotient is negative. Cleared otherwise. Undefined if overflow or divide by zero occurs.
Z Set if the quotient is zero. Cleared otherwise. Undefined if overflow or divide by zero occurs.
V Set if division overflow occurs; undefined if divide by zero occurs. Cleared otherwise.
C Always cleared

Instruction Format (word form):

15	14	13	12	11	10	9	8	7	6	5	4	3	2	1	0
										EFFECTIVE ADDRESS					
1	0	0	0	REGISTER			1	1	1	MODE			REGISTER		

B

Instruction Fields:

Register field — Specifies any of the eight data registers. This field always specifies the destination operand.

Effective Address field — Specifies the source operand. Only data addressing modes are allowed as shown:

Addressing Mode	Mode	Register
Dn	000	reg. number:Dn
An	—	—
(An)	010	reg. number:An
(An)+	011	reg. number:An
−(An)	100	reg. number:An
(d_{16},An)	101	reg. number:An
(d_8,An,Xn)	110	reg. number:An

Addressing Mode	Mode	Register
(xxx).W	111	000
(xxx).L	111	001
#⟨data⟩	111	100
(d_{16},PC)	111	010
(d_8,PC,Xn)	111	011

NOTE

Overflow occurs if the quotient is larger than a 16-bit signed integer. The instruction checks for overflow at the start of execution. If the upper word of the dividend is greater than or equal to the divisor, the overflow bit is set in the condition codes, and the instruction terminates with the operands unchanged.

B

DIVU Unsigned Divide

Operation: Destination/Source → Destination

Assembler Syntax: DIVU.W ⟨ea⟩,Dn 32/16 → 16r:16q

Attributes: Size = (Word)

Description: Divides the unsigned destination operand by the unsigned source operand and stores the unsigned result in the destination. The instruction divides a long word by a word. The result is a quotient in the lower word (least-significant 16 bits) and the remainder is in the upper word (most significant 16 bits) of the result.

Two special conditions may arise during the operation:

1. Division by zero causes a trap
2. Overflow may be detected and set before the instruction completes. If the instruction detects an overflow, it sets the overflow condition code, and the operands are unaffected.

Condition Codes:

X	N	Z	V	C
—	*	*	*	0

X Not affected

N Set if the quotient is negative. Cleared otherwise. Undefined if overflow or divide by zero occurs.

Z Set if the quotient is zero. Cleared otherwise. Undefined if overflow or divide by zero occurs.

V Set if division overflow occurs; undefined if divide by zero occurs. Cleared otherwise.

C Always cleared

Instruction Format (word form):

15	14	13	12	11	10	9	8	7	6	5	4	3	2	1	0
1	0	0	0	REGISTER			TYPE	1	1	EFFECTIVE ADDRESS					
										MODE			REGISTER		

Instruction Fields:

Register field — Specifies any of the eight data registers. This field always specifies the destination operand.

Effective Address field — Specifies the source operand. Only data addressing modes are allowed as shown:

Addressing Mode	Mode	Register
Dn	000	reg. number:Dn
An	—	—
(An)	010	reg. number:An
(An)+	011	reg. number:An
−(An)	100	reg. number:An
(d_{16},An)	101	reg. number:An
(d_8,An,Xn)	110	reg. number:An

Addressing Mode	Mode	Register
(xxx).W	111	000
(xxx).L	111	001
#⟨data⟩	111	100
(d_{16},PC)	111	010
(d_8,PC,Xn)	111	011

NOTE

Overflow occurs if the quotient is larger than a 16-bit signed integer. The instruction checks for overflow at the start of execution. If the upper word of the dividend is greater than or equal to the divisor, the overflow bit is set in the condition codes, and the instruction terminates with the operands unchanged.

B

EOR — Exclusive OR Logical

Operation:

Source ⊕ Destination ➧ Destination

Assembler Syntax: EOR Dn,⟨ea⟩

Attributes: Size = (Byte, Word, Long)

Description: Performs an exclusive OR operation on the destination operand using the source operand and stores the result in the destination location. The size of the operation may be specified to be byte, word, or long. The source operand must be a data register. The destination operand is specified in the effective address field.

Condition Codes:

X	N	Z	V	C
—	*	*	0	0

X Not affected
N Set if the most-significant bit of the result is set. Cleared otherwise.
Z Set if the result is zero. Cleared otherwise.
V Always cleared
C Always cleared

Instruction Format (word form):

15	14	13	12	11	10	9	8	7	6	5	4	3	2	1	0
1	0	1	1	REGISTER			OP-MODE			EFFECTIVE ADDRESS MODE			EFFECTIVE ADDRESS REGISTER		

Instruction Fields:

Register field — Specifies any of the eight data registers

Op-Mode field —

Byte	Word	Long	Operation
100	101	110	(⟨ea⟩) ⊕ (⟨Dn⟩) ➧ ⟨ea⟩

B

Effective Address field — Specifies the destination operand. Only data alterable addressing modes are allowed as shown:

Addressing Mode	Mode	Register
Dn	000	reg. number:Dn
An	—	—
(An)	010	reg. number:An
(An)+	011	reg. number:An
–(An)	100	reg. number:An
(d_{16},An)	101	reg. number:An
(d_8,An,Xn)	110	reg. number:An

Addressing Mode	Mode	Register
(xxx).W	111	000
(xxx).L	111	001
#⟨data⟩	—	—
(d_{16},PC)	—	—
(d_8,PC,Xn)	—	—

NOTE

Memory to data register operations are not allowed. Most assemblers use EORI when the source is immediate data.

Exclusive OR Immediate

EORI

Operation:
Immediate Data ⊕ Destination ▶ Destination

Assembler Syntax: EORI #⟨data⟩,⟨ea⟩

Attributes: Size = (Byte, Word, Long)

Description: Performs an exclusive OR operation on the destination operand using the immediate data and the destination operand and stores the result in the destination location. The size of the operation may be specified as byte, word, or long. The size of the immediate data matches the operation size.

Condition Codes:

X	N	Z	V	C
—	*	*	0	0

X Not affected
N Set if the most significant bit of the result is set. Cleared otherwise.
Z Set if the result is zero. Cleared otherwise.
V Always cleared
C Always cleared

Instruction Format:

<table>
<tr><td>15</td><td>14</td><td>13</td><td>12</td><td>11</td><td>10</td><td>9</td><td>8</td><td>7</td><td>6</td><td>5</td><td>4</td><td>3</td><td>2</td><td>1</td><td>0</td></tr>
<tr><td rowspan="2">0</td><td rowspan="2">0</td><td rowspan="2">0</td><td rowspan="2">0</td><td rowspan="2">1</td><td rowspan="2">0</td><td rowspan="2">1</td><td rowspan="2">0</td><td colspan="2" rowspan="2">SIZE</td><td colspan="6">EFFECTIVE ADDRESS</td></tr>
<tr><td colspan="3">MODE</td><td colspan="3">REGISTER</td></tr>
<tr><td colspan="8">WORD DATA (16 BITS)</td><td colspan="8">BYTE DATA (8 BITS)</td></tr>
<tr><td colspan="16">LONG DATA (32 BITS)</td></tr>
</table>

Instruction Fields:

Size field — Specifies the size of the operation:
00 — Byte operation
01 — Word operation
10 — Long operation

B

Effective Address field — Specifies the destination operand. Only data alterable addressing modes are allowed as shown:

Addressing Mode	Mode	Register
Dn	000	reg. number:Dn
An	—	—
(An)	010	reg. number:An
(An)+	011	reg. number:An
−(An)	100	reg. number:An
(d_{16},An)	101	reg. number:An
(d_8,An,Xn)	110	reg. number:An

Addressing Mode	Mode	Register
(xxx).W	111	000
(xxx).L	111	001
#⟨data⟩	—	—
(d_{16},PC)	—	—
(d_8,PC,Xn)	—	—

Immediate field — (Data immediately following the instruction):
If size = 00, the data is the low-order byte of the immediate word
If size = 01, the data is the entire immediate word
If size = 10, the data is next two immediate words

B

EORI to CCR

Exclusive OR Immediate to Condition Code

EORI to CCR

Operation: Source ⊕ CCR ▸ CCR

Assembler Syntax: EORI #⟨data⟩,CCR

Attributes: Size = (Byte)

Description: Performs an exclusive OR operation on the condition code register using the immediate operand and stores the result in the condition code register (low-order byte of the status register). All implemented bits of the condition code register are affected.

Condition Codes:

X	N	Z	V	C
*	*	*	*	*

X Changed if bit 4 of immediate operand is one. Unchanged otherwise.
N Changed if bit 3 of immediate operand is one. Unchanged otherwise.
Z Changed if bit 2 of immediate operand is one. Unchanged otherwise.
V Changed if bit 1 of immediate operand is one. Unchanged otherwise.
C Changed if bit 0 of immediate operand is one. Unchanged otherwise.

Instruction Format:

15	14	13	12	11	10	9	8	7	6	5	4	3	2	1	0
0	0	0	0	1	0	1	0	0	0	1	1	1	1	0	0
0	0	0	0	0	0	0	0	BYTE DATA (8 BITS)							

B

EORI to SR

Exclusive OR Immediate to the Status Register (Privileged Instruction)

EORI to SR

Operation: If supervisor state
then Source ⊕ SR ➧ SR

else TRAP

Assembler Syntax: EORI #⟨data⟩,SR

Attributes: Size = (Word)

Description: Performs an exclusive OR operation on the contents of the status register using the immediate operand and stores the result in the status register. All implemented bits of the status register are affected.

Condition Codes:

X	N	Z	V	C
*	*	*	*	*

X Changed if bit 4 of immediate operand is one. Unchanged otherwise.
N Changed if bit 3 of immediate operand is one. Unchanged otherwise.
Z Changed if bit 2 of immediate operand is one. Unchanged otherwise.
V Changed if bit 1 of immediate operand is one. Unchanged otherwise.
C Changed if bit 0 of immediate operand is one. Unchanged otherwise.

Instruction Format:

15	14	13	12	11	10	9	8	7	6	5	4	3	2	1	0
0	0	0	0	1	0	1	0	0	1	1	1	1	1	0	0
WORD DATA (16 BITS)															

B

Operation: Rx ⟷ Ry

Assembler Syntax:
EXG Dx,Dy
EXG Ax,Ay
EXG Dx,Ay
EXG Ay, Dx

Attributes: Size = (Long)

Description: Exchanges the contents of two 32-bit registers. The instruction performs three types of exchanges:

1. Exchange data registers
2. Exchange address registers
3. Exchange a data register and an address register

Condition Codes:

Not affected

Instruction Format:

15	14	13	12	11	10	9	8	7	6	5	4	3	2	1	0
1	1	0	0	REGISTER Rx			1	OP-MODE					REGISTER Ry		

Instruction Fields:

Register Rx field — Specifies either a data register or an address register depending on the mode. If the exchange is between data and address registers, this field always specifies the data register.

Op-Mode field — Specifies the type of exchange:
01000 — Data registers
01001 — Address registers
10001 — Data register and address register

Register Ry field — Specifies either a data register or an address register depending on the mode. If the exchange is between data and address registers, this field always specifies the address register.

B

EXT — Sign Extend

Operation: Destination Sign-Extended ➧ Destination

Assembler Syntax:
EXT.W Dn — Extend byte to word
EXT.L Dn — Extend word to long word

Attributes: Sizes (Word, Long)

Description: Extends a byte in a data register to a word or a word in a data register to a long word, by replicating the sign bit to the left. If the operation extends a byte to a word, bit [7] of the designated data register is copied to bits [15:8] of that data register. If the operation extends a word to a long word, bit [15] of the designated data register is copied to bits [31:16] of the data register.

Condition Codes:

X	N	Z	V	C
—	*	*	0	0

X Not affected
N Set if the result is negative. Cleared otherwise.
Z Set if the result is zero. Cleared otherwise.
V Always cleared
C Always cleared

Instruction Format:

15	14	13	12	11	10	9	8	7	6	5	4	3	2	1	0
0	1	0	0	1	0	0	OP-MODE			0	0	0	REGISTER		

Instruction Fields:

Op-Mode field — Specifies the size of the sign-extension operation:
010 — Sign-extend low-order byte of data register to word
011 — Sign-extend low-order word of data register to long

Register field — Specifies the data register is to be sign-extended

B

ILLEGAL — Take Illegal Instruction Trap — ILLEGAL

Operation: SSP − 2 ➧ SSP; Vector Offset ➧ (SSP);
SSP − 4 ➧ SSP; PC ➧ (SSP);
SSP − 2 ➧ SSP; SR ➧ (SSP);
Illegal Instruction Vector Address ➧ PC

Assembler Syntax: ILLEGAL

Attributes: Unsized

Description: Forces an illegal instruction exception, vector number 4. All other illegal instruction bit patterns are reserved for future extension of the instruction set and should not be used to force an exception.

Only the MC68010 stores a four-word exception stack frame by first writing the exception vector offset and format code to the system stack. All processors write the PC, followed by the SR, to the system stack.

Condition Codes:
Not affected

Instruction Format:

15	14	13	12	11	10	9	8	7	6	5	4	3	2	1	0
0	1	0	0	1	0	1	0	1	1	1	1	1	1	0	0

Operation: Destination Address ➧ PC

Assembler Syntax: JMP ⟨ea⟩

Attributes: Unsized

Description: Program execution continues at the effective address specified by the instruction. The addressing mode for the effective address must be a control addressing mode.

Condition Codes:
Not affected

Instruction Format:

15	14	13	12	11	10	9	8	7	6	5	4	3	2	1	0
0	1	0	0	1	1	1	0	1	1	EFFECTIVE ADDRESS					
										MODE			REGISTER		

Instruction Fields:
Effective Address field — Specifies the address of the next instruction. Only control addressing modes are allowed as shown:

Addressing Mode	Mode	Register
Dn	—	—
An	—	—
(An)	010	reg. number:An
(An)+	—	—
−(An)	—	—
(d_{16},An)	101	reg. number:An
(d_8,An,Xn)	110	reg. number:An

Addressing Mode	Mode	Register
(xxx).W	111	000
(xxx).L	111	001
#⟨data⟩	—	—
(d_{16},PC)	111	010
(d_8,PC,Xn)	111	011

B

Operation: SP – 4 ➧ Sp; PC ➧ (SP)
Destination Address ➧ PC

Assembler Syntax: JSR ⟨ea⟩

Attributes: Unsized

Description: Pushes the long word address of the instruction immediately following the JSR instruction onto the system stack. Program execution then continues at the address specified in the instruction.

Condition Codes:
Not affected

Instruction Format:

15	14	13	12	11	10	9	8	7	6	5	4	3	2	1	0
										EFFECTIVE ADDRESS					
0	1	0	0	1	1	1	0	1	0	MODE			REGISTER		

Instruction Fields:
Effective Address field — Specifies the address of the next instruction. Only control addressing modes are allowed as shown:

Addressing Mode	Mode	Register
Dn	—	—
An	—	—
(An)	010	reg. number:An
(An)+	—	—
–(An)	—	—
(d_{16},An)	101	reg. number:An
(d_8,An,Xn)	110	reg. number:An

Addressing Mode	Mode	Register
(xxx).W	111	000
(xxx).L	111	001
#⟨data⟩	—	—
(d_{16},PC)	111	010
(d_8,PC,Xn)	111	011

B

LEA — Load Effective Address — 

Operation: ⟨ea⟩ ➧ An

Assembler Syntax: LEA ⟨ea⟩,An

Attributes: Size = (Long)

Description: Loads the effective address into the specified address register. All 32 bits of the address register are affected by this instruction.

Condition Codes:
Not affected

Instruction Format:

15	14	13	12	11	10	9	8	7	6	5	4	3	2	1	0
0	1	0	0	REGISTER			1	1	1	EFFECTIVE ADDRESS					
										MODE			REGISTER		

Instruction Fields:

Register field — Specifies the address register to be updated with the effective address

Effective Address field — Specifies the address to be loaded into the address register. Only control addressing modes are allowed as shown:

Addressing Mode	Mode	Register
Dn	—	—
An	—	—
(An)	010	reg. number:An
(An)+	—	—
−(An)	—	—
(d_{16},An)	101	reg. number:An
(d_8,An,Xn)	110	reg. number:An

Addressing Mode	Mode	Register
(xxx).W	111	000
(xxx).L	111	001
#⟨data⟩	—	—
(d_{16},PC)	111	010
(d_8,PC,Xn)	111	011

B

LINK — Link and Allocate — 

Operation: Sp − 4 → Sp; An → (SP);
SP → An; SP + d → SP

Assembler Syntax: LINK An, #⟨displacement⟩

Attributes: Size = Unsized

Description: Pushes the contents of the specified address register onto the stack. Then loads the updated stack pointer into the address register. Finally, adds the 16-bit sign-extended displacement operand to the stack pointer. The address register occupies one long word on the stack. The user should specify a negative displacement in order to allocate stack area.

Condition Codes:
Not affected

Instruction Format:

15	14	13	12	11	10	9	8	7	6	5	4	3	2	1	0
0	1	0	0	1	1	1	0	0	1	0	1	0	REGISTER		
WORD DISPLACEMENT															

Instruction Fields:
Register field — Specifies the address register for the link
Displacement field — Specifies the twos complement integer to be added to the stack pointer

NOTE

LINK and UNLK can be used to maintain a linked list of local data and parameter areas on the stack for nested subroutine calls.

Operation: Destination Shifted by ⟨count⟩ ➧ Destination

Assembler Syntax:
LSd Dx,Dy
LSd #⟨data⟩,Dy
LSd ⟨ea⟩
where d is direction, L or R

Attributes: Size = (Byte, Word, Long)

Description: Shifts the bits of the operand in the direction specified (L or R). The carry bit receives the last bit shifted out of the operand. The shift count for the shifting of a register is specified in two different ways:

1. Immediate — The shift count (1-8) is specified in the instruction.
2. Register — The shift count is the value in the data register specified in the instruction modulo 64.

The size of the operation for register destinations may be specified as byte, word, or long. The contents of memory, ⟨ea⟩, can be shifted one bit only, and the operand size is restricted to a word.

The LSL instruction shifts the operand to the left the number of positions specified as the shift count. Bits shifted out of the high order bit go to both the carry and the extend bits; zeros are shifted into the low-order bit.

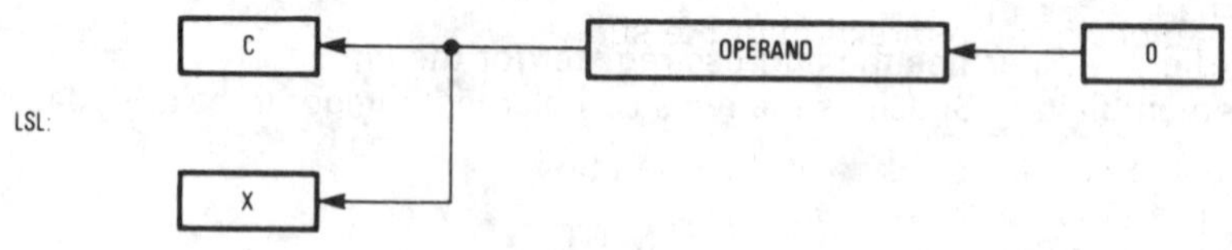

The LSR instruction shifts the operand to the right the number of positions specified as the shift count. Bits shifted out of the low order bit go to both the carry and the extend bits; zeros are shifted into the high order bit.

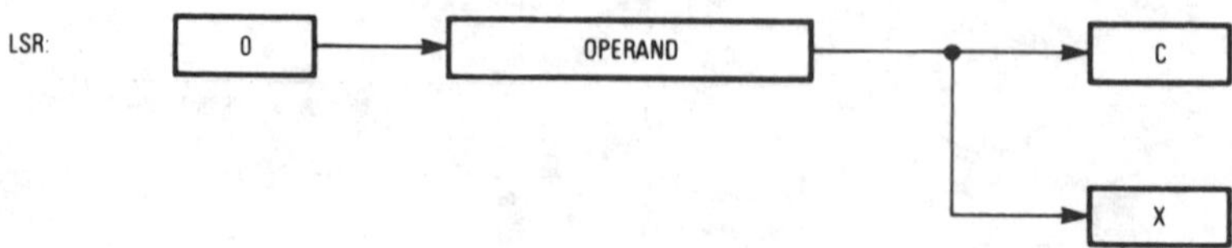

Condition Codes:

X	N	Z	V	C
*	*	*	0	*

X Set according to the last bit shifted out of the operand. Unaffected for a shift count of zero.
N Set if the result is negative. Cleared otherwise.
Z Set if the result is zero. Cleared otherwise.
V Always cleared
C Set according to the last bit shifted out of the operand. Cleared for a shift count of zero.

Instruction Format (Register Shifts):

15	14	13	12	11	10	9	8	7	6	5	4	3	2	1	0
1	1	1	0	COUNT/REGISTER			dr	SIZE		i/r	0	1	REGISTER		

Instruction Field (Register Shifts):

Count/Register field:
If i/r = 0, this field contains the shift count. The values 1-7 represent shifts of 1-7; value of 0 specifies a shift count of 8.
If i/r = 1, the data register specified in this field contains the shift count (modulo 64).

dr field — Specifies the direction of the shift:
0 — Shift right
1 — Shift left

Size field — Specifies the size of the operation:
00 — Byte operation
01 — Word operation
10 — Long operation

i/r field:
If i/r = 0, specifies immediate shift count
If i/r = 1, specifies register shift count

Register field — Specifies a data register to be shifted

Instruction Format (Memory Shifts):

15	14	13	12	11	10	9	8	7	6	5	4	3	2	1	0
										EFFECTIVE ADDRESS					
1	1	1	0	0	0	1	dr	1	1	MODE			REGISTER		

B

Instruction Fields (Memory Shifts):

dr field — Specifies the direction of the shift:
- 0 — Shift right
- 1 — Shift left

Effective Address field — Specifies the operand to be shifted. Only memory alterable addressing modes are allowed as shown:

Addressing Mode	Mode	Register
Dn	—	—
An	—	—
(An)	010	reg. number:An
(An)+	011	reg. number:An
−(An)	100	reg. number:An
(d_{16},An)	101	reg. number:An
(d_8,An,Xn)	110	reg. number:An

Addressing Mode	Mode	Register
(xxx).W	111	000
(xxx).L	111	001
#⟨data⟩	—	—
(d_{16},PC)	—	—
(d_8,PC,Xn)	—	—

B

MOVE **Move Data from Source to Destination**

Operation: Source → Destination

Assembler Syntax: MOVE ⟨ea⟩,⟨ea⟩

Attributes: Size = (Byte, Word, Long)

Description: Moves the data at the source to the destination location, and sets the condition codes according to the data. The size of the operation may be specified as byte, word, or long.

Condition Codes:

X	N	Z	V	C
—	*	*	0	0

X Not affected
N Set if the result is negative. Cleared otherwise.
Z Set if the result is zero. Cleared otherwise.
V Always cleared
C Always cleared

Instruction Format:

15	14	13	12	11	10	9	8	7	6	5	4	3	2	1	0
0	0	SIZE		DESTINATION						SOURCE					
				REGISTER			MODE			MODE			REGISTER		

Instruction Fields:

Size field — Specifies the size of the operand to be moved:
- 01 — Byte operation
- 11 — Word operation
- 10 — Long operation

Destination Effective Address field — Specifies the destination location. Only data alterable addressing modes are allowed as shown:

Addressing Mode	Mode	Register
Dn	000	reg. number:Dn
An	—	—
(An)	010	reg. number:An
(An)+	011	reg. number:An
−(An)	100	reg. number:An
(d_{16},An)	101	reg. number:An
(d_8,An,Xn)	110	reg. number:An

Addressing Mode	Mode	Register
(xxx).W	111	000
(xxx).L	111	001
#⟨data⟩	—	—
(d_{16},PC)	—	—
(d_8,PC,Xn)	—	—

Source Effective Address field — Specifies the source operand. All addressing modes are allowed as shown:

Addressing Mode	Mode	Register
Dn	000	reg. number:Dn
An*	001	reg. number:An
(An)	010	reg. number:An
(An)+	011	reg. number:An
−(An)	100	reg. number:An
(d_{16},An)	101	reg. number:An
(d_8,An,Xn)	110	reg. number:An

Addressing Mode	Mode	Register
(xxx).W	111	000
(xxx).L	111	001
#⟨data⟩	111	100
(d_{16},PC)	111	010
(d_8,PC,Xn)	111	011

*For byte size operation, address register direct is not allowed.

Notes:

1. Most assemblers use MOVEA when the destination is an address register.
2. MOVEQ can be used to move an immediate 8-bit value to a data register.

B

MOVEA — Move Address

Operation: Source ➧ Destination

Assembler Syntax: MOVEA ⟨ea⟩,An

Attributes: Size = (Word, Long)

Description: Moves the contents of the source to the destination address register. The size of the operation is specified as word or long. Word-size source operands are sign-extended to 32-bit quantities.

Condition Codes:
Not affected

Instruction Format:

15	14	13	12	11	10	9	8	7	6	5	4	3	2	1	0
0	0	SIZE		DESTINATION REGISTER			0	0	1	SOURCE MODE			SOURCE REGISTER		

Instruction Fields:

Size field — Specifies the size of the operand to be moved:
- 11 — Word operation. The source operand is sign-extended to a long operand and all 32 bits are loaded into the address register.
- 10 — Long operation

Destination Register field — Specifies the destination address register

Effective Address field — Specifies the location of the source operand. All addressing modes are allowed as shown:

Addressing Mode	Mode	Register
Dn	000	reg. number:Dn
An	001	reg. number:An
(An)	010	reg. number:An
(An)+	011	reg. number:An
−(An)	100	reg. number:An
(d_{16},An)	101	reg. number:An
(d_8,An,Xn)	110	reg. number:An

Addressing Mode	Mode	Register
(xxx).W	111	000
(xxx).L	111	001
#⟨data⟩	111	100
(d_{16},PC)	111	010
(d_8,PC,Xn)	111	011

B

MOVE from CCR

Move from the Condition Code Register

MOVE from CCR

Operation: CCR ➧ Destination

Assembler Syntax: MOVE CCR,⟨ea⟩

Attributes: Size = (Word)

Description: Moves the condition code bits (zero extended to word size) to the destination location. The operand size is a word. Unimplemented bits are read as zeros.

Condition Codes:
Not affected

Instruction Format:

15	14	13	12	11	10	9	8	7	6	5	4	3	2	1	0
0	1	0	0	0	0	1	0	1	1	EFFECTIVE ADDRESS MODE			EFFECTIVE ADDRESS REGISTER		

Instruction Fields:

Effective Address field — Specifies the destination location. Only data alterable addressing modes are allowed as shown:

Addressing Mode	Mode	Register
Dn	000	reg. number:Dn
An	—	—
(An)	010	reg. number:An
(An)+	011	reg. number:An
−(An)	100	reg. number:An
(d_{16},An)	101	reg. number:An
(d_8,An,Xn)	110	reg. number:An

Addressing Mode	Mode	Register
(xxx).W	111	000
(xxx).L	111	001
#⟨data⟩	—	—
(d_{16},PC)	—	—
(d_8,PC,Xn)	—	—

NOTE

MOVE from CCR is a word operation. ANDI, ORI, and EORI to CCR are byte operations.

MOVE to CCR — Move to Condition Codes

MOVE to CCR

Operation: Source → CCR

Assembler Syntax: MOVE ⟨ea⟩,CCR

Attributes: Size = (Word)

Description: Moves the low-order byte of the source operand to the condition code register. The upper byte of the source operand is ignored; the upper byte of the status register is not altered.

Condition Codes:

X	N	Z	V	C
*	*	*	*	*

X Set to the value of bit 4 of the source operand
N Set to the value of bit 3 of the source operand
Z Set to the value of bit 2 of the source operand
V Set to the value of bit 1 of the source operand
C Set to the value of bit 0 of the source operand

Instruction Format:

15	14	13	12	11	10	9	8	7	6	5	4	3	2	1	0
0	1	0	0	0	1	0	0	1	1	EFFECTIVE ADDRESS MODE			REGISTER		

Instruction Fields:

Effective Address field — Specifies the location of the source operand. Only data addressing modes are allowed as shown:

Addressing Mode	Mode	Register
Dn	000	reg. number:Dn
An	—	—
(An)	010	reg. number:An
(An)+	011	reg. number:An
−(An)	100	reg. number:An
(d_{16},An)	101	reg. number:An
(d_8,An,Xn)	110	reg. number:An

Addressing Mode	Mode	Register
(xxx).W	111	000
(xxx).L	111	001
#⟨data⟩	111	100
(d_{16},PC)	111	010
(d_8,PC,Xn)	111	011

NOTE

MOVE to CCR is a word operation. ANDI, ORI, and EORI to CCR are byte operations.

MOVE from SR

Move from the Status Register
(Privileged Instruction – MC68010 Only)

MOVE from SR

Operation: SR ➧ Destination
MC68010 only:
If Supervisor state
then SR ➧ Destination
else TRAP

Assembler Syntax: MOVE SR,⟨ea⟩

Attributes: Size = (Word)

Description: Moves the data in the status register to the destination location. The destination is word length. Unimplemented bits are read as zeros.

Condition Codes:
Not affected

Instruction Format:

15	14	13	12	11	10	9	8	7	6	5	4	3	2	1	0
0	1	0	0	0	0	0	0	1	1	EFFECTIVE ADDRESS					
										MODE			REGISTER		

Instruction Fields:

Effective Address field — Specifies the destination location. Only data alterable addressing modes are allowed as shown:

Addressing Mode	Mode	Register
Dn	000	reg. number:Dn
An	—	—
(An)	010	reg. number:An
(An)+	011	reg. number:An
–(An)	100	reg. number:An
(d_{16},An)	101	reg. number:An
(d_8,An,Xn)	110	reg. number:An

Addressing Mode	Mode	Register
(xxx).W	111	000
(xxx).L	111	001
#⟨data⟩	—	—
(d_{16},PC)	—	—
(d_8,PC,Xn)	—	—

B

NOTE

Use the MOVE from CCR instruction to access only the condition codes. In the MC68000, MC68HC000, and MC68008, memory destination is read before it is written to.

Move to the Status Register (Priviledged Instruction)

MOVE
to SR

Operation: If supervisor state
then Source ➧ SR
else TRAP

Assembler Syntax: MOVE ⟨ea⟩,SR

Attributes: Size = (Word)

Description: Moves the data in the source operand to the status register. The source operand is a word and all implemented bits of the status register are affected.

Condition Codes:
Set according to the source operand

Instruction Format:

15	14	13	12	11	10	9	8	7	6	5	4	3	2	1	0
										EFFECTIVE ADDRESS					
0	1	0	0	0	1	1	0	1	1	MODE			REGISTER		

Instruction Fields:
Effective Address field — Specifies the location of the source operand. Only data addressing modes are allowed as shown:

Addressing Mode	Mode	Register
Dn	000	reg. number:Dn
An	—	—
(An)	010	reg. number:An
(An)+	011	reg. number:An
−(An)	100	reg. number:An
(d_{16},An)	101	reg. number:An
(d_8,An,Xn)	110	reg. number:An

Addressing Mode	Mode	Register
(xxx).W	111	000
(xxx).L	111	001
#⟨data⟩	111	100
(d_{16},PC)	111	010
(d_8,PC,Xn)	111	011

B

MOVE USP

Move User Stack Pointer (Privileged Instruction)

Operation: If supervisor state
then USP ➧ An or An ➧ USP
else TRAP

Assembler Syntax: MOVE USP,An
MOVE An,USP

Attributes: Size = (Long)

Description: Moves the contents of the user stack pointer to or from the specified address register

Condition Codes:
Not affected

Instruction Format:

15	14	13	12	11	10	9	8	7	6	5	4	3	2	1	0
0	1	0	0	1	1	1	0	0	1	1	0	dr	REGISTER		

Instruction Fields:
dr field — Specifies the direction of transfer:
0 — Transfer the address register to the USP
1 — Transfer the USP to the address register
Register field — Specifies the address register for the operation

B

Move Control Register
(Privileged Instruction)

MOVEC

Operation: If supervisor state
then Rc ➧ Rn or Rn ➧ Rc
else TRAP

Assembler Syntax: MOVEC Rc,Rn
MOVEC Rn,Rc

Attributes: Size = (Long)

Description: Moves the contents of the specified control register (Rc) to the specified general register (Rn) or copies the contents of the specified general register to the specified control register. This is always a 32-bit transfer even though the control register may be implemented with fewer bits. Unimplemented bits are read as zeros.

Condition Codes:
Not affected

Instruction Format:

15	14	13	12	11	10	9	8	7	6	5	4	3	2	1	0
0	1	0	0	1	1	1	0	0	1	1	1	1	0	1	dr
A/D	REGISTER			CONTROL REGISTER											

Instruction Fields:

dr field — Specifies the direction of the transfer:
- 0 — Control register to general register
- 1 — General register to control register

A/D field — Specifies the type of general register:
- 0 — Data register
- 1 — Address register

Register field — Specifies the register number
Control Register field — Specifies the control register

Hex	Control Register
000	Source Function Code (SFC) register
001	Destination Function Code (DFC) register
800	User Stack Pointer (USP)
801	Vector Base Register (VBR)

Any other code causes an illegal instruction exception.

B

MOVEM — Move Multiple Registers — MOVEM

Operation: Registers → Destination
Source → Registers

Assembler Syntax: MOVEM register list,⟨ea⟩
MOVEM ⟨ea⟩,register list

Attributes: Size = (Word, Long)

Description: Moves the contents of selected registers to or from consecutive memory locations starting at the location specified by the effective address. A register is selected if the bit in the mask field corresponding to that register is set. The instruction size determines whether 16 or 32 bits of each register are transferred. In the case of a word transfer to either address or data registers, each word is sign-extended to 32 bits, and the resulting long word is loaded into the associated register.

Selecting the addressing mode also selects the mode of operation of the MOVEM instruction, and only the control modes, the predecrement mode, and the postincrement mode are valid. If the effective address is specified by one of the control modes, the registers are transferred starting at the specified address, and the address is incremented by the operand length (2 or 4) following each transfer. The order of the registers is from data register 0 to data register 7, then from address register 0 to address register 7.

If the effective address is specified by the predecrement mode, only a register to memory operation is allowed. The registers are stored starting at the specified address minus the operand length (2 or 4), and the address is decremented by the operand length following each transfer. The order of storing is from address register 7 to address register 0, then from data register 7 to data register 0. When the instruction has completed, the decremented address register contains the address of the last operand stored.

If the effective address is specified by the postincrement mode, only a memory to register operation is allowed. The registers are loaded starting at the specified address; the address is incremented by the operand length (2 or 4) following each transfer. The order of loading is the same as that of control mode addressing. When the instruction has completed, the incremented address register contains the address of the last operand loaded plus the operand length.

Condition Codes:
Not affected

Instruction Format:

<table>
<tr><td>15</td><td>14</td><td>13</td><td>12</td><td>11</td><td>10</td><td>9</td><td>8</td><td>7</td><td>6</td><td>5</td><td>4</td><td>3</td><td>2</td><td>1</td><td>0</td></tr>
<tr><td rowspan="2">0</td><td rowspan="2">1</td><td rowspan="2">0</td><td rowspan="2">0</td><td rowspan="2">1</td><td rowspan="2">dr</td><td rowspan="2">0</td><td rowspan="2">0</td><td rowspan="2">1</td><td rowspan="2">SIZE</td><td colspan="6">EFFECTIVE ADDRESS</td></tr>
<tr><td colspan="3">MODE</td><td colspan="3">REGISTER</td></tr>
<tr><td colspan="16">REGISTER LIST MASK</td></tr>
</table>

Instruction Field:

dr field — Specifies the direction of the transfer:
- 0 — Register to memory
- 1 — Memory to register

Size field — Specifies the size of the registers being transferred:
- 0 — Word transfer
- 1 — Long transfer

Effective Address field — Specifies the memory address for the operation. For register to memory transfers, only control alterable addressing modes or the predecrement addressing mode are allowed as shown:

Addressing Mode	Mode	Register
Dn	—	—
An	—	—
(An)	010	reg. number:An
(An)+	—	—
−(An)	100	reg. number:An
(d_{16},An)	101	reg. number:An
(d_8,An,Xn)	110	reg. number:An

Addressing Mode	Mode	Register
(xxx).W	111	000
(xxx).L	111	001
#⟨data⟩	—	—
(d_{16},PC)	—	—
(d_8,PC,Xn)	—	—

For memory to register transfers, only control addressing modes or the postincrement addressing mode are allowed as shown:

Addressing Mode	Mode	Register
Dn	—	—
An	—	—
(An)	010	reg. number:An
(An)+	011	reg. number:An
−(An)	—	—
(d_{16},An)	101	reg. number:An
(d_8,An,Xn)	110	reg. number:An

Addressing Mode	Mode	Register
(xxx).W	111	000
(xxx).L	111	001
#⟨data⟩	—	—
(d_{16},PC)	111	010
(d_8,PC,Xn)	111	011

Register List Mask field — Specifies the registers to be transferred. The low order bit corresponds to the first register to be transferred; the high-order bit corresponds to the last register to be transferred. Thus, both for control modes and for the postincrement mode addresses, the mask correspondence is:

15	14	13	12	11	10	9	8	7	6	5	4	3	2	1	0
A7	A6	A5	A4	A3	A2	A1	A0	D7	D6	D5	D4	D3	D2	D1	D0

B

For the predecrement mode addresses, the mask correspondence is reversed:

15	14	13	12	11	10	9	8	7	6	5	4	3	2	1	0
D0	D1	D2	D3	D4	D5	D6	D7	A0	A1	A2	A3	A4	A5	A6	A7

NOTE

An extra read bus cycle occurs for memory operands. This accesses an operand at one address higher than the last register image required.

B

Operation: Source → Destination

Assembler Syntax: MOVEP Dx,(d,Ay)
MOVEP (d,Ay),Dx

Attributes: Size = (Word, Long)

Description: Moves data between a data register and alternate bytes within the address space (typically assigned to a peripheral), starting at the location specified and incrementing by two. This instruction is designed for 8-bit peripherals on a 16-bit data bus. The high-order byte of the data register is transferred first and the low order byte is transferred last. The memory address is specified in the address register indirect plus 16-bit displacement addressing mode. If the address is even, all the transfers are to or from the high order half of the data bus; if the address is odd, all the transfers are to or from the low order half of the data bus. The instruction also accesses alternate bytes on an 8-bit bus.

Example: Long transfer to/from an even address

Byte Organization in Register

31–24	23–16	15–8	7–0
HI-ORDER	MID-UPPER	MID-LOWER	LOW-ORDER

Byte Organization in Memory (Low Address at Top)

15–8	7–0
HI-ORDER	
MID-UPPER	
MID-LOWER	
LOW-ORDER	

Example: Word transfer to/from an odd address

Byte Organization in Register

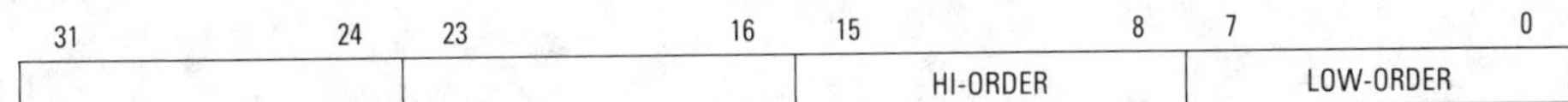

Byte Organization in Memory (Low Address at Top)

15–8	7–0
	HI-ORDER
	LOW-UPPER

Condition Codes:
Not affected

Instruction Format:

15	14	13	12	11	10	9	8	7	6	5	4	3	2	1	0
0	0	0	0	DATA REGISTER			OP-MODE			0	0	1	ADDRESS REGISTER		
DISPLACEMENT (16 BITS)															

Instruction Fields:

Data Register field — Specifies the data register for the instruction

Op-Mode field — Specifies the direction and size of the operation:

- 100 — Transfer word from memory to register
- 101 — Transfer long from memory to register
- 110 — Transfer word from register to memory
- 111 — Transfer long from register to memory

Address Register field — Specifies the address register which is used in the address register indirect plus displacement addressing mode

Displacement field — Specifies the displacement used in the operand address

Operation: Immediate Data ➧ Destination

Assembler Syntax: MOVEQ #⟨data⟩,Dn

Attributes: Size = (Long)

Description: Moves a byte of immediate data to a 32-bit data register. The data in an 8-bit field within the operation word is sign extended to a long operand in the data register as it is transferred.

Condition Codes:

X	N	Z	V	C
—	*	*	0	0

X Not affected
N Set if the result is negative. Cleared otherwise.
Z Set if the result is zero. Cleared otherwise.
V Always cleared
C Always cleared

Instruction Format:

15	14	13	12	11	10	9	8	7	6	5	4	3	2	1	0
0	1	1	1	REGISTER			0	DATA							

Instruction Fields:

Register field — Specifies the data register to be loaded
Data field — 8 bits of data, which are sign extended to a long operand

B

MOVES

Move Address Space
(Privileged Instruction)

MOVES

Operation: If supervisor state
then Rn → Destination [DFC] or Source [SFC] → Rn
else TRAP

Assembler Syntax:
MOVES Rn,⟨ea⟩
MOVES ⟨ea⟩,Rn

Attributes: Size = (Byte, Word, Long)

Description: Moves the byte, word, or long operand from the specified general register to a location within the address space specified by the destination function code (DFC) register; or, moves the byte, word, or long operand from a location within the address space specified by the source function code (SFC) register to the specified general register.

If the destination is a data register, the source operand replaces the corresponding low-order bits of that data register, depending on the size of the operation. If the destination is an address register, the source operand is sign extended to 32 bits and then loaded into that address register.

Condition Codes:
Not affected

Instruction Format:

15	14	13	12	11	10	9	8	7	6	5	4	3	2	1	0
0	0	0	0	1	1	1	0	SIZE		EFFECTIVE ADDRESS MODE			EFFECTIVE ADDRESS REGISTER		
A/D	REGISTER			dr	0	0	0	0	0	0	0	0	0	0	0

Instruction Fields:
Size field — Specifies the size of the operation:
- 00 — Byte operation
- 01 — Word operation
- 10 — Long operation

Move Address Space
(Privileged Instruction)

MOVES

Effective Address Field — Specifies the source or destination location within the alternate address space. Only memory alterable addressing modes are allowed as shown:

Addressing Mode	Mode	Register
Dn	—	—
An	—	—
(An)	010	reg. number:An
(An)+	011	reg. number:An
−(An)	100	reg. number:An
(d_{16},An)	101	reg. number:An
(d_8,An,Xn)	110	reg. number:An

Addressing Mode	Mode	Register
(xxx).W	111	000
(xxx).L	111	001
#⟨data⟩	—	—
(d_{16},PC)	—	—
(d_8,PC,Xn)	—	—

A/D field — Specifies the type of general register:
0 — Data register
1 — Address register
Register field — Specifies the register number
dr field — Specifies the direction of the transfer:
0 — From ⟨ea⟩ to general register
1 — From general register to ⟨ea⟩

NOTE

For either of the two following examples with the same address register as both source and destination

MOVES.x An,(An)+
MOVES.x An,−(An)

the value stored is undefined. The current implementation of the MC68010 stores the incremented or decremented value of An.

B

MULS Signed Multiply MULS

Operation: Source * Destination ➧ Destination

Assembler Syntax: MULS.W ⟨ea⟩,Dn 16×16 ➧ 32

Attributes: Size = (Word)

Description: Multiplies two signed operands yielding a signed result. The multiplier and multiplicand are both word operands, and the result is a long word operand. A register operand is the low order word; the upper word of the register is ignored. All 32 bits of the product are saved in the destination data register.

Condition Codes:

X	N	Z	V	C
—	*	*	0	0

X Not affected
N Set if the result is negative. Cleared otherwise.
Z Set if the result is zero. Cleared otherwise.
V Always cleared
C Always cleared

Instruction Format (word form):

15	14	13	12	11	10	9	8	7	6	5	4	3	2	1	0
1	1	0	0	REGISTER			1	1	1	EFFECTIVE ADDRESS MODE			EFFECTIVE ADDRESS REGISTER		

Instruction Fields:

Register field — Specifies a data register as the destination
Effective Address field — Specifies the source operand. Only data addressing modes are allowed as shown:

Addressing Mode	Mode	Register
Dn	000	reg. number:Dn
An	—	—
(An)	010	reg. number:An
(An)+	011	reg. number:An
−(An)	100	reg. number:An
(d_{16},An)	101	reg. number:An
(d_8,An,Xn)	110	reg. number:An

Addressing Mode	Mode	Register
(xxx).W	111	000
(xxx).L	111	001
#⟨data⟩	111	100
(d_{16},PC)	111	010
(d_8,PC,Xn)	111	011

B

MULU Unsigned Multiply

Operation: Source * Destination ➧ Destination

Assembler Syntax: MULU.W ⟨ea⟩,Dn   16×16 ➧ 32

Attributes: Size = (Word)

Description: Multiplies two unsigned operands yielding an unsigned result. The multiplier and multiplicand are both word operands, and the result is a long word operand. A register operand is the low-order word; the upper word of the register is ignored. All 32 bits of the product are saved in the destination data register.

Condition Codes:

X	N	Z	V	C
—	*	*	0	0

X Not affected
N Set if the result is negative. Cleared otherwise.
Z Set if the result is zero. Cleared otherwise.
V Always cleared
C Always cleared

Instruction Format (word form):

15	14	13	12	11	10	9	8	7	6	5	4	3	2	1	0
										EFFECTIVE ADDRESS					
1	1	0	0	REGISTER			0	1	1	MODE			REGISTER		

Instruction Fields:

Register field — Specifies a data register as the destination
Effective Address field — Specifies the source operand. Only data addressing modes are allowed as shown:

Addressing Mode	Mode	Register
Dn	000	reg. number:Dn
An	—	—
(An)	010	reg. number:An
(An)+	011	reg. number:An
–(An)	100	reg. number:An
(d_{16},An)	101	reg. number:An
(d_8,An,Xn)	110	reg. number:An

Addressing Mode	Mode	Register
(xxx).W	111	000
(xxx).L	111	001
#⟨data⟩	111	100
(d_{16},PC)	111	010
(d_8,PC,Xn)	111	011

B

NBCD Negate Decimal with Extend

NBCD

Operation: 0 − (Destination$_{10}$) − X ➧ Destination

Assembler Syntax: NBCD ⟨ea⟩

Attributes: Size = (Byte)

Description: Subtracts the destination operand and the extend bit from zero. The operation is performed using binary coded decimal arithmetic. The packed BCD result is saved in the destination location. This instruction produces the tens complement of the destination if the extend bit is zero, or the nines complement if the extend bit is one. This is a byte operation only.

Condition Codes:

X	N	Z	V	C
*	U	*	U	*

X Set the same as the carry bit
N Undefined
Z Cleared if the result is non-zero. Unchanged otherwise.
V Undefined
C Set if a decimal borrow occurs. Cleared otherwise.

NOTE

Normally the Z condition code bit is set via programming before the start of the operation. This allows successful tests for zero results upon completion of multiple precision operations.

Instruction Format:

15	14	13	12	11	10	9	8	7	6	5	4	3	2	1	0
0	1	0	0	1	0	0	0	0	0	EFFECTIVE ADDRESS					
										MODE			REGISTER		

Instruction Fields:

Effective Address field — Specifies the destination operand. Only data alterable addressing modes are allowed as shown:

Addressing Mode	Mode	Register
Dn	000	reg. number:Dn
An	—	—
(An)	010	reg. number:An
(An)+	011	reg. number:An
−(An)	100	reg. number:An
(d_{16},An)	101	reg. number:An
(d_8,An,Xn)	110	reg. number:An

Addressing Mode	Mode	Register
(xxx).W	111	000
(xxx).L	111	001
#⟨data⟩	—	—
(d_{16},PC)	—	—
(d_8,PC,Xn)	—	—

B

NEG — Negate

NEG

Operation: 0 − (Destination) ➧ Destination

Assembler Syntax: NEG ⟨ea⟩

Attributes: Size = (Byte, Word, Long)

Description: Subtracts the destination operand from zero and stores the result in the destination location. The size of the operation is specified as byte, word, or long.

Condition Codes:

X	N	Z	V	C
*	*	*	*	*

X Set the same as the carry bit
N Set if the result is negative. Cleared otherwise.
Z Set if the result is zero. Cleared otherwise.
V Set if an overflow occurs. Cleared otherwise.
C Cleared if the result is zero. Set otherwise.

Instruction Format:

15	14	13	12	11	10	9	8	7	6	5	4	3	2	1	0
										EFFECTIVE ADDRESS					
0	1	0	0	0	1	0	0	SIZE		MODE			REGISTER		

Instruction Fields:

Size field — Specifies the size of the operation:
- 00 — Byte operation
- 01 — Word operation
- 10 — Long operation

Effective Address field — Specifies the destination operand. Only data alterable addressing modes are allowed as shown:

Addressing Mode	Mode	Register
Dn	000	reg. number:Dn
An	—	—
(An)	010	reg. number:An
(An)+	011	reg. number:An
−(An)	100	reg. number:An
(d_{16},An)	101	reg. number:An
(d_8,An,Xn)	110	reg. number:An

Addressing Mode	Mode	Register
(xxx).W	111	000
(xxx).L	111	001
#⟨data⟩	—	—
(d_{16},PC)	—	—
(d_8,PC,Xn)	—	—

B

Operation: 0 − (Destination) − X ➧ Destination

Assembler Syntax: NEGX ⟨ea⟩

Attributes: Size = (Byte, Word, Long)

Description: Subtracts the destination operand and the extend bit from zero. Stores the result in the destination location. The size of the operation is specified as byte, word, or long.

Condition Codes:

X	N	Z	V	C
*	*	*	*	*

- X Set the same as the carry bit
- N Set if the result is negative. Cleared otherwise.
- Z Cleared if the result is non-zero. Unchanged otherwise.
- V Set if an overflow occurs. Cleared otherwise.
- C Set if a borrow occurs. Cleared otherwise.

NOTE

Normally the Z condition code bit is set via programming before the start of the operation. This allows successful tests for zero results upon completion of multiple precision operations.

Instruction Format:

15	14	13	12	11	10	9	8	7	6	5	4	3	2	1	0
0	1	0	0	0	0	0	0	SIZE		EFFECTIVE ADDRESS MODE			EFFECTIVE ADDRESS REGISTER		

Instruction Fields:

Size field — Specifies the size of the operation:
- 00 — Byte operation
- 01 — Word operation
- 10 — Long operation

B

Effective Address field — Specifies the destination operand. Only data alterable addressing modes are allowed as shown:

Addressing Mode	Mode	Register
Dn	000	reg. number:Dn
An	—	—
(An)	010	reg. number:An
(An)+	011	reg. number:An
−(An)	100	reg. number:An
(d_{16},An)	101	reg. number:An
(d_8,An,Xn)	110	reg. number:An

Addressing Mode	Mode	Register
(xxx).W	111	000
(xxx).L	111	001
#⟨data⟩	—	—
(d_{16},PC)	—	—
(d_8,PC,Xn)	—	—

B

No Operation

NOP

Operation: None

Assembler Syntax: NOP

Attributes: Unsized

Description: Performs no operation. The processor state, other than the program counter, is unaffected. Execution continues with the instruction following the NOP instruction.

Condition Codes:
Not affected

Instruction Format:

15	14	13	12	11	10	9	8	7	6	5	4	3	2	1	0
0	1	0	0	1	1	1	0	0	1	1	1	0	0	0	1

Operation: ~ Destination ▶ Destination

Assembler Syntax: NOT ⟨ea⟩

Attributes: Size = (Byte, Word, Long)

Description: Calculates the ones complement of the destination operand and stores the result in the destination location. The size of the operation is specified as byte, word, or long.

Condition Codes:

X	N	Z	V	C
—	*	*	0	0

X Not affected
N Set if the result is negative. Cleared otherwise.
Z Set if the result is zero. Cleared otherwise.
V Always cleared
C Always cleared

Instruction Format:

15	14	13	12	11	10	9	8	7	6	5	4	3	2	1	0
0	1	0	0	0	1	1	0	SIZE		EFFECTIVE ADDRESS					
										MODE			REGISTER		

Instruction Fields:

Size field — Specifies the size of the operation:
- 00 — Byte operation
- 01 — Word operation
- 10 — Long operation

Effective Address field — Specifies the destination operand. Only data alterable addressing modes are allowed as shown:

Addressing Mode	Mode	Register
Dn	000	reg. number:Dn
An	—	—
(An)	010	reg. number:An
(An)+	011	reg. number:An
−(An)	100	reg. number:An
(d_{16},An)	101	reg. number:An
(d_8,An,Xn)	110	reg. number:An

Addressing Mode	Mode	Register
(xxx).W	111	000
(xxx).L	111	001
#⟨data⟩	—	—
(d_{16},PC)	—	—
(d_8,PC,Xn)	—	—

B

OR

Inclusive OR Logical

Operation: Source V Destination ➧ Destination

Assembler Syntax: OR ⟨ea⟩,Dn
OR Dn,⟨ea⟩

Attributes: Size = (Byte, Word, Long)

Description: Performs an inclusive OR operation on the source operand and the destination operand and stores the result in the destination location. The size of the operation is specified as byte, word, or long. The contents of an address register may not be used as an operand.

Condition Codes:

X	N	Z	V	C
—	*	*	0	0

X Not affected
N Set if the most significant bit of the result is set. Cleared otherwise.
Z Set if the result is zero. Cleared otherwise.
V Always cleared
C Always cleared

Instruction Format:

15	14	13	12	11	10	9	8	7	6	5	4	3	2	1	0
1	0	0	0	REGISTER			OP-MODE			EFFECTIVE ADDRESS					
										MODE			REGISTER		

Instruction Fields:

Register field — Specifies any of the eight data registers
Op-Mode field —

Byte	Word	Long	Operation
000	001	010	(⟨ea⟩) V (⟨Dn⟩) ➧ ⟨Dn⟩
100	101	110	(⟨Dn⟩) V (⟨ea⟩) ➧ ⟨ea⟩

B

Effective Address field — If the location specified is a source operand, only data addressing modes are allowed as shown:

Addressing Mode	Mode	Register
Dn	000	reg. number:Dn
An	—	—
(An)	010	reg. number:An
(An)+	011	reg. number:An
−(An)	100	reg. number:An
(d_{16},An)	101	reg. number:An
(d_8,An,Xn)	110	reg. number:An

Addressing Mode	Mode	Register
(xxx).W	111	000
(xxx).L	111	001
#⟨data⟩	111	100
(d_{16},PC)	111	010
(d_8,PC,Xn)	111	011

If the location specified is a destination operand, only memory alterable addressing modes are allowed as shown:

Addressing Mode	Mode	Register
Dn	—	—
An	—	—
(An)	010	reg. number:An
(An)+	—	—
−(An)	100	reg. number:An
(d_{16},An)	101	reg. number:An
(d_8,An,Xn)	110	reg. number:An

Addressing Mode	Mode	Register
(xxx).W	111	000
(xxx).L	111	001
#⟨data⟩	—	—
(d_{16},PC)	—	—
(d_8,PC,Xn)	—	—

Notes:

1. If the destination is a data register, it must be specified using the destination Dn mode, not the destination ⟨ea⟩ mode.
2. Most assemblers use ORI when the source is immediate data.

B

Operation: Immediate Data V Destination ➧ Destination

Assembler Syntax: ORI #⟨data⟩,⟨ea⟩

Attributes: Size = (Byte, Word, Long)

Description: Performs an inclusive OR operation on the immediate data and the destination operand and stores the result in the destination location. The size of the operation is specified as byte, word, or long. The size of the immediate data matches the operation size.

Condition Codes:

X	N	Z	V	C
—	*	*	0	0

X Not affected
N Set if the most significant bit of the result is set. Cleared otherwise.
Z Set if the result is zero. Cleared otherwise.
V Always cleared
C Always cleared

Instruction Format:

15	14	13	12	11	10	9	8	7	6	5	4	3	2	1	0
0	0	0	0	0	0	0	0	SIZE		EFFECTIVE ADDRESS MODE			EFFECTIVE ADDRESS REGISTER		
WORD DATA (16 BITS)								BYTE DATA (8 BITS)							
LONG DATA (32 BITS)															

Instruction Fields:

Size field — Specifies the size of the operation.
00 — Byte operation.
01 — Word operation.
10 — Long operation.

B

Effective Address field — Specifies the destination operand. Only data alterable addressing modes are allowed as shown:

Addressing Mode	Mode	Register
Dn	000	reg. number:Dn
An	—	—
(An)	010	reg. number:An
(An)+	011	reg. number:An
−(An)	100	reg. number:An
(d_{16},An)	101	reg. number:An
(d_8,An,Xn)	110	reg. number:An

Addressing Mode	Mode	Register
(xxx).W	111	000
(xxx).L	111	001
#⟨data⟩	—	—
(d_{16},PC)	—	—
(d_8,PC,Xn)	—	—

Immediate field — (Data immediately following the instruction):
If size = 00, the data is the low-order byte of the immediate word
If size = 01, the data is the entire immediate word
If size = 10, the data is the next two immediate words

B

ORI to CCR

Inclusive OR Immediate to Condition Codes

ORI to CCR

Operation: Source V CCR ➧ CCR

Assembler Syntax: ORI #⟨data⟩,CCR

Attributes: Size = (Byte)

Description: Performs an inclusive OR operation on the immediate operand and the condition codes and stores the result in the condition code register (low-order byte of the status register). All implemented bits of the condition code register are affected.

Condition Codes:

X	N	Z	V	C
*	*	*	*	*

X Set if bit 4 of immediate operand is one. Unchanged otherwise.
N Set if bit 3 of immediate operand is one. Unchanged otherwise.
Z Set if bit 2 of immediate operand is one. Unchanged otherwise.
V Set if bit 1 of immediate operand is one. Unchanged otherwise.
C Set if bit 0 of immediate operand is one. Unchanged otherwise.

Instruction Format:

15	14	13	12	11	10	9	8	7	6	5	4	3	2	1	0
0	0	0	0	0	0	0	0	0	0	1	1	1	1	0	0
0	0	0	0	0	0	0	0	BYTE DATA (8 BITS)							

B

ORI to SR

Inclusive OR Immediate to the Status Register (Privileged Instruction)

ORI to SR

Operation: If supervisor state
then Source V SR ➧ SR
else TRAP

Assembler Syntax: ORI #⟨data⟩,SR

Attributes: Size = (Word)

Description: Performs an inclusive OR operation of the immediate operand and the contents of the status register and stores the result in the status register. All implemented bits of the status register are affected.

Condition Codes:

X	N	Z	V	C
*	*	*	*	*

X Set if bit 4 of immediate operand is one. Unchanged otherwise.
N Set if bit 3 of immediate operand is one. Unchanged otherwise.
Z Set if bit 2 of immediate operand is one. Unchanged otherwise.
V Set if bit 1 of immediate operand is one. Unchanged otherwise.
C Set if bit 0 of immediate operand is one. Unchanged otherwise.

Instruction Format:

15	14	13	12	11	10	9	8	7	6	5	4	3	2	1	0
0	0	0	0	0	0	0	0	0	1	1	1	1	1	0	0
WORD DATA (16 BITS)															

B

Operation: Sp − 4 ➧ SP; ⟨ea⟩ ➧ (SP)

Assembler Syntax: PEA ⟨ea⟩

Attributes: Size = (Long)

Description: Computes the effective address and pushes it onto the stack. The effective address is a long word address.

Condition Codes:
Not affected

Instruction Format:

15	14	13	12	11	10	9	8	7	6	5	4	3	2	1	0
0	1	0	0	1	0	0	0	0	1	EFFECTIVE ADDRESS					
										MODE			REGISTER		

Instruction Fields:

Effective Address field — Specifies the address to be pushed onto the stack. Only control addressing modes are allowed as shown:

Addressing Mode	Mode	Register
Dn	—	—
An	—	—
(An)	010	reg. number:An
(An)+	—	—
−(An)	—	—
(d_{16},An)	101	reg. number:An
(d_8,An,Xn)	110	reg. number:An

Addressing Mode	Mode	Register
(xxx).W	111	000
(xxx).L	111	001
#⟨data⟩	—	—
(d_{16},PC)	111	010
(d_8,PC,Xn)	111	011

B

RESET

Reset External Devices (Privileged Instruction)

Operation: If supervisor state
then Assert $\overline{\text{RESET}}$ Line
else TRAP

Assembler Syntax: RESET

Attributes: Unsized

Description: Asserts the $\overline{\text{RESET}}$ signal for 124 clock periods, resetting all external devices. The processor state, other than the program counter, is unaffected and execution continues with the next instruction.

Condition Codes:
Not affected

Instruction Format:

15	14	13	12	11	10	9	8	7	6	5	4	3	2	1	0
0	1	0	0	1	1	1	0	0	1	1	1	0	0	0	0

Rotate (Without Extend)

ROL
ROR

Operation: Destination Rotated by ⟨count⟩ → Destination

Assembler Syntax:
ROd Dx,Dy
ROd #⟨data⟩,Dy
ROd ⟨ea⟩
where d is direction, L or R

Attributes: Size = (Byte, Word, Long)

Description: Rotates the bits of the operand in the direction specified (L or R). The extend bit is not included in the rotation. The rotate count for the rotation of a register is specified in either of two ways:

1. Immediate — The rotate count (1-8) is specified in the instruction.
2. Register — The rotate count is the value in the data register specified in the instruction, modulo 64.

The size of the operation for register destinations is specified as byte, word, or long. The contents of memory, ⟨ea⟩; can be rotated one bit only, and operand size is restricted to a word.

The ROL instruction rotates the bits of the operand to the left; the rotate count determines the number of bit positions rotated. Bits rotated out of the high-order bit go to the carry bit and also back into the low-order bit.

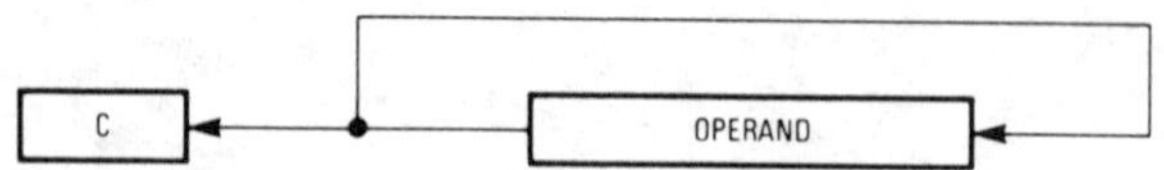

The ROR instruction rotates the bits of the operand to the right; the rotate count determines the number of bit positions rotated. Bits rotated out of the low-order bit go to the carry bit and also back into the high-order bit.

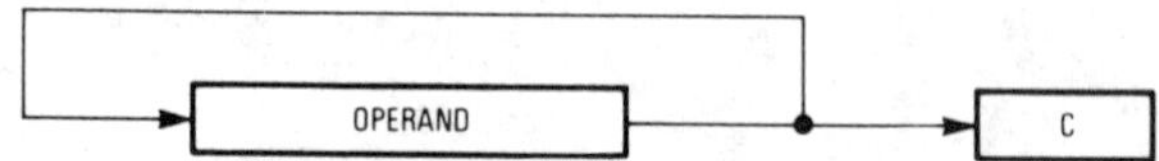

B

Rotate (Without Extend)

Condition Codes:

X	N	Z	V	C
—	*	*	0	*

X Not affected
N Set if the most significant bit of the result is set. Cleared otherwise.
Z Set if the result is zero. Cleared otherwise.
V Always cleared
C Set according to the last bit rotated out of the operand. Cleared when the rotate count is zero.

Instruction Format (Register Rotate):

15	14	13	12	11	10	9	8	7	6	5	4	3	2	1	0
1	1	1	0	COUNT/ REGISTER			dr	SIZE		i/r	1	1	REGISTER		

Instruction Fields (Register Rotate):

Count/Register field:
- If i/r = 0, this field contains the rotate count. The values 1-7 represent counts of 1-7, and 0 specifies a count of 8.
- If i/r = 1, this field specifies a data register that contains the rotate count (modulo 64).

dr field — Specifies the direction of the rotate:
- 0 — Rotate right
- 1 — Rotate left

Size field — Specifies the size of the operation:
- 00 — Byte operation
- 01 — Word operation
- 10 — Long operation

i/r field — Specifies the rotate count location:
- If i/r = 0, immediate rotate count
- If i/r = 1, register rotate count

Register field — Specifies a data register to be rotated

Instruction Format (Memory Rotate):

15	14	13	12	11	10	9	8	7	6	5	4	3	2	1	0
										EFFECTIVE ADDRESS					
1	1	1	0	0	1	1	dr	1	1	MODE			REGISTER		

B

Rotate (Without Extend)

ROL
ROR

Instruction Fields (Memory Rotate):

dr field — Specifies the direction of the rotate:
0 — Rotate right
1 — Rotate left

Effective Address field — Specifies the operand to be rotated. Only memory alterable addressing modes are allowed as shown:

Addressing Mode	Mode	Register
Dn	—	—
An	—	—
(An)	010	reg. number:An
(An)+	011	reg. number:An
−(An)	100	reg. number:An
(d_{16},An)	101	reg. number:An
(d_8,An,Xn)	110	reg. number:An

Addressing Mode	Mode	Register
(xxx).W	111	000
(xxx).L	111	001
#⟨data⟩	—	—
(d_{16},PC)	—	—
(d_8,PC,Xn)	—	—

B

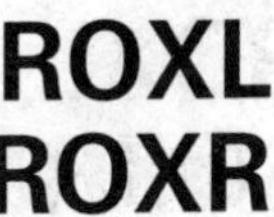

ROXL ROXR

Rotate with Extend

ROXL ROXR

Operation: Destination Rotated with X by ⟨count⟩ ➧ Destination

Assembler Syntax:
ROXd Dx,Dy
ROXd #⟨data⟩,Dy
ROXd ⟨ea⟩
where d is direction, L or R

Attributes: Size = (Byte, Word, Long)

Description: Rotates the bits of the operand in the direction specified (L or R). The extend bit is included in the rotation. The rotate count for the rotation of a register is specified in either of two ways:

1. Immediate — The rotate count (1-8) is specified in the instruction.
2. Register — The rotate count is the value in the data register specified in the instruction, modulo 64.

The size of the operation for register destinations is specified as byte, word, or long. The contents of memory, ⟨ea⟩, can be rotated one bit only, and operand size is restricted to a word.

The ROXL instruction rotates the bits of the operand to the left; the rotate count determines the number of bit positions rotated. Bits rotated out of the high-order bit go to the carry bit and the extend bit; the previous value of the extend bit rotates into the low-order bit.

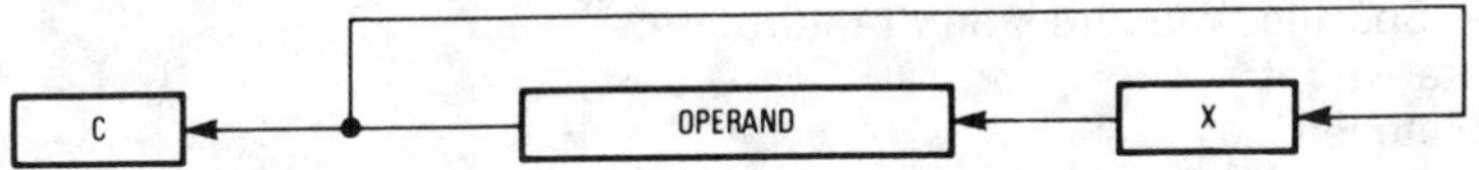

The ROXR instruction rotates the bits of the operand to the right; the rotate count determines the number of bit positions rotated. Bits rotated out of the low order bit go to the carry bit and the extend bit; the previous value of the extend bit rotates into the high order bit.

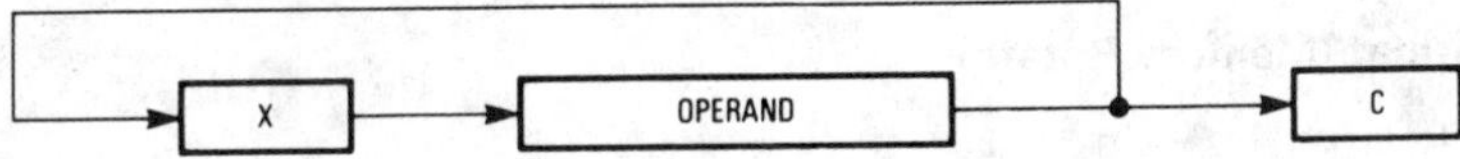

Condition Codes:

X	N	Z	V	C
*	*	*	0	*

X Set to the value of the last bit rotated out of the operand. Unaffected when the rotate count is zero.
N Set if the most significant bit of the result is set. Cleared otherwise.
Z Set if the result is zero. Cleared otherwise.
V Always cleared
C Set according to the last bit rotated out of the operand. When the rotate count is zero, set to the value of the extend bit.

Instruction Format (Register Rotate):

15	14	13	12	11	10	9	8	7	6	5	4	3	2	1	0
1	1	1	0	COUNT/ REGISTER			dr	SIZE		i/r	1	0	REGISTER		

Instruction Fields (Register Rotate):

Count/Register field:
If i/r = 0, this field contains the rotate count. The values 1-7 represent counts of 1-7, and 0 specifies a count of 8.
If i/r = 1, this field specifies a data register that contains the rotate count (modulo 64).

dr field — Specifies the direction of the rotate:
0 — Rotate right
1 — Rotate left

Size field — Specifies the size of the operation:
00 — Byte operation
01 — Word operation
10 — Long operation

i/r field — Specifies the rotate count location:
If i/r = 0, immediate rotate count
If i/r = 1, register rotate count

Register field — Specifies a data register to be rotated

Instruction Format (Memory Rotate):

B

15	14	13	12	11	10	9	8	7	6	5	4	3	2	1	0
										EFFECTIVE ADDRESS					
1	1	1	0	0	1	0	dr	1	1	MODE			REGISTER		

Instruction Fields (Memory Rotate):

dr field — Specifies the direction of the rotate:
0 — Rotate right
1 — Rotate left

Rotate with Extend

ROXL
ROXR

Effective Address field — Specifies the operand to be rotated. Only memory alterable addressing modes are allowed as shown:

Addressing Mode	Mode	Register
Dn	—	—
An	—	—
(An)	010	reg. number:An
(An)+	011	reg. number:An
−(An)	100	reg. number:An
(d_{16},An)	101	reg. number:An
(d_8,An,Xn)	110	reg. number:An

Addressing Mode	Mode	Register
(xxx).W	111	000
(xxx).L	111	001
#⟨data⟩	—	—
(d_{16},PC)	—	—
(d_8,PC,Xn)	—	—

B

Operation: (SP) ➧ PC; SP + 4 + d ➧ SP

Assembler Syntax: RTD #⟨displacement⟩

Attributes: Unsized

Description: Pulls the program counter value from the stack and adds the sign-extended 16-bit displacement value to the stack pointer. The previous program counter value is lost.

Condition Codes:
Not affected

Instruction Format:

15	14	13	12	11	10	9	8	7	6	5	4	3	2	1	0
0	1	0	0	1	1	1	0	0	1	1	1	0	1	0	0
DISPLACEMENT (16 BITS)															

Instruction Field:
Displacement field — Specifies the twos complement integer to be sign extended and added to the stack pointer

RTE — Return from Exception (Privileged Instruction)

RTE

Operation: If supervisor state
then (SP) ➧ SR; SP + 2 ➧ SP; (SP) ➧ PC;
SP + 4 ➧ SP;
restore state and deallocate stack according to (SP)
else TRAP

Assembler Syntax: RTE

Attributes: Unsized

Description: Loads the processor state information stored in the exception stack frame located at the top of the stack into the processor. The instruction examines the stack format field in the format/offset word to determine how much information must be restored.

Condition Codes:
Set according to the condition code bits in the status register value restored from the stack

Instruction Format:

15	14	13	12	11	10	9	8	7	6	5	4	3	2	1	0
0	1	0	0	1	1	1	0	0	1	1	1	0	0	1	1

Format/Offset word (in stack frame):

15	14	13	12	11	10	9	8	7	6	5	4	3	2	1	0
FORMAT				0	0	VECTOR OFFSET									

Format Field of Format/Offset Word:
Contains the format code, which implies the stack frame size (including the format/offset word):
0000 — Short Format, removes four words. Loads the status register and the program counter from the stack frame.
1000 — MC68010 Long Format, removes 29 words
Any other value in this field causes the processor to take a format error exception.

B

Operation: (SP) ➧ CCR; SP + 2 ➧ SP;
(SP) ➧ PC; SP + 4 ➧ SP

Assembler Syntax: RTR

Attributes: Unsized

Description: Pulls the condition code and program counter values from the stack. The previous condition codes and program counter values are lost. The supervisor portion of the status register is unaffected.

Condition Codes:
Set to the condition codes from the stack

Instruction Format:

15	14	13	12	11	10	9	8	7	6	5	4	3	2	1	0
0	1	0	0	1	1	1	0	0	1	1	1	0	1	1	1

B

RTS — Return from Subroutine — RTS

Operation: (SP) ➧ PC; SP + 4 ➧ SP

Assembler Syntax: RTS

Attributes: Unsized

Description: Pulls the program counter value from the stack. The previous program counter value is lost.

Condition Codes:
Not affected

Instruction Format:

15	14	13	12	11	10	9	8	7	6	5	4	3	2	1	0
0	1	0	0	1	1	1	0	0	1	1	1	0	1	0	1

B

Operation: $Destination_{10} - Source_{10} - X \blacktriangleright Destination$

Assembler Syntax:
SBCD Dx,Dy
SBCD −(Ax),−(Ay)

Attributes: Size = (Byte)

Description: Subtracts the source operand and the extend bit from the destination operand and stores the result in the destination location. The subtraction is performed using binary coded decimal arithmetic; the operands are packed BCD numbers. The instruction has two modes:

1. Data register to data register: The data registers specified in the instruction contain the operands.
2. Memory to memory: The address registers specified in the instruction access the operands from memory using the predecrement addressing mode.

This operation is a byte operation only.

Condition Codes:

X	N	Z	V	C
*	U	*	U	*

X Set the same as the carry bit
N Undefined
Z Cleared if the result is non-zero. Unchanged otherwise.
V Undefined
C Set if a borrow (decimal) is generated. Cleared otherwise.

NOTE

Normally the Z condition code bit is set via programming before the start of an operation. This allows successful tests for zero results upon completion of multiple-precision operations.

Instruction Format:

15	14	13	12	11	10	9	8	7	6	5	4	3	2	1	0
1	0	0	0	REGISTER Ry			1	0	0	0	0	R/M	REGISTER Rx		

Instruction Fields:

Register Ry field — Specifies the destination register
If R/M = 0, specifies a data register
If R/M = 1, specifies an address register for the predecrement addressing mode
R/M field — Specifies the operand addressing mode:
0 — The operation is data register to data register
1 — The operation is memory to memory
Register Rx field — Specifies the source register:
If R/M = 0, specifies a data register
If R/M = 1, specifies an address register for the predecrement addressing mode

Scc — Set According to Condition

Scc

Operation: If Condition True
then 1s ➧ Destination
else 0s ➧ Destination

Assembler Syntax: Scc ⟨ea⟩

Attributes: Size = (Byte)

Description: Tests the specified condition code; if the condition is true, sets the byte specified by the effective address to TRUE (all ones). Otherwise, sets that byte to FALSE (all zeros). Condition code cc specifies one of the following conditions:

CC	carry clear	0100	$\overline{C}$	LS	low or same	0011	C+Z
CS	carry set	0101	C	LT	less than	1101	$N\cdot\overline{V}+\overline{N}\cdot V$
EQ	equal	0111	Z	MI	minus	1011	N
F	never true	0001	0	NE	not equal	0110	$\overline{Z}$
GE	greater or equal	1100	$N\cdot V+\overline{N}\cdot\overline{V}$	PL	plus	1010	$\overline{N}$1
GT	greater than	1110	$N\cdot V\cdot\overline{Z}+\overline{N}\cdot\overline{V}\cdot\overline{Z}$	T	always true	0000	$\overline{V}$
HI	high	0010	$\overline{C}\cdot\overline{Z}$	VC	overflow clear	1000	V
LE	less or equal	1111	$Z+N\cdot\overline{V}+\overline{N}\cdot V$	VS	overflow set	1001	

Condition Codes:
Not affected

Instruction Format:

15	14	13	12	11	10	9	8	7	6	5	4	3	2	1	0
0	1	0	1	CONDITION				1	1	EFFECTIVE ADDRESS					
										MODE			REGISTER		

Instruction Fields:
Condition field — The binary code for one of the conditions listed in the table
Effective Address field — Specifies the location in which the true/false byte is to be stored. Only data alterable addressing modes are allowed as shown:

Addressing Mode	Mode	Register
Dn	000	reg. number:Dn
An	—	—
(An)	010	reg. number:An
(An)+	011	reg. number:An
–(An)	100	reg. number:An
(d_{16},An)	101	reg. number:An
(d_8,An,Xn)	110	reg. number:An

Addressing Mode	Mode	Register
(xxx).W	111	000
(xxx).L	111	001
#⟨data⟩	—	—
(d_{16},PC)	—	—
(d_8,PC,Xn)	—	—

Note: A subsequent NEG.B instruction with the same effective address can be used to change the Scc result from TRUE or FALSE to the equivalent arithmetic value (TRUE = 1, FALSE = 0). In the MC68000, MC68HC000, and MC68008 a memory destination is read before it is written to.

B

Load Status Register and Stop (Privileged Instruction)

STOP

Operation: If supervisor state
then Immediate Data ➧ SR; STOP
else TRAP

Assembler Syntax: STOP #⟨data⟩

Attributes: Unsized

Description: Moves the immediate operand into the status register (both user and supervisor portions), advances the program counter to point to the next instruction, and stops the fetching and executing of instructions. A trace, interrupt, or reset exception causes the processor to resume instructions execution. A trace exception occurs if instruction tracing is enabled when the STOP instruction begins execution. If an interrupt request is asserted with a priority higher than the priority level set by the new status register value, an interrupt exception occurs; otherwise, the interrupt request is ignored. External reset always initiates reset exception processing.

Condition Codes:

Set according to the immediate operand

Instruction Format:

15	14	13	12	11	10	9	8	7	6	5	4	3	2	1	0
0	1	0	0	1	1	1	0	0	1	1	1	0	0	1	0
IMMEDIATE DATA															

Instruction Fields:

Immediate field — Specifies the data to be loaded into the status register

B

SUB — Subtract

Operation: Destination − Source ➧ Destination

Assembler Syntax:
SUB ⟨ea⟩,Dn
SUB Dn,⟨ea⟩

Attributes: Size = (Byte, Word, Long)

Description: Subtracts the source operand from the destination operand and stores the result in the destination. The size of the operation is specified as byte, word, or long. The mode of the instruction indicates which operand is the source, which is the destination, and which is the operand size.

Condition Codes:

X	N	Z	V	C
*	*	*	*	*

X Set to the value of the carry bit
N Set if the result is negative. Cleared otherwise.
Z Set if the result is zero. Cleared otherwise.
V Set if an overflow is generated. Cleared otherwise.
C Set if a borrow is generated. Cleared otherwise.

Instruction Format:

15	14	13	12	11	10	9	8	7	6	5	4	3	2	1	0
										EFFECTIVE ADDRESS					
1	0	0	1	REGISTER			OP-MODE			MODE			REGISTER		

Instruction Fields:

Register field — Specifies any of the eight data registers

Op-Mode field —

Byte	Word	Long	Operation
000	001	010	(⟨Dn⟩) − (⟨ea⟩) ➧ ⟨Dn⟩
100	101	110	(⟨ea⟩) − (⟨Dn⟩) ➧ ⟨ea⟩

B

Effective Address field — Determines the addressing mode. If the location specified is a source operand, all addressing modes are allowed as shown:

Addressing Mode	Mode	Register
Dn	000	reg. number:Dn
An*	001	reg. number:An
(An)	010	reg. number:An
(An)+	011	reg. number:An
−(An)	100	reg. number:An
(d_{16},An)	101	reg. number:An
(d_8,An,Xn)	110	reg. number:An

Addressing Mode	Mode	Register
(xxx).W	111	000
(xxx).L	111	001
#⟨data⟩	111	100
(d_{16},PC)	111	010
(d_8,PC,Xn)	111	011

*For byte size operation, address register direct is not allowed.

If the location specified is a destination operand, only memory alterable addressing modes are allowed as shown:

Addressing Mode	Mode	Register
Dn	—	—
An	—	—
(An)	010	reg. number:An
(An)+	011	reg. number:An
−(An)	100	reg. number:An
(d_{16},An)	101	reg. number:An
(d_8,An,Xn)	110	reg. number:An

Addressing Mode	Mode	Register
(xxx).W	111	000
(xxx).L	111	001
#⟨data⟩	—	—
(d_{16},PC)	—	—
(d_8,PC,Xn)	—	—

Notes:

1. If the destination is a data register, it must be specified as a destination Dn address, not as a destination ⟨ea⟩ address.
2. Most assemblers use SUBA when the destination is an address register, and SUBI or SUBQ when the source is immediate data.

SUBA

Subtract Address

Operation: Destination − Source ➧ Destination

Assembler Syntax: SUBA ⟨ea⟩,An

Attributes: Size = (Word, Long)

Description: Subtracts the source operand from the destination address register and stores the result in the address register. The size of the operation is specified as word or long. Word size source operands are sign extended to 32-bit quantities prior to the subtraction.

Condition Codes:
Not affected

Instruction Format:

15	14	13	12	11	10	9	8	7	6	5	4	3	2	1	0
1	0	0	1	REGISTER			OP-MODE			EFFECTIVE ADDRESS MODE			EFFECTIVE ADDRESS REGISTER		

Op-Mode Field:

Word	Long	Operation
011	111	(⟨An⟩) − (⟨ea⟩) ➧ ⟨An⟩

Instruction Fields:

Register field — Specifies the destination, any of the eight address registers

Op-Mode field — Specifies the size of the operation:

011 — Word operation. The source operand is sign extended to a long operand and the operation is performed on the address register using all 32 bits.

111 — Long operation

Effective Address field — Specifies the source operand. All addressing modes are allowed as shown:

Addressing Mode	Mode	Register
Dn	000	reg. number:Dn
An	001	reg. number:An
(An)	010	reg. number:An
(An)+	011	reg. number:An
−(An)	100	reg. number:An
(d_{16},An)	101	reg. number:An
(d_8,An,Xn)	110	reg. number:An

Addressing Mode	Mode	Register
(xxx).W	111	000
(xxx).L	111	001
#⟨data⟩	111	100
(d_{16},PC)	111	010
(d_8,PC,Xn)	111	011

B

Operation: Destination − Immediate Data ➧ Destination

Assembler Syntax: SUBI #⟨data⟩,⟨ea⟩

Attributes: Size = (Byte, Word, Long)

Description: Subtracts the immediate data from the destination operand and stores the result in the destination location. The size of the operation is specified as byte, word, or long. The size of the immediate data matches the operation size.

Condition Codes:

X	N	Z	V	C
*	*	*	*	*

X Set to the value of the carry bit
N Set if the result is negative. Cleared otherwise.
Z Set if the result is zero. Cleared otherwise.
V Set if an overflow occurs. Cleared otherwise.
C Set if a borrow occurs. Cleared otherwise.

Instruction Format:

15	14	13	12	11	10	9	8	7	6	5	4	3	2	1	0
0	0	0	0	0	1	0	0	SIZE		EFFECTIVE ADDRESS MODE			EFFECTIVE ADDRESS REGISTER		
WORD DATA (16 BITS)								BYTE DATA (8 BITS)							
LONG DATA (32 BITS)															

Instruction Fields:

Size field — Specifies the size of the operation:
00 — Byte operation
01 — Word operation
10 — Long operation

Effective Address field — Specifies the destination operand. Only data alterable addressing modes are allowed as shown:

Addressing Mode	Mode	Register
Dn	000	reg. number:Dn
An	—	—
(An)	010	reg. number:An
(An)+	011	reg. number:An
−(An)	100	reg. number:An
(d_{16},An)	101	reg. number:An
(d_8,An,Xn)	110	reg. number:An

Addressing Mode	Mode	Register
(xxx).W	111	000
(xxx).L	111	001
#⟨data⟩	—	—
(d_{16},PC)	—	—
(d_8,PC,Xn)	—	—

Immediate field — (Data immediately following the instruction)
If size = 00, the data is the low order byte of the immediate word
If size = 01, the data is the entire immediate word
If size = 10, the data is the next two immediate words

SUBQ — Subtract Quick

Operation: Destination − Immediate Data ➧ Destination

Assembler Syntax: SUBQ #⟨data⟩,⟨ea⟩

Attributes: Size = (Byte, Word, Long)

Description: Subtracts the immediate data (1-8) from the destination operand. The size of the operation is specified as byte, word, or long. Only word and long operations are allowed with address registers, and the condition codes are not affected. When subtracting from address registers, the entire destination address register is used, regardless of the operation size.

Condition Codes:

X	N	Z	V	C
*	*	*	*	*

X Set to the value of the carry bit
N Set if the result is negative. Cleared otherwise.
Z Set if the result is zero. Cleared otherwise.
V Set if an overflow occurs. Cleared otherwise.
C Set if a borrow occurs. Cleared otherwise.

Instruction Format:

15	14	13	12	11	10	9	8	7	6	5	4	3	2	1	0
0	1	0	1	DATA			1	SIZE		EFFECTIVE ADDRESS					
										MODE			REGISTER		

Instruction Fields:

Data field — Three bits of immediate data; 1-7 represent immediate values of 1-7, and 0 represents 8

Size field — Specifies the size of the operation:
- 00 — Byte operation
- 01 — Word operation
- 10 — Long operation

Effective Address field — Specifies the destination location. Only alterable addressing modes are allowed as shown:

Addressing Mode	Mode	Register
Dn	000	reg. number:Dn
An*	001	reg. number:An
(An)	010	reg. number:An
(An)+	011	reg. number:An
−(An)	100	reg. number:An
(d_{16},An)	101	reg. number:An
(d_8,An,Xn)	110	reg. number:An

*Word and Long only.

Addressing Mode	Mode	Register
(xxx).W	111	000
(xxx).L	111	001
#⟨data⟩	—	—
(d_{16},PC)	—	—
(d_8,PC,Xn)	—	—

B

SUBX — Subtract with Extend — SUBX

Operation: Destination − Source − X ➧ Destination

Assembler Syntax:
SUBX Dx,Dy
SUBX −(Ax),−(Ay)

Attributes: Size = (Byte, Word, Long)

Description: Subtracts the source operand and the extend bit from the destination operand and stores the result in the destination location. The instruction has two modes:

1. Data register to data register: The data registers specified in the instruction contain the operands.
2. Memory to memory: The address registers specified in the instruction access the operands from memory using the predecrement addressing mode.

The size of the operand is specified as byte, word, or long.

Condition Codes:

X	N	Z	V	C
*	*	*	*	*

X Set to the value of the carry bit
N Set if the result is negative. Cleared otherwise.
Z Cleared if the result is non-zero. Unchanged otherwise.
V Set if an overflow occurs. Cleared otherwise.
C Set if a carry occurs. Cleared otherwise.

NOTE

Normally the Z condition code bit is set via programming before the start of an operation. This allows successful tests for zero results upon completion of multiple-precision operations.

Instruction Format:

15	14	13	12	11	10	9	8	7	6	5	4	3	2	1	0
1	0	0	1	REGISTER Ry			1	SIZE		0	0	R/M	REGISTER Rx		

Instruction Fields:

Register Ry field — Specifies the destination register:
If R/M = 0, specifies a data register
If R/M = 1, specifies an address register for the predecrement addressing mode

Size field — Specifies the size of the operation:
00 — Byte operation
01 — Word operation
10 — Long operation

R/M field — Specifies the operand addressing mode:
0 — The operation is data register to data register
1 — The operation is memory to memory

Register Rx field — Specifies the source register:
If R/M = 0, specifies a data register
If R/M = 1, specifies an address register for the predecrement addressing mode

B

SWAP — Swap Register Halves

Operation: Register [31:16] ⟷ Register [15:0]

Assembler Syntax: SWAP Dn

Attributes: Size = (Word)

Description: Exchange the 16-bit words (halves) of a data register

Condition Codes:

X	N	Z	V	C
—	*	*	0	0

X Not affected
N Set if the most-significant bit of the 32-bit result is set. Cleared otherwise.
Z Set if the 32-bit result is zero. Cleared otherwise.
V Always cleared
C Always cleared

Instruction Format:

15	14	13	12	11	10	9	8	7	6	5	4	3	2	1	0
0	1	0	0	1	0	0	0	0	1	0	0	0	REGISTER		

Instruction Fields:
Register field — Specifies the data register to swap

B

Operation: Destination Tested ➧ Condition Codes; 1 ➧ bit 7 of Destination

Assembler Syntax: TAS ⟨ea⟩

Attributes: Size = (Byte)

Description: Tests and sets the byte operand addressed by the effective address field. The instruction tests the current value of the operand and sets the N and Z condition bits appropriately. TAS also sets the high order bit of the operand. The operation uses a read-modify-write memory cycle that completes the operation without interruption. This instruction supports use of a flag or semaphore to coordinate several processors.

Condition Codes:

X	N	Z	V	C
—	*	*	0	0

X Not affected
N Set if the most significant bit of the operand is currently set. Cleared otherwise.
Z Set if the operand was zero. Cleared otherwise.
V Always cleared
C Always cleared

Instruction Format:

15	14	13	12	11	10	9	8	7	6	5	4	3	2	1	0
0	1	0	0	1	0	1	0	1	1	EFFECTIVE ADDRESS					
										MODE			REGISTER		

Instruction Fields:

Effective Address field — Specifies the location of the tested operand. Only data alterable addressing modes are allowed as shown:

Addressing Mode	Mode	Register
Dn	000	reg. number:Dn
An	—	—
(An)	010	reg. number:An
(An)+	011	reg. number:An
−(An)	100	reg. number:An
(d_{16},An)	101	reg. number:An
(d_8,An,Xn)	110	reg. number:An

Addressing Mode	Mode	Register
(xxx).W	111	000
(xxx).L	111	001
#⟨data⟩	—	—
(d_{16},PC)	—	—
(d_8,PC,Xn)	—	—

B

Operation: 1 ▶ S bit of SR
SSP − 2 ▶ SSP; Format/Offset ▶ (SSP); — MC68010 only
SSP − 4 ▶ SSP; PC ▶ (SSP); SSP − 2 ▶ SSP;
SR ▶ (SSP); Vector Address ▶ PC

Assembler Syntax: TRAP #⟨vector⟩

Attributes: Unsized

Description: Causes a TRAP #⟨vector⟩ exception. The instruction adds the immediate operand (vector) of the instruction to 32 to obtain the vector number. The range of vector values is 0-15, which provides 16 vectors.

Condition Codes:
Not affected

Instruction Format:

15	14	13	12	11	10	9	8	7	6	5	4	3	2	1	0
0	1	0	0	1	1	1	0	0	1	0	0	VECTOR			

Instruction Fields:
Vector field — Specifies the trap vector to be taken

B

Operation: If V then TRAP

Assembler Syntax: TRAPV

Attributes: Unsized

Description: If the overflow condition is set, causes a TRAPV exception (vector number 7). If the overflow condition is not set, the processor performs no operation and execution continues with the next instruction.

Condition Codes:
Not affected

Instruction Format:

15	14	13	12	11	10	9	8	7	6	5	4	3	2	1	0
0	1	0	0	1	1	1	0	0	1	1	1	0	1	1	0

Operation: Destination Tested ▶ Condition Codes

Assembler Syntax: TST ⟨ea⟩

Attributes: Size = (Byte, Word, Long)

Description: Compares the operand with zero and sets the condition codes according to the results of the test. The size of the operation is specified as byte, word, or long.

Condition Codes:

X	N	Z	V	C
—	*	*	0	0

X Not affected
N Set if the operand is negative. Cleared otherwise.
Z Set if the operand is zero. Cleared otherwise.
V Always cleared
C Always cleared

Instruction Format:

15	14	13	12	11	10	9	8	7	6	5	4	3	2	1	0
0	1	0	0	1	0	1	0	SIZE		EFFECTIVE ADDRESS					
										MODE			REGISTER		

Instruction Fields:

Size field — Specifies the size of the operation:
- 00 — Byte operation
- 01 — Word operation
- 10 — Long operation

Effective Address field — Specifies the destination operand. If the operation size is word or long, all addressing modes are allowed. If the operation size is byte, only data addressing modes are allowed as shown:

Addressing Mode	Mode	Register
Dn	000	reg. number:Dn
An	—	—
(An)	010	reg. number:An
(An)+	011	reg. number:An
−(An)	100	reg. number:An
(d_{16},An)	101	reg. number:An
(d_8,An,Xn)	110	reg. number:An

Addressing Mode	Mode	Register
(xxx).W	111	000
(xxx).L	111	001
#⟨data⟩	—	—
(d_{16},PC)	111	010
(d_8,PC,Xn)	111	011

B

Operation: An ➧ SP; (SP) ➧ An; SP + 4 ➧ SP

Assembler Syntax: UNLK An

Attributes: Unsized

Description: Loads the stack pointer from the specified address register then loads the address register with the long word pulled from the top of the stack.

Condition Codes:
Not affected

Instruction Format:

15	14	13	12	11	10	9	8	7	6	5	4	3	2	1	0
0	1	0	0	1	1	1	0	0	1	0	1	1	REGISTER		

Instruction Fields:
Register field — Specifies the address register for the instruction

B

APPENDIX C
INSTRUCTION FORMAT SUMMARY

This appendix provides a summary of the primary words of each instruction of the instruction set. The complete instruction consists of the primary words followed by the addressing mode operands such as immediate data fields, displacements, and index operands. Table C-1 is an operation code (opcode) map that illustrates the use of bits 15 through 12 to specify the operations.

Table C-1. Operation Code Map

Bits 15 through 12	Operation
0000	Bit Manipulation/MOVEP/Immediate
0001	Move Byte
0010	Move Long
0011	Move Word
0100	Miscellaneous
0101	ADDQ/SUBQ/Scc/DBcc
0110	Bcc/BSR
0111	MOVEQ
1000	OR/DIV/SBCD
1001	SUB/SUBX
1010	(Unassigned, Reserved)
1011	CMP/EOR
1100	AND/MUL/ABCD/EXG
1101	ADD/ADDX
1110	Shift/Rotate
1111	Coprocessor Interface (MC68020)

ORI

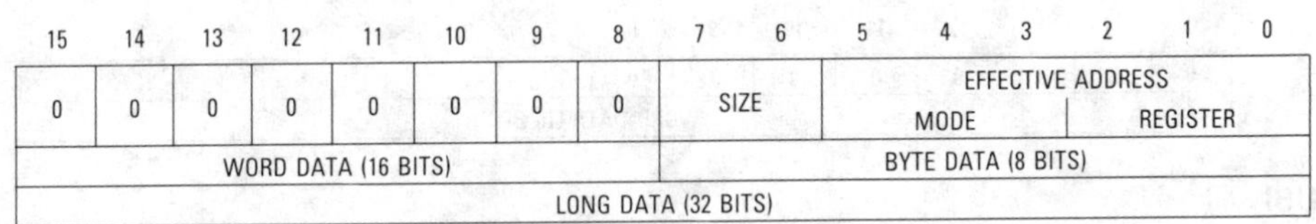

15	14	13	12	11	10	9	8	7	6	5	4	3	2	1	0
0	0	0	0	0	0	0	0	SIZE		EFFECTIVE ADDRESS MODE			EFFECTIVE ADDRESS REGISTER		
WORD DATA (16 BITS)								BYTE DATA (8 BITS)							
LONG DATA (32 BITS)															

Size Field: 00 = Byte 01 = Word 10 = Long

ORI to CCR

15	14	13	12	11	10	9	8	7	6	5	4	3	2	1	0
0	0	0	0	0	0	0	0	0	0	1	1	1	1	0	0
0	0	0	0	0	0	0	0	BYTE DATA (8 BITS)							

ORI to SR

15	14	13	12	11	10	9	8	7	6	5	4	3	2	1	0
0	0	0	0	0	0	0	0	0	1	1	1	1	1	0	0
WORD DATA (16 BITS)															

Bit (Dynamic)

15	14	13	12	11	10	9	8	7	6	5	4	3	2	1	0
0	0	0	0	DATA REGISTER			1	TYPE		EFFECTIVE ADDRESS MODE			EFFECTIVE ADDRESS REGISTER		

Type Field: 00 = TST 10 = CLR 01 = CHG 11 = SET

MOVEP

15	14	13	12	11	10	9	8	7	6	5	4	3	2	1	0
0	0	0	0	DATA REGISTER			OP-MODE			0	0	1	ADDRESS REGISTER		
DISPLACEMENT (16 BITS)															

Op-Mode Field: 100 = Transfer Word from Memory to Register
101 = Transfer Long from Memory to Register
110 = Transfer Word from Register to Memory
111 = Transfer Long from Register to Memory

ANDI

15	14	13	12	11	10	9	8	7	6	5	4	3	2	1	0
0	0	0	0	0	0	1	0	SIZE		EFFECTIVE ADDRESS MODE			EFFECTIVE ADDRESS REGISTER		
WORD DATA (16 BITS)								BYTE DATA (8 BITS)							
LONG DATA (32 BITS)															

Size Field: 00 = Byte 01 = Word 10 = Long

ANDI to CCR

15	14	13	12	11	10	9	8	7	6	5	4	3	2	1	0
0	0	0	0	0	0	1	0	0	0	1	1	1	1	0	0
0	0	0	0	0	0	0	0	BYTE DATA (8 BITS)							

ANDI to SR

15	14	13	12	11	10	9	8	7	6	5	4	3	2	1	0
0	0	0	0	0	0	1	0	0	1	1	1	1	1	0	0
WORD DATA (16 BITS)															

SUBI

15	14	13	12	11	10	9	8	7	6	5	4	3	2	1	0
0	0	0	0	0	1	0	0	SIZE		EFFECTIVE ADDRESS MODE			EFFECTIVE ADDRESS REGISTER		
WORD DATA (16 BITS)								BYTE DATA (8 BITS)							
LONG DATA (32 BITS)															

Size Field: 00 = Byte 01 = Word 10 = Long

ADDI

15	14	13	12	11	10	9	8	7	6	5	4	3	2	1	0
0	0	0	0	0	1	1	0	SIZE		EFFECTIVE ADDRESS MODE			EFFECTIVE ADDRESS REGISTER		
WORD DATA (16 BITS)								BYTE DATA (8 BITS)							
LONG DATA (32 BITS)															

Size Field: 00 = Byte 01 = Word 10 = Long

Bit (Static)

15	14	13	12	11	10	9	8	7	6	5	4	3	2	1	0
0	0	0	0	1	0	0	0	TYPE		EFFECTIVE ADDRESS MODE			EFFECTIVE ADDRESS REGISTER		
0	0	0	0	0	0	0	0	BIT NUMBER							

Type Field: 00 = TST 10 = CLR 01 = CHG 11 = SET

EORI

15	14	13	12	11	10	9	8	7	6	5	4	3	2	1	0
0	0	0	0	1	0	1	0	SIZE		EFFECTIVE ADDRESS MODE			EFFECTIVE ADDRESS REGISTER		
WORD DATA (16 BITS)								BYTE DATA (8 BITS)							
LONG DATA (32 BITS)															

Size Field: 00 = Byte 01 = Word 10 = Long

EORI to CCR

15	14	13	12	11	10	9	8	7	6	5	4	3	2	1	0
0	0	0	0	1	0	1	0	0	0	1	1	1	1	0	0
0	0	0	0	0	0	0	0	BYTE DATA (8 BITS)							

EORI to SR

15	14	13	12	11	10	9	8	7	6	5	4	3	2	1	0
0	0	0	0	1	0	1	0	0	1	1	1	1	1	0	0
WORD DATA (16 BITS)															

CMPI

15	14	13	12	11	10	9	8	7	6	5	4	3	2	1	0
0	0	0	0	1	1	0	0	SIZE		EFFECTIVE ADDRESS MODE			EFFECTIVE ADDRESS REGISTER		
WORD DATA (16 BITS)								BYTE DATA (8 BITS)							
LONG DATA (32 BITS)															

Size Field: 00 = Byte 01 = Word 10 = Long

MOVES

15	14	13	12	11	10	9	8	7	6	5	4	3	2	1	0
0	0	0	0	1	1	1	0	SIZE		EFFECTIVE ADDRESS MODE			EFFECTIVE ADDRESS REGISTER		
D/A	REGISTER			dr	0	0	0	0	0	0	0	0	0	0	0

dr Field: 0 = EA to Register 1 = Register to EA

C

MOVE Byte

15	14	13	12	11	10	9	8	7	6	5	4	3	2	1	0
0	0	0	1	DESTINATION REGISTER			DESTINATION MODE			SOURCE MODE			SOURCE REGISTER		

Note Register and Mode Locations

MOVEA Long

15	14	13	12	11	10	9	8	7	6	5	4	3	2	1	0
0	0	1	0	DESTINATION REGISTER			0	0	1	SOURCE MODE			SOURCE REGISTER		

MOVE Long

15	14	13	12	11	10	9	8	7	6	5	4	3	2	1	0
0	0	1	0	DESTINATION REGISTER			DESTINATION MODE			SOURCE MODE			SOURCE REGISTER		

Note Register and Mode Locations

MOVEA Word

15	14	13	12	11	10	9	8	7	6	5	4	3	2	1	0
0	0	1	1	DESTINATION REGISTER			0	0	1	SOURCE MODE			SOURCE REGISTER		

MOVE Word

15	14	13	12	11	10	9	8	7	6	5	4	3	2	1	0
0	0	1	1	DESTINATION REGISTER			DESTINATION MODE			SOURCE MODE			SOURCE REGISTER		

Note Register and Mode Locations

NEGX

15	14	13	12	11	10	9	8	7	6	5	4	3	2	1	0
0	1	0	0	0	0	0	0	SIZE		EFFECTIVE ADDRESS MODE			EFFECTIVE ADDRESS REGISTER		

Size Field: 00 = Byte 01 = Word 10 = Long

MOVE from SR

15	14	13	12	11	10	9	8	7	6	5	4	3	2	1	0
0	1	0	0	0	0	0	0	1	1	EFFECTIVE ADDRESS MODE			EFFECTIVE ADDRESS REGISTER		

CHK

15	14	13	12	11	10	9	8	7	6	5	4	3	2	1	0
0	1	0	0	REGISTER			1	1	0	EFFECTIVE ADDRESS MODE			EFFECTIVE ADDRESS REGISTER		

LEA

15	14	13	12	11	10	9	8	7	6	5	4	3	2	1	0
										EFFECTIVE ADDRESS					
0	1	0	0	REGISTER			1	1	1	MODE			REGISTER		

CLR

15	14	13	12	11	10	9	8	7	6	5	4	3	2	1	0
										EFFECTIVE ADDRESS					
0	1	0	0	0	0	1	0	SIZE		MODE			REGISTER		

Size Field: 00 = Byte 01 = Word 10 = Long

MOVE from CCR

15	14	13	12	11	10	9	8	7	6	5	4	3	2	1	0
										EFFECTIVE ADDRESS					
0	1	0	0	0	0	1	0	1	1	MODE			REGISTER		

NEG

15	14	13	12	11	10	9	8	7	6	5	4	3	2	1	0
										EFFECTIVE ADDRESS					
0	1	0	0	0	1	0	0	SIZE		MODE			REGISTER		

Size Field: 00 = Byte 01 = Word 10 = Long

MOVE to CCR

15	14	13	12	11	10	9	8	7	6	5	4	3	2	1	0
										EFFECTIVE ADDRESS					
0	1	0	0	0	1	0	0	1	1	MODE			REGISTER		

NOT

15	14	13	12	11	10	9	8	7	6	5	4	3	2	1	0
										EFFECTIVE ADDRESS					
0	1	0	0	0	1	1	0	SIZE		MODE			REGISTER		

Size Field: 00 = Byte 01 = Word 10 = Long

MOVE to SR

15	14	13	12	11	10	9	8	7	6	5	4	3	2	1	0
										EFFECTIVE ADDRESS					
0	1	0	0	0	1	1	0	1	1	MODE			REGISTER		

NBCD

15	14	13	12	11	10	9	8	7	6	5	4	3	2	1	0
										EFFECTIVE ADDRESS					
0	1	0	0	1	0	0	0	0	0	MODE			REGISTER		

SWAP

15	14	13	12	11	10	9	8	7	6	5	4	3	2	1	0
0	1	0	0	1	0	0	0	0	1	0	0	0	REGISTER		

C

BKPT

15	14	13	12	11	10	9	8	7	6	5	4	3	2	1	0
0	1	0	0	1	0	0	0	0	1	0	0	1	VECTOR		

PEA

15	14	13	12	11	10	9	8	7	6	5	4	3	2	1	0
0	1	0	0	1	0	0	0	0	1	EFFECTIVE ADDRESS					
										MODE			REGISTER		

Size Field: 00 = Byte 01 = Word 10 = Long

EXT

15	14	13	12	11	10	9	8	7	6	5	4	3	2	1	0
0	1	0	0	1	0	0	OP-MODE			0	0	0	REGISTER		

Op-Mode Field: 010 = Extend Word 011 = Extend Word

MOVEM Registers to EA

15	14	13	12	11	10	9	8	7	6	5	4	3	2	1	0
0	1	0	0	1	0	0	0	1	SIZE	EFFECTIVE ADDRESS					
										MODE			REGISTER		
REGISTER LIST MASK															

Size Field: 0 = Word Transfer 1 = Long Transfer

TST

15	14	13	12	11	10	9	8	7	6	5	4	3	2	1	0
0	1	0	0	1	0	1	0	SIZE		EFFECTIVE ADDRESS					
										MODE			REGISTER		

Size Field: 00 = Byte 01 = Word 10 = Long

TAS

15	14	13	12	11	10	9	8	7	6	5	4	3	2	1	0
0	1	0	0	1	0	1	0	1	1	EFFECTIVE ADDRESS					
										MODE			REGISTER		

ILLEGAL

15	14	13	12	11	10	9	8	7	6	5	4	3	2	1	0
0	1	0	0	1	0	1	0	1	1	1	1	1	1	0	0

MOVEM EA to Registers

15	14	13	12	11	10	9	8	7	6	5	4	3	2	1	0
0	1	0	0	1	1	0	0	1	SIZE	EFFECTIVE ADDRESS					
										MODE			REGISTER		
REGISTER LIST MASK															

Size Field: 0 = Word Transfer 1 = Long Transfer

TRAP

15	14	13	12	11	10	9	8	7	6	5	4	3	2	1	0
0	1	0	0	1	1	1	0	0	1	0	0	VECTOR			

LINK Word

15	14	13	12	11	10	9	8	7	6	5	4	3	2	1	0
0	1	0	0	1	1	1	0	0	1	0	1	0	REGISTER		
WORD DISPLACEMENT															

UNLK

15	14	13	12	11	10	9	8	7	6	5	4	3	2	1	0
0	1	0	0	1	1	1	0	0	1	0	1	1	REGISTER		

MOVE to USP

15	14	13	12	11	10	9	8	7	6	5	4	3	2	1	0
0	1	0	0	1	1	1	0	0	1	1	0	0	REGISTER		

MOVE from USP

15	14	13	12	11	10	9	8	7	6	5	4	3	2	1	0
0	1	0	0	1	1	1	0	0	1	1	0	1	REGISTER		

RESET

15	14	13	12	11	10	9	8	7	6	5	4	3	2	1	0
0	1	0	0	1	1	1	0	0	1	1	1	0	0	0	0

NOP

15	14	13	12	11	10	9	8	7	6	5	4	3	2	1	0
0	1	0	0	1	1	1	0	0	1	1	1	0	0	0	1

STOP

15	14	13	12	11	10	9	8	7	6	5	4	3	2	1	0
0	1	0	0	1	1	1	0	0	1	1	1	0	0	1	0
IMMEDIATE DATA															

RTE

15	14	13	12	11	10	9	8	7	6	5	4	3	2	1	0
0	1	0	0	1	1	1	0	0	1	1	1	0	0	1	1

C

RTD

15	14	13	12	11	10	9	8	7	6	5	4	3	2	1	0
0	1	0	0	1	1	1	0	0	1	1	1	0	1	0	0
DISPLACEMENT (16 BITS)															

RTS

15	14	13	12	11	10	9	8	7	6	5	4	3	2	1	0
0	1	0	0	1	1	1	0	0	1	1	1	0	1	0	1

TRAPV

15	14	13	12	11	10	9	8	7	6	5	4	3	2	1	0
0	1	0	0	1	1	1	0	0	1	1	1	0	1	1	0

RTR

15	14	13	12	11	10	9	8	7	6	5	4	3	2	1	0
0	1	0	0	1	1	1	0	0	1	1	1	0	1	1	1

MOVEC

15	14	13	12	11	10	9	8	7	6	5	4	3	2	1	0
0	1	0	0	1	1	1	0	0	1	1	1	1	0	1	dr
A/D	REGISTER			CONTROL REGISTER											

dr Field: 0 = Control Register to General Register
1 = General Register to Control Register

Control Register Field: $000 = SFC
$001 = DFC
$800 = USP
$801 = VBR

JSR

15	14	13	12	11	10	9	8	7	6	5	4	3	2	1	0
0	1	0	0	1	1	1	0	1	0	EFFECTIVE ADDRESS					
										MODE			REGISTER		

JMP

15	14	13	12	11	10	9	8	7	6	5	4	3	2	1	0
0	1	0	0	1	1	1	0	1	1	EFFECTIVE ADDRESS					
										MODE			REGISTER		

ADDQ

15	14	13	12	11	10	9	8	7	6	5	4	3	2	1	0
0	1	0	1	DATA			0	SIZE		EFFECTIVE ADDRESS					
										MODE			REGISTER		

Data Field: Three bits of immediate data, 1-7 represent immediate values of 1-7, and 0 represents 8.
Size Field: 00 = Byte 01 = Word 10 = Long

Scc

15	14	13	12	11	10	9	8	7	6	5	4	3	2	1	0
0	1	0	1	CONDITION				1	1	EFFECTIVE ADDRESS					
										MODE			REGISTER		

DBcc

15	14	13	12	11	10	9	8	7	6	5	4	3	2	1	0
0	1	0	1	CONDITION				1	1	0	0	1	REGISTER		
DISPLACEMENT (16 BITS)															

SUBQ

15	14	13	12	11	10	9	8	7	6	5	4	3	2	1	0
0	1	0	1	DATA			1	SIZE		EFFECTIVE ADDRESS					
										MODE			REGISTER		

Data Field: Three bits of immediate data; 1-7 represent immediate values of 1-7, and 0 represents 8.
Size Field: 00=Byte 01=Word 10=Long

Bcc

15	14	13	12	11	10	9	8	7	6	5	4	3	2	1	0
0	1	1	0	CONDITION				8-BIT DISPLACEMENT							
16-BIT DISPLACEMENT IF 8-BIT DISPLACEMENT = $00															

BRA

15	14	13	12	11	10	9	8	7	6	5	4	3	2	1	0
0	1	1	0	0	0	0	0	8-BIT DISPLACEMENT							
16-BIT DISPLACEMENT IF 8-BIT DISPLACEMENT = $00															

BSR

15	14	13	12	11	10	9	8	7	6	5	4	3	2	1	0
0	1	1	0	0	0	0	1	8-BIT DISPLACEMENT							
16-BIT DISPLACEMENT IF 8-BIT DISPLACEMENT = $00															

MOVEQ

15	14	13	12	11	10	9	8	7	6	5	4	3	2	1	0
0	1	1	1	REGISTER			0	DATA							

Data Field: Data is sign extended to a long operand and all 32 bits are transferred to the data register.

C

OR

15	14	13	12	11	10	9	8	7	6	5	4	3	2	1	0
1	0	0	0	REGISTER			OP-MODE			EFFECTIVE ADDRESS MODE			EFFECTIVE ADDRESS REGISTER		

Op-Mode Field:

Byte	Word	Long	Operation
000	001	010	(⟨ea⟩)v(⟨Dn⟩) ➧ ⟨Dn⟩
100	101	110	(⟨Dn⟩)v(⟨ea⟩) ➧ ⟨ea⟩

DIVS/DIVU Word

15	14	13	12	11	10	9	8	7	6	5	4	3	2	1	0
1	0	0	0	REGISTER			TYPE	1	1	EFFECTIVE ADDRESS MODE			EFFECTIVE ADDRESS REGISTER		

Type Field: 0 = DIVU 1 = DIVS

SBCD

15	14	13	12	11	10	9	8	7	6	5	4	3	2	1	0
1	0	0	0	REGISTER Ry			1	0	0	0	0	R/M	REGISTER Rx		

R/M Field: 0 = Data Register to Data Register 1 = Memory to Memory

If R/M = 0, Both Registers are Data Registers
If R/M = 1, Both Registers are Address Registers for the Predecrement Addressing Mode

SUB

15	14	13	12	11	10	9	8	7	6	5	4	3	2	1	0
1	0	0	1	REGISTER			OP-MODE			EFFECTIVE ADDRESS MODE			EFFECTIVE ADDRESS REGISTER		

Op-Mode Field:

Byte	Word	Long	Operation
000	001	010	(⟨Dn⟩) – (⟨ea⟩) ➧ ⟨Dn⟩
100	101	110	(⟨ea⟩) – (⟨Dn⟩) ➧ ⟨ea⟩

SUBA

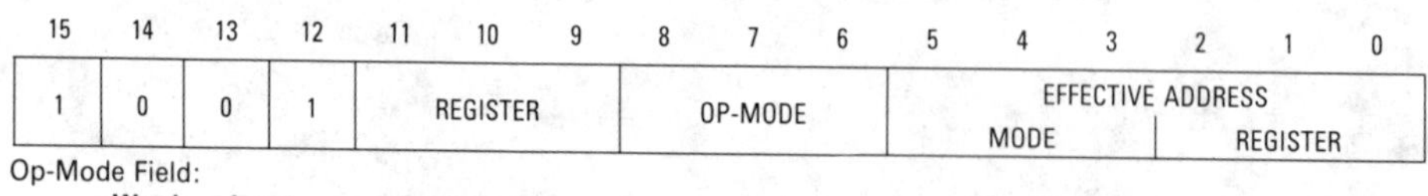

Op-Mode Field:

Word	Long	Operation
011	111	(⟨An⟩) – (⟨ea⟩) ➧ ⟨An⟩

SUBX

15	14	13	12	11	10	9	8	7	6	5	4	3	2	1	0
1	0	0	1	REGISTER Ry			1	SIZE		0	0	R/M	REGISTER Rx		

Size Field: 00 = Byte 01 = Word 10 = Long
R/M Field: 0 = Data Register to Data Register 1 = Memory to Memory

If R/M = 0, Both Registers are Data Registers
If R/M = 1, Both Registers are Address Registers for the Predecrement Addressing Mode

CMP

15	14	13	12	11	10	9	8	7	6	5	4	3	2	1	0
1	0	1	1	REGISTER			OP-MODE			EFFECTIVE ADDRESS					
										MODE			REGISTER		

Op-Mode Field:

Byte	Word	Long	Operation
000	001	010	(⟨Dn⟩) − (⟨ea⟩)

CMPA

15	14	13	12	11	10	9	8	7	6	5	4	3	2	1	0
1	0	1	1	REGISTER			OP-MODE			EFFECTIVE ADDRESS					
										MODE			REGISTER		

Op-Mode Field:

Word	Long	Operation
011	111	(⟨An⟩) − (⟨ea⟩)

EOR

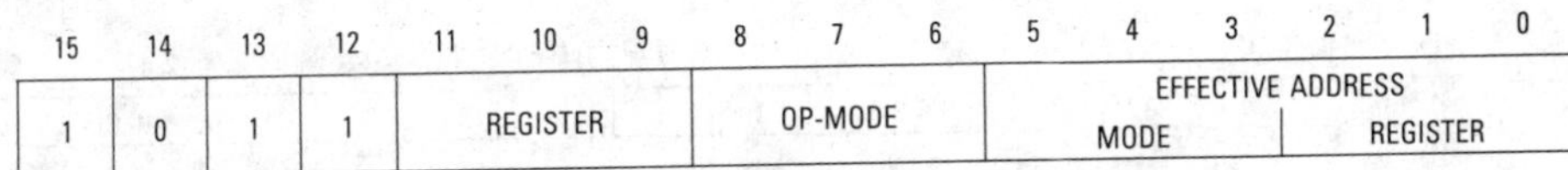

15	14	13	12	11	10	9	8	7	6	5	4	3	2	1	0
1	0	1	1	REGISTER			OP-MODE			EFFECTIVE ADDRESS					
										MODE			REGISTER		

Op-Mode Field:

Byte	Word	Long	Operation
100	101	110	(⟨ea⟩) ⊕ (⟨Dn⟩) ➧ ⟨ea⟩

CMPM

15	14	13	12	11	10	9	8	7	6	5	4	3	2	1	0
1	0	1	1	REGISTER Ax			1	SIZE		0	0	1	REGISTER Ay		

Size Field: 00 = Byte 01 = Word 10 = Long

AND

15	14	13	12	11	10	9	8	7	6	5	4	3	2	1	0
1	1	0	0	REGISTER			OP-MODE			EFFECTIVE ADDRESS					
										MODE			REGISTER		

Op-Mode Field:

Byte	Word	Long	Operation
000	001	010	(⟨ea⟩)Λ(⟨Dn⟩) ➧ ⟨Dn⟩
100	101	110	(⟨Dn⟩)Λ(⟨ea⟩) ➧ ⟨ea⟩

MULS/MULU Word

15	14	13	12	11	10	9	8	7	6	5	4	3	2	1	0
1	1	0	0	REGISTER			TYPE	1	1	EFFECTIVE ADDRESS					
										MODE			REGISTER		

Type Field: 0 = MULU 1 = MULS

C

ABCD

15	14	13	12	11	10	9	8	7	6	5	4	3	2	1	0
1	1	0	0	REGISTER Rx			1	0	0	0	0	R/M	REGISTER Ry		

R/M Field: 0 = Data Register to Data Register 1 = Memory to Memory

If R/M = 0, Both Registers are Data Registers
If R/M = 1, Both Registers are Address Registers for the Predecrement Addressing Mode

EXG Data Registers

15	14	13	12	11	10	9	8	7	6	5	4	3	2	1	0
1	1	0	0	REGISTER Dx			1	0	1	0	0	0	REGISTER Dy		

EXG Address Registers

15	14	13	12	11	10	9	8	7	6	5	4	3	2	1	0
1	1	0	0	REGISTER Ax			1	0	1	0	0	1	REGISTER Ay		

EXG Data Register and Address Register

15	14	13	12	11	10	9	8	7	6	5	4	3	2	1	0
1	1	0	0	REGISTER Dx			1	1	0	0	0	1	REGISTER Ay		

ADD

15	14	13	12	11	10	9	8	7	6	5	4	3	2	1	0
1	1	0	1	REGISTER			OP-MODE			EFFECTIVE ADDRESS					
										MODE			REGISTER		

Op-Mode Field:

Byte	Word	Long	Operation
000	001	010	(⟨ea⟩) + (⟨Dn⟩) → ⟨Dn⟩
100	101	110	(⟨Dn⟩) + (⟨ea⟩) → ⟨ea⟩

ADDA

15	14	13	12	11	10	9	8	7	6	5	4	3	2	1	0
1	1	0	1	REGISTER			OP-MODE			EFFECTIVE ADDRESS					
										MODE			REGISTER		

Op-Mode Field:

Word	Long	Operation
011	111	(⟨ea⟩) + (⟨An⟩) → ⟨An⟩

ADDX

15	14	13	12	11	10	9	8	7	6	5	4	3	2	1	0
1	1	0	1	REGISTER Rx			1	SIZE		0	0	R/M	REGISTER Ry		

Size Field: 00 = Byte 01 = Word 10 = Long
R/M Field: 0 = Data Register to Data Register 1 = Memory to Memory

If R/M = 0, Both Registers are Data Registers
If R/M = 1, Both Registers are Address Registers for the Predecrement Addressing Mode

Shift/Rotate Register

15	14	13	12	11	10	9	8	7	6	5	4	3	2	1	0
1	1	1	0	COUNT/REGISTER			dr	SIZE		I/R	TYPE		REGISTER		

Count/Register Field:
If I/R Field = 0, Specifies Shift Count
If I/R Field = 1, Specifies a Data Register that Contains the Shift Count
dr Field: 0 = Right 1 = Left
Size Field: 00 = Byte 01 = Word 10 = Long
I/R Field: 0 = Immediate Shift Count 1 = Register Shift Count
Type Field: 00 = Arithmetic Shift 01 = Logical Shift 10 = Rotate with Extend 11 = Rotate

Shift/Rotate Memory

15	14	13	12	11	10	9	8	7	6	5	4	3	2	1	0
										EFFECTIVE ADDRESS					
1	1	1	0	0	TYPE		dr	1	1	MODE			REGISTER		

Type Field: 00 = Arithmetic Shift 01 = Logical Shift 10 = Rotate with Extend 11 = Rotate
dr Field: 0 = Right 1 = Left

C

C

APPENDIX D
MC68010 LOOP MODE OPERATION

In the loop mode of the MC68010, a single instruction is executed repeatedly under control of the test condition, decrement, and branch (DBcc) instruction without any instruction fetch bus cycles. The execution of a single-instruction loop without fetching an instruction provides a highly efficient means of repeating an instruction because the only bus cycles required are those that read and write the operands.

The DBcc instruction uses three operands: a loop counter, a branch condition, and a branch displacement. When this instruction is executed in the loop mode, the value in the low-order word of the register specified as the loop counter is decremented by one and compared to minus one. If the result after decrementing the value is equal to minus one, the result is placed in the loop counter, and the next instruction in sequence is executed. Otherwise, the condition code register is checked against the specified branch condition. If the branch condition is true, the result is discarded, and the next instruction in sequence is executed. When the count is not equal to minus one and the branch condition is false, the branch displacement is added to the value in the program counter, and the instruction at the resulting address is executed.

Figure D-1 shows the source code of a program fragment containing a loop that executes in the loop mode in the MC68010. The program moves a block of data at address SOURCE to a block starting at address DEST. The number of words in the block is labeled LENGTH. If any word in the block at address SOURCE contains zero, the move operation stops, and the program performs whatever processing follows this program fragment.

```
        LEA      SOURCE, A0       Load A Pointer To Source Data
        LEA      DEST, A1         Load A Pointer To Destination
        MOVE.W   #LENGTH, D0      Load The Counter Register
LOOP    MOVE.W   (A0)+, (A1)+     Loop To Move The Block Of Data
        DBEQ     D0, LOOP         Stop If Data Word Is Zero
```

Figure D-1. DBcc Loop Mode Program Example

The first load effective address (LEA) instruction loads the address labeled SOURCE into address register A0. The second instruction, also an LEA instruction, loads the address labeled DEST into address register A1. Next, a move data from source to destination (MOVE) instruction moves the number of words into data register D0, the loop counter. The last two instructions, a MOVE and a test equal, decrement, and branch (DBEQ), form the loop that moves the block of data. The bus activity required to execute these instructions consists of the following cycles:

1. Fetch the MOVE instruction.
2. Fetch the DBEQ instruction.
3. Read the operand at the address in A0.
4. Write the operand at the address in A1.
5. Fetch the displacement word of the DBEQ instruction.

D

Of these five bus cycles, only two move the data. However, the MC68010 has a two-word prefetch queue in addition to the one-word instruction decode register. The loop mode uses the prefetch queue and the instruction decode register to eliminate the instruction fetch cycles. The procesor places the MOVE instruction in the instruction decode register and the two words of the DBEQ instruction in the prefetch queue. With no additional opcode fetches, the processor executes these two instructions as required to move the entire block or to move all non-zero words that precede a zero.

The MC68010 enters the loop mode automatically when the conditions for loop mode operation are met. Entering the loop mode is transparent to the programmer. The conditions are that the loop count and branch condition of the DBcc instruction must result in looping, the branch displacement must be minus four, and the branch must be to a one-word loop mode instruction preceding the DBcc instruction. The looped instruction and the first word of the DBcc instruction are each fetched twice when the loop is entered. When the processor fetches the looped instruction the second time and determines that the looped instruction is a loop mode instruction, the processor automatically enters the loop mode, and no more instruction fetches occur until the count is exhausted or the loop condition is true.

In addition to the normal termination conditions for the loop, several abnormal conditions cause the MC68010 to exit the loop mode. These abnormal conditions are

- Interrupts
- Trace Exceptions
- Reset Operations
- Bus Errors

Any pending interrupt is taken after each execution of the DBcc instruction, but not after each execution of the looped instruction. Taking an interrupt exception terminates the loop mode operation; loop mode operation can be restarted on return from the interrupt handler. While the T bit is set, a trace exception occurs at the end of both the looped instruction and the DBcc instruction, making loop mode unavailable while tracing is enabled. A reset operation aborts all processing, including loop mode processing. A bus error during loop mode operation is handled the same as during other processing; however, when the return from exception (RTE) instruction continues execution of the looped instruction, the three-word loop is not fetched again.

Table D-1 lists the loop mode instructions of the MC68010. Only one-word versions of these instructions can operate in the loop mode. One-word instructions use the three address register indirect modes: (An), (An)+, and −(An).

D

Table D-1. MC68010 Loop Mode Instructions

Opcodes	Applicable Addressing Modes
MOVE [BWL]	(Ay) to (Ax) (Ay) to (Ax)+ (Ay) to −(Ax) (Ay)+ to (Ax) (Ay)+ to (Ax)+ (Ay)+ to −(Ax) −(Ay) to (Ax) −(Ay) to (Ax)+ −(Ay) to −(Ax) Ry to (Ax) Ry to (Ax)+
ADD [BWL] AND [BWL] CMP [BWL] OR [BWL] SUB [BWL]	(Ay) to Dx (Ay)+ to Dx −(Ay) to Dx
ADDA [WL] CMPA [WL] SUBA [WL]	(Ay) to Ax −(Ay) to Ax (Ay)+ to Ax
ADD [BWL] AND [BWL] EOR [BWL] OR [BWL] SUB [BWL]	Dx to (Ay) Dx to (Ay)+ Dx to −(Ay)

Opcodes	Applicable Addressing Modes
ABCD [B] ADDX [BWL] SBCD [B] SUBX [BWL]	−(Ay) to −(Ax)
CMP [BWL]	(Ay)+ to (Ax)+
CLR [BWL] NEG [BWL] NEGX [BWL] NOT [BWL] TST [BWL] NBCD [B]	(Ay) (Ay)+ −(Ay)
ASL [W] ASR [W] LSL [W] LSR [W] ROL [W] ROR [W] ROXL [W] ROXR [W]	(Ay) by #1 (Ay)+ by #1 −(Ay) by #1

NOTE
[B, W, or L] indicate an operand size of byte, word, or long word.

D

D

INDEX

I

— I —

— J —

— K —

— L —

— M —

— R —

— S —

— S —

I

— T —

I

— T —

— U —

— V —

— W —